P9-DVU-934

DATE DUE

06/18/07 AR 18 09			

DEMCO 38-296

Perfectionist Politics

Religion and Politics

Michael Barkun, *Series Editor*

Perfectionist Politics

Abolitionism and the Religious Tensions

of American Democracy

Douglas M. Strong

 Syracuse University Press

K

Copyright © 1999 by Syracuse University Press, Syracuse, New York 13244-5160

All Rights Reserved

First Edition 1999

99 00 01 02 03 04   6 5 4 3 2 1

The paper used in this publication meets the minimum requirements of American National Standard for Information Sciences—Permanence of Paper for Printed Library Materials, ANSI z39.48-1984. ∞

Library of Congress Cataloging-in-Publication Data

Strong, Douglas M., 1956–
    Perfectionist politics : abolitionism and the religious tensions of American democracy / Douglas M. Strong. — 1st ed.
        p.   cm. — (Religion and politics)
        Includes bibliographical references and index.
        ISBN 0-8156-2793-9 (cloth : alk. paper)
        1. Antislavery movements—United States—History—19th century.
        2. Abolitionists—United States—History—19th century.   3. Slavery and the church—United States—History—19th century   4. Evangelicalism—United States—History—19th century.   5. Perfection—Religious aspects—Protestant churches.   6. United States—Church history—19th century.   7. Liberty Party (N.Y.)   8. New York (State)—Politics and government—1775–1865.   I. Title. II. Series.
E449.S917 1998
973.7'114—dc21   98-37928

Manufactured in the United States of America

To Clinton and Mary Strong

and to the memory of
Howard A. Strong (1890–1982)
and
Jennie M. Strong (1896–1990)

raconteurs of yesteryear,
models of holiness.

They followed in the footsteps
of Ezra Brewster Strong
(Howard's great-grandfather).
Ezra was born in Thetford, Vermont, in 1798
and baptized as an infant
at the Thetford Congregational Church.
A restless young man, Ezra left New England and migrated west,
settling in Farmersville, New York, in 1832.
There–in the burned-over district–
he discarded the established theology
and social ethos of his childhood.
Ezra became a Free Baptist
and, eventually, an antislavery voter.

This is his story.

DOUGLAS M. STRONG is professor of the history of Christianity at Wesley Theological Seminary in Washington, D.C. He is the author of *Reading Christian Ethics: A Historical Sourcebook* and *They Walked in the Spirit: Personal Faith and Social Action in America.*

Contents

Illustrations

Tables and Maps

Tables

Maps

Acknowledgments

William Goodell, the author of an early historical account of abolitionism and a prominent figure in this book, stated that "it would be interesting to trace the history of anti-slavery church agitation," for "there are materials sufficient for volumes." While doing his own research, however, Goodell found that "the items lie so scattered among different sects, and in various localities, that it would be a great task to collect, to classify, and to present them."[1] What was "a great task" in 1853 is even more difficult today, partly because neither the political party nor most of the congregations that were formed as a part of the ecclesiastical abolitionist movement still exist. Thus I am grateful to the staffs of numerous community libraries, historical societies, denominational archives, and local churches who have assisted me in locating these materials.

I wish to express my deep gratitude to the readers, mentors, colleagues, and friends whose critical reflection, instruction, assistance, and motivation have facilitated the completion of this project: Michael Barkun, Sandra Hughes Boyd, William H. Brackney, Kenneth W. Brewer, N. Burton Brooks, Jr., Steven C. Bullock, Ronald K. Burke, Mark S. Burrows, Ted A. Campbell, Kit Carlson, Donald W. Dayton, Melvin E. Dieter, Will Gravely, William N. A. Greenway, Jr., Mary Kelley, Doris Kirsch, William C. Kostlevy, Katherine W. Lindley, Doris H. and Herbert D. Luxon, Robert W. Lyon, Stephen A. Marini, Jeffrey C. Mason, M. Douglas Meeks, John M. Mulder, Lynn Pedigo, Cynthia L. Rigby, Milton C. Sernett, Kathleen Henderson Staudt, and Arthur D. Thomas, Jr.; the congregation of Aldersgate United Methodist Church (East Brunswick, N.J.); students and faculty colleagues at Wesley Theological Seminary; and Cynthia Maude-Gembler and the staff at Syracuse University Press. Particular thanks is extended to James M. McPherson, James H. Moorhead, and Ronald C. White, Jr.

The original inspiration for this book came from the stories of my forebears, as told and as lived by my parents and grandparents. More immediate inspiration comes from my spouse, Cynthia, and my sons, Timothy and Nathanael. It is they who encourage me, and it is they who challenge me to make history relevant.

Perfectionist Politics

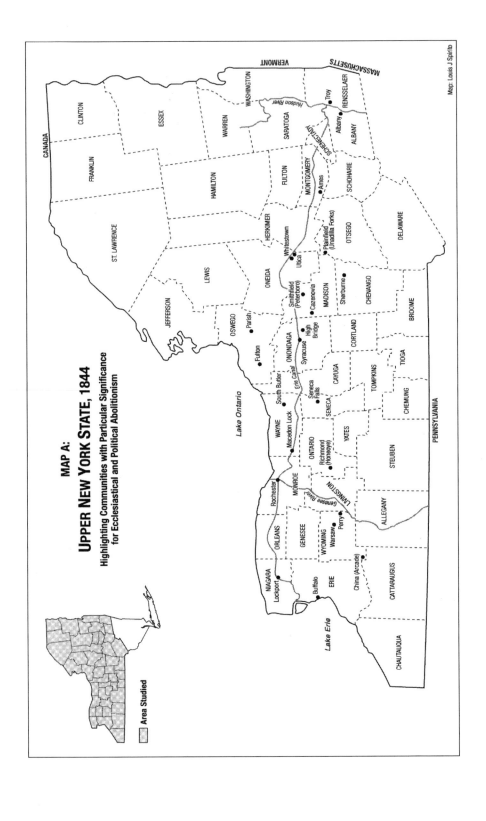

MAP A:
UPPER NEW YORK STATE, 1844
Highlighting Communities with Particular Significance
for Ecclesiastical and Political Abolitionism

Area Studied

Map: Louis J Spirito

Introduction

I N 1839, Calvin Colton, a former Presbyterian clergyman turned conservative Whig commentator, warned his colleagues that certain antislavery advocates were attempting to "remodel political society" according to fanatical perfectionist religious notions. Colton was referring to a group of evangelical abolitionists who were preparing to organize a new antislavery political party, soon to be known as the Liberty Party. The earliest formal deliberations of this group of "political abolitionists" took place in a church in Warsaw, New York—a church that Colton knew firsthand to be saturated with perfectionist teaching. Although Colton was not averse to individuals preaching the doctrine of Christian perfection in the confines of their own congregations (even if he did not believe in the concept himself), he felt that it was reckless for moral reformers to try "to introduce perfectionism into the social system." Colton's anxiety had been provoked by recent statements and actions from the abolitionists, who confidently believed that their antislavery endeavors were helping to fulfill God's design for "a perfect state of society."[1]

In their efforts to bring about the consummation of a sanctified, millennial society, political abolitionists broadened their familiar tactic of noncoercive moral suasion to include a more activistic strategy. Because their traditional Whig and Democratic parties were unwilling to take a firm stand against slavery, these activists formed a third political party; Liberty Party supporters sought the abolition of slavery and other social evils as a preliminary step to the establishment of the government of God on earth. For his part, Colton feared this intrusion of a religious agenda into the realm of civil affairs, believing it to be the insidious result of "the application of perfectionism to politics."[2]

By 1844, Colton was deeply concerned. The vote totals of the Liberty Party were expanding by geometric proportions every year; Liberty advocates were hopeful that theirs would be the majority party in the North by 1848. Because Liberty votes were drawn away from the traditional parties, both Whig and Democratic political pundits were alarmed.[3] To Colton, however, even more ominous than the electoral strength of political abolitionism was the threat caused by its combination with "ecclesiastical abolitionism."

Beginning in the mid-1830s, ecclesiastical abolitionism (also referred to as antislavery church reform) was a movement among evangelical activists to withdraw from their denominations and to reorganize themselves into independent, locally controlled antislavery congregations, often known informally as "abolition churches."[4] Although the struggle against African American slavery was basic to the self-definition of the abolition churches, it was not their only issue of concern, as the concept of abolitionism came to include much more than antislavery sentiment. According to perfectionist reasoning, the abolition of chattel slavery was only one illustration of the "immediate abolition of iniquity" required in one's personal life and in the nation.[5] That is, the "peculiar institution" became a paradigm for tyrannical institutions that existed throughout the society; in particular, the legal despotism enslaving African Americans was compared to the "spiritual despotism" enslaving evangelical Americans. The fact that the major denominations and political parties refused to condemn slaveholders was simply a specific example of the fetters that such institutions imposed generally upon the human conscience.

This "ecclesiastical slavery," according to the seceders, was vividly demonstrated by the prescribed dogma and the authoritative judicatories of the denominations. In the opinion of ecclesiastical abolitionists, "[T]he chains of sectarianism bind the souls of God's children as the chains of Southern tyrants bind the bodies of men."[6] Translocal religious institutions were considered inherently sinful—especially large, connectional denominations such as the Presbyterian Church and the Methodist Episcopal Church. God's government could not be established through the instrumentality of these faulty human constructs. Since traditional denominations were deemed sinful, the only recourse for Christians seeking to live a holy life was to secede from such religious institutions. The spiritual despotism of old, impure denominations was to be replaced with the "spiritual democracy" of reorganized, purified congregations.[7] Because ecclesiastical abolitionists believed that Christians should "come out" of unsanctified structures, many of the new congregations they established were referred to as "comeouter churches."[8]

First and foremost, as church reformers ecclesiastical abolitionists were interested in restructuring the culture of American religion. This would be accomplished by abolishing the institutional hierarchies that stifled their attempts to work for the elimination of slavery and for other holy endeavors. Building upon this first objective, ecclesiastical abolitionists further developed an interest in restructuring the culture of American politics. The religious despotism perceived within the established denominations had its corollary in a corresponding political despotism perceived within the established Whig and Democratic parties—hence the initiative for the founding of the "pure" Liberty Party.

From his perspective, Colton accused the abolition churches of being "chiefly devoted" to the advancement of the Liberty Party. It was they, he charged, who "have taken lead, and are at the head of the [political abolitionist] movement." Such ecclesiastical partisanship, Colton believed, was a dangerous "junction of religion and political power." He felt that the Liberty Party deserved to be publicly stigmatized as an abolition church—a derogatory epithet, for him—rather than treated as a traditional political party.[9]

Colton's accusation was designed as a criticism, but the ecclesiastical abolitionists were not bothered by it. They were proud of any identification of the Liberty Party with the abolition churches. Abolitionist congregations were unabashed in their political promotion of the Liberty Party, and the party was straightforward regarding the religious motivation for its political agenda. William Goodell, a prominent Liberty leader, agreed with Colton that "Anti-Slavery secession and re-organization of churches" was "the fundamental principle upon which the Liberty party [was] founded." In regions where ecclesiastical abolitionism was strong, it was nearly identical with political abolitionism; Goodell noted that "the 'political abolitionists,' especially in Central and Western New York, where that movement originated, are the very men who have . . . tak[en] measures for seceding and organizing new churches."[10] Abolition churches served as the political headquarters and campaign pulpits of Liberty candidates, and Liberty Party leaders were usually members and often pastors of these congregations.

Ecclesiastical abolitionists were committed to sanctifying the political process and the religious practice of antebellum America. They expressed this commitment by establishing new, purified organizations, specifically the Liberty Party and antislavery congregations. In this way, the polities of both church and state were to be made holy—a perfectionist politics.

As Colton noted, the underlying theological impetus that drove the ecclesiastical abolitionists was their belief in Christian perfection, the present attainability of complete personal and social holiness. Perfectionist motifs were not new within American Christianity; they can be seen, at least implicitly, in much of the religious rhetoric of the early Republic. By the late 1830s, however, the propagation of perfectionism acquired a new urgency and was preached more frequently and explicitly. Among evangelicals, the particular theological form of perfectionism that became popular was the doctrine of entire sanctification. Christians could receive God's "second blessing" of entire sanctification when they took an additional convictional step beyond their initial "new birth" conversion. Through the experiential spirituality and volitional commitment of entire sanctification, it was possible for each believer—and, by extrapolation, all of society—to obey the moral law of God completely. Every person needed to renounce his or her known sins and to give concrete evidence of a reformed life. Ecclesiastical abolitionists, fueled by the powerful religious experience of evangelical perfection, were convinced that a sanctified life and a sanctified society could be realized after Christians separated from impure institutions.[11]

Several historians have demonstrated how the abolitionists of the early 1830s appropriated the then-current theological discourse of revivalistic evangelicalism, drawing parallels between their conversion experience and their acceptance of antislavery; as reborn persons, the abolitionists repented of past proslavery behavior and vowed to lead a renewed life of antislavery agitation.[12] Going further, we can see that those ecclesiastical abolitionists who argued for the more specific tactic of political action in the 1840s also appropriated a more specific theological discourse, that of evangelical perfectionism. Many Liberty advocates drew a parallel between their entire sanctification and their antislavery voting. The abolition vote was a recording of a person's spiritual choice against sin and for holiness, analogous to one's entire sanctification; a Liberty ballot became a practical and definitive way for ecclesiastical abolitionists to exhibit their sanctified resolve.

For a brief period in the 1840s—a "perfectionist moment," if you will—

ecclesiastical abolitionists were united in the hope that they could bring about a perfect state of society by the establishment of sanctified civil and religious organizations. This effort, however, required a personal moral rigor that was difficult to maintain for very long, particularly as the optimism of the agrarian population in the region diminished due to economic uncertainty and to rural demographic decline. Consequently, by the 1850s there was a splintering of the movement. Some ecclesiastical abolitionists deviated from the idealism of principled religious purity and adopted the pragmatic realism of expedient political compromise, eventually merging into the Free Soil Party; others maintained a small evangelical perfectionist remnant of the Liberty Party that continued to espouse a radical political agenda through the Civil War.

By 1847, William Goodell realized that the unique religious/political alliance known as ecclesiastical abolitionism had disintegrated into separate factions. He was fearful lest the noble testimony of these antislavery church reformers slip into oblivion; their story was, Goodell wrote, "an item in the ecclesiastical history of our times, that should not be lost."[13] The story, however, has been lost—and our task is to recover it.

The process of narrating the story of ecclesiastical abolitionism requires a reconfiguration of the historiographies of antebellum religion and social reform. Instead of the sharp dichotomies characteristic of previous scholarship, a more balanced perspective emerges—challenging, for example, the reductionistic polarities of Garrisonian liberalism versus evangelical conservativism and of moral suasion versus political action.[14]

The formative historiography of abolitionism, written during the "bloody shirt" triumphalism of the postbellum era, contended that the Liberty Party was a direct antecedent of the Republican Party. Little attention was given to those characteristics of the Liberty supporters—such as their pervasive religiosity and their distaste for electioneering—that set them apart from typical political parties.[15] Later, even revisionist studies of abolitionism tended to accept the premise that the Liberty Party was a conventional and therefore unprincipled political movement, contrasting it to the ostensibly purer, noncoercive abolitionist impulse of the early 1830s. In her 1967 study of the abolitionist movement, for example, Aileen Kraditor stressed the role played by William Lloyd Garrison and therefore viewed the development of political schemes as the very antithesis of virtuous antislavery action. From her perspective, Liberty

Party advocates were conservative clerics bent on destroying the true abolition-ist movement by their unswerving support for traditional institutions and by their opposition to Garrison's threateningly "radical" goals.[16]

From a different angle, Gilbert Barnes's study of Theodore Dwight Weld and other antislavery reformers encouraged historians to consider the perva-sive evangelical commitment of early abolitionists. According to Barnes, the later political abolitionists had little connection to the single-minded religious motivations of the antislavery pioneers; like Kraditor, Barnes perceived politi-cal antislavery activists as compromisers of pure abolitionist principles. Thus, he described the Liberty Party as "the most pathetic residue" of the antislavery movement, a "fiasco" that was merely a desperation tactic developed by a few politically ambitious abolitionists.[17]

Indeed, in Weld's Cincinnati and in Garrison's Boston, political abolition-ists were often professional office-seekers or religious traditionalists who were not interested in a drastic alteration of the civil and ecclesiastical status quo.[18] Among the comeouter churches of upper New York, however, a different kind of political abolitionism was prevalent—one that was both explicitly evangeli-cal in its rhetoric and (though Garrison denied it) a challenge to institutional power. As evangelicals, New York Liberty activists believed in the necessity of a conversion experience, in the Bible as the primary source of religious truth, and in traditional Christian doctrines such as the Trinity and the divinity of Christ. Unlike many of their evangelical contemporaries, however, they ques-tioned the legitimacy of the established political and ecclesiastical structures. For instance, although a common caricature of political abolitionists is that they were defenders of the patriarchal social order, many Liberty Party mem-bers in New York state were deeply involved in the women's rights movement from its beginning.[19] Moreover, unlike conservative abolitionists—whose con-cern was primarily the protection of white "free labor"—the evangelical perfec-tionist Liberty leaders, animated by their religious convictions, adamantly insisted on full civil rights for African Americans.

These Liberty men and women were political eccentrics who practiced a radical spirituality distinct from the religion of those who were at the center of Protestant power. Studying them, therefore, runs counter to the work of the many historians of antebellum reform who have concentrated their attention on certain prominent "great men" of the religious establishment. In contrast to this traditional approach, Lawrence Friedman has challenged scholars to "learn more about Northern churches at the local level" in order to understand the actual lived experience of religious reformers.[20] When such local sources are used, we are able to reconstruct the cultural history of common men and women—many of whom were motivated by their experience of Christian holiness to stand up against the dominant institutions of church and state.

Through considering the beliefs and actions of individuals at the local level, we gain a fuller appreciation of the wide range of views present within the antislavery movement.[21] This book, for example, highlights the continuum between anti-institutionalism and institutional support, a fundamental tension in American society that was evident in the disputes between antislavery factions. Ecclesiastical abolitionists had to contend with this prevailing tension in the organization of their churches and in their political activities.

As Nathan Hatch has pointed out, Americans in the early republic were faced with a religious debate over the nature of democracy.[22] They questioned how far and how fast the democratization of society should take place, and how society should reconcile its twofold desire for liberty and for order. On one side were those (such as Garrison) who favored the dismantling of any coercive human authorities that mediated between the individual and God. On the other side were those (such as the leaders of traditional political parties and denominations) who feared that the abandonment of God-ordained institutional supports for the society would loosen all social restraints. For their part, the ecclesiastical abolitionists tried to steer a "middle course" between these positions that was neither anarchistic nor supportive of traditional institutions.[23] Instead, they hoped to establish sanctified civil and religious structures—a mediating, but precariously unstable strategy.

The use of sanctification terminology was a means by which individuals in the religiously oriented culture of the antebellum rural North expressed their views of human nature and of social relations. Contrary to the compartmentalization developing within much of American society, ecclesiastical abolitionists did not separate their lives into distinct sacred and secular spheres; rather, politics, commercial endeavors, and religious faith were understood in a holistic way, all framed by what may be termed an evangelical perfectionist worldview.[24] At the heart of the religious and social vision of the ecclesiastical abolitionists, evangelical perfectionism committed them both to ethical purity and to political pragmatism. As perfectionists, they affirmed the potential of living without sin and thus the formation of a truly free society; as evangelicals, however, they affirmed the enduring possibility of sin and thus the continued need for governmental restraint. Holiness was the goal for which they strived, yet a relapse into sin was also an ever present reality. They insistently maintained that God's government and human government could coexist, despite the seeming incongruity of the two concepts. The reformers' acceptance of the doctrine of entire sanctification heightened their moral resolve to hold these ideas concurrently without qualifying either one. Once convinced that a divinely inspired liberty and a humanly derived order ought to function together, sanctified ecclesiastical abolitionists tolerated no compromise in the mutual pursuit of their dual commitment.

Such a conflation of apparently conflicted goals provided the reformers with a unique vantage point from which they could view the similarly conflicted goals of antebellum democracy. Many Americans realized that there were paradoxes inherent within democratic ideology, but the self-scrutinizing demands of evangelical perfectionism forced ecclesiastical abolitionists to examine the internal logic of these paradoxes with an unusual intensity. They were bound by their theological proclivities to practice all of their ideals with holy, undiluted fervor—even ideals that seemed mutually exclusive. By simultaneously embracing diverse precepts with rigorous conviction, ecclesiastical abolitionists were able to understand with singular insight the basic tensions that existed within antebellum culture. They articulated the inner contradictions of American democratic principles better than most of their contemporaries because their theological rhetoric and reform activity manifested those contradictions so clearly.[25]

In the process of examining ecclesiastical abolitionism in relation to antebellum culture, another division in the historiography of nineteenth-century reform becomes apparent: the relative weight that one assigns to causation due to particular social processes. Which aspect of American society was most influential in the development of the reform impulse? Was it due to a peculiar regional demographic profile? Was it caused by the market economy? Was a specific faith perspective the essential element? Religious historians often assert that the theological character of revivalism provided the primary impetus for mid-nineteenth-century social reform.[26] Lee Benson concluded that the ethnocultural makeup of religious reformers determined their unusual political behavior.[27] Other historians have interpreted the success of revivalism almost solely as the product of a particular social location, and more specifically as the moral legitimation of hegemonic social control by declining elites[28] or by an upwardly mobile bourgeoisie.[29] By integrating these perspectives, perhaps the rise of revivalistic reform can be best understood as resulting from a combination of conditions, environmental, commercial, and religious—a richly textured cultural fabric in which both the socioeconomic situation and the belief system of the Liberty constituency formed integral components of a whole picture.[30]

One important factor, for example, was the geographic setting in which both the abolition churches and the Liberty Party arose. It is important to understand the distinctive regional locus of ecclesiastical abolitionism—an area of the country that had gained a reputation for being "burned over" by the recurrent revival fires kindled by the preaching of Charles G. Finney and others.[31] This so-called burned-over district is difficult to locate precisely. One could include any of the newly settled areas of predominantly Yankee origin in which markets were expanding and "where enthusiasts flourished": northern and western New England; portions of New York, Pennsylvania, and Ontario; and the Old Northwest of Ohio, Indiana, Michigan, Illinois, Wisconsin, and Iowa. Although each of these areas had a burned-over character, historians have noted that the most concentrated region of religiously intense social reform was upper New York state.[32]

The central and western sections of New York became the wellspring of revivalistic fervor; more especially, in regard to ecclesiastical abolitionism, the region was the birthplace and the heartland of the Liberty Party and of the abolition churches. The forty-five counties of New York state that lay north of the Catskill Mountains cast approximately one-quarter of all Liberty votes polled nationally during the years from 1840 to 1846, and even larger percentages of the national membership of the various abolition church groups came from this area. Thus, although ecclesiastical abolitionism could be studied profitably in the other burned-over regions, upper New York provides a logical (and manageable) geographical base for the research included in this book.[33]

Another closely related factor in interpreting the social location of the ecclesiastical abolitionists is their economic position in the society. Many people in the burned-over district were appreciative yet fearful of the emerging market-driven society. In a similar way, ecclesiastical abolitionists provided both encouragement and criticism of the commercial culture of the period.[34] In particular, ecclesiastical abolitionists manifested this ambivalence by their support of a strategy that was simultaneously outwardly focused and parochial; that is, they devised broad social reform goals but planned to achieve those goals through the restructuring of local institutions.

As important as these demographic and economic conditions were for the evolution of ecclesiastical abolitionism, the movement could not have arisen without the development of particular theological convictions. Thus, I join those historians who view religion as an important independent variable in the study of antislavery, not just a dependent one. Although this book ascribes importance to the interpretative relevance of the abolitionists' social location, its most significant contribution is its careful analysis of the religious experience—and therefore, the distinctive beliefs—of the reformers.

Some recent monographs have begun to take seriously the faith commitments of Liberty advocates; in this regard, the work of Lewis Perry, John McKivigan, and Richard Carwardine offers instructive insight into the interrelation of antislavery religion and politics.[35] While following in the historiographical trajectory of these scholars, this book also extends their arguments in two substantive ways. First, we must analyze the specific theological content of the Liberty members' religious commitments. It is not sufficient to indicate that Liberty supporters were revivalistic or even that they were perfectionistic in a general sense;[36] rather, a detailed understanding of the doctrine and experience of entire sanctification helps us to comprehend more clearly the ideological basis for their strategic move to political action. Indeed, the unique aspect of this analysis is its description of the religious practice and the worldview of evangelical perfectionism, especially as it related to church reform and to political antislavery. Previous scholarship has not distinguished the particular beliefs of evangelical perfectionists from the wider perfectionism of the era.

To be sure, those Liberty members who were ecclesiastical abolitionists were similar (in some respects) to other antebellum perfectionists, especially in the common struggle to challenge the prerogatives of corrupt institutional authorities. As evangelicals, however, many of the beliefs of the ecclesiastical abolitionists were quite different from those of the Garrisonian perfectionists; specifically, the ecclesiastical abolitionists' adherence to evangelical doctrines regarding human frailty caused them to insist on the essentiality of human structures such as churches and political parties. In addition, evangelicalism's stress on definitive affective religious experiences provided ecclesiastical abolitionist Liberty leaders with an enthusiastic passion to obey the divine will—a spiritually empowered motivation that included but went beyond the moral imperatives that were characteristic of Garrisonian perfectionism.

Second, we must explore the nature and the significance of the linkage between the abolition churches and the Liberty Party. The Liberty Party became a kind of surrogate denomination—undergirded by the theology of evangelical perfectionism—that united the various comeouters in a common ecclesiastical abolitionist network of hundreds of congregations and political cells. This coalition succeeded in bringing together denominationally diverse abolitionists into a single reform crusade dedicated to the complete overhaul of civil and religious institutions. Ecclesiastical secession was not simply coincidental with political secession; it offered a preexistent model and theological grounding for political involvement.

The recovery of the lost story of ecclesiastical abolitionism adds to our basic understandings of religious benevolence and of antislavery political action. Previously unrecognized, the impulse toward democratic church reform can now be seen as a significant benevolent movement in its own right, one which substantially influenced the broader antislavery movement by supplying a religious foundation for the politicization of abolitionism. The development of alternative ecclesiastical structures in the 1830s provided a precedent for alternative political structures in the 1840s—and for the eventual schism of the nation. Perhaps Calvin Colton was accurate after all when he determined that perfectionism applied to the political process would result in the complete remodeling of the society.

ONE

A Middle Course *The Mediating Role of*

Evangelical Perfectionism

ARSAW, New York, was a small and isolated frontier settlement when the Reverend John Lindsay, a home missionary sent by the Connecticut Missionary Society, officiated at an organizational meeting of the town's first religious body in 1808. The ten original members called the new congregation the Union Society of Warsaw, indicating their intention that the church would be the unifying religious institution of the young community. In 1817, they built a sturdy, Federal-style edifice similar to the church buildings that they had known back home. The Warsaw congregants were reflecting the desire of their colleagues in Connecticut that the churches of the new western settlements would be foundations of New England orthodoxy and stability. In great measure, their desire was realized; during the first three decades of the town's history, the original Union Society projected an image of endurance and of authority within the community.[1]

By the late 1830s, however, Warsaw was a community in religious turmoil. The Union Society, by then called Warsaw Presbyterian Church, was fraught with disputes over doctrine, ecclesiology, and social reform. The two factions that had developed within the Warsaw church were illustrative of differing religious views regarding the proper extent of American democracy. The conservative faction sought to continue the restrained and sober revival efforts of traditional Calvinist theology—a pattern of religious behavior long familiar to

Presbyterians. In contrast, the "reforming" faction promoted "new measures" of religious revival, innovative and emotional means of reaching potential converts; based on the egalitarian concept of personal free will, these new measures were intended to lead people toward an experience of regeneration and entire sanctification. The reforming faction was also abolitionist, demanding that church members campaign for antislavery politicians and that the church sever its ecclesiastical ties with what it saw as a proslavery Presbyterian denomination. The final straw for the conservatives occurred in November 1839, when the reformers used the church building to hold a political convention— the first ever to nominate an abolitionist candidate for president.

Although the conservatives interpreted the actions of the reformers as disorderly fanaticism, the Warsaw reformers were actually less anti-institutional than other Northern abolitionists, particularly the anarchistic followers of William Lloyd Garrison. However, the very presence of the Garrisonians provided a convenient foil for religious conservatives, exemplifying for them the worst attributes and potential heresies of all ultraist reformers.[2] Consequently, Warsaw conservatives instituted church trials and dismissals against the reformers, forcing the latter to secede from the parent church in January 1840. This seceding faction of ecclesiastical abolitionists organized a new, antislavery congregation named The Church of Warsaw, which—in order to demonstrate its antidenominational inclinations—refused to join any regional judicatory. Within a year, The Church of Warsaw met in a new meetinghouse built (for spite?) directly adjacent to the old church.[3]

The two buildings stood side-by-side, a visible testimony to the nineteenth-century religious struggle over the scope of democratization. Among the religiously oriented people of Warsaw and of scores of other New York towns, the conflicting claims of liberty and of order often played out against a background of perfectionistic reform. In exploring the history of the ecclesiastical abolitionists—men and women such as the reformers who established The Church of Warsaw—we must begin by surveying the larger religious and social landscapes of which they were a part. Out of the wide range of revivalist, abolitionist, and perfectionist views that characterized the antebellum North, the ecclesiastical abolitionists steered a middle course—theological and political— in pursuit of their ideals. The depth and complexity of their mediating perspective makes their story a microcosm of the cultural tensions facing American society at the time.

Warsaw Presbyterian Church, Warsaw, New York. Built in 1817; it was one of the earliest "Presbygational" **congregations organized in western New York.** *Courtesy of Warsaw Historical Society.*

The Religious Search for Order

Upper New York state was the largest recipient of extensive outmigration from New England during the early national period. The westward expansion of New England began immediately after the close of the Revolutionary War, but fear of Native Americans and of the British in Canada kept the numbers small until the Treaty of Ghent (1815) ended the final round of hostilities with the British. Many younger Yankees heard of and responded to the allure of the

The Church of Warsaw, Warsaw, New York. An independent Congregational church built next to the Warsaw Presbyterian Church (dedicated in January 1841). *Courtesy of Warsaw Historical Society.*

fertile and relatively unsettled lands in the "Genesee country" of the New York frontier.[4]

At first, the New England settlers established towns that greatly resembled their native communities. To begin with, emigrants from a particular Yankee village often settled near each other, causing new neighborhoods and even entire towns to take on the character of that older New England community. Residents of Pawlet, Vermont, for example, migrated as a group to Pulaski, New York; eager to retain their familiar religious forms after they arrived in the new settlement, the emigrants organized the First Congregationalist Church of Pulaski before they ever left Vermont, even bringing their own minister with them.[5]

Churches, as exemplified by the original Union Society of Warsaw, were intended to provide community cohesion to emigrant settlements. Villages were described as "church-going, order-loving communities." Churches offered social interaction, entertainment, and common activities for the populace of the new towns. The congregations "represented the very core" of village social structure.[6]

The immigrant churches incorporated customary New England ecclesiastical usages. Each Congregationalist church adopted articles of faith, a church covenant, and rules of admission; the articles and covenants were generally borrowed from established Calvinistic doctrinal guidelines such as those the settlers knew in New England. Those wishing admission to the newly constituted frontier churches had to meet with the elders and to be examined regarding the Reformed "doctrines of the gospel and views and motives to Christian conduct."[7] These familiar New England forms also encouraged prudently controlled revivalism. Popular religion in New England and in frontier New York had been invigorated since the 1790s by the recurrent revivalism collectively referred to as the Second Great Awakening; many Yankee emigrants were products of this awakened spiritual emphasis and desired to perpetuate it.[8] The revivalism culminated, according to a standard denominational history of the region, in what "proved to be many stable, enduring churches and in the setting of a pattern of revivals that influenced the religious life of New York" for many years.[9]

Moreover, a unique arrangement between the Congregationalists and their potential rivals, the Presbyterians, helped to ensure ecclesiastical order on the frontier. The New England settlers were largely Congregationalist in background, but most of the frontier churches were not referred to as Congregationalist. Rather, as in the case of the Union Society of Warsaw, the churches were nominally Presbyterian, due to various "plans of union" and "accommodation plans." These churches of mixed polity were often colloquially referred to as "Presbygational."[10] The cooperative agreements between the Presbyterian General Assembly and various Congregationalist associations (regional judicatories) provided a basis for mutual home missionary endeavors in frontier areas bereft of available clergy. In the early days of settlement, denominational leaders welcomed the opportunity "to promote union and harmony" and to prevent competition in evangelization; such cooperation was possible because the two denominations shared "affinity in creed and disposition."[11] They did, however, differ in regard to church government. Presbyterians viewed the church as the universal body of Christians, locally manifested in particular assemblies; in contrast, Congregationalists understood the church primarily as each individual congregation, and so the designation of "church" was not to be applied to any translocal ecclesiastical organization.

In the implementation of the accommodation plans, Congregationalism was almost completely overwhelmed by Presbyterianism. A Presbyterian commentator asserted that the plans of union "made Central and Western New York the Lebanon of our church, and turned Congregationalism here into a nursery for Presbyterianism."[12] The accommodation plans were designed to be reciprocal, but Congregationalists did most of the accommodating; in fact, a survey in 1836 found that several hundred Presbyterian churches had originally been, in some measure, Congregationalist.[13]

However, the settlers did not always turn to the Presbygational churches for their spiritual direction, as increasingly they were drawn to newer and more ambitious churches, particularly Methodist and Baptist. Berkshire, New York, was a typical town: its first settlers were New England Congregationalists; as the Methodists began to attract more members, they "met with opposition and persecution from the Congregational society," who "considered the Methodists as intruders."[14] Almost every community harbored several competing religious groups, and divergent interpretations of Christian doctrine and practice inevitably led to an erosion of Presbygationalist preeminence.

The Methodists and Baptists grew dramatically in upper New York state and, together with the Presbygationalists, made up the vast majority of churches.[15] Baptist societies were usually pastored by local farmer-preachers, subsisting primarily on their own husbandry and ordained on the basis of their hortatory skills rather than on any formal academic qualifications. The Methodists, although highly structured, also provided down-to-earth lay leadership on a local level, informal and emotive worship, and a flexible organization capable of expanding quickly to reach new settlements. Another attraction of Methodism, and a challenge to New England orthodoxy, was the Wesleyan stress on each individual's ability, due to God's prevenient grace, to respond to the offer of salvation. This Arminian understanding of human ability was easier to reconcile with the frontier evangelists' plea for immediate conversion and with the democratic tendencies of the settlers than was the traditional Calvinist belief that God predetermined when and how people responded to the offer of grace.[16]

Initially, Methodists and Baptists were particularly well suited to perpetuate and to benefit from the more exuberant aspects of the second Awakening that Presbygationalists shunned. The earliest Methodist and Baptist revivals and camp meetings were noted for their wild preaching, their "eccentricities," their "vehemence of manners, and their ability to scandalize their staid Presbygationalist neighbors."[17] Within a generation, however, Baptists and Methodists became "respectable," their enthusiasm so subdued by the late 1820s that their revival meetings were described as "perfectly orderly."[18] As a sure sign of their acceptance, Presbygationalists began to cooperate—first informally, then officially—with Methodists and with Baptists, grudgingly receiving them as true evangelical brethren.[19]

By the 1830s, the largest denominations in upper New York—the Presbygationalists, Methodists, and Baptists—recognized each other as fellow Christians. They shared a vaguely conceived but generally recognized concept of being "evangelical"; that is, they all believed in the need for a dramatic personal conversion as the initiatory regenerative (new birth) experience of every Christian's life, and they depended on the Bible as their primary source of religious authority. Because these churches all advocated biblical authority and the normativeness of a conversion experience, they considered one another to be relatively like-minded Christians.[20]

The Religious Search for Liberty

Despite harmony of thought concerning the necessity of an evangelical experience, there was little agreement on any common doctrinal core among the major churches in upper New York. The large majority of evangelical folk were willing to acknowledge that members of some other denominations were Christians, but acceptance of even a limited pluralism opened up a Pandora's box of possible doctrinal and ecclesiastical leniencies. Each religious group had a different interpretation of scriptural orthodoxy, interpretations that often seemed to be in flux. The relatively stable and unified religious order to which New Englanders had formerly been accustomed (or, at least, which they nostalgically imagined) was mitigated by the more pluralistic religious configurations that followed the second Awakening.[21]

To add to the ecclesiastical confusion, by 1830 several smaller evangelical offshoots existed alongside the major denominations in upper New York: the Reformed Methodists and the Methodist Protestants (both secessions from the Methodist Episcopal Church) and the Freewill Baptist Connection, the Free Communion Baptists, and the Christian Connection (all secessions from the so-called Regular or Calvinistic Baptists). Not surprisingly, this popular religiosity began to flourish just as the Methodists and the Baptists were being accepted into the dominant social order; the new religious bodies had common concerns that led them to leave their respective denominations—concerns that demonstrated the level of social respectability to which the mainstream Methodists and Baptists had come. In particular, all of these groups were eager to exercise greater theological or structural freedom than they had experienced in their former churches. Doctrinal egalitarianism (as expressed in the Arminian belief in freedom of the human will) and ecclesiological egalitarianism (as expressed in the church polity of congregational independence) were viewed as logical and necessary corollaries. The new sects sought to establish religious structures that combined democratically methodistic doctrine (individual free will) with democratically baptistic polity (congregationalism).

The two Methodist schisms (Reformed Methodists and Methodist Protestants) broke away because, in their view, Methodism's episcopal polity led to a "monopoly of power by the ministry." Bishops and most clergy were considered "religious tyrants" who repressed "honest convictions and free inquiry" among the laity.[22] The Freewill Baptist Connection, as its name implies, advocated the doctrine of human ability, in contrast to the Calvinism that was traditional among the Regular Baptists. The Free Communion Baptists were similar to Freewill Baptists, stressing the full extension of Christian fellowship to all evangelical (that is, regenerated) persons, regardless of denominational affiliation. The Christian Connection also believed in a more democratic, Arminian theology; they emphasized their democratic inclinations by desiring to be known only as "Christians."[23]

To a greater or lesser degree, all five of these minor offshoots attempted to apply democratic principles to church structures or theology that they perceived as undemocratic. Ecclesiastical judicatories, religious hierarchies of any kind, distinctions between clergy and laity, reliance on creeds rather than on the Bible alone, and membership or communion requirements based on adherence to denominational formularies of doctrine rather than on simple profession of faith in Christ—all were seen as evidence of how arbitrary human authority crushed the freedom of individual conscience.

Moreover, the issues with which these various schismatic groups grappled typified the general crisis of authority occurring throughout American culture. Many Americans realized that the rhetoric of liberty often failed to match the reality of experience. Thus, these movements participated in the quest for an answer to a fundamental question of America's early national period: With the desire both to extend personal liberty and to conduct an orderly society, what form would American democracy take? Such questioning launched a widespread debate in the early Republic over the meaning of freedom.

This clash of opinions was itself a byproduct of the quest for greater liberty. True liberty, it seemed, must result from unobstructed freedom of conscience. Every person, "exercising the Protestant right of private judgment," was left "each to his own conclusions." Democracy opened immediate access to truth for all people. Doctrinal investigation among Christians, if pursued with an open mind, would result in agreement on essentials (such as moral and ethical behavior), while nonessential disagreements would fall by the wayside. Many Americans confidently thought that this unrestricted discussion of ideas would free individuals from bondage to ignorance and to superstition, creating the natural harmony of thought inherent in a true democracy.[24] They did not seem to anticipate that the actual outcome might be acrimonious controversy.

Antebellum evangelicals held up the Christian religion as a model of democratic liberty. According to William Goodell, Christians were originally the vanguard of the principle of democratic equality. At its best, Goodell believed, Christianity was the ally of American democracy: both affirmed the natural rights of all persons, both asserted the benefits of free investigation, both proclaimed the necessity of ethical action above speculative philosophy, and both desired the construction of a godly, harmonious, and democratic society. Only a corruption of its original ideals could make Christianity undemocratic. Church history has shown us, Goodell stated, that "Christianity degraded became the ally of despotism," and the justification of slavery by the church was an example of Christianity's descent into despotic darkness.[25]

Like Goodell, reform-minded evangelicals believed that liberty could exist only among citizens living in relative equality, unrestrained by the arbitrary authority either of church or of state. Institutional hierarchies, unmerited and distinguishing titles, deference expected to certain professions due to prescribed status alone, one's livelihood secured through the labors of someone else, or monopolistic control over certain goods—all produced unfair advantage of one person over another. These things interjected someone or something between individuals and their natural right to personal liberty. What was demanded instead was equal opportunity for all.

Vestiges of aristocratic authority remained in American institutions and society, particularly the churches and the civil government. Certain privileged elites still held sway and needed to be stripped of their unnatural advantages. In the popular mind, these elites represented the decadence and superstition of Europe, still tyrannized by its papacy and aristocracy; for many Northerners, the slave economy of the South seemed similarly feudal and corrupt. Many Americans felt that they were now on the brink of a new, momentous age, an "age of light," of endless possibilities. All that was needed was for Americans to throw off their undemocratic fetters and to discover their natural virtue.[26]

An Ordered Liberty

Opinion differed greatly on how best to promote greater personal liberty while at the same time establishing an orderly and harmonious Christian society. The desire for freedom from restraint stood in tension with the desire for restrained freedom. Those who hoped to strip power from arbitrary authorities believed that they could create a society in which all people lived and acted in cooperative tranquility. But how should one organize a society without traditional checks and social parameters? On the one side were those who stressed concepts such as liberty, democracy, and freedom over against despotic authority, tyranny, and slavery. Others emphasized order, established institutions, and harmony over against anarchy, fanaticism, disorganization, and ultraism.

The Whig propagandist Calvin Colton was a prominent spokesperson for the properly ordered society. A particularly astute observer of the burned-over district, Colton had served for several years as a Presbyterian pastor in LeRoy, Genesee County, and he knew New York state and its people well. By the late 1830s, what he observed alarmed him: religious "fanaticism" was trying to restructure the political order in accordance with "exaggerated" concepts of democracy. "Good sense," he argued, dictated certain restraints on democratic tendencies as well as determination to check the excesses of democracy. "Radical reformism," as portrayed by Colton, knew no such caution.[27]

In truth, few of Colton's identified radical reformers were as deficient in order and in restraint as he maintained, and not all of the so-called arbitrary authorities mentioned by those advocating greater liberty were completely devoid of democratic sympathies. Many religious people in upper New York, especially those who became ecclesiastical abolitionists, sought a society that was both democratized and organized—an ordered liberty. Those who held such a viewpoint, such as the abolitionist seceders from the Warsaw Presbyterian Church, were self-consciously trying to steer between the Scylla of despotic institutionalism and the Charybdis of anarchistic disorganization.

Their middle course was difficult to maintain, however. Conservatives considered the reformers to be ultraists, while others (Garrisonian abolitionists, for instance) thought that they were perpetuating hierarchical abuses. Evangelical New Yorkers recognized the pitfalls in their attempts to resolve this tension; as an astute observer noted, to determine "precisely where liberty ends and licentiousness begins is a delicate act."[28]

A Fertile Soil for New Measures Revivalism

Exuberant revivalism was attended by demands for greater democratization in theology and in ecclesiology. In the late 1820s, just as the Methodists and Baptists were backing away from this relatively democratic gospel, some Presbygationalist revivalists began to embrace it. Presbygationalists were unaccustomed to such direct and unconventional methods; consequently, among them the more extreme revivalistic tactics seemed to be "*new* measures."[29]

Charles G. Finney—who became a religious symbol for the age, much as Andrew Jackson became a political symbol[30]—was not the first, even among Presbygationalists, to use the new measures. He was, rather, a popularizer of novel methods among the more established denominations, a mainstream representative of numerous lesser known but very effective new measures revivalists in central and western New York. Beyond the celebrated Finney revivals in the large population centers, countless revivals in smaller communities were led by popular preachers hailing from all of the region's evangelical denominations. One local narrative from Madison County reported that "every little hamlet of this part of the country felt the pulsations of religious life that throbbed with conscious force in the larger towns and cities of the State." By the mid-1830s, new measures revivalism brought religious vitality into most of the hills and hollows of central and western New York, marking the area as the prototypical burned-over district.[31]

The region was certainly afire with religious enthusiasm—and debate. While one conservative opponent warned other Presbygationalists that "fanaticism and false doctrines . . . prevail in this section of country,"[32] other observers viewed the results more favorably. A contemporary of Finney recalled the revivalistic era approvingly: "The scene of these revivals lies before us, and their effects . . . and what do we see? No 'burnt district,' certainly . . . but a quick and fertile soil, a harvest field, a beautiful garden. Revivals have made it a land for revivals."[33]

It is appropriate that commentators used such metaphors as "fertile soil" and "a harvest field" in their descriptions, for the revivalism of the region flourished in a context of rapid agricultural gain, expanding farm markets, and substantial population increase. In this environment, revival preachers were optimistic about their religious future; when they surveyed the situation, they saw a region of economic and demographic expansion, coupled with the evangelical earnestness of the Yankee settlers.[34]

Beginning with Whitney Cross's landmark study, historians have tried to explain the prevalence of revivalistic reform in upper New York. Some writers have proposed that a unique set of religious elements resulted in the high-pitched level of revivalistic fervor.[35] In contrast, Paul E. Johnson offers an economic interpretation, contending that evangelical revivalism, temperance reform, and sabbatarianism were useful for the development of a stable entrepreneurial class dependent on employed wage labor.[36] Clearly, however, the most satisfactory explanations posit an intermingling of factors, where interpretative credence is given both to the rise of new religious expressions and to the development of particular social conditions.

Specifically, various historians have demonstrated that the reformers were tentatively engaged in the emerging market revolution—accepting some aspects of the commercial culture while rejecting other aspects.[37] On the one hand, upper New York evangelicals paid much attention to external markets and to the broader, nationally oriented culture that went along with them, a positive interest manifested in the effective use of new transportation and communication developments such as canal and train travel and cheaply produced periodicals. In the minds of church people, the spread of the gospel often was connected to these technological advances. The Freewill Baptists, for instance, viewed their new, widely distributed denominational paper as God's medium "to diffuse the rich blessings of the kingdom of Christ" to the "far-spread field . . . [of] the world."[38]

In the village of China, New York, a small community fifty miles south of the Erie Canal, revival interests and market interests were promoted simultaneously. Charles O. Shepard, a merchant and Congregationalist elder, made a trip to the prosperous canal city of Rochester, which impressed him in two ways: its revivalistically oriented populace, represented by several thriving evangelical churches, and its business success, represented most obviously by the brand new Reynolds Arcade Building—a four-story commercial edifice with a covered concourse. He returned home convinced that his town could participate in the region's religious and economic prosperity. Under Shepard's influence, town leaders changed the name of their village from the remote-sounding "China" to the commercially directed "Arcade." During the same period, Shepard persuaded his fellow townspeople to participate in Finneyite new measures revivals.[39] Revivalistic energy and market potential were mutually reinforcing. As Daniel Walker Howe has pointed out, the faith commitments of antebellum evangelicals often predisposed them toward particular attitudes about current economic issues.[40]

At the same time, burned-over district evangelical reformers were not uncritical of the emerging market economy. In fact, revivalistic New Yorkers were ambivalent about the effects of commercialization, the "grasping commercial spirit [which] seemed to predominate" during this period. They challenged the selfish, impersonal, market-driven ethos of both Southern slaveholders and Northern businessmen that "elevate[d] property above humanity—matter above spirit."[41] While open to the benefits of the wider culture, they were still firmly tied to their community-centered social structures, embracing the new prosperity, while still striving to maintain a measure of local autonomy and stability.

Revivalistic Reform Strategy

The temperance movement was the first widely accepted activistic reform tied to new measures revivalism. Gerrit Smith, a temperance advocate who was

soon to be a prominent ecclesiastical abolitionist, clearly articulated the connection between benevolent reform and revivalistic religion. Smith said the
idea of temperance was to be diffused, first by personal regeneration, then in
local reformation, and finally in national transformation: "An individual adopts
the principle of total abstinence from ardent spirits. The principle is soon extended from himself to his family—from his family to the neighborhood—and
thence over the whole town." Smith continued: "One town after another
would confirm and rivet its advancement in the work of temperance, until
speedily the whole land" would be transformed.[42]

Huntington Lyman of Arcade (Charles Shepard's brother-in-law, later to be
the first pastor of the abolitionist Church of Warsaw) agreed with his friend
Smith. Benevolent activity, Lyman believed, began in each regenerated home,
and "from thence goes forth a general influence, pervading society."[43] For
Smith, Lyman, and their burned-over district counterparts, the entire nation
would be the object of social redemption, a redemption accomplished first
through individual conversion and then through the reformation of their own
small communities.

Temperance and other benevolent causes persisted from the 1820s through
the Civil War, but it was the antislavery crusade that most deeply seized revivalistic Northerners. Although the idea of an immediate (as opposed to a gradual)
abolition of slavery was first popularized by Garrison and other New Englanders, upstate New Yorkers assumed a prominent role in the movement by the
mid-1830s. These New Yorkers soon would challenge Garrison's strategy of individual moral influence.

The reform activity of the burned-over district abolitionists was sustained
by their religious fervor. Many, such as Huntington Lyman, prepared for the
ministry at Finney's activistic training school in Oberlin, Ohio, or at Beriah
Green's radically oriented Oneida Institute in Whitesboro (Whitestown), New
York. Along with their evangelistic work, Lyman and others who would soon
become leading ecclesiastical abolitionists—William Goodell, John Lawyer,
Luther Lee, Samuel Ringgold Ward, and Hiram Whitcher, for example—often
served as traveling preachers and as lecturers for antislavery societies. As they
traveled, these antislavery "agents" connected the rural towns and villages of
the region with the broader forum of the national benevolent societies.[44]

The intermediary role of the traveling agents demonstrates the way in
which new measures revivalists constructed their social reform strategy, pro-

moting translocal ends through local means. Reform advocacy helped to expand both their knowledge about social evils and the responsibility that evangelicals felt for eliminating such sins within American society. Through various
social reform endeavors, burned-over district evangelicals may have thought
globally, but they acted locally.

On one level, revivalistic reformers were enamored with the broader national culture, as demonstrated by their development of a popular religious press to
spread their message and the mass distribution of inexpensive tracts. They also
employed itinerating agents and extended the so-called benevolent empire of
nationally based voluntary societies into the hinterland through the establishment of local societies.

However, as revivalistic reformers engaged the broader culture, their individualistic view of reality (derived from their evangelical preoccupation with
personal conversion) prevented them from seeing the need for structural
changes within society. They insisted on redeeming the world one person at a
time: communities would be reformed only when redeemed individuals banded together, and the spread of reformed communities would eventually create a
transformed society. "The millennium would commence in America," the revivalists believed, by the Christianization of the country.[45] No longer were
preachers to be concerned with the regeneration of their own congregants
alone; revival preaching now had a much more ambitious goal, based on the
belief that converting each American would ultimately convert the nation. Although this vision was broad, the strategy to effect it was locally centered and
individually based. Equipped with a carefully balanced strategy of national redemption through personal regeneration, burned-over district abolitionists
were ready to lead the moral charge into the thick of antislavery politics—both
in the church and in the state.

The Theological Basis for New Measures Revivalism and Immediate Abolition

To new measures revivalists, individuals were either reformed or unreformed. According to Finney, "[S]in and holiness . . . both consist in supreme,
ultimate, and opposite choices, or intentions, and cannot, by any possibility,
co-exist." There was, in the words of revivalist Luther Myrick, "no neutrality
on the part of moral beings. . . . God desires no neutrals, but either for or

against."[46] This theology was particularly well suited to revivalistic social reform: the evangelical emphasis on the need for immediate repentance fit well with the reformers' insistence that one's conversion experience be demonstrated by ethical action and the evangelical stress on individual free will corresponded to the reformers' belief that ultimate, eternal consequences resulted from each person's daily moral choices.

These revivalistic emphases were appropriated from the theological system developed by Nathaniel W. Taylor and other Yale divines.[47] Taylor's views, simplified for popular consumption, circulated widely among the new measures Presbygationalist churches of New York; Oberlin-educated pastors from the region, for example, were trained in the New Haven mold, and many of Finney's disciples in upper New York viewed the great revivalist as "the true successor of Dr. Taylor."[48] Taylor's theology centered on the concept of the "moral government of God"—a term that referred to the extent of God's jurisdiction over human activities. According to Taylor, God instituted the moral law for the regulation of divine government. It corresponded to the law of nature, in which God's eternal design could be discerned. The moral law also had an approximate equivalent in civil law—if the civil law was democratically administered.[49]

Using this theological structure, new measures preaching provided a religious vocabulary that coincided with prevailing political discourse regarding the extent of democratization. Those nurtured under such preaching, particularly revivalistic reformers, appropriated the moral government language to frame their deliberations concerning the civil government. Among social reformers such as the abolitionists, the imminent "government of God" might be effected through the government of the United States—once the latter was democratically reformed and freed from the sin of slavery.[50]

God's government could not be established until all persons gave free obedience to the moral law. The revivalists insisted, in contrast to traditional Calvinism, that there must be true freedom of choice. Humans did not sin due to an inherited depravity—the Calvinist understanding—but due to moral depravity, a volitional disposition to selfishness. "Sin is in the sinning" was the phrase associated with Taylor's theology; that is, an individual became sinful by his or her own willful actions. Thus it was theoretically possible not to sin.[51]

The opposite of human selfishness was holiness. Once someone comprehended his or her own disposition to sin, it was an individual's obligation to repent immediately. The new birth occurred when a person repented, causing a shift of one's volitional allegiance from selfish actions to virtuous actions. The continuous choosing of the good, through the self-mastery of sinful desires, constituted the process of sanctification. Holiness resulted from a continuous conformity to the moral law following conversion. When practiced by regenerated individuals throughout the whole society, such obedience would eventually effect, or at least closely approximate, the harmonious millennial government of God.[52]

Among new measures revivalists, this meant that less importance was placed on precise doctrinal correctness than on ethical action. Moral reform activity became the barometer of one's spiritual state. As William Goodell preached to his ecclesiastical abolitionist congregation, "In order to leave off sinning, men must labor in the divine service. There is no neutrality or inactivity in the case."[53] However, although Taylor believed that one *could* keep the law (theoretical ability), he was convinced that no one actually *would* keep it (practical inability). Therefore "entire sanctification"—defined as "entire obedience to the moral law"—might be attained, ought to be attained, and should be aimed at, but it "is not attainable in this life in such a sense as to make its attainment an object of rational pursuit, with the expectation of attaining it."[54] Taylor stopped short of his own seemingly logical conclusions regarding the possibility of perfection. It was merely common sense, he believed, to realize that people will not cease sinning.

In the 1830s, New York abolitionists, most of whom were products of new measures revivalism, appropriated Taylor's theology for their cause.[55] They "thought favorably" of Taylor's system because they "found in it that doctrine of *immediate repentance* which makes consistent abolitionists of all who truly embrace it." A person's acceptance of immediate abolition became identified with his or her immediate repentance; in a typical statement, one reformer proudly declared: "From the hour of my spiritual birth I have been an 'Abolitionist.'" Combining the phraseologies of abolitionism and of new measures revivalism, religious reformers were urged to strive for the "immediate abolition of all iniquity." Slavery represented the sin of despotic tyranny, and emancipation represented the holiness of democratic freedom. A person's public repudiation of "the principle of slavery" correlated with his or her repudiation of sin. Northerners as well as Southern slaveholders needed to renounce "the principle of slavery," because that sinful "principle" controlled the political and ecclesiastical institutions of the nation.[56]

According to abolitionists who accepted Taylor's theological system, sanctification was the "carrying out" of conversion. Correspondingly, emancipation should have been the spontaneous outgrowth of holy activity following the promotion of abolition—a "carrying out of the new principle of action." If converted Christians throughout the society repented of the sin of slavery, emancipation would result as a matter of course; a detailed strategic program for the demise of slavery was not necessary.[57]

By 1840, however, frustrated abolitionists learned that emancipation was not so easily accomplished and that the "carrying out of the new principle of action" was more difficult than expected. Taylor's doctrines were now seen as a theological hindrance to substantive reform. Abolitionists noticed a certain indefiniteness in Taylor's doctrine of sanctification, diluting the urgency and full impact of its appeal. Additionally, the abolitionists' perception of the utility of Taylor's theology was affected by the well-known fact that Taylor had publicly disparaged the antislavery movement for being too radical. What was needed, the abolitionists believed, was a more definitive doctrine of entire sanctification, one that would undergird the demand for a more definitive strategy of political action.[58]

Therefore, Finney and other new measures Presbygationalist revivalists in the burned-over district, aided by Arminian ideas borrowed from their Methodist friends, took the traditional New England doctrines one step further than had Taylor. They asserted that regenerated individuals—and, collectively, a regenerated society—could consistently live without willful sin; that is, there could be an attainable entire sanctification.

This development of evangelical perfectionist doctrine was not surprising. The revivalistic milieu of the burned-over district was a tinderbox just waiting to be ignited with the fires of perfectionist reform. The potential had been implicit already in the social reality of the region; in the late 1830s, it became explicit.

A Soil Exactly Adapted to Its Needs

The environment of upper New York was ripe for the growth of perfectionism. In that region, according to one contemporary commentator, "perfectionism found a soil exactly adapted to its needs"; similarly, historian Whitney Cross observed that "perfectionism was practically predestined to arise" in the burned-over context.[59] The prevailing influence of millennialism and of common sense realism encouraged the special propagation of holiness doctrine. Moreover, the financial panic of 1837 provided a material incentive that helped to stimulate interest in sanctification.

A general spirit of optimistic millennial expectation prevailed among the religious segment of the population. Millennialism is a theological concept regarding the prophesied reign of God on earth; the most prevalent antebellum expression of this concept was postmillennialism, which asserted that Christ's second coming would occur after an idyllic thousand-year period. According to this belief, human beings are presently in the penultimate time prior to the millennium, and it is humanity's responsibility to help usher in the impending millennium by approximating God's government as closely as possible. On a personal level, the postmillennial goal assumes that individuals will become holy in the fullness of time. By extension, the collated holiness of many individuals will eventually result in the millennial society.[60]

Perfectionist thought fit particularly well with postmillennialism. According to perfectionists, the aggregation of personal holiness would result in a perfected society, a concept that was very similar to the vision of a millennial society. The United States was viewed as the most suitable arena for God's unfolding millennial drama; perfectionist abolitionist Jonathan Blanchard was convinced that "the world is on its return to God," with America leading the way. Though there was a great amount of work to be done, there was an exuberance and a certainty that it would be accomplished, because it was God's work. Already, as revivalistic reformers pointed out, the temperance reformation had produced widespread results. Such success encouraged the reformers toward ever more ambitious preparations for the millennium. For abolitionists, this meant creating a society free from slavery and from other restraints placed on the human conscience.[61]

The advancement of religious perfectionism was also encouraged by the influence of common sense realism. Common sense thought, which in its American form was rather crudely adapted from its original Scottish expression, stressed the self-evident application of the law of God to the moral duty of individuals. A moral simplicity was presumed, in which God's will for persons and for human society would be readily discernible. Everyone could have an intuitive certainty that their ethical actions were divinely commissioned.[62] When this common sense emphasis on intuitive moral behavior was joined with the empirical stress on affective experience, it was easy for nineteenth-century people to accept perfectionism. This was especially true because in its antebellum form, the theological concept of Christian perfection was simultaneously described as a religious experience (consistent with empiricism) and as a personal commitment to live out ethical principles (consistent with the precepts of common sense realism).

The greater appeal of the doctrine of perfection was also occasioned by the panic of 1837, a sudden economic downturn that came after several years of relative prosperity. Earlier, expanding markets had encouraged religious as well as financial optimism among revivalistic New Yorkers; God's work was proceeding well, it seemed, especially as churches and benevolent organizations reaped the monetary fruits of business success. When the depression hit, however, these same benevolent institutions suffered. As a result, the panic exacerbated the ambivalence many felt about the rapid changes in the region's assimilation of a market economy.[63]

Along with their fiscal problems, and perhaps because of them, evangelicals felt that their revivalistic experiences needed to be more definite and secure. Entire sanctification—a special effusion of God's grace that made individuals more holy—would seem to reinforce and to solidify personal religiosity despite economic difficulties. It is not surprising, then, that the panic was contemporaneous with an increasing interest in the possibility of sanctified living. The shortage of money was but a divine reminder of the transitory nature of this world and of the consequent need for greater efforts to bring in the rule of God; one perfectionist was convinced that "as money goes down, holiness goes up." An ecclesiastical abolitionist paper similarly charged that "our country has been in too great haste to be rich. . . . Will not Christians be led by passing events, to repent and aim at an increase of holiness rather than wealth?"[64]

The Resurgence of the Doctrine of Perfection

By the late 1830s, although prevalent social conditions and particular intellectual currents inclined religious reformers to appropriate perfectionist ideas, they had not yet actually promoted the specific doctrine—and experience—of entire sanctification. Soon, however, the general perfectionist strain in burned-over district culture would be transformed into the specific advocacy of evangelical perfectionism.

Christian perfection, or "perfect love" (as Methodist founder John Wesley called it), was the culmination of a postconversion religious process in which the believer came to love God completely, with all one's "heart, mind, soul, and strength." Wesley's belief in perfection was qualified—he did not imply absolute sinlessness or an absence of infirmities. He focused, rather, on the fullness of the individual's consistent intention to love God and neighbor. Entire sanctification—the gift of perfect love—was understood to be the result both of God's grace and of the free choice of the believer. Wesley taught that one's entire sanctification could be received in a moment, but he never mapped out the specifics of what that experience would look like. Nonetheless, Wesley's teaching invited all Christians to participate in God's holiness, offering believers the concrete goal that they could actually "expect to be made perfect in love in this life." Wesley was convinced that the lifting up of Christian perfection was the Methodist movement's most important contribution to Christendom.[65]

This doctrine traveled with Methodism to the New World—where it acquired new nuances of expression that stretched the original Wesleyan understanding. Entire sanctification was expected to be experienced as an existential crisis similar to one's new birth, an additional experience often referred to as the second blessing. American preachers also encouraged regenerate believers to anticipate entire sanctification at increasingly earlier stages of their Christian life. Christian perfection, it seemed, could be achieved almost on demand.[66]

Even with this distinctly American expression of entire sanctification, the preaching of the doctrine began to decline after the frontier period of Methodist expansion. Most evidence indicates that a generation of Methodist ministers from approximately 1815 to 1835 were more concerned about the pressing needs of church development and the new responsibilities incumbent upon a settled ministry than the promulgation of perfect love.[67] The upwardly mobile adherents of the growing denomination drew back from the promotion of holiness because of the doctrine's perceived association with older, less respectable styles of Methodist exuberance and enthusiasm. By 1832, the bishops' pastoral address to the denomination's General Conference took note of this widespread neglect. "Why," they asked, "have we so few living witnesses that 'the blood of Jesus Christ cleanseth from all sin?'" The earlier American Methodists had commonly experienced "this high attainment in religion," the bishops lamented, but "now, a profession of it is rarely to be met among us." Few Methodists preached or wrote on the theme. Although Christian perfection was an official doctrine of the Methodist Episcopal church, it generally was not emphasized among Methodists—nor advocated at all by other denominations—until the mid-1830s.[68]

Within just a few years, however, the preaching of perfection emerged again. Timothy Merritt inaugurated the *Guide to Christian Perfection* in 1839 with a call for a new specialization in the propagation of holiness, because "the importance of the subject demands special attention and extra effort at this time." Calvin Colton wrote the same year that "perfectionism is an old doctrine in the religious world, but has recently been revived in this country." A movement was afoot to encourage persons of all denominations to a higher level of Christian commitment. It is not surprising that burned-over district revivalists and abolitionists were many of those leading the way.[69]

As early as 1828, James Latourette and a few of his fellow Methodist revivalists in New York state began to put a renewed emphasis on the doctrine of entire sanctification in their preaching. They encouraged emotional and physical outbursts as attestations to the experience. These preachers were even willing to assume the hitherto derogatory term "perfectionist." Probably due to a lack of support from the hierarchy for his excessive measures, Latourette broke away from the Methodist establishment and pastored an independent perfectionist congregation in New York City. A group soon migrated from Latourette's congregation to Albany, and from there to the town of Delphi in central New York; subsequently, Delphi became a center for perfectionists drawn from various denominations. By these actions, the early perfectionists presaged the comeouterism that would typify later ecclesiastical abolitionists.[70]

Luther Myrick

Reports of doctrinal irregularity among the Presbygational churches of the burned-over district caused great consternation among the powerful conservative Presbyterian leaders in New York City and in Philadelphia. The conservatives charged their denominational counterparts in upper New York state with a lack of diligence in controlling theological errors festering within the region. By 1834, central New York Presbyterian ministers realized that "something must be done to stop the clamors of the men down east, who had begun to think that Oneida Presbytery had all run crazy." The presbytery concluded that "the state of things demanded that there should be an example to deter others"—a denominational prosecution of one of the agitators. They chose as their example a minister named Luther Myrick.[71]

Myrick could claim no innocence regarding his role in the religious turmoil. Pertaining to the "fanaticism and false doctrine which was said to prevail in this section of country," wrote an eyewitness, "the name of Luther Myrick occupied a very conspicuous place in the public mind." The specific "false doctrine" that Myrick articulated was the theological concept of entire sanctification, and the most serious of the several formal charges levied against Myrick was that he had been "preaching the doctrine of perfection." To be precise, the presbytery was actually accusing Myrick of promoting a more extreme and controversial type of perfectionism, antinomian perfectionism. He was being blamed for "all the sins and all the stupidity" of certain "Mysticks" and "Antinomians," who believed that holiness implied complete moral license.[72] Myrick, however, was an evangelical perfectionist, rejecting the ethical libertinism of the antinomians and insisting that Christians follow God's moral law. Nonetheless, he was guilty as charged on the count of teaching entire sanctification (in its evangelical form), and he did not disclaim it.

At his trial, the presbytery gave Myrick an opportunity to clear his name and to demonstrate his Calvinist orthodoxy by preaching a sermon to them. So he did preach to his Presbyterian colleagues—on their personal need for entire sanctification. Not surprisingly, "the presbytery members were very uneasy and restless" while he preached. Following his sermon, he was summarily suspended from the Presbyterian ministry.[73]

Myrick was a key transitional figure, introducing Methodist conceptions of evangelical perfection into traditionally Calvinist, Presbygationalist circles. An ordained preacher and itinerant revivalist, Myrick pastored several Presbygational churches in central New York from 1827 to 1833 before his trial and suspension from the ministry. His last official Presbyterian pastorate was in Cazenovia, Madison County, only four miles from the perfectionist center at Delphi; Myrick's holiness ideas may have supplemented those at Delphi, or his ideas may have been partially derived from theirs. Whatever the case, the theology that he preached clearly had Wesleyan inclinations, causing a conservative opponent to charge him with denying "every doctrine which distinguishes the Presbyterian church from the Methodist."[74]

Myrick's brand of perfectionism implanted the Methodist concept of perfect love into the prevailing theology of Nathaniel Taylor. For American Methodists, perfect love for God and for neighbor could be realized when a person experienced God's gracious gift of entire sanctification; for Taylor, perfect moral obedience was a worthy goal for which one was obligated to strive but which one would never reach. Myrick combined these concepts to argue that Christians can and ought to attain total conformity to the moral law of God by being entirely sanctified by the Spirit. He taught "the doctrine of Perfection, not merely as a matter of obligation, but of personal experience," believing that a dramatic spiritual experience could give one the necessary power to fulfill one's duty of entire obedience to God's law.[75] In his early career, Myrick applied the doctrine of Christian perfection to issues of individual morality; by 1836, however, he had extended the idea of complete sanctification to the whole of society, including attacks on the "tyranny" of southern slavery, of denominational judicatories, and of religious patriarchy—thus challenging some of the most fundamental assumptions about civil and ecclesiastical institutions in the United States.

As a result of Myrick's influence, many new independent perfectionist congregations sprang up in central New York, most of them the result of "disruptions" and secessions from Presbygationalist churches.[76] Myrick also encouraged the public participation of women in revival meetings and in congregational decision-making, challenging the way that women were being treated in Presbyterian churches—treated, he contended, "as if they had no souls."[77] The anti-institutionalist theme in all of these actions, derived from his espousal of evangelical perfectionism, would later bear fruit in ecclesiastical abolitionism.

Oberlin Perfectionism

Evangelical perfectionist theology was also in bloom at Oberlin College, Charles G. Finney's revivalistic school in Ohio.[78] Given the extensive contacts between Oberlin and the burned-over district of New York, the affinity of Finney and his colleagues for holiness doctrine was to be expected. Finney's initial sphere of operations was upper New York state; he had worked closely with Myrick and others from the region who were now promoting the new doctrines. The president of Oberlin, Asa Mahan, had continuing connections with his native region. Also, a large proportion of the college's enrollment hailed from central and western New York, and these idealistic young men and women were particularly receptive to the religious developments of their home region.[79]

The new interest in promoting evangelical perfectionism at Oberlin grew from the practical need for retaining revivalistic enthusiasm. Finney was characteristically frank about his expediency in adopting the doctrine; his encouragement to believers that they should now experience entire sanctification was more strategic than dogmatic. Finney was troubled that many of his converts were falling away from their earlier commitments. Greater spiritual stamina was needed to accomplish the enormous tasks that faced Christians if they were to bring in the millennium. Although he believed that his earlier efforts had resulted in "genuine" revivals, he was concerned that the majority of converts were "a disgrace to religion," having abandoned any attempt to obey the moral law. Finney viewed this abandonment of moral living as the logical result of an acceptance of Taylor's theological limitations on the actual attainability of Christian perfection. Desiring to be practical in all matters of theology, Finney could not help but be attracted by perfectionist logic, which held out the promise of an attained sanctification.[80]

Initially, Finney had disregarded the doctrine of holiness as held by "our Methodist brethren," misinterpreting Wesley's doctrine of sanctification "to relate almost altogether to states of the sensibility"—to emotional experiences unrelated to ethical resolve. By 1837, however, the Oberlinites looked anew at the doctrine of Christian perfection, and over the next decade Finney, Mahan, and their colleagues taught a rather generic version of the Methodist concept of perfect love combined with Taylor's view of moral obligation. Like Myrick, the Oberlinites believed that a second, higher religious experience after conversion (akin to the experience of entire sanctification as preached by early American Methodists) provided the power necessary for living a consistently consecrated life—perfect obedience to the moral law. Indeed, the moral duty of "entire consecration" was made equivalent and coterminous with the gracious gift of entire sanctification. They also held the Wesleyan view that "constant growth in holiness" should occur after a sanctification experience, so that Christian perfection became a spiral of holiness for the believer.[81]

After Finney's 1837 acceptance of the concept of entire sanctification, "Oberlin perfectionism" became commonplace among many Northern churches and communities. Scores of students were trained at Oberlin, then sent to pulpits impressed with the stamp of evangelical perfectionist theology.

Oberlin-led perfectionist tent meetings and church conferences were held throughout the burned-over district, and in 1839 the *Oberlin Evangelist* began publication with the expressed purposes of disseminating holiness doctrine and of encouraging reform activity.[82]

Garrisonian Perfectionism

In the same year that Finney accepted entire sanctification—1837—the antinomian perfectionist leader John Humphrey Noyes paid a visit to William Lloyd Garrison's antislavery office in Boston, where Garrison was having a lively discussion with leading abolitionists regarding "political matters"—presumably about the appropriateness of abolitionists getting involved in the political process in order to further the antislavery cause. Noyes and Garrison talked about the doctrine of perfection and, more significantly, the application of perfectionist ideas to the exercise of governmental power.[83] Garrison, influenced by the nonresistant doctrines of his friend Henry C. Wright, was preoccupied with these questions.

Viewing slavery as an unwarranted infringement on the natural right of an individual to personal freedom, Wright deduced that slaveholders were despotic authorities who held unnatural control over slaves. Slavery, at its root, was coercive subjugation of one person by another, a compulsory system that denied human liberty. Going further, Wright postulated that coercion in any form was wrong; not only was slavery evil, but so was war, and so was any human government that used force for the enactment of laws. Even a democracy used the threat of force to back up its claims, and so obedience to such a government was compulsory, and compulsion denied the basic maxim of individual freedom. Consistent with nonresistance, Wright did not advocate forceful disobedience to coercive human governments, but he did suggest that any active support of a government, such as political involvement, only served to buttress its inherently despotic authority.[84]

As Garrison grappled with these ideas, they seemed to resonate with Noyes's antinomian brand of perfectionism. Noyes expressed to Garrison his belief that the U.S. government was denying God-given liberty to millions of the nation's inhabitants by its legal acceptance of slavery; the American people were sinfully trying to perpetuate a human government that was opposed to God's government. Moreover, Noyes made the daring suggestion that Garrison could "set Anti-slavery in the sunshine only by making it tributary to Holiness," that is, by becoming preoccupied with the "UNIVERSAL EMANCIPATION FROM SIN." Noyes considered antislavery and other reform movements as only "preliminary skirmishes which precede a general engagement." Garrison could become a commanding officer in "the hottest battle of righteousness" if he set his "face toward *perfect* holiness."

Garrison was now provided with a larger panorama of the sovereign rule of God in all aspects of human society, rather than the relatively limited picture of the emancipation of slaves. Consequently, he became committed to nonresistance, renounced human governments, and asserted his agreement with "practical holiness"—the doctrine "that total abstinence from sin, in this life, is not only commanded but necessarily obtainable." Although he never claimed to have had a religious experience of entire sanctification, Garrison nonetheless believed that a holy life was "practically attainable."[85]

Garrison's acceptance of perfectionism marked a turning point in his career. He realized that slavery could not be attacked in isolation from other personal and societal sins and he became antagonistic toward institutions in church and state. Given his antinomian tendencies and his thoroughgoing repudiation of institutional structures, Garrison should be understood as an anarchistic perfectionist, a descriptive type which was both similar to, and different from, the evangelical perfectionism of Myrick and Finney.[86]

"Perfectionists Differ among Themselves"

During the 1830s and 1840s, perfectionism in the burned-over district was growing beyond its original Methodist bailiwick, most dramatically among nontraditional adherents to the doctrine who were perfectionists by disposition rather than by custom.[87] Their fundamental theological proclivity was rebellion against authority, dogmatism, and doctrinal systemization, stressing instead freedom of private judgment, openness to innovation, and the value of individual investigation unmediated by creeds, confessions, or ecclesiastical hierarchies. Thus, antebellum perfectionists had a reputation for being inherently anti-institutional. According to them, the unnatural structures of slavery, denominational hierarchies, and traditional Calvinist dogma were obviously sinful, kept in power by immoral persons—and destined to be dismantled by sanctified persons.

Although burned-over district perfectionists united in their distrust of institutions, they divided over the extent of that anti-institutionalism. The desired result of the free investigation of ideas was a harmonic and simplified core of Christian faith, but the actual result was an ideological bedlam in which nearly as many varieties of perfectionism were produced as there were perfectionists. According to one antinomian, "perfectionists differ among themselves on almost all points."[88]

In studying perfectionism, several historians have described a range or "spectrum" of perfectionist views;[89] similarly, historians of abolition have identified an "institutionalization continuum," a scale of differing views regarding the appropriate amount of institutionalization.[90] Actually, the abolitionist "continuum" and the perfectionist "spectrum" were closely aligned. Lewis Perry, for example, has demonstrated a "doctrinal link between antislavery and anarchism" among the Garrisonians; when Garrison embraced nonresistant thought, his abolitionism was subsumed under the rubric of anarchistic perfectionism.[91]

Abolitionists varied broadly along the institutionalization continuum. For example, Luther Myrick surveyed the divergent opinions regarding the role of religious organizations: at one extreme were the anarchistic perfectionists who "withdr[ew] from all church organizations" because they were inherently evil; at the other extreme were nonperfectionists who supported the existing "corrupt" ecclesiastical authorities out of concern that well-established social structures were needed to provide guidance and control for the society. In between were the ecclesiastical abolitionists, who suggested that church organizations were impure as presently constituted but could be redeemed by being drastically restructured. Those who held to this moderate viewpoint, including Myrick himself, believed that it was the duty of sanctified Christians "to break away from the present corrupt organizations and establish a new organization."[92]

Myrick's survey demonstrates that the societal debate concerning the proper scope of freedom in America, expressed earlier in the discourse of new measures revivalism, was by the late 1830s expressed in the more emphatic rhetoric of perfectionism. The dialogue about perfectionism became the "more powerful means" by which religious abolitionists participated in the larger cultural dialogue about democratization.[93] Their differences were articulated in the language of their theological discussions concerning the appropriate structures for a democratic society. These differences can be seen as defining three generalized groups of abolitionists—the anarchists, the institutionalists, and the reformers.

Anarchists

Antebellum perfectionists believed that human society could approximate the millennium—the eventual and inevitable rule of the government of God on earth. Anarchistic perfectionists articulated a more specific application of this belief. For them, all human structures stood in the way of the establishment of the divine order; therefore, such structures should be abolished in preparation for the millennium. For anarchists that meant severing all connections with human structures, including support for political activities or local Christian congregations, because they imposed unnatural restraints upon individuals.[94]

Anarchists claimed that their actual goal was not anarchy but order—God's millennial order.[95] The type of government that they proposed was to be "immediately exercised by God" rather than organized by humans, because any human structure would inevitably be based on coercive restraint. The harmony of this divine government would result in a new society in which individual self-mastery held sway and in which the moral law was obeyed on a purely voluntary basis.[96] According to the anarchists, any attempt at reforming or restructuring human organizations was not only wrongheaded but wicked; a somewhat improved situation brought on by reforms would only delay the eventual necessary destruction of all human devices and thus delay the harmonized society of the millennium.

In line with these beliefs, the Garrisonians withdrew from most institutions and developed a strong antipathy toward all those who continued to support the established structures. Because "government is upheld by physical strength, and its laws are enforced at the point of the bayonet," the nonresistants repudiated "all human politics." Churches, which were shams of true religion, were also to be discarded. Organized religion was to be replaced by each individual's own religion of the heart, unmediated by any creed or clergyman.[97]

Institutionalists

At the other end of the abolitionist continuum were nonperfectionists who supported conventional structures and who endorsed existing churches and traditional politics. As one might have suspected, the perfectionist abolitionists who left "sinful" structures denounced the institutionalists as traitors to the antislavery cause.

While perfectionist abolitionists considered slavery to be just one symptom of a cancerously oppressive society, dying from institutional tyranny, institution-supporting abolitionists felt that slavery was merely an evil blemish that needed to be removed from a generally healthy society. By advocating antislavery from an insider's position, they could raise the religious consciousness of the people within their churches and political parties and at the same time control the anarchists' social disorder. They were also concerned about achieving practical results, which—they hoped—could be obtained more readily by working within established structures.

Along with their pragmatism, many institution-supporting abolitionists were convinced that existing human organizations were ordained by God. People needed to be controlled by coercive governments until the millennial government of God put an end to inherent human sinfulness. Furthermore, they insisted, citizens must submit to their leaders as instruments of God's law on earth, for the external human law was equivalent to the law of God.[98] These abolitionists were dedicated to working through extant structures, remaining committed to the Whig or Democratic parties as the most realistic means to achieve their ends. As Christian citizens obligated to obey the civil law as if it were God's law, their task was to convince the majority to legislate change through conventional channels.[99]

Perfectionist abolitionists (whether anarchistic or evangelical) were as hostile toward institutional antislavery advocates as they were toward their outright proslavery opponents. They regarded the institutionalists as wolves in sheep's clothing.

Reformers

The major portion of abolitionists in upper New York state were found somewhere between the two extremes of this continuum. Neither wholly antiorganizational nor wholly institution-supporting, they were instead reformers. Contrary to those who maintained traditional institutions, the reformers felt that political parties and churches must be rigorously altered to limit the organizational power of human structures; contrary to anarchistic perfectionists, reformers argued that civic order required some human institutions. Thus the reformers were evangelical perfectionists: as evangelicals, they believed in the primacy of affective religious experience and in the biblical idea of the inevitability of sin, with its consequent need to order human behavior; as perfectionists, they believed that intentional sin could be overcome and that the authority granted to institutional structures should be restricted. Their tactic was to come out from existing "despotic" institutions and to "re-form" them along sanctified lines. They described their strategy as "secession and re-organization."[100]

The reformers' ideal of democratic freedom as an ordered (or organized) liberty typified their moderate viewpoint. Myrick, for instance, advocated a type of "Christian Liberty" that was derived from "the heavenly doctrines of Christian Union and Holiness." Such liberty, as perceived by Myrick, implied freedom from hierarchical authorities but still left a place for localized, voluntary external structures. William Goodell likewise called for Christian liberty, which he defined as a democratic principle existing in between the extremes of "DISORGANIZATION and DESPOTISM."[101] He felt that true democracy would provide for a "government in accordance with the principles of liberty and human rights, yet, at the same time, effective in the maintenance of a strict discipline." The abolitionists at Oberlin agreed with Myrick and with Goodell. They contrasted true freedom—the "freedom of holiness"—with the false "liberty of atheists" (i.e., anarchists), which did not recognize necessary social restraints based on the "laws of mutual dependence." Some external laws were needed to hold together the fabric of society.[102]

The reformers were convinced that human cooperation with God was essential for the successful establishment of the divine government on earth. They believed that human governments should be reordered to correspond with God's democratic moral government. When that occurred, the millennium would commence, for God's government would be coterminous with human government.[103]

Both in religious and in political matters, the reformers thought that it was important to find "middle ground." In Goodell's opinion, the middle ground was clearly fixed by a "Bible line of demarkation [*sic*] between despotic authority on the one hand, and disorganization on the other."[104]

In actual practice, it was difficult for the reformers to reach consensus regarding the biblical boundaries that were appropriate for their centrist stance.

Goodell himself realized that there were "threatening errors, on the right hand and on the left." Like most middle-of-the-road strategies, the reforming position was precariously unstable. There was only "a slender railing" to keep reformers from falling off the precipice into antinomian anarchism on the one side or institutional despotism on the other.[105]

The difficulty that the reformers faced in maintaining a balanced middle course provided them with an immediate personal example of the balancing act that was going on more broadly within antebellum culture. American democracy was caught in a basic and unresolvable tension between two conflicting ideals, the freedom of individual conscience and the social order of corporate compromise. Many Americans did not try to keep these ideals together simultaneously; Garrisonians, for example, rejected institutional involvement altogether, while institutionalists sacrificed religious purity for partisan success. Only the reforming position—the evangelical perfectionists who called themselves ecclesiastical abolitionists—sought to hold together both moral principle and political action. As such, among their contemporaries, the ecclesiastical abolitionists were able to articulate with particular clarity the inherent ambivalences of antebellum democracy.

TWO

Spiritual Democracy  *The Development*
of Antislavery Church Reform

WHEN SAMUEL RINGGOLD WARD moved to the small village of South Butler, New York, in 1841 to assume his position as the new pastor of the Congregational church, he and his young family were the only African Americans in the community. Ward's presence brought much more than racial diversity to South Butler, however. His interest in equal rights for his fellow African Americans and his dedication to evangelical perfectionist reform led him to work for the expansion of democracy in all aspects of the town's religious and political life. For example, Ward's preaching that denominational authorities and sectarian distinctions were antidemocratic convinced the South Butler church members to sever their ties to the presbytery; the congregation became a center for church reform agitation by hosting regional "Christian Union" conventions. Ward was also an avid Liberty man, provoking the congregation to support the Liberty Party organizationally and electorally. As a result, South Butler was reputed to contain "political abolitionists of the most frantic and rabid kind."[1]

Ward's successors in South Butler during the 1840s continued his commitment to alternative religious and political structures. Thus, the congregation was accustomed to notoriety and to unconventional leadership when, in 1852, it called its most famous pastor—Antoinette Brown, usually considered to be the first ordained clergywoman. Like the other pastors at the Congregational

Samuel Ringgold Ward (1817–1866?). *From I. Garland Penn,* The Afro-American Press and Its Editors *(Springfield, Mass.: Willey and Co., 1891).*

church of South Butler, Brown was a student of Oberlin perfectionism, a supporter of Christian union, and a Liberty Party leader—in short, an ecclesiastical abolitionist.[2]

In its concern for church reform, the South Butler congregation was part of a distinct benevolent reform movement designed to democratize religious institutions.[3] Church reformers were committed to the goal of a spiritual democracy, defined as Christian fellowship that was free from hierarchical restraint and factional division. As ecclesiastical abolitionists, they believed that spiritual democracy would occur when sanctified Christians seceded from denominationally bound churches and reorganized themselves into democratically structured antislavery congregations. The achievement of this religious de-

Antoinette Brown (1825–1921). *Courtesy of Schlesinger Library, Radcliffe College.*

mocratization for Christian Americans would help usher in political democratization for all Americans. The pursuit of a perfected politics in ecclesiastical matters was intended to provide an example for the concurrent pursuit of a perfected politics in civil matters.

Because William Lloyd Garrison's views regarding the progress of abolitionism often prevailed in the literature about the antislavery movement, the comeouter churches' impact was "overlooked," according to William Goodell. Garrisonian abolitionists denied the legitimacy of all human structures, including antislavery congregations; thus, despite the emergence of hundreds of comeouter churches by 1850, their preeminent role in furthering abolitionism was "wholly ignored" in the journals and reports of the Garrisonians. As early as 1853, Goodell warned future scholars of abolitionism to be cognizant of this Garrisonian bias: "The historian must look elsewhere than to the columns of their [Garrisonian] journals . . . for information concerning this [church reform] movement. He must seek it in the papers of the Liberty party, and in the religious papers conducted by those engaged in these enterprises."[4]

When the periodicals mentioned by Goodell are investigated, along with congregational records and other local sources, it becomes apparent that church reform was a popular and influential movement, and that the way in which church reformers reorganized their congregations furnished abolitionists with a model for reorganizing the political landscape.

Typical of ecclesiastical abolitionists, Luther Myrick was fond of calling church reform the "cause of Christian Liberty."[5] Likewise, other church reformers styled themselves "the friends of liberty."[6] This desire to create egalitarian religious institutions was not new: the Christian Connection, the Methodist Protestant church, and other small religious bodies had encouraged greater doctrinal and organizational liberty for several decades. Thus, ecclesiastical abolitionists were part of an already-established pattern of religious democratization, a second generation of those on the quest for a spiritual democracy.[7]

The two generations of Christian democratizers, however, differed significantly from one another. Earlier groups such as the Christian Connection were interested in liberating the structures of the church but often were ambivalent about other movements for liberation, such as antislavery.[8] The later church reformers—the ecclesiastical abolitionists—were interested in extending freedom to the whole society, not just to the church. Their evangelical perfectionist theology enlarged and intensified the already existing impulse for greater spiritual democracy.

Most ecclesiastical abolitionists were introduced to the broad vision of establishing a sanctified "government of God" through their interest in the proposal that Christians should be unfettered from the authority of powerful denominations. The logic of perfectionism then compelled them to expand their concern for democratic reform beyond their original interest in securing freedom from denominational oppression to include additional issues of freedom from oppression. The struggle for greater democratization was now applied to enslaved African Americans—and eventually to other marginalized people, such as women, Native Americans, and industrial laborers. They came to believe that there was a direct linkage between the various interlocking oppressions so characteristic of institutional structures; slavery was evil, but so were religious hierarchies, traditional partisan politics, patriarchy, and other forms of oppression.[9]

Abolitionist Frustration with Traditional Denominations

Before the mid-1830s, most religiously active abolitionists were not interested in withdrawing from the established churches; they were committed to moving their denominations toward the immediatist position. Given their confident belief that the power of persuasive education would naturally create a morally pure society, abolitionists had every reason to expect that, with sufficient information, their denominations would embrace immediatism; theoretically, professing Christians were more open than was the general populace to investigating new truths that would lead to greater moral purity.[10] The abolitionists discovered, however, that the major denominations seemed to have more interest in limiting and inhibiting antislavery activity than in accepting the antislavery agenda.

Denominational officials sought to restrict abolitionist agitation for several reasons. Foremost was the pervasiveness of racial prejudice. The vast majority of churchmen, South and North, stubbornly persisted in their racist "contempt . . . maintain[ed] towards the Negro." Religious leaders also disliked abolitionists' use of harsh language; antislavery advocates had the reputation of making their "zeal for liberty a cloak of pharisaic arrogance and uncharitableness." Abolitionists often refused to admit any integrity in the motives of those who disagreed with them. Many Northern judicatories were already on record as opposing slavery; religious leaders were offended that abolitionists did not consider their mild antislavery statements strong enough. Additionally, those within the mainstream denominations saw abolitionist contentiousness as a threat to ecclesiastical harmony. Leaders of the religious establishment worried that denunciatory statements would alienate Southerners. This would hinder their evangelization efforts in the South and, consequently, lessen their group's overall influence relative to other denominations. Furthermore, abolitionists threatened the privileged position of the leaders themselves by attacking "the constituted authorities of the church."[11]

The abolitionists of the Methodist church of Seneca Falls perceptively analyzed the reasons for ecclesiastical restriction of antislavery activities. They wrote in their minutes that many "ministers and people are so startled at what they deem wrong and precipitate among abolitionists that, fearing for the unity of the church, they have so directed all their councils for the suppression of abolitionism, that they have not as heretofore so deeply realized and deplored the great evil of slavery." Unfortunately for the abolitionists in such churches, the majority of persons in the large denominations continued to support the "suppression of abolitionism"—including antiabolitionist mob attacks and the disruption of antislavery church services—more than they "deplored the great evil of slavery."[12]

Ecclesiastical censures and proscriptive legislation became commonplace at denominational meetings. Methodist leaders were especially eager to silence the abolitionists under their supervision. In 1836, the New York Annual Conference of the Methodist Episcopal Church censured the abolitionist paper *Zion's Watchman* and prosecuted its editor, La Roy Sunderland (later to become an antislavery comeouter). The *Watchman* had a great amount of support from upstate Methodist abolitionists, and these abolitionists condemned the denominational censuring as high-handed and despotic.

Most galling to abolitionists within the denominations were "gag rules" that forbade the discussion of slavery at church meetings. First, the (Congregationalist) General Association of Connecticut prohibited itinerating agents from speaking to members of churches "without the advice and consent of the pastors and regular ecclesiastical bodies." Several New York state conferences, presbyteries, and associations took their cue from the General Association's action and passed their own prohibitory regulations. William Goodell echoed the protest of the New York State Anti-Slavery Society when he declared that the judicatories exercised "a prerogative comprising in essence one of the most despotic powers claimed by the slave-master over the slave."[13]

Within Presbyterianism, the restrictions on abolitionist activities were compounded by concurrent denominational anxieties over perfectionism and church polity. These anxieties resulted first in the 1837 schism between "New School" and "Old School" factions, and later in the further proscription of abolitionists within the New School.[14]

Various historians have attempted to isolate one factor as primarily responsible for the 1837 schism. Some point to antislavery agitation.[15] Others find that the Presbyterian split was the ultimate consequence of a longstanding doctrinal controversy growing out of revisions to their traditional "federal theology," the final straw for conservative Old School Presbyterians being the popularity of Nathaniel Taylor's "free will" ideas among New Schoolers.[16] A more nuanced interpretation would conclude that a combination of factors led to the division. Indeed, according to those most directly affected by the schism, the controversy was a coalescence of several interrelated issues: perfectionism, abolitionism, and church reform.[17]

To Presbyterian leaders, Luther Myrick's trial in 1834 symbolized the seemingly despicable condition of the Presbygational churches in upper New York state and on the Western Reserve of northeastern Ohio. Old School opponents of that region's rampant new measures identified two problems: the pervasiveness of Taylor's theology (which was believed to lead "directly to Perfectionism"), and the extremes to which some burned-over district preachers would go to promote revivals and moral reforms.[18] According to the conservative Old School faction of the Warsaw Presbyterian church, for example, the opposing faction was advancing "false doctrine" (specifically perfectionism) and "fanaticism" (which referred to their strong support of ultraist reform movements, particularly abolition). In the minds of the Old Schoolers, perfectionist theology and extremist advocacy of radical reforms were intertwined.[19]

However, it was not just the existence of perfectionist "false doctrine" and abolitionist "fanaticism" that caused Old School Presbyterians to force out the New Schoolers; they also disliked the polity of the Presbygational churches. Due to the accommodation agreements between Presbyterians and Congregationalists, the presbyteries had no effective jurisdiction over a large number of their churches and pastors. Some of those identified as heretics, such as

Myrick, were within Presbyterian jurisdiction and could be disciplined, but conservative leaders had no control over many other nominally Presbyterian preachers and congregations. A troublemaker such as Finney could simply affiliate with the Congregationalists, thereby escaping disciplinary action and remaining at liberty to influence Presbyterian churches with his bothersome beliefs.

Similarly, an entire church that declared itself Congregationalist could ignore the admonitions of the presbytery. The church in Oran, New York, for example, asked Myrick to preach for them after his suspension from the Presbyterian ministry—deliberately scoffing at presbyterial authority. The presbytery was aghast, but because of the accommodation agreement, "they had no command over the church at Oran." Such embarrassments were just what Old School Presbyterians hoped to remedy by declaring the accommodation plans null and void in 1837, thereby excising nearly half of the denomination's membership.[20]

The situation, however, did not get any better for perfectionist Presbygationalists following the split in the denomination. After the excision, the now-severed New School branch was not about to be accused of harboring dangerous beliefs and practices within its own ranks. New Schoolers in central New York were informed that Old Schoolers "charged the Presbytery with countenancing" unorthodox perfectionist and abolitionist preachers "because they did not lay their hands upon them and put a stop to their mad careers." The New School Presbyterians hoped to put an end to their reputation as extremists in doctrine and reform. As perfectionism spread during the late 1830s and early 1840s, several New School judicatories officially censured all perfectionists found within their bounds, repeating the previous actions taken by the Old Schoolers.[21]

Many burned-over district Presbygationalists preferred an independent congregational church government and were angered by assertions of Presbyterian dominance over their local church affairs (whether Old School or New School). Their resentment drove them toward the views of democratic church reform being advanced by Luther Myrick and others. William Goodell spoke for many when he complained that the "Congregationalists have consented to such a connexion and affinity with Presbyterians, as have led to the compromise of their distinctive principles of religious liberty, [and] of church independency." Ironically, Goodell explained, many churches that were

Congregationalist in name were not actually structured according to a demo-cratically congregational polity. In addition, those attracted to a locally based church government were often the same persons who were censured for their abolitionist and perfectionist agitation. After the 1837 schism, then, there exist-ed a conflation of interests among many independently minded New York Presbygationalists and, eventually, among their friends from other denomina-tions: the advocacy of ultraist reforms such as abolition, the espousal of Finney's and Myrick's brand of evangelical perfectionism, and the promotion of democratic church reform. All the components were in place for the devel-opment of a unified ecclesiastical abolitionist agenda.[22]

Spiritual Despotism Versus Spiritual Democracy

Ecclesiastical abolitionists perceived that their denominations and political parties catered to Southern despotism by accommodating proslavery con-stituencies for the sake of institutional harmony. They began to question whether their affiliation with proslavery denominations and parties was consis-tent with a holy life. When denominational judicatories with whom they were "connected by ecclesiastical ties," wrote the Seneca Falls Methodists, "adopt measures and sanction principles, which, by their tendency, are subversive of the dearest interests of humanity and religion," then they were duty-bound to act in a way that would clear them of their guilt by association. Preoccupied as they were with questions of purity and principle, the abolitionists resonated with the evangelical perfectionist doctrinal emphasis on pure and uncompro-mising obedience to the moral law. "You cannot stand too erect," wrote Beriah Green for the New York State Anti-Slavery Society: "A righteous cause de-mands uprightness in its supporters." The acceptance of entire sanctification included one's absolute personal disentanglement with evil, "coming out" from institutions that were perceived as sinful was a particularly imperative dis-entanglement.[23]

Religious abolitionists believed that their fellow Christians would become abolitionists if they were free to investigate the slavery issue. It was observed, however, that most individuals within the denominations were so driven by sectarian loyalty that their "bigoted partiality . . . close[d] up the mind to im-partial investigation." Petty sectarian jealousies were inhibiting professing Christians from becoming consistent abolitionists. Their "unnatural" attachment to pet doctrinal distinctives and religious traditions constrained them from living righteously. Perhaps, they reasoned, the very structures of the institutions were intrinsically despotic, a result of the denominations' demand that their constituents adhere to authoritative creeds or practices, thereby blocking the direct investigative access existing naturally between an individual and God.[24]

Denominational hierarchies exercised a despotism not unlike that of slaveholders. Conventional ecclesiastical (and political) institutions hindered Christians from living perfected lives of obedience to the moral law, and prevented them from establishing the democratized government of God in American society. Ecclesiastical abolitionists concluded that the entire structures of those institutions must be fundamentally flawed. The only suitable response to such tyranny was to come out from the impurity. Unlike the complete rejection of those institutions by the anarchists, however, the ecclesiastical abolitionists sought to restructure and purify their churches, based on their distinctively moderating interpretation of the perfected moral government of God. They sought to establish new organizations that would allow unmediated investigation and unrestricted moral activity.[25]

Unionists and Other Presbygationalist Comeouters

Luther Myrick was the primary formative influence on early ecclesiastical abolitionist thought. Following his 1834 suspension from the Oneida Presbytery, Myrick and three other ministers created their own evangelical perfectionist judicatory, the Central Evangelical Association. Within two years, even the Central Evangelical Association was too binding for Myrick's evolving views on church polity, so he organized an independent Free Church in Cazenovia, New York, unaffiliated with any judicatory. To propagate further his anti-institutionalist ideas, he established in May 1836 the *Union Herald,* a weekly paper that promoted the formation of locally based churches, free from any institutional restraint that could bind individual conscience or tie a congregation to a denomination. Myrick hoped to replace the spiritual despotism of religious hierarchies with the spiritual democracy of community-centered congregational government—a purified ecclesiastical polity. Because his intention was to break down denominational parochialism and to unify all sanctified Christians, Myrick's ecclesiological ideas became known as "Unionism," and churches established on his model were dubbed Unionist or Union churches. Critics, however, claimed that Myrick's ideas led to "disunion" rather than to union and that Unionism was simply another denomination composed of those who allegedly did not believe in any denomination.[26]

Unionist churches—the earliest ecclesiastical abolitionist congregations in the burned-over district[27]—multiplied rapidly in the late 1830s and 1840s. Seven churches were connected to Myrick's Central Evangelical Association in 1835; a decade later, one hundred and one Unionist churches had been established in upper New York state alone.[28] Myrick facilitated communication between the independent-minded Unionists through the *Union Herald,* making it a forum for the exchange of news and ideas about antislavery church reform. Until his death in 1843, Myrick travelled constantly, preaching on the topic of church reform and providing leadership at periodic Christian Union conventions.

Unionist churches were composed of persons who left their denominational (usually Presbygational) churches. Often, these new churches abandoned any traditional labels—such as "Presbyterian"—so that they would not mistakenly be identified as belonging to a denomination. The comeouter congregations adopted a variety of new names for themselves, depending on what phrase each local group felt was the most scripturally valid and the least denominational-sounding—the Free Meeting House in Apulia, The Church of Christ in Preble, the Independent Church in Canastota, the Anti-Slavery Church in Cato, the Abolition Church in Moravia, and the Church of Equal Rights in Randolph Center.[29] Others referred to themselves as did the evangelical perfectionists of Warsaw, who believed themselves to be the only true church in the community, uniting all sanctified reformers—and thus matter-of-factly called themselves *The* Church of Warsaw.[30]

Myrick was hesitant to employ any name for the group of congregations associated with his ideas of church reform, for fear that a distinguishing designation would be interpreted as condoning the existence of a denominational faction. "We have no name. People call us just what they please. . . . We have assumed no particular name, as a body, and we do not intend to." Nonetheless, he did acquiesce to using the term "Unionist" for the sake of convenience.[31]

Some entire Presbygational churches accepted Myrick's ideas, declared their independence, and pulled out of their presbyteries. Many of the seceding local churches called themselves Congregational or Free Congregational as a way of repudiating the institutional encroachments of Presbyterianism; though called "Congregational," many of these churches were also free of any association with traditional New England Congregationalism.

It is important to understand the subtle distinctions between the various professed Congregationalists. Some so-called Congregational churches were completely independent church bodies made up of antislavery church reformers. Others were Presbygational churches that reasserted their old denominational identity as Congregationalists after the 1837 breakup of the accommodation plans—out of loyalty to their Yankee heritage, for instance, or to escape the perceived deficiencies of the now-splintered Presbyterian denomination. Indeed, among some of these traditional Congregationalists, their renewed denominational consciousness was linked to a Calvinist repudiation of perfectionism. Thus, nonperfectionist Congregationalist abolitionists such as Joshua Leavitt felt comfortable supporting the trend toward a growing institutional identity because the national Congregational denomination was doctrinally Calvinist and also because it satisfied their desire to be removed from any complicity with the "proslavery" position of Presbyterianism.[32] Of course, to perfectionist church reformers, Congregationalism of this nonperfectionist, institutionalized variety merely replaced the "ecclesiastical slavery" of one centralized judicatory with that of another.

The perfectionist Congregational and Free Congregational churches in the burned-over district, following Myrick's model, were completely independent of all translocal associations. They held to a policy of antislavery agitation and a polity of strict congregational autonomy.[33] Antoinette Brown and the South Butler church she served, for example, are usually labeled "Congregationalist," but neither she nor the church were Congregationalist in any denominational sense; the church was a comeouter organization that happened to be congregational in its organizational structure.[34] Thus, the South Butler Congregational church and other Free Congregational churches became veritable Unionist churches without actually calling themselves "Unionists."

Myrick had intended that Union churches would unify all comeouter abolitionists; in practice, however, the Union and Free Congregational churches were composed predominantly of ex-Presbygationalists.[35] Instead of joining the Union churches, abolitionists from the other evangelical denominations formed their own groups of antislavery churches during the decade after 1837: the Franckean Lutherans, the Wesleyan Methodists, and various antislavery

Baptists. Given the variety of comeouter groups, it was difficult for church reformers to establish their desired union of sanctified abolitionists. Comeouter
groups differed over how a truly democratic church polity should function; all
ecclesiastical abolitionists adopted the tactic of "secession and re-organization" regarding proslavery institutions, but they disagreed with one another on
the amount of reorganization that was appropriate. Among ecclesiastical abolitionists, a range of perspectives reflected their diverse views on institutional
structures, although that range was relatively narrow when compared with the
sharp disagreements that ecclesiastical abolitionists had with the anarchists on
the one side and with the leaders of traditional institutions on the other. All ecclesiastical abolitionists were in the middle of the institutionalization continuum, but the various comeouters manifested a narrow spectrum of their own
within the larger spectrum of views regarding institutional structures.

The differences among ecclesiastical abolitionists were most noticeable between Myrick and some of the leaders of the other comeouter groups, such as
John Lawyer of the Franckean Lutherans. Like Myrick, Lawyer rejected the authority of denominational hierarchy; unlike Myrick, however, he and some of
the other ecclesiastical abolitionist leaders were willing to maintain a few "denominational distinctions," such as the continued use of traditional names
(Lutheran, Methodist, or Baptist). Lawyer defended the Franckean Lutherans'
use of their denominational title by contending that "a mere change of name
will never effect the establishment of Christian Union."[36]

Although they retained some limited denominational traits, the other comeouter groups were nearly identical to the Unionists in most respects. They
based their activism on the concept of Christian holiness. They strenuously
sought to eliminate factional divisions among sanctified abolitionists. They
were committed to supporting the Liberty Party. And, concurring with Myrick
that denominational hierarchies were divisive and despotic, they promoted the
goal of a spiritual democracy. (These groups will be discussed more thoroughly in chapter 4.)

This concept of spiritual democracy—particularly as it became associated
with evangelical perfectionism, political abolitionism, and the radical overhaul
of ecclesiastical structures—was the mutual theme of the several abolitionist
comeouter groups centered in upstate New York.[37] As the principles of spiritual democracy became more prevalent, the various abolitionist churches gave
increasingly less weight to the peculiar distinctives of their parent denomina-

tions, abandoned their traditional identities, and grew in solidarity with other abolitionist seceders, regardless of denominational background. Although most antislavery congregations still had particular designations, the term "abolition churches" and the movement known as "antislavery church reform" or "ecclesiastical abolitionism" came to be broadly representative of all who withdrew from the major evangelical denominations. Increasingly, antislavery congregations were an amalgamation of denominationally diverse people. By the early 1840s, this sense of unity nearly created a merger of ecclesiastical abolitionists into one antislavery church organization.[38]

The Church Reform Agenda

The church reformers' concept of Christian union was based on a paradox: Christians would be spiritually united only after they seceded from "anti-Christian" denominational churches. Myrick asserted that established religious bodies—not antislavery seceders—were the ones guilty of schism, because the denominational churches were divided into separate sects. Ecclesiastical abolitionists believed that their small congregations of denominationally diverse reformers foreshadowed the eventual millennial union of all true Christians. They were convinced that like-minded Christian communities would be created if people had unbridled access to information and were unhindered by hierarchical authorities in their quest for truth.[39]

The ecclesiastical abolitionist revolt against oppressive hierarchies took several forms. In contrast to the power of denominational bureaucracies, church reformers stressed congregational initiative. In contrast to the domination of white men in every aspect of church governance, they encouraged the participation and eventually the leadership of African Americans and women. And in contrast to clerical authority, they emphasized the decision-making ability of all church members.

Although antislavery church reformers did not reject the office of pastor (as did the Garrisonians), they did place definite checks on ministerial power. Furthermore, because of their anti-institutional distaste for sacerdotal distinctions between lay and clergy, they minimized the importance of ordination. Church reformers felt that such a rite implied a differentiation of status among Christians and the inherent power of a "clerical caste." William Goodell, for example, served as a Unionist minister but was never ordained, and Antoinette

Brown was "installed" as a pastor rather than formally ordained; in typical ec-clesiastical abolitionist language, it was stated that she was installed because the "authority by any one to 'ordain' [was] disclaimed and denied."[40]

Finally, in contrast to the "spirit of exclusiveness" characteristic of most de-nominations, church reformers condemned "sectarianism"—defined as the adoption of religious tenets that would further the power and authority of one's particular group. Church reformers disapproved of membership stan-dards that required a person's assent to doctrines not deemed "fundamental" to salvation. Since harmony in essential doctrines would occur naturally if peo-ple were free to investigate truth, Myrick thought doctrinal tests should not be required of church members. Unanimity of belief would occur when past su-perstitions and dogmatic "bondage" were swept away. Thus, Unionist preach-ing ridiculed or gave scant treatment to traditional Reformed doctrines. In their experience, these doctrines were merely the shackles of denominational creedalism.[41]

The lack of a regularized doctrinal system among Unionists led critics, par-ticularly Presbyterians, to accuse Union churches of being "unorthodox."[42] Many Unionist leaders, such as Goodell and David Plumb, worried about these accusations of doctrinal irregularity and suggested that Union churches formulate simple declarations of faith. Such voluntary confessions would demonstrate evangelical soundness while repudiating or neglecting elements of Calvinist dogma that were associated with doctrinal oppression. The pro-posal to develop Unionist confessions of faith precipitated heated arguments between the majority of church reformers who felt comfortable with a basic affirmation of fundamental beliefs and those who felt that any formal doctrinal statements were inherently coercive.[43]

Most ecclesiastical abolitionists believed that simple common sense led Christians to collate the scattered doctrines of the Bible into an organized form. Such a collation was not viewed as coercive as long as adherence to it was not compulsory. Traditional creeds had often been used to exclude certain Christians, particularly perfectionists, and so ecclesiastical abolitionist formu-laries of doctrine were not called creeds, a term that still had authoritarian con-notations. Instead, church reformers labeled their statements of faith with other terms, describing them as a "summary statement" or a "synoptical view of sentiments."[44] At the same time that ecclesiastical abolitionists were devel-oping affirmations of basic evangelical beliefs, they rejected nonessential "doc-

trines or customs" that they believed distinguished Christians from one another and led to separation. The subtle differences, however, between "essential"
or "fundamental" beliefs and nonessential ones were open to diverse interpretations and ended up dividing ecclesiastical abolitionists.[45]

The only distinguishing characteristic that Myrick permitted was the differentiation of believers into separate communities of faith based on geographical
proximity. "God's children belong to one family," he declared, "and have no
right to countenance any other distinction than locality." This one "distinction"—of "locality"—indicated the importance that Myrick placed on community-based governance.[46] In contrast, Garrison espoused an individualistic
ecclesiology: persons could best perform their religious duty without participating in a structured church body at all. "Outward visible organization[s]"
were not appropriate for Christians. Garrison believed any association of humans, even on a local level, would impose rules on its members.[47]

The polity advocated by ecclesiastical abolitionists lay between the authoritarian institutionalism characteristic of the denominations and the self-govern-
ing anti-institutionalism characteristic of the Garrisonians. On the one hand,
ecclesiastical abolitionists opposed the encroachments on personal liberty inherent in traditional, nationally based church governments. Denominational
hierarchies substituted translocal authority for the democratic governance of
individual congregations. Abolitionists from the small villages of the burned-
over district were attracted to a local critique of arbitrary national power. For
antislavery church reformers, the image of a perfected ecclesiastical structure
consisted of a regional organization that could advise congregations but would
not have any prescribed jurisdiction over local churches.[48]

On the other hand, however, Garrison went too far when he advocated an
ecclesiology with no need for a community of believers. Church reformers
feared that he sought not only the destruction of corrupt proslavery denominations, but also the "annihilation of the *true* Christian church." The ecclesiastical abolitionists sensed the need for some church order, albeit one in which the
power of the organization was rigorously circumscribed. Certain Christian duties could not be fulfilled except in "a collective capacity." Although they did
not accept the validity of existing denominational structures, they encouraged
sanctified abolitionists to worship together in purified local churches and to
meet together in conventions of like-minded reformers.[49]

Church reformers agreed on the propriety of having a representative assem-

bly of sanctified comeouter congregations in order to establish a stable and
continuing structure for the scattered ecclesiastical abolitionists. Unionists met
together, for example, in church reform "conventions." Some Free Congregational churches grouped themselves into abolitionist "associations." The
Franckean Lutherans convened in a "synod," although they were hesitant to
use the term for fear that others would presume that they were governed by an
authoritative judicatory. The Wesleyan Methodists carefully called themselves
a connection rather than a church. When the Wesleyan Methodist connection
grew into a relatively large national organization, many of the Wesleyans felt the
need to split their group into two regional connections, expressing the typical
church reformers' anxiety regarding translocal power.[50]

To avoid the errors of the denominations from which they seceded, these
variously titled assemblies held no power over individual comeouter congregations. The abolition churches were proud of their newfound freedom from hierarchical control. Myrick clearly stated the antislavery church reformers'
position on the appropriate amount of institutional structure:

We believe in associations, or, if you please, organization. We do not believe that we can
act efficiently in an isolated capacity. . . . We do not war against *Christian associations,*
but against *sectarian* [denominational] *organizations.* A church association, for the
purpose of efficient action in advancing the cause of Christ is not "wicked *per se*"; but a
sectarian organization is, because it is a violation of God's moral law.

This religious democratization was an ordered liberty, reflective of a middle
course and characterized by a combination of "true conservatism and true radicalism."[51]

Although ecclesiastical abolitionists developed structures of authority, the
power ascribed to these structures was carefully qualified. The church reformers' preoccupation with the proper shape and order of ecclesiological polity reveals a fine line between the amount of organization considered coercive and
that considered voluntary—a tenuous balance between individual freedom of
religious conscience and the need for common expressions of religious belief
and practice.

Church reformers believed that spiritual democracy would be achieved by a
structure that emphasized both personal liberty and social order. William
Goodell wrote that when ecclesiastical government and civil government were
"perverted" by the elitist control of undemocratic hierarchies, church and state
"should not be abandoned" (which was the Garrisonian position), "nor their

perversion sanctioned" (which was the position of those who remained within their "proslavery" denominations and political parties). Rather, in place of the existing institutions, new organizations, "on the true Bible model, should be established in their stead." [52]

"A New Heart Evinced by a Holy Life"

Despite the claim that they had no religious tests, ecclesiastical abolitionists had one mandatory membership requirement: evidence of "Christian character." Christian character was defined as "a new heart evinced by a holy life"—a regenerative (new birth) experience of faith in Jesus Christ manifested by sanctified actions. Personal "faith in the Savior" and evidence of "holy living" were always considered prerequisites for membership in abolition churches, as Myrick and the other church reformers based all their activism on that evangelical foundation.[53]

The religious experience of Christian perfection was characterized by ecclesiastical abolitionists in terms of particular actions. Secession from denominational churches and, later, political abolition became indispensable proofs of one's holiness, thus declaring a specifically ethical interpretation of the concept of entire sanctification.[54]

Compared with the formulations of sanctification doctrine developed by the postbellum Holiness movement, the ecclesiastical abolitionist descriptions of Christian perfection lacked theological precision. They did not dwell on the details of receiving entire sanctification; as William Goodell said, "[I]t is our duty to labor & pray for entire sanctification of all believers . . . without demanding to know precisely when & how" it occurs. The controversies on the subject, Goodell concluded, were "less profitable than curious."[55]

Nonetheless, the ecclesiastical abolitionist use of the doctrine of holiness was much more explicit than the generalized perfectionist themes prevalent in antebellum culture. Specifically, ecclesiastical abolitionists affirmed that the religious experience of entire sanctification was attainable in this life and that total obedience to the known law of God was an obligation for Christians. The common motif in these holiness statements was their stress on moral earnestness as the visible fruit of entire sanctification. Goodell criticized those who tried to make entire sanctification "consist mainly . . . in sensations or emotions" without "being perfect in obedience." Likewise, Myrick wrote that holiness made Unionists "efficient laborers in the kingdom of Christ." Ecclesiastical abolitionists spoke about Christian perfection in terms of its practical effect on their efforts for reform.[56]

Ecclesiastical abolitionists such as Myrick and Goodell were sure that sanctification was immediately available, but they always emphasized the pursuit of the ethical goal of holiness over any normative description of how to reach entire sanctification. John Keep, one of the pastors of the independent Congregational church of Arcade, New York, encouraged ecclesiastical abolitionists to "press on for the attainment of entire sanctification," but they were to "show their attainments by their works rather than by their declarations."[57] Because they stressed the practical results of sanctification, ecclesiastical abolitionists from extremely varied denominational backgrounds were able to work together in the task of social transformation.

Sources of Church Reform Activism

The broad appeal of this praxis-oriented rendering of the doctrine of Christian perfection was especially important as the church reform movement began to grow in the late 1830s and early 1840s. A plethora of literature was written on the issue of church reform,[58] and hundreds of comeouter congregations dotted the landscape. The ethical understanding of Christian perfection was used as the theological basis for these endeavors.

Oberlin became a strong proponent of church reform sentiment, and it was natural for Oberlinites to link the reorganization of congregations with their activistic emphasis on holiness.[59] Though Finney himself was often cautious about the social implications of reform movements,[60] Oberlin's graduates (particularly those who returned to their native New York state) had no such caution. Oberlin alumni were some of the leading ecclesiastical abolitionists in the burned-over district. Many of them were ministers in the region's perfectionistic Free Congregational churches. John Keep, for example, one of these fervent Oberlinite church reformers, traveled extensively throughout New York state and pastored several comeouter congregations.[61]

Beriah Green's Oneida Institute in Whitesboro, New York, was also a hub of church reform activism. The pattern set by the comeouter Congregational church of Whitesboro—the antislavery church attended by Oneida's multiracial student body—served as an example for the Institute's graduates as they abolitionized churches throughout central New York.[62] Green's close associate Gerrit Smith also had a great impact on church reform, organizing a perfectionist antislavery church in his home village of Peterboro and encouraging others to follow his lead. The so-called Peterboro Platform of church reform principles became a model for many independent congregations of both white and black abolitionists.[63]

African American ecclesiastical abolitionists as well provided leadership for the nascent church reform movement. A number of black comeouter preachers and congregations functioned as equal partners with whites in the work of establishing God's moral government, and black and white cooperation in reorganizing churches was lifted up as a shining example of the possibility of racial reconciliation. Moreover, African American ecclesiastical abolitionists challenged their colleagues to live up to the uncompromising standards of their perfectionist faith. The powerful preaching of Samuel Ringgold Ward, Willis A. Hodges, and others served to remind white perfectionists who were tempted to become preoccupied solely with the reform of church structures that they had a moral responsibility to continue the fight against slavery and the struggle to obtain civil rights for African Americans.[64]

Over and above these important sources of church reform agitation, it was William Goodell's advocacy of ecclesiastical abolitionism during the 1840s that produced an explosion of interest in the democratization of church structures. In 1842, Goodell left his post as editor of the antislavery paper *The Friend of Man* in order to begin the *Christian Investigator,* a paper specifically devoted to church reform. He also became the pastor of the Independent Abolition Church in Honeoye (town of Richmond), New York. When Luther Myrick died in 1843, Goodell's persuasive personality filled the resulting leadership vacuum.[65]

Goodell solidified the ecclesiastical abolitionist movement in two ways. First, in conjunction with those Unionists who wanted to construct a formal statement of doctrine, Goodell maintained that the Christian character of each individual was based on his or her adherence to certain foundational evangelical beliefs. These beliefs included an affirmation of the Trinity, the divinity of Christ, the authority of the Bible, the need for a regenerative faith experience, and (in contrast to the antinomian perfectionists) the persistence of some of the effects of human depravity—even among persons who were entirely sanctified. In accordance with these convictions, meetings held under Goodell's direction

William Goodell (1792–1878). *Courtesy of Berea College.*

were clearly announced as "evangelical" Christian union conventions. Lewis C. Lockwood, a disciple of Goodell, stated his belief that "'evangelical Christian' is the only appropriate name for a Christian union church" and "evidence of evangelical Christianity the only test of membership."[66]

Second, it was Goodell who unequivocally linked ecclesiastical abolitionism with political abolitionism. Luther Myrick supported the Liberty Party as early as 1841, but he was never involved in the party leadership.[67] Goodell, however, was a prominent Liberty leader. He consistently encouraged religious comeouters to become active in the Liberty Party, and nearly every issue of the *Christian Investigator* contained admonitions for political abolitionists to become ecclesiastical abolitionists. To Liberty voters, he declared that democra-

cy for all Americans would not occur with political reformation alone; it must
begin with spiritual democracy within the churches.

Goodell used the concept of Christian perfection as his justification both
for church reform and for political action. To be sure, some historians have
characterized Goodell as a nonperfectionist; it is true that he was on guard
against unorthodox antinomian perfectionism and was also suspicious of some
of Finney's teachings.[68] In Goodell's mind, Finney's reluctance to become
thoroughly committed to ecclesiastical and political reform must have been related to some deficiency in the Oberlin theology.[69] Goodell's disagreements
with Oberlin, though, did not mean that he considered evangelical perfectionism to be unorthodox. In fact, he often promoted the doctrine of entire sanctification. He grew up going to a Methodist class meeting and devoured the
writings of John Wesley and of John Fletcher while still a child. His preaching
and writing regularly affirmed the doctrine. To be specific, Goodell described
Christian perfection as a higher level of religious commitment in which the believer fully obeyed the moral law of God. "To be wholly sanctified," he
preached, "is to be wholly free from sin." In this respect, he did not differ at all
from the standard evangelical perfectionism of the period.[70]

The innovation that Goodell introduced into antebellum perfectionism was
his contention that entire sanctification was directly connected to political abolition. He defined obedience to God's law in a way that required each sanctified person's involvement in political action. Goodell submitted that entire
sanctification, when properly understood, would always result in the right discharge of "political duties," and he was critical of any constructions of sanctification that did not include specific social reform activity. He was especially
angered by those "clerical pretenders to a holiness that cannot preach politics—that cannot mingle with politics." Goodell's brand of holiness was defi-
nitely mingled with politics, and this particular formulation of evangelical
perfectionism became the theological basis for the ecclesiastical abolitionists'
support of the Liberty Party.[71]

THREE

Liberty Party Theology

Perfectionist Undergirding for Political Activity

I N AUGUST 1843, a "majestic" white tent was pitched in front of the courthouse in Buffalo, New York. High above the canvas, flapping in the breeze, was a blue banner inscribed with the words "HOLINESS TO THE LORD." This was Charles G. Finney's "Big Tent," a symbol of evangelical perfectionist revivalism, used for holiness meetings throughout the burned-over district since the mid-1830s.[1] For two days and nights under the canopy, pastors of comeouter churches prayed fervently as nearly three thousand congregants sang rousing hymns and orators preached on God's law and on the obligations of a sanctified life.

A casual observer could easily have assumed that the event in the Big Tent that summer was simply another protracted meeting held in order to promote spiritual regeneration and holy living.[2] Such an observer would not have been wrong, even though the occasion for this tent meeting was the national nominating convention of a political party—for the Liberty Party was a most unusual political organization. Liberty supporters, accustomed to combining expressions of evangelical perfectionist belief with antislavery advocacy, viewed the use of the Oberlin tent for the party's national convention as especially fitting.[3] As one abolitionist responded to critics who feared the "mixing up" of politics and religion, "Mix them, and mix them, and mix them, and keep mixing, until they ceased to be mixed, and politics became religion and reli-

Oberlin's "Big Tent." Used for Liberty Party conventions and other events aligned with Oberlin's evangelical perfectionist convictions. *From James H. Fairchild,* Oberlin: The Colony and the College, 1833–1883 *(Oberlin, Ohio: E. J. Goodrich, 1883).*

gion, politics." In the *Liberty Press,* the New York state party's semiofficial paper, the explicit conjunction of piety and politics was referred to as "Liberty Party Theology."[4]

Many prominent leaders at the Buffalo meeting and at other Liberty Party conventions were ecclesiastical abolitionists.[5] These perfectionist Liberty activists believed in the democratic restructuring of religious institutions as an essential part of the democratic restructuring of political institutions; to them, the end result of their efforts would be the establishment of God's government both in church and in state—a sanctified society. Even opponents of abolition-ism recognized that church reformers were the ones leading the political aboli-tionist activity. Writing some years later, proslavery apologist David Christy was convinced that the actions of Northern churches had provided the "most efficient basis for the organization of the Abolition party." Among upper New York state Liberty leaders, antislavery church reform activity corresponded to, and often prefigured, antislavery political activity. Indeed, the peculiar reli-gious sentiments of the ecclesiastical abolitionists provided the essential moti-vation for their political behavior.[6]

Potent Means, Specific Tactics

In the late 1830s, renewed emphasis on the doctrine of Christian perfection and the movement to democratize church structures coincided with the period when antislavery goals and tactics underwent redefinition. Initially, abolition-ists agreed that their principle task was simply to persuade others that slavery must be ended immediately. Within a few years, though, more definitive strate-gies were broached. As William Goodell reflected some years later regarding this important tactical juncture, "When a large body of the people were con-vinced of the truths abolitionists had taught them, the question arose, How shall they best be led to put their principles in practice?" Engrossed as many of them were in theological discussions that challenged basic presuppositions re-garding the nature of civil and of ecclesiastical institutions, it was to be expect-ed that the debates concerning abolitionist strategy would be related to questions of political theory and practice. Thus, the infamous 1840 divisions among abolitionists resulted in no small degree from "differences in theology, having a bearing on ethics, on politics, and on reformatory measures."[7]

Despite the charge by critics that the antislavery movement "was only gath-ering strength to become a political body for ambitious, unprincipled aspi-rants," abolitionists invariably affirmed before 1837 that they desired only to influence American Christians to repent of the national sin of slavery; they had no interest in personal political advancement. Their tack was simply moral suasion through the pulpit, various forms of education, and legislative peti-tions. Up to that point, abolitionists—at least in their role as officers of antislav-ery societies—had eschewed overt political campaigning.[8]

By 1837, however, many abolitionists questioned the effectiveness of moral suasion. It seemed that more and more efforts were required just to produce the same results. One of their original goals—persuading slaveholders to emancipate their own slaves—was a dismal failure. In some ways, the South was more unyielding than it had been prior to the rise of abolitionism; the North was equally intolerant, as evidenced by unremitting mob violence directed against abolitionists.[9]

Moral suasion was dealt a decisive blow by the onset of widespread financial difficulties in the spring of 1837. While the panic created interest in perfectionism, it also seriously disabled many religious institutions, including churches, evangelical colleges, volunteer benevolent societies, and the religious press. Hit especially hard were the major benefactors of abolitionist organizations. During "this season of distress and discouragement," the American Anti-Slavery Society (AASS) had to trim its budget severely, as did its sister benevolent societies. The AASS released many of its itinerating abolitionist preachers from their agencies and limited its publishing endeavors. Soon it was evident that the AASS was in a weak condition both in its finances and in its morale.[10]

One consequence of the weakening of the national society was a greater emphasis on the work done by local societies, resulting in the decentralization of abolitionist activities. Beginning in 1836, the number of smaller societies multiplied rapidly; new ones were organized in counties, towns, and neighborhoods. Individual abolitionists began to be less dependent on the larger Society and concentrated more of their efforts locally.[11]

Also during this time—and following the lead of ecclesiastical judicatories—proscriptive laws against abolitionists were passed by civil legislative bodies. In May 1836, the New York state legislature adopted a "gag law" which detained any abolitionist papers and pamphlets sent South, because they might incite "insurrection and sedition in a sister state." The Whig Party (the party of most New York abolitionists) kept antislavery off its agenda for fear of its divisiveness. More ominously, Congress passed a resolution declaring "that all petitions, memorials, and papers touching the subject of slavery" be laid on the table without being debated, printed, read, or referred; by that one enactment, Congress effectively sealed off the single most utilized moral suasion tactic of the abolitionists. In reply, the Rochester Anti-Slavery Society resolved that the Congressional rejection of abolitionist petitions was "a wanton assumption of power over the people."

Goodell was convinced that prohibitive civil legislation was possible only because of the success of its ecclesiastical sibling. "The legislative gag law," he wrote, resulted from "apathy upon the strides of ecclesiastical usurpation." Ecclesiastical abolitionists believed that, tolerated in the church, arbitrary authority would soon spread to the state and eventually all liberties would be curtailed. They believed that despotism must be checked both in religious and in political institutions; with the petition route blocked, duty demanded that other avenues of action be explored.[12]

Abolitionists realized that moral suasion had failed. Their representative legislatures, their political parties, and even their denominations had not moved any closer to the abolitionist position. In fact, the opposite had occurred; those institutions were firmly committed not to antagonize the proslavery interests of the country.

If it were true, as the reformers firmly believed, that "the people of this country who prize liberty, will become abolitionists, as soon as the necessary information is extended to them," then something must have hindered individuals from the free investigation that would change moral attitudes and behavior on the issue of slavery. More specifically, something must have been inherently wrong with their political and ecclesiastical institutions—an unnatural loyalty preventing the members of those institutions from denouncing tyranny. Just as the major denominations were inhibited from taking controversial stands on ethical issues as a result of their "sectarian" pride and attachment to pet doctrines and practices, likewise, within political organizations, strong party identification and the desire for national intraparty harmony led Whigs and Democrats to accommodate proslavery interests. Party loyalty caused Christian voters to succumb to moral compromise when they supported their party's nominee regardless of the candidate's stance on slavery.[13] Ecclesiastical abolitionists were anxious "lest abolitionists should prove themselves faithless to their principle at the polls—lest they should incur guilt and disgrace by voting for slavery, in order to vote with their party."[14]

Although their persuasive efforts were now hampered and their expectations for the reform of existing political structures were waning, ecclesiastical abolitionists were not stymied. They merely adopted the same perfectionist logic that they had already used to reform church structures, blaming the ineffectiveness of suasion on the moral intransigence of "impure" institutions. Moreover, they also placed some of the burden on themselves, feeling that they needed to do their reform work better and more thoroughly, with greater personal purity and renewed moral vigor for the task at hand. Just as the revivalists pleaded for "more powerful means" to enhance the staying power of conversions, so ecclesiastical abolitionists such as Beriah Green believed that they had need of "the most powerful motives, which Heaven itself has furnished." They obtained the powerful motives that they needed for their new strategy of "definite action" from evangelical perfectionism.[15]

Two specific characteristics of the doctrine of entire sanctification were linked to the strategic shift toward more concrete measures. First, the Wesleyan belief that individuals should be steadily growing in the power of God's righteousness was reflected in the ecclesiastical abolitionists' agitation for a strategy that was more righteous and more powerful. Perfectionists demanded constantly expanding levels of holy living and ethical commitment, insisting that the character of every reformer ought to be "measured in degrees of moral worth, upon a scale of simple holiness"; that is, the extent of consecrated living should continually increase. This sent sanctified abolitionists on a vigorous quest towards higher and higher goals. Antislavery activists, however, were then faced with a predicament: At the same time as they strove toward greater consecration in achieving abolitionist objectives, they bogged down in the ineffective tactics of moral suasion. Because "the motto of abolitionists should be '*onward,*'" wrote a contributor to the *Friend of Man,* "greater force should be immediately brought into the field." A critic of abolitionism perceptively observed that, for such reformers, the power "of moral persuasion" was no longer "potent enough, for their cause. Hence they are hurried onward, like mad men, to grasp the civil arm to aid in accomplishing their purpose." Ecclesiastical abolitionists were provoked to try unconventional tactics.[16]

A second characteristic of the doctrine of entire sanctification—the attainability of holiness—was also related to the strategic struggle within abolitionism. The religious arguments originally given for the support of immediate abolitionism were based on ideas promulgated by Nathaniel W. Taylor and other Yale theologians, and New York reformers in particular "had identified . . . [the] New Haven theology . . . with the cause of abolition." Immediatism was often described with the same limitations that Taylor had used to qualify the attainability of perfection. Taylor urged immediate repentance but hedged on the possibility of an entirely holy life; likewise, abolitionists in the early 1830s urged Christians to "repent" of their proslavery support but were unsure how the particular fulfillment of the effects of this repentance would take place. They confidently believed that having right principles and pure motives somehow would cause the demise of slavery; once converted Christians repented of the sin of supporting slavery, emancipation would result naturally, and so a detailed strategic program was not needed. Like Taylor's concept of sanctification, then, emancipation was the real but vaguely indefinite culmination of repentant behavior. The means for reaching emancipation, like the Taylorite means for reaching perfection, were left indistinct. As Donald Scott has said about early abolitionism, "Immediatism was less a program of what to do about slavery than, in evangelical terms, a 'disposition,' a state of being in which the heart and will were set irrevocably against slavery." Reflecting some years later, Alvan Stewart wrote that before the rise of the Liberty Party he and his fellow reformers "spent our energies in establishing our abstractions as first principles, and gave but little time to the practical carrying out of the same, [which was] infinitely the most important."[17]

The implementation of antislavery principles—which the abolitionists of the early 1830s expected to occur almost automatically—seemed, in the frustration of the latter part of the decade, to be troublingly remote. By 1837, precisely when revival preaching was judged inadequate for achieving lasting conversions, the original vague "disposition" against slavery was judged to be inadequate for achieving abolition's goals. And just as Finney and other preachers opted for the more powerful strategy of entire sanctification to consolidate flagging evangelistic energies, many abolitionists of the same period and region likewise were ready to choose a more powerful strategy to consolidate antislavery efforts. Expressing a typical sentiment, the abolitionists of the Seneca Falls Methodist church determined to develop decisive plans for "carrying out the principles of immediate emancipation," plans that were lacking in their earlier disposition toward moral suasion.[18]

At the same time, Taylor determined that the antislavery movement had become too fanatical; much to the consternation of his former disciples, he was "putting down abolitionism." Taylor's vocal opposition gave abolitionists yet another reason to question his doctrines, and William Goodell spoke for many of his colleagues when he expressed the conviction that Taylor was "not proceeding along the reform route." At this crucial juncture, ecclesiastical abolitionists found the need to appropriate a theology that was more sufficient for their task, a theology that would proceed along with them on their journey toward a practical, politically active faith.[19]

Goodell and his colleagues determined that the recently revived doctrine of entire sanctification was particularly suited for their strategic advancement to antislavery political action, in much the same way that that doctrine had already been useful for the advancement of revivalism and democratic church reform. In order for them to fulfill their sacred "political duties," it was necessary for them to be entirely sanctified, to be "perfect in obedience." By adopting the language and the experience of entire sanctification—an intentional step toward greater holiness—they provided a means by which they could (in Colton's words) "introduce perfectionism into the social system" and apply "the principle of perfectionism [to] the political structure of [the] society."[20]

Thus evangelical perfectionism provided ecclesiastical abolitionists in the late 1830s with the more definitive framework necessary for the politicization of antislavery. The theological arguments of the earlier abolitionists were built upon Taylor's rather abstract demands for holiness; they assumed that the pursuit of sanctification was a noble but elusive goal. The later arguments of the ecclesiastical abolitionists, dependent on the exuberant preaching of Finney, Myrick, and others, asserted that it was reasonable for each Christian believer to expect to be entirely sanctified in this life. Complete obedience to the moral law was attainable—and would be attained immediately if Christians would truly act on the principles that they claimed to hold. Evangelical perfectionists assumed that the prophesied millennium—the idealized future period of God's reign on earth—could actually be reached. In fact, a sanctified society could be achieved almost immediately, if only believers would practice moral obedience.

Evangelical perfectionist categories provided the drive and theological grounding for abolitionists in the late 1830s and the 1840s to become more focused. Antislavery advocacy was now imbued with a new energy and specificity—a specificity that was interpreted to mean political action. The acceptance of immediate abolition, formerly identified with the first-level religious experience of evangelical conversion, became in its newly politicized form identified with the second-level religious experience of evangelical perfection. This newfound connection between entire sanctification and abolitionist political action was simply stated by the Franckean Lutherans, one of the comeouter groups of church reformers: "Holiness," defined as a complete "consecration to God, and devotion to his service," would provide the resolution that was needed for "carrying out our political principles." In 1840, the carrying out of these evangelical perfectionist political principles resulted in the formation of the Liberty Party.[21]

Justifying the Use of Political Power

Politics was a popular pastime among mid-nineteenth-century Americans. Campaigns were full of symbolism and enthusiasm; election seasons furnished revelry and entertainment for many isolated communities; in small villages, the boisterousness of political rallies provided an excitement similar to that provided by revival meetings. There was great faith in the democratic process and a confidence that the electoral system could be used to reform the nation.[22]

In particular, the Whigs believed that the federal government could be the vehicle for creating a more moral society. In the Whig understanding of a "positive state," the government had a responsibility to act on behalf of the entire community. The state must act to purge society of moral evils in order to sustain a virtuous populace, which alone could perpetuate a democracy; democratic virtues were possible only if there were no "artificial" monopolies of power or privileged classes. Because of a natural human tendency toward unrestrained power, certain checks were needed on human behavior, usually in the form of collective, structured action. The government needed broad national powers if it were to secure a healthy balance between democratic freedom and social order.[23]

Many abolitionists supported the Whigs. The abolitionists' evangelical stress on moral virtue corresponded to the Whig emphasis on collective moral responsibility, and the abolitionist belief that slaveholders represented a privileged class seemed to be directly correlative with Whig principles regarding the abuse of power. Moreover, Whigs often portrayed their party as against slavery—at least in principle. In order to try to appease abolitionist voters, New York Whig politicians such as William Seward voiced antislavery sentiments when speaking unofficially, as individuals. Meanwhile, however, the national Whig Party declared slavery to be constitutional, failed to call for any governmental action to hasten its demise, nominated a slaveholder for vice president, and publicly denounced abolitionism. Among ecclesiastical abolitionists, such duplicity confirmed that "unsanctified hands" controlled conventional party politics. They desired concrete results but saw that none were in the offing in the two major parties.[24]

Earlier, when abolitionists advanced the strategy of moral suasion alone, they believed that individuals would become righteous voters through evangelical conversion, but the expected purification of the political system was not happening. Ecclesiastical abolitionists came to recognize that even if individuals became more holy, the candidates and platforms of the parties were still proslavery. Christians who wished to vote had no righteous alternatives from which to choose. They were being forced to compromise their principles at the polls.[25]

As abolitionists became more organized, they became more of an electoral force with which to be reckoned. Abolitionists began to demand that—in order to receive their votes—candidates for office had to state their position on slavery unambiguously. The result was the practice of questioning (or "interrogating") candidates regarding their views, a tactic that became popular among abolitionists in 1838.[26]

This new tactic did not suffice for long, however. Voters—even antislavery voters—had amazing loyalty to their respective parties. Although a few candidates were willing to submit to interrogation by abolitionists, most voters continued to support the candidates of their own party, regardless of the candidates' antislavery qualifications. A perfected government could certainly not be effected by the allegiance of Christians to such imperfect political institutions; a purer party was needed.[27]

Myron Holley, a Rochester abolitionist, is often credited with founding the antislavery third party in 1839, but ecclesiastical abolitionists in Utica had proposed a distinctly Christian, antislavery "liberty-party" as early as March 1838. Alvan Stewart, a prominent Utica church reformer, declared that the organization of the new party would allow ecclesiastical abolitionists to "honor their principles at the polls." A few antislavery candidates ran on independent tickets for local offices in 1839, free from any "sinful" association with the conventional political parties.[28]

Soon it was determined that antislavery candidates should also campaign for national offices. The first independent abolitionist nominations for president were made at an antislavery convention held in November 1839 at the Presbyterian church in Warsaw, New York (the same church that split a few months later over the doctrine of evangelical perfection, the democratization of ecclesiastical polity, and the insistence by some members that the church take a definitive political stand on abolition). A similar action supporting abolitionist nominations was taken at a state convention held in January 1840 at the independent antislavery Congregational church of Arcade. Finally, another convention took place in Albany in April 1840, formally constituting the Liberty Party and nominating James G. Birney for the presidency.[29] Although a few original Liberty leaders (such as Joshua Leavitt and Elizur Wright) were not interested in perfectionism,[30] upper New York state evangelical perfectionists predominated at the formative meetings of the party.

The establishment of the Liberty Party produced a swift reaction, as institutional authorities—both sectarian and secular—were uncomfortable with the notion of an unapologetically religious power block. Officials from the traditional political parties and denominations were convinced that theological beliefs and party platforms belonged within entirely separate "spheres." The leaders of religious and of civil institutions agreed that there was to be a clear division between the expression of one's religious faith and one's activity in the affairs of government. This dichotomy was related to the common nineteenth-century view that there were particularly appropriate areas of influence for various groups of people within society; differentiated roles were established, for example, for women in contrast to men and for clergy in contrast to laity. Moreover, religious practice and partisan politics had definite, prescribed boundaries.[31]

From the political perspective, party leaders were fearful of clerical domination in civil government. Supporters of the dominant power structures realized that political abolitionism was primarily a religious movement, a seemingly new development that frightened them greatly. Whig leader Calvin Colton was shocked that Liberty activists "invoked Divine authority to justify a use of political power in upsetting political society, or reforming the state."[32]

From the religious perspective, most clergymen believed that Christianity was too spiritually minded to be tangled up in political wrangling. Church officials viewed politics with suspicion. Before the 1840 election, Charles G. Finney—echoing the sentiments of others—declared: "I am no politician. I have for a long time been too deeply disgusted with the political course of things in the U.S. to have any hope with either of the political parties." Ministers and other professing Christians should not become immersed in "the dirty waters of politics," given that moral compromise seemed inevitable in the context of the American political system. For evangelicals, even the cause of antislavery was "a religious and moral question [that] was too sacred to be mingled with politics." Beriah Green confessed that before the late 1830s, evangelical antislavery reformers "treated politics . . . as a smutty concern, with which our clean hands had nothing to do."[33]

By 1839, however, Green and his fellow ecclesiastical abolitionists were convinced that they had a responsibility to "elevate politics to their *proper* sphere." The entire democratic process could be perfected if reformers would enlarge the arena traditionally considered acceptable for evangelical benevolence to incorporate political campaigning. Ecclesiastical abolitionists challenged the suitability of the prevailing notion of separate spheres because they resented the reduced status that was ascribed to religion in such a scheme. Their expansion of the range of activities deemed to be proper for the religious sphere had important implications for the political roles both of abolitionist clergy and of women, the two groups that were presumed to be the caretakers of that sphere. Ecclesiastical abolitionists contended that all Christians, whatever their present social status, were obliged to engage in politics, because all aspects of one's life were subject to God's law.[34]

The creation of the Liberty Party in 1840 provided an opportunity for evangelical reformers to change their minds about political participation. Finney, for example, had unapologetically stated that "the course which the politics of this nation has taken has prevented my voting altogether," but when he heard about the formation of the Liberty Party, he was willing to be convinced otherwise. "If a party will arise who will take consistent ground," Finney declared, then "I shall go to the polls." Likewise, in 1840, Samuel Ringgold Ward "became, for the first time, a member of a political party." Ecclesiastical abolitionists believed that Christians would not be corrupted by such politicking, as opponents charged, but that just the opposite would occur: their involvement would raise the moral tone of the entire political culture.[35]

Meanwhile, Garrisonian abolitionists continued to assert that the only legitimate strategic measure for religious reformers was personal moral suasion and that coercive actions of any kind were sinful. Because human governments are based on the premise that legalized compulsion can be used to back up their legislative actions, nonresistants defined such structures as inherently wrong: "Political action, by voting, even for the abolition of slavery, under a civil government based on physical force" was thus regarded as sinful by the Garrisonians. As one might expect, the Garrisonians had "a holy horror of the Liberty party."[36] According to the Garrisonians, it was fruitless to attempt to legislate change, because human institutions (both civil and ecclesiastical) would never be purified. God's moral government would be actuated in God's time, and only through the agency of individual moral influence. According to Garrison,

"[P]olitical reformation is to be effected solely by a change in the moral vision of the people, not by attempting to prove that it is the duty of every voter to be an abolitionist."[37]

In response, ecclesiastical abolitionists declared that perfectionist religious convictions and purified political principles were correlative duties. In direct contrast to the charge that piety and politics were irreconcilable, Liberty advocates perceived their "righteous" political action as a different and higher type of moral influence. They claimed that their political work was no more coercive than individual suasion had been; it was simply the "moral effect of numbers."[38] Along with their earlier goal of perfecting the component parts of the nation (individual voters), they were now committed to perfecting the political apparatus of the nation (parties, candidates, and campaigning). Moreover, rather than destroying human structures (the professed goal of the Garrisonian nonresistants), political abolitionists sought to "purify, invigorate, [and] immortalize" churches and the government, which they saw as merely following through on the original intentions of the AASS.[39] In spite of Garrison's oft-repeated accusation that they were not true abolitionists, the members of the Liberty Party insisted that their political activity was consistent with the radical goals of the movement. The Liberty activists did disavow certain Garrisonian ideas—particularly the anarchistic rejection of organized Christianity and of democratic government—but on other issues they agreed with the Garrisonians, specifically with their condemnation of the existing proslavery institutions and their support for universal reform measures, such as racial equality and women's rights.[40]

God's Government Embodied in Human Form

Much of the historiography of abolitionism has assumed that the antislavery movement divided into two easily distinguishable groups by 1840. The first group, concentrated within the Garrison-controlled AASS, was anti-clerical, supportive of women's rights, and against political action; the opposing group, centered among conservative abolitionists who operated concurrently within the Liberty Party and the American and Foreign Anti-Slavery Society (AFASS), was united by its antagonism toward women's rights and its clerical support for traditional churches. The Garrisonians were motivated by a desire to rid the nation of various forms of oppression, while the conservative abolitionists were interested only in restricting the influence of slavery in order to promote the growth of white free labor in the North.[41]

This division is too facile—the unintentional result of historians' overdependence on Garrisonian sources. According to Garrison, people were either with him or against him, and no differentiation was made between the various abolitionists with whom he disagreed. As early as 1852, William Goodell realized that although the Liberty Party was "distinct" in its origins and political ethics from the AFASS, it had been "perseveringly identified with it" by misrepresentations made in Garrisonian publications.[42]

Most Liberty members differed both from the Garrisonian anarchists and from the institution-supporting abolitionists who clustered in the AFASS. They were admittedly disturbed by Garrison's nonresistant criticism of political action; nonetheless, they were in much greater sympathy with Garrison's broad reform objectives than they were with some of the positions promoted by the conservative abolitionists active in the AFASS, particularly when prominent members of the AFASS disapproved of the formation of independent antislavery churches.[43] Far from being a branch of the AFASS, as Garrison charged, the New York state Liberty Party declared its official "neutrality" in the disputes between the two national antislavery societies. A few Liberty leaders did join the AFASS, but others remained in the AASS.[44] The majority of the original Liberty Party members stayed aloof from the controversy altogether, particularly those ecclesiastical abolitionist Liberty leaders who were from central and western New York. In their characteristically mediating manner, the Liberty advocates were against institutional hierarchies and in favor of a "broad platform" of universal reform (similar to Garrison) at the same time as they were evangelically "orthodox" and politically active (similar to Garrison's opponents).[45]

Like the Garrisonians, for example, and unlike the conservative abolitionists, most upper New York Liberty activists were firmly committed to women's rights.[46] James C. Jackson, an ecclesiastical abolitionist and a close colleague of Luther Myrick, was convinced that if the conservative abolitionists "who left the old society [the AASS] for the women question, could only catch a glimpse of our radicalism, they would feel aggrieved at our womanish propensities." As early as 1841, Jackson noted that women actively participated at Liberty Party conventions; following one such convention, he commented that if the conservative abolitionists could have spent just "one hour in our meeting," they "would have left it with new ideas of woman." Jackson proudly declared that in the burned-over district of New York "are found none who wish to exclude woman from a participation in our Anti-Slavery gatherings, and more especially in our *political* Anti-Slavery meetings." This political abolitionist support for women's rights is understandable when one remembers that many Liberty Party leaders learned their lessons in strategy from their earlier education in church reform agitation, in which Myrick and others challenged human hierarchies of all kinds. It also explains why, only six years later, some of the same perfectionist Liberty leaders would help to initiate the movement for women's suffrage.[47]

As another indication of their dialectical approach to opposing abolitionist perspectives, perfectionist Liberty advocates accepted Garrison's critique of the oppressive tyranny operating within religious and political institutions but rejected Garrison's increasingly strident repudiation of all Christian churches and of organized government. Similar to the anarchists, the Liberty Party was strongly antidenominational (i.e., against "sectarianism"), declaring that "the present organized church associations and organizations, *as they are,* are not only in the way of humanity . . . but in the way of Christianity itself." At the same time, however, Liberty leaders wanted sanctified Christians to restructure themselves into purified antislavery churches, so long as the jurisdiction of these new ecclesiastical organizations was carefully circumscribed.[48] Similarly, Liberty supporters were against the factionalism of traditional partisan politics, yet they affirmed the need for a limited party organization. Significantly, the organizational name that they chose—the Liberty Party—was a rather oxymoronic phrase that reflected the ecclesiastical abolitionist desire for an ordered liberty, a mixture of freedom and structure.

Liberty Party leaders believed that democratic governments in church and state were divinely established institutions, a part of God's moral government. God's influence, they asserted, is exerted "through the instrumentality of human governments." The Liberty Party stated explicitly that their vision of the moral government of God was "the foundation of all [their] enactments and political arrangements." If the American government were democratically reorganized, it had the potential to become the visible government of God—a foreshadowing of God's millennial rule "embodied in human forms."[49] Not only would temporal organizations in church and state be necessary "as long as human beings exist in this world," but they would be required even after "the world is holy" (i.e., during the millennial society). Therefore, it was imperative for Christians to work within governing structures, both civil and ecclesiastical. Christians were obligated to aid and to support human governments; voting was "the highest moral power" that could be exercised, and it was the duty of each sanctified believer to vote righteously and to secure "legislation that is in accordance with the law of God."[50]

Ecclesiastical abolitionists affirmed the divine intention for political structures at the same time as they condemned the existing structures as immoral. In the words of Finney, "Instead of destroying human governments, Christians are bound to reform them. To attempt to destroy, instead of reforming human governments, is the same in principle as is often pled by those who are attempting to destroy, rather than reform the Church. . . . What mad policy is this!" Rather than following the "mad policy" of the Garrisonians, Finney urged abolitionists to "set about the moral reformation of government," which would "be brought about by promoting union among Christians and by extending correct views on the subject of Christian responsibility in regard to their relation to government." If the Garrisonians were "mad," however, Finney thought the leaders of the established political parties were downright sinful; Whigs and Democrats conducted politics "in a selfish or ungodly manner." In contrast, ecclesiastical abolitionists were "bound to meddle with politics in popular governments" in the holy manner that befitted their evangelical perfectionist convictions.[51]

Was the political meddling of the ecclesiastical abolitionists a serious strategy of party formation or simply a slightly altered version of antislavery religious idealism? James Brewer Stewart and others have concluded that Liberty advocates were intrigued by the benefits of political power but were not interested in developing a structured political apparatus; thus, the Liberty leaders engaged in "political antipolitics." This description is useful, especially when comparing the Liberty Party with other contemporary parties. The Liberty constituency was repelled by the crass, unprincipled tactics typical of antebellum partisan rivalry and distrusted the hierarchical institutionalization of the Whig and the Democratic parties.[52]

Nonetheless, Liberty supporters were engrossed in the details of campaigning and of political mobilization. They campaigned through an extremely unconventional political strategy, however, using the interconnected network of local antislavery congregations. This confirmed the ecclesiastical abolitionist

The Liberty Press.

Utica, Saturday, Feb. 7, 1846.

"The righteous shall grow like a Cedar in Lebanon."
Ps. xcii. 12.

THE CEDAR OF LEBANON.

The Cedar is the emblem of Constancy, of Protection, of Renown, of Immortality.

Will ye despise the acorn,
  Just thrusting out its shoot,
Ye monarchs of the forest,
  That strike the deepest root?

Will ye despise the streamlets,
  Upon the mountain side,
Ye broad and mighty rivers,
  On sweeping to the tide?

Time now his scythe is whet
    ting,
  Ye giant oaks, for you;
Ye floods, the sea is thirsting
  To drink you like the dew.

Of what is small, but *living*,
  God makes himself the nurse,
While 'ONWARD,' cry the voices
  Of all his universe.

Our plant is of the *Cedar*,
  That knoweth not decay,
Its growth shall bless the moun-
    tains,
  Till mountains pass away.

Its top shall greet the sunshine,
  Its leaves shall drink the rain,
While on its lower branches,
  The slave shall hang his chain.

Masthead of *The Liberty Press* (1846). Edited by Wesley Bailey, a founder of the Wesleyan Methodist Connection. *Courtesy of Utica Public Library.*

contention that "the Liberty Party was born . . . to demonstrate the maxim that religion has everything to do with politics."[53] Liberty political rallies took on the form of the revival meetings from which most Liberty men and women had been spiritually nurtured.[54] The party's platforms sounded remarkably like the "synoptical view of [religious] sentiments" formulated by the Unionists. Supporters were recruited from among antislavery congregations. Liberty Party editors such as J. N. T. Tucker and Wesley Bailey used the columns of their papers to support church reform. They also borrowed well-known religious symbols to proclaim the righteousness of their political cause; in contrast to the Democrats' oft-used image of a hickory tree, for instance, abolitionists adopted the biblical image of a cedar of Lebanon as the insignia of the Liberty Party.

Campaigners such as Gerrit Smith, Samuel Ringgold Ward, and William Goodell went from town to town, abolition church to abolition church, preaching the political "antislavery gospel" on behalf of particular Liberty candidates. Liberty Party conventions were held in comeouter churches and revivalistic pavilions, such as Oberlin's Big Tent, where antislavery hymns were sung and bountiful dinners were prepared by the women of the host congregations. And—consistent with their image as temperate religious reformers—cold water was the beverage served at Liberty Party functions, in stark contrast to the hard cider offered at Whig and at Democratic gatherings.[55]

Consecrated Votes

Interpreters of abolitionism have noted that Liberty advocates were religious, but there has been little discussion of the particular content of their religiosity.[56] What was the actual religious sentiment of Liberty Party members? Because Liberty supporters in upper New York relied on the experience and commitment of entire sanctification, it is essential to plumb the depths of this theological concept if we are to understand their moral earnestness and their passion. For example, entire sanctification was both an emotive experience of God's perfecting grace and a volitional commitment to particular ethical actions, thus providing its proponents with evangelical fervor along with the typical reformers' sense of religious obligation. Moreover, the individual's acceptance of entire sanctification was stated in unapologetically evangelical terms; for example, each person was expected to narrate a prior experience of the new birth, to affirm his or her belief in the truths of the Bible, and to recognize the ever present possibility of a return to sinful behavior. Given such blatantly evangelical convictions, the specific brand of perfectionism associated with the Liberty Party was subtly but profoundly different from the anarchistic perfectionism characteristic of the Garrisonians and from the Romantic perfectionism prevalent in antebellum culture. It was this evangelical perfectionism, as preached in the abolition churches, that formed the motivational base for Liberty Party voting.

Liberty supporters were very open about their evangelical perfectionist stance. The party's ultimate intent was to keep "all men from all sin." It was claimed that Liberty candidates had a more "righteous moral character" than those endorsed by other parties. Liberty Party conventions assumed that those who ran for office under their label would "walk in a perfect way" before God, and at least some Liberty voters were convinced "that their favorite candidates [were] absolutely sinless."[57] When Finney held a perfectionist meeting in Rochester in 1841, none of the establishment secular or religious papers took note of it except for the *American Citizen,* a Liberty Party paper—indicating the close affinity of the party to holiness teaching.[58]

Among evangelical perfectionist Liberty advocates, entire sanctification was demonstrated by the purity of political comeouterism. In the revivalistic milieu of the burned-over district, moral choices were considered unambiguous; a person's actions were either holy or sinful. Because abolitionists defined slavery as sin, then separation from this sin was required in one's political as well as in one's ecclesiastical relationships. "No neutral ground" was permissible. When someone withdrew from one of the established parties (Whig or Democratic), that person was considered to be taking higher ground "in favor of correct political action." "Coming out" and joining the Liberty Party represented an individual's "thorough conversion."[59]

Coming out of impure political institutions, however, was just the first step; actually voting for Liberty Party candidates was considered an individual's most overt and specific demonstration of holiness. By Liberty voting, each sanctified abolitionist was "enter[ing] his protest before public opinion." Just as they had consecrated their lives to God, ecclesiastical abolitionists were regularly urged to "consecrate your votes" to God's cause of universal liberty. An antislavery ballot was proof of one's unqualified allegiance to God.

The evangelical perfectionist reasoning underlying the political activism of ecclesiastical abolitionists was plainly stated by a Rev. Thurston, a Liberty Party–supporting pastor:

We are to be holy always, in all that we do. . . . We are required to be as holy in one place as another . . . at the town house, as at the church. We are to be as holy . . . in depositing our vote for the election of offices for the state or nation, as in lifting up our hands in prayer to God. . . . We are to obey God. . . . To depart from it [that is, to depart from obedience to God by voting unrighteously] would be to commit moral evil, to sin.

A vote in favor of a Liberty Party candidate was a vote against sin. Liberty voting became a practical and definitive way for abolitionists to exhibit their sanctified resolve. Abolitionists were encouraged to elect Liberty Party candidates so that they could "walk up to the polls, and deposite [*sic*] your votes, without a twinge of conscience." Entirely sanctified individuals were required to act on the highest moral principles possible, and abolitionist voting was "the highest moral power we can exercise, as individuals."[60]

Not all evangelical ministers who preached about entire sanctification agreed with the political implications of the doctrine insisted upon by ecclesiastical abolitionists. Goodell was harshly critical of those who advocated holiness but who thought that they were "too spiritually minded to plead the cause of the oppressed"—those who "consider[ed] it quite too profane and secular, to discharge the duties of political life."[61] For Goodell, the experience of entire sanctification resulted in an active obedience that included direct political involvement. He agreed with his colleague Luther Lee, who urged his fellow comeouters "to vote the Liberty ticket as a religious duty." For ecclesiastical abolitionists who were going on to perfection, their religious duty required a particular political act.[62]

According to Goodell and other ecclesiastical abolitionists, it was crucial not only to put abolitionists in office but also to promote sanctified principles among an unsanctified electorate. The uncompromising example of Liberty members who voted in a holy manner was considered to be the greatest strength of the party; such modeling of moral purity would persuade fellow townspeople to act righteously and to vote similarly. Alvan Stewart challenged his fellow abolitionists to vote consistently for Liberty tickets—even for "the lowest town officer"—because it was "the principle we call on our neighbors to witness." Although they knew that they constituted only "a small minority," Liberty voters in the 1840s were persuaded that their antislavery polling would eventually "exert an influence that is felt through the length and breadth of this mighty nation against oppression." The political principle of the Liberty Party would "go on, steadily increasing, till it embraces the majority of the nation." Just as casting a Liberty ballot demonstrated the entire sanctification of each abolitionist, likewise such balloting was essential for the entire sanctification of the society; the actions of every voter had a millennial impact. Stewart was convinced that "in the act of voting, [the abolitionist] acts not for himself alone, but for . . . his neighbors, his country—and indirectly, for the world."[63]

Liberty leaders such as Stewart were committed to nothing less than the moral transformation of the world, prefigured by the moral transformation of their own communities. Their first task was to reform the towns of the burned-over district into what historian Curtis Johnson has called "islands of holiness."[64] They thought that they could best demonstrate the imminent inbreaking of God's divine rule on earth by restructuring the churches and electoral politics of their small towns. Their job was not completed with the creation of sanctified, self-contained villages, however, for ecclesiastical abolitionists intended their "island" communities to be linked together into a vast archipelago of evangelical perfection, until the entire social order was sanctified. Their social reform efforts, though locally based, would be instrumental in abolitionizing the entire nation. In this way, ecclesiastical abolitionists articulated the same ideal they had advanced earlier through antislavery church reform—an ideal in which the aggregate holiness of local Christians would result in a sanctified community, and the multiplication of many sanctified communities would result in a sanctified society.

Liberty supporters knew full well that they were not prominent figures in national politics; nonetheless they believed that they had an indispensable role to play in God's politics. They considered themselves to be "the rank and file of the Anti-Slavery infantry." Individuals understood that their righteous actions had momentous consequences; the success of God's cause would "depend on his vote." They were ordinary folk from obscure little towns, but they were emboldened by the hope that their activities would actually result in a reconstructed society.[65]

Locating the Liberty Constituency

In the minds of the ecclesiastical abolitionists, the anticipated millennium seemed destined to begin in the vicinity of upper New York. This supposition was based on the fact that the core constituency of the Liberty Party came from the central and western sections of the Empire State. The most influential of the party's original members[66] and about one-quarter of the national Liberty electorate resided in the region.[67] Moreover, the portion of the Liberty Party membership that came from outside of New York state hailed to a large extent from communities in other burned-over areas—northern New England, western Massachusetts, and Yankee-settled sections of northeastern Ohio, southern Michigan, northern Illinois, southeastern Wisconsin, and Iowa.[68]

Liberty advocates were not surprised that the burned-over district was such a fertile ground for evangelical perfectionist political action. Samuel Ringgold Ward remarked that the ecclesiastical abolitionists with whom he worked in New York had a "peculiar character"; their unusual interest in radical reform was due to the fact that they were "God-fearing descendants of New England Puritans . . . living . . . apart from the allurements" of the emerging consumer-oriented culture. Rather than following the dictates of urban bourgeois society, they "felt at liberty to hear, judge, and determine for themselves" the right course of action.[69]

Ward's careful observations enabled him to describe with particular insight the cultural and social location of politically minded ecclesiastical abolitionists—the demographic context, the religious character, and the social profile of the perfectionist Liberty constituency. Ward described them as rural transplanted Yankees of revivalistic heritage who felt ambivalent about the values of the market revolution.[70] He understood that the beliefs that gave meaning to their lives were closely bound up with the temporal matters of their everyday existence.[71]

The reformers' religious convictions developed within the larger burned-over environment, an environment that Judith Wellman has described as "a context but not a cause of reform."[72] Liberty supporters' views regarding the commercial economy, for example, were shaped by the social circumstances of the region. A rapid expansion of agricultural markets was followed by financial panic; consequently, an uncertainty developed regarding the effects of commercialization. An apprehensive, yet risk-taking business climate existed. When such fluctuating attitudes regarding the economy were combined with the reformers' perfectionist proclivities, the spiritually revived portion of the populace responded with ultraist behavior—behavior that, collectively, resulted in the creation of the burned-over setting. The extent to which upper New York was more burned-over than other areas simply attests to the region's somewhat larger concentration of revivalistically oriented Yankees and the earlier maturity of (and hence the greater impact of the financial panic on) its agricultural economy.[73]

The social standing of the perfectionist Liberty activists reflected the ambiguous economic situation that prevailed in the burned-over district. Many New York Liberty leaders held a middling status in society and were engaged in relatively humble careers such as husbandry, small commercial enterprises, and the ministry. The editor of a Liberty Party paper declared that in contrast to Whig and Democratic leaders, who tended to be affluent professional politicians, "most of our leaders and political speakers have been and are ministers— not statesmen or politicians." Politically active ecclesiastical abolitionists were regularly described as "poor men" or "common people," and some of the most prominent perfectionist Liberty leaders—Goodell, Green, Ward, Luther Lee, and Charles Torrey, for example—often found themselves destitute.[74]

Moreover, in fundamental contrast to the major political parties, the Liberty Party included socially marginalized persons in prominent positions—the rural working class, African Americans, and women. James C. Jackson characterized Liberty meetings as consisting of "farmers, mechanics, working-men, and their wives and daughters." Luther Myrick described a state Liberty convention in Syracuse similarly: it was composed of "hundreds of working men and women, the bone and muscle of the community, [gathered] from various portions of the Empire State." African Americans were active in the party from its beginnings, and the 1843 Liberty convention marked the first time in American history that blacks had official leadership status in a national political assembly. The Liberty Party was thus the first interracial political party. Women too achieved a measure of political power, as they held positions of influence in the party structure and were nominated for office.[75]

At the same time, some Liberty advocates had substantial means: Alvan Stewart, Charles O. Shepard, and Archibald Griffith were in the process of becoming successful entrepreneurs,[76] and one Liberty leader, Gerrit Smith, was wealthy. The relative prosperity of these Liberty men put them at the same social level as the major party politicians, but their preoccupation with moral principles distinguished them from the behavior of Whig and Democratic politicos. They gave liberally in support of benevolent causes and they consistently worked on behalf of the oppressed. This self-denying attitude of solidarity with the slaves, according to Ward, demonstrated that evangelical perfectionist Liberty supporters were among the very few white persons who honestly attempted to be "identified" with "coloured people." Gerrit Smith, at one time the largest landowner in New York, gave away 120,000 acres of his property in 1846 in a real estate venture intended to assist African Americans to become self-sufficient. He also provided the Liberty Party, Oneida Institute, Oberlin College, and various ecclesiastical abolitionist papers, comeouter churches, and African American organizations with substantial funding.[77]

Despite their entrepreneurial involvement, even relatively prosperous Liberty leaders had mixed feelings about their role in the expansion of the market economy, especially when it became evident that such expansion introduced the influence of an external culture on their rural environment. On the one hand, they participated in the national culture that was developing beyond the boundaries of their villages, for example by welcoming new marketing techniques such as the inexpensive printing of tracts and newspapers.[78] Many reformers also became involved in state and national politics for the first time through their Liberty Party activities.[79]

On the other hand, perfectionistic Liberty advocates were uneasy about their connections with the wider commercializing culture. They condemned the avaricious "acquisition of money and the pursuit of pleasure" that prevailed among the majority of Americans, and they were fearful that forces beyond their control were impinging on their efforts to sanctify their villages, thereby hindering the establishment of God's government. Lawrence Friedman has described how the "institutional transition toward consolidated and centralized structures" in the North threatened "voluntaristic community-centered existence." The market culture provided access to goods and services for the rural people of upper New York but it also caused them considerable worry.[80] As urban areas became increasingly dominant, ecclesiastical abolitionists were concerned that the apparently loose morals of the "cities and large towns" would infect them. They preferred to engage in the "pure and simple" agrarian life with which they were familiar, and which seemed to be more easily reformable than the "corrupt and complex" urban world beyond their influence. It did not surprise Liberty Party members when their neighboring rural communities delivered large numbers of abolitionist votes. Conversely, when the urban centers of New York state produced few Liberty votes, they were not disappointed, for they "expected very little from any of our cities." God's sanctified society would begin in the small towns of the Republic.[81]

Village culture centered around a few independent local structures—the church, the school, and the town government—all of which were governed on the basis of close interpersonal relationships. Ecclesiastical abolitionists believed that such small-scale institutions were God's ideal for humanity. Localized, independent government in church and in state represented God's order—"the democracy of Christianity and the Christianity of democracy"— which was "destined to revolutionize and bless the whole earth." So naturally, the centerpiece of their strategy for social and political transformation was community organization.[82] Only in the late 1840s did Liberty activists begin to promote a broadly based reform strategy that addressed social problems through more collective means.

During the heyday of evangelical perfectionist reform in the early to mid-1840s, ecclesiastical abolitionists dreamed of model moral communities that would be nationally promoted through decentralized agencies—individualistic means used to effect wide-ranging goals. They believed that their towns could have a millennial impact through their involvement in church reform and political antislavery. They had captured a vision of the government of God on earth; even more importantly, they were convinced that they had a personal stake in making that vision become a reality. The primary decentralized agencies that ecclesiastical abolitionists used to advance the cause of the Liberty Party were the hundreds of antislavery churches springing up throughout the burned-over regions of New York state and beyond. As a result, a loose but very effective network of congregation-based political activists was formed, dedicated to living out an uncompromised perfectionist credo.

FOUR

The Abolition Church  *Expanding*

the Ecclesiastical Abolitionist Network

U NUSUALLY TREACHEROUS winter weather prevented the anticipated complement of abolitionists from attending a long-scheduled
church reform convention in Syracuse in December 1843; "the trav-
elling," one participant noted, "was very bad." Nothing, however, impeded the
single-minded enthusiasm of those who were able to make their way there—an
excitement generated by the potential significance of the assembly. Although
there had been many previous gatherings, the purpose of this Syracuse convention was to bring together the widest possible diversity of ecclesiastical abolitionists. William Goodell and other designers of the convention intended to
lay the groundwork for a grand, inclusive "General Evangelical Secession" of
all politically minded comeouters—thereby setting the stage for the unfolding
of the millennial society. They hoped that this meeting would help unify the
disparate antislavery churches that had previously separated from several different denominations.[1] Among those who organized and attended the Syracuse Church Reform Convention were all of the major Liberty Party leaders in
upper New York, as well as the best-known public figures from each of the
largest ecclesiastical abolitionist groups—the Unionists, the Free Baptists, and
the Wesleyan Methodists.[2] Such a high level of transdenominational interaction was extraordinary.[3]

In the end, the Syracuse convention did not succeed in structurally uniting the comeouters. The unified General Evangelical Secession did not materialize because the seceders found themselves caught in the democratic tension between liberty and order: they could not agree on the amount of organizational structure allowable in the newly united group.[4] Ecclesiastical abolitionists were on the horns of a dilemma between their fondness for familiar religious traditions and their commitment to achieving a nonhierarchical "Union" of antislavery comeouters. On the one hand, interested as they were in maintaining a measure of recognizable order, they were unwilling to relinquish all their customary sectarian usages—modes of baptism and denominational titles, for example. On the other hand, desiring freedom from heavy-handed religious institutionalization, the seceders proposed a new organization with a decentralized polity and no overarching authority. This lack of ongoing structure eventually caused the disintegration of the movement by the 1860s.

In the 1840s, however, ecclesiastical abolitionists were able to thrive without formal organizational unity, for they were bound by their cooperative social action within the Liberty Party. Partisan identification as Liberty members enabled ecclesiastical abolitionists to get beyond the ideological impasse of "liberty versus order." For those who were fearful of too much religious institutionalization, the Liberty organization provided an (ostensibly) nonreligious structure through which they could work. Moreover, for those who wanted to retain some of their particular sectarian distinctiveness, the Liberty Party offered a common cause for comeouter groups to support without forcing them to abandon all of their respective traditions. Newfound political allegiances created an esprit de corps that extended across the whole gamut of seceding groups, allowing the Liberty Party to function as a kind of surrogate denominational structure.[5]

No wonder critic Calvin Colton contemptuously dubbed the Liberty Party the "Abolition Church." He characterized the Liberty organization as a multiform hydra of numerous religious components operating as a uniform political party.[6] Though not denominationally ordered in the usual sense, the antislavery congregations were intricately interrelated by a vast, expanding network of agencies linked together by their mutual interest in a perfected politics. These interlocking agencies included educational institutions (especially Oberlin and Oneida), itinerating church reform lecturers and Liberty Party campaigners (often the same people), and a score of religious and political newspapers (the *Union Herald,* the *Abolitionist,* the *Christian Investigator,* the *Liberty Press,* the *Impartial Citizen,* the *Liberty Party Paper,* and others). The elaborate network of ecclesiastical abolitionist interconnectedness grew extensively during the 1840s, especially through the use of periodic meetings such as the Syracuse convention. Advertised under different headings—"Antislavery Church Reform Convention," "Christian Union Convention," "Anti-Sectarian Convention," and "Perfectionist Convention"—a similar collection of persons nonetheless attended them all.[7]

Religious historians have tended to view the so-called antislavery sects[8]—Wesleyan Methodists, Franckean Lutherans, Free Baptists, Unionists, and others—as unique products of particular denominational factors. When one reads the narrative histories of these groups, it appears as if each abolitionist sect arose almost spontaneously, in splendid isolation from the other comeouters. This historiographical record fails to note the theological concepts and praxis that connected antislavery religious groups.[9] In fact, what is most remarkable in tracing the stories of each of the various comeouter sects is that so little distinguished one from the other. Their similarity was predicated on a common theological understanding of evangelical perfectionism—an amazing religious congruence when one remembers the traditional doctrinal rejection of perfectionist ideas by Presbyterians, Congregationalists, Lutherans, and Baptists. They were drawn together by a shared ethical interpretation of entire sanctification as a theological justification for innovative activities such as the reorganizing of churches and outright political campaigning. Even in an age of intense denominational rivalry,[10] the antislavery religious groups shared facilities, practiced open communion, and promoted the mutual recognition of members and ministers. The abolitionist congregations overcame their sectarian parochialism through their work in the Liberty Party and realized that they had more in common with each other than they did with their former "proslavery" denominational associates.[11]

Franckean Lutherans

Soon after the first Presbygationalist antislavery comeouters reorganized into Union churches, Lutheran antislavery comeouters also reorganized. Beginning in 1837, individual abolitionist Lutheran congregations in New York withdrew from the Hartwick Synod (the regional judicatory)—and, later, from the Lutheran General Synod (the national judicatory)—to form a new, purified

"Franckean Synod." This so-called synod was dramatically unlike the seced-ers' previous denominational structures, however: its actions were only "advi-sory," and the members of each congregation voluntarily determined if they would adhere to the advice of the collective will. Though others referred to them by the term "synod," the Franckeans called themselves "Independent Evangelic Lutheran Churches," thus hoping to make clear that they were not subject to any higher judicatory—including their own.[12] The precipitating cause of the Franckeans' withdrawal was their uncompromising commitment to antislavery church reform. Like the Unionists, the main issue for the Franck-eans was the reluctance of their parent denomination (in this case, the estab-lished Lutheran synods) to take a firm stand against the tyranny of either slavery or "ecclesiastical jurisdiction."[13]

The Franckeans were inheritors of the rich Lutheran pietist tradition of the German Palatines who settled in the Schoharie and Mohawk valleys of east-central New York and in Rensselaer County, east of Troy.[14] (Their use of the name "Franckean" honored the tradition of German pietist leader A. H. Francke.) The pietist heritage included a distrust of formalized doctrine, a stress on experiential faith, and the obligation of living a holy life following regeneration. However, just as the evangelical awakenings of the eighteenth century differed in many respects from antebellum revivalism, so too the eighteenth-century inheritance of continental pietism was transformed in the burned-over district context into the "radical-radicalism" of the Franckean comeouters.[15] While retaining some of their traditional Lutheran beliefs and practices, the Franckeans also appropriated the doctrine and social agenda common to the other ecclesiastical abolitionists of the region.[16]

Throughout the antebellum period, burned-over district revivalistic reform influenced the leaders and members of the Franckean Synod. As one of the Franckean pastors explained, "Between different churches, located side by side and operating in the same field, there must be mutual influence"; such mutuality, he concluded, resulted in many "common characteristics" between the Franckeans and other New York evangelicals. One of the Franckean founders, for example, was converted at a revival led by Charles G. Finney. He and other Franckean pastors became itinerant revivalists, promoting all the new measures common to Finneyite enthusiasm; such measures caused Franckeans to be accused of "Methodism" by their opponents within the Lutheran church. The Franckeans were also strong supporters of the evangelical benevolent voluntary societies and of the Sunday School movement.[17] Most significant were their direct involvement in abolitionism and the networking with other revivalistic evangelicals that occurred through that involvement. Non-Lutheran abolitionists (such as Wesleyan Methodist leader Luther Lee) were invited to preach at Franckean churches,[18] and one of the organizers of the Franckean Synod, John Lawyer, was a traveling agent for the New York State Anti-Slavery Society who preached abolitionism in churches of varied denominations.[19]

The intense revivalistic milieu of the burned-over district led many evangelicals to embrace the doctrine of Christian perfection, and the members of the Franckean Synod were no exception.[20] The Franckeans' emphasis on holy living was partly derived from their pietist heritage, but the explicit evangelical perfectionism of the Franckeans was much more dependent on their interaction with other ecclesiastical abolitionists in upper New York. Several evangelical perfectionists from the region, such as Beriah Green, Luther Myrick, and Luther Lee, had an especially strong influence.[21]

Like other antislavery comeouters, the Franckeans specifically affirmed their belief in the doctrine of entire sanctification—certainly not a typical Lutheran theological tenet. They proudly promoted "modern perfectionism as taught at Oberlin," and the preaching of the Oberlin doctrine became a major piece in the Franckeans' theological repertoire.[22] In contrast to the general emphasis on perfection then current in the society—as well as to the general stress on sanctified living common to their pietist heritage—the Franckeans established a distinct doctrine of Christian holiness that was stated directly and without qualification: "*Resolved,* That we believe in, and embrace the doctrine of *Christian holiness,* and that we feel called upon . . . to not only receive and preach it in the *abstract,* but to reduce it to practice, and urge it upon our people as a gospel requirement." Similar to William Goodell, the Franckeans defined entire sanctification in ethical terms as obedience to the moral law. They had no use for a nominal belief in the concept of holiness—"in the *abstract*"— that was devoid of moral obligation. Entire sanctification, as described by the Franckeans, was a distinctive doctrine ready-made for justifying radical moral reforms such as political abolition.[23]

The Franckean Synod developed a comprehensive social reform program characteristic of the perfectionist agenda of ecclesiastical abolitionism. This included many reforms that were not traditional among pietists but were typical among their fellow revivalistic reformers in the burned-over district, such as women's rights, opposition to secret societies, opposition to capital punishment, and pacifistic opposition to the Mexican War. The Franckeans also attempted to break down the racial barriers of antebellum society, and they were especially proud of their ordination of an African American, Daniel A. Payne, to the Christian ministry. Although Payne later transferred his credentials to a black denomination, the time he spent preaching and teaching among the Franckeans significantly affected their attitudes in favor of integration.[24]

The Franckeans' propensity for sanctified ethical action is not surprising, considering that many young Franckean clergy were trained at Oneida Institute—Beriah Green's "hot-bed" of evangelical perfectionism, political abolitionism, and ecclesiastical restructuring—rather than at a Lutheran seminary.[25] This connection helps explain why Franckeans supported antislavery church reform; their own rationale for secession from the Hartwick Synod was based on the kind of evangelical perfectionist reasoning common to the other abolitionist comeouters.[26] They contrasted the spiritual democracy of their congregations to the "ecclesiastical despotism" of the Lutheran General Synod and other national denominational judicatories. Just as they would not accept the civil oppression of slaves, so too they would "bow to no ecclesiastical tyranny or oppression."[27]

The Franckeans insisted on "the independency of each particular church or society"—a congregational polity that emphasized local self-government. Translocal religious organizations had "no right to exercise any ecclesiastical jurisdiction or legislative power over any portion of the church." The Franckeans thus viewed their own "synod" as "no judicatory but only an advisory body," a sort of annual convention in which ministers united to consult each other on the "most effectual means" of promoting God's perfected society. This system was similar to Goodell's plan for regular conventions of ecclesiastical abolitionists (although it differed somewhat from that of Myrick, who was suspicious of any organization beyond the local church). Some translocal organization was necessary, the Franckeans believed, but such organization could not impose any hierarchical restrictions on its participants.[28] Unlike the Garrisonians, they believed in the need for "positive institutions" such as civil government and church structure, although the power exercised by those institutions was to be severely limited.[29]

The Franckeans balked at the binding of the human conscience that occurred when members of the major denominations were obliged to subscribe to sectarian creeds. They contrasted such creedalism to the free investigation that resulted when persons had the Bible as their only guide.[30] Consequently, the Franckean Synod disregarded the Augsburg Confession, the traditional standard of Lutheran orthodoxy, and in its place formulated their own evangelical perfectionist statements of faith. They felt that some parts of the Augsburg Confession were "manifestly unscriptural"; when asked outright whether they believed all of the confession, they "frankly and candidly" declared that they did not.[31] The Franckeans' selective acceptance of the doctrines of the Augsburg Confession and their denial of its ultimate authority, combined with their perfectionist theology and social reform agitations, caused various other Lutheran synods to charge that the Franckean Synod was fanatical and unorthodox. These charges only drew the Franckeans farther away from their old Lutheran associations and closer to their comeouter comrades.[32]

It is not surprising, therefore, that the Franckeans were enamored with the prospects of an ecclesiastical union with other sanctified abolitionists. Resolutions were passed and sermons preached on the topic of Christian union at nearly every annual session of the synod—John Lawyer being the most visible proponent of these actions. The Franckeans were certain that there was "scarcely a shade of difference" between the "fundamental" doctrines of sanctified evangelicals. Thus, they did not require a doctrinal test as a qualification for membership in their churches but rather used the usual ecclesiastical abolitionist membership criteria of Christian character: evangelical experience and holy living, demonstrated in social reform.[33]

The Franckeans were at the center of efforts to unite the various antislavery comeouters. They were leaders at the church reform conventions of the region, due in part to the strong impact that ecclesiastical abolitionists Luther Myrick, Beriah Green, and William Goodell had on the Franckean Synod. Many of their church buildings housed multidenominational abolitionist congregations, and Unionists and other comeouters shared their pastors and their facilities with the Franckeans.[34] In the village of Parish, New York, for example, abolitionists seceded from several denominational churches, combined into one antislavery congregation, and constructed their own building. Although the pastor selected by this new congregation was a Franckean, the antislavery seceders of Parish adopted a generic form of independent local church government suitable for all abolitionist comeouters.[35]

The ecclesiastical abolitionism of the Franckeans led them naturally into avid promotion of the Liberty Party. Voting for Liberty candidates was seen to be "a sacred duty," consistent with their desire to reorganize political and religious institutions to match the pattern of the government of God. Frequent support for the Liberty Party appeared in the pages of their paper, the *Lutheran Herald*.[36] Towns with a strong Franckean presence had high Liberty vote tallies relative to their neighboring towns,[37] and political abolitionism was advocated in the synod's official resolutions.[38] The Franckeans also provided leadership for regional gatherings sponsored by the party; one of these Liberty Party gatherings, held in the Free Baptist church of Ames, was jointly led by Beriah Green and several Franckean pastors.[39]

Each comeouter group struggled to find an appropriate balance between organizational structure and personal liberty. At best, that balance was precarious and short-lived. The "liberty versus order" tension in the Franckean Synod was expressed in the interactions of two of its leaders, Philip Wieting and John Lawyer. Lawyer, like many perfectionists, continually pressed the abolitionist agenda toward higher, holier ground; he urged the Franckeans to adopt a comprehensive social program and became increasingly dissatisfied with even a minimal amount of Lutheran "denominational distinctions."[40] Wieting, however, was described as "a radical, but not an extremist"—an indication of his caution concerning the pace of social reform. His relative conservatism prompted him to warn against "the fatal consequence in undertaking to do too much," in direct contrast to uncompromising perfectionists such as Lawyer, who thought sanctified believers could never do too much to achieve a perfected society. Wieting's "regard for order" led him to call for measures that would "sustain our languishing institutions"—at the same time as Lawyer was attempting to dismantle the synod's remaining institutional structures.[41] The Franckean Synod, like other comeouter groups, eventually opted to follow Wieting on the path toward institution-building. John Lawyer—frustrated with the synod and officially accused of preaching unorthodox doctrine—left the Franckeans in 1849.[42]

Wesleyan Methodists

Following the admonitions of their founder, John Wesley, Methodists were traditionally opposed to slavery. American Methodism maintained this conviction briefly, originally calling for the expulsion of any slaveholding member; almost immediately, however, this vigorous stance was whittled away as the Methodist Episcopal Church grew into the largest denomination in the United States. By 1808, and even more egregiously by the 1820s and 1830s, Methodists accommodated to slavery so as not to interrupt denominational growth in the South. The church kept a nominal disapproval of slavery in its *Discipline,* but in practice it abandoned Wesley's firm antislavery position. As a result, dedicated Methodist Episcopal abolitionists such as Orange Scott, La Roy Sunderland, Cyrus Prindle, George Storrs, and Luther Lee were able to build a large antislavery constituency, particularly in New England and in upper New York state. In the late 1830s, this abolitionist constituency felt the wrath of the denomination's hierarchy, and these oppressive experiences led them to conclude that the civil despotism of slavery was aided and abetted by a concurrent religious despotism.[43] So, like other antislavery agitators in the burned-over district, Methodist abolitionists linked advocacy for civil rights to the advocacy for greater spiritual democracy within the churches.

Long before the organization of Methodist abolitionism, two groups with a strong base in the burned-over district seceded from the Methodist Episcopal Church over the issue of greater spiritual democracy: the Reformed Methodists in 1814 and the Methodist Protestants in 1830.[44] By the early 1840s, many members of these groups in New York state sympathized with the church reform concerns of the region's flourishing ecclesiastical abolitionist movement. Predictably, these two older groups discovered a kinship with the erstwhile group of Methodist Episcopal antislavery agitators; Reformed Methodists such as Wesley Bailey and Methodist Protestants such as George Pegler allied themselves with discontented antislavery members of the Methodist Episcopal Church in one common venture to establish ecclesiastical abolitionism among the various brands of Methodism. This resulted in the formation of the Wesleyan Methodist Connection, the largest abolitionist comeouter group.[45]

As early as 1841, abolitionist Methodists from upper New York held "Seceding Methodist Conventions" in High Bridge (Wesley Bailey's home) and in Utica. At the time, Bailey was publishing an abolitionist paper in cooperation with Myrick, the *Madison County Abolitionist* (later called simply *The Abolitionist*). Myrick was pleased that Bailey used this paper to support "the cause of Christian Union" and political abolition.[46] The next year, a prominent Methodist Liberty man, James C. DeLong, invited Bailey to move to Utica and to become editor of the *Liberty Press,* the mouthpiece of the Liberty Party in central New York.[47] Comeouter abolitionism among Methodists in New York was now centered in Utica and was closely aligned with the Liberty Party leadership there. At just this time, a general secession of Methodist Episcopal abolitionists throughout the North was orchestrated by New Englander Orange Scott; Bailey, Lee, and other New Yorkers joined forces with this broader movement and hosted its organizing convention at Utica in May 1843, where the Wesleyan Methodist Connection was established. The new connection exemplified the goal of Christian union by including in its ranks abolitionist Methodist Protestants, Reformed Methodists, Free Baptists, and Presbygationalists, as well as former members of the Methodist Episcopal Church; the first two pastors of the Wesleyan Methodist congregation in Utica were a former Methodist Protestant (George Pegler) and a former Reformed Methodist (Wesley Bailey). Bailey was also the chairman of the Wesleyan Methodist Connection's Utica district.[48]

An emphasis on Christian perfection was the theological base of the Wesleyan Methodists' reform endeavors. Like the Franckeans, the Wesleyan Methodists drew holiness themes out of their own tradition—but also like the Franckeans, the Wesleyans' stress on entire sanctification and on the urgency of applying that doctrine to political and to religious structures resulted from their collaboration with other similarly inclined ecclesiastical abolitionists.[49]

The Wesleyan Methodist conception of evangelical perfection parallelled that of other comeouter groups. For instance, the first General Conference of the new connection added an article on "Sanctification" to their *Discipline,* much like the evangelical perfectionist statements of other antislavery comeouters.[50] The article affirmed that sanctified believers could be delivered from the "pollution and reigning power of sin," enabling persons to live out their lives as continual reformers. This definitive statement of entire sanctification gave theological specificity to abolitionist calls for explicit action.[51]

The Wesleyan Methodists also developed an evangelical perfectionist approach toward social problems that resembled the broadening reform interests of their fellow ecclesiastical abolitionists. Antislavery efforts were no longer enough; according to Lee, "the Gospel is so radically reformatory, that to preach it fully and clearly, is to attack and condemn all wrong, and to assert and defend all righteousness."[52] Wesleyan Methodists supported temperance, women's rights, the abolition of secret societies, and the abolition of war. They also resisted the pervasive racial prejudice of the period; in Wesleyan Methodist churches, African Americans were welcomed as equals. In Syracuse, for instance, Lee's Wesleyan meetinghouse was the only white church in town that did not segregate African Americans who came to worship.[53]

The Wesleyan Methodists' concept of entire sanctification stressed purity of life, including the purity of social institutions. Comeouterism became a visible and unqualified way to separate themselves from sin. In seceding from impurity, they purged themselves from their sinful association with the old "proslavery" structures. At the same time, comeouterism became a way of creating new, holier institutions that would lead the way toward the millennial society.[54]

Wesleyan Methodist interest in reorganizing and in perfecting institutional structures was especially evident in their sweeping support for and leadership in the Liberty Party.[55] Bailey's Wesleyan Methodist and Liberty Party connections resulted in publicity for both comeouter groups in the pages of the *Liberty Press*.[56] The Liberty Party in Vermont was said to have had a "predominantly Wesleyan Methodist leadership." Regional representative assemblies of the connection and local congregations took strong stands in favor of political abolitionism. The Wesleyan Methodists supported the Liberty Party by political advertising and campaigning, particularly in their paper, the *True Wesleyan;* some reference to the third party appeared in nearly every issue, and the editor was convinced that "in most cases" Wesleyan Methodists were Liberty Party voters.[57]

Luther Lee,[58] the leading figure of New York state Wesleyan Methodism, argued so forcefully for political action at the 1839 convention where the idea of the Liberty Party took shape that he claimed to have "turned the scale in favor of a political anti-slavery party." He "boldly urged men to vote for James G. Birney" and he referred to the third party as "our Liberty Party." Lee insisted that he "never had any politics which was not a part of [his] religion, and [he] urged men to vote the Liberty ticket." It seems that individual members clearly felt this "urging" to vote for Liberty candidates, sometimes in not so subtle ways: one Wesleyan Methodist who had neglected to vote in the 1844 election felt obliged to print a public apology for his laxity in not supporting the Liberty slate![59]

Although strongly committed to the Liberty Party, Wesleyan Methodists still thought that purification of the church was the "first efficient step in the work of reform." Wesleyan Methodist comeouters felt that their secession from established political parties correlated to their similar secession from the hierarchical polity of Methodism. Lee's "Pastoral Address" to the Utica organizing convention of the Wesleyan Methodists tied these two issues together; their "repudiation of all connection with Slavery," he declared, had its parallel in a "rejection of the prerogative system of Episcopacy." The Wesleyan Methodists believed that no hierarchies of privilege—over African Americans or over individual Christians—were to be tolerated. Denominational aristocracies, as represented in Methodist Episcopacy, denied the "inalienable right to private judgment in matters of religion."[60]

Wesleyan Methodists also desired to break down the "artificial" barrier of denominational divisions. They were attracted to the idea of a sanctified "union" of all abolitionists in each community. Antislavery advocates in Watertown, for instance, built a Free Church intended to accommodate all "the friends of the abolition cause"; almost as an afterthought, it was noted that the Free Church happened to be "under the supervision of the Wesleyan Society." Likewise, the abolitionist congregants in the town of Ashford were not denominationally discriminating. Even though they were supplied by a Wesleyan Methodist preacher, they did not refer to themselves as a Wesleyan church; rather, they called themselves simply the Anti-Slavery Church Society of Ashford. Wesleyan Methodists also tried to join forces with the Reformed Methodists and with the Methodist Protestants.[61]

The ideal of spiritual democracy among Wesleyan Methodists was expressed most clearly by Luther Lee. From his days as a lecturer for the New York State Anti-Slavery Society, Lee developed close relations with other ecclesiastical abolitionists. These wider antislavery connections opened up Lee to the possibility of eliminating denominational divisions and uniting diverse abolitionists. At the 1843 Syracuse Church Reform Convention, he explored the idea that the Wesleyan Methodists might join William Goodell and the Unionists in a broadly based alliance of all abolition churches.[62] The Wesleyan Methodists informed Goodell that if the Unionists would only give up their remaining vestiges of denominational pride, the Wesleyan Methodists in New York state would "try to do the same, and join" them.[63] However, this General Evangelical Secession of former Methodists, former Presbygationalists, and others never came to pass, because the Wesleyan Methodists desired to keep a few limited "denominational distinctions." Lee, still proud of his heritage as a

Luther Lee (1800–1889). Wesleyan Methodist leader and political abolitionist, as an older man.
Courtesy of the Library of Congress.

follower of John Wesley, was fearful that Goodell's plan was merely an attempt to organize "a Presbyterian Anti-Slavery Church." Despite their ecclesiastical abolitionist affinities for Christian union, the Wesleyan Methodists could not quite bring themselves to forego all of their familiar denominational identity.[64]

Differences emerged among Methodist abolitionists regarding the proper balance to be struck between individual rights and institutional prerogatives. These differences were evident in the varied ways in which the leading Methodist abolitionists dealt with questions of church order, illustrating the slippery nature of the middle course taken by ecclesiastical abolitionists. For instance, a few Methodist abolitionists did not secede with the Wesleyan Methodists but rather continued to promote antislavery from within the Methodist Episcopal

Church and were not concerned with changing the governance of the institution.[65] Toward the other end of the institutionalization continuum were abolitionists such as George Storrs, who renounced the Methodist name, embraced Luther Myrick's brand of Unionism, and established an independent, abolitionist Church of God in Albany.[66] The majority of Methodist abolitionists in the burned-over district, however, became part of the Wesleyan Methodist Connection. They maintained "moderate views" regarding church government; that is, they were convinced of the necessity of "coming out" of the Methodist Episcopal Church, but they disapproved of any type of religious anarchism that did not combine comeouterism with a pragmatically reorganized church structure.[67]

Even *within* the Wesleyan Methodist Connection, as within the Franckean Synod, the tension between institutional support and anarchism created instability. While all Wesleyan Methodists avoided the extremes of continued support of the Methodist Episcopal Church or an anarchistic rejection of all church organization, various Wesleyan Methodists had differing plans for structuring the ideal ecclesiastical organization in between those extremes. Some leaned toward institutional consolidation, while others wanted to mix local control with a voluntary national organization. Orange Scott, for example, encouraged the continuation of institutional privileges within the new Wesleyan Methodist organization. Scott favored the retention of a centralized form of episcopal polity with only slight alterations, because he believed that the structure of the parent church was not inherently evil but was simply "overgrown."[68] In contrast, two of the leading Wesleyan Methodists from upper New York—Lee and Prindle—held a decentralized view of church reform closer to the views of their ecclesiastical abolitionist associates in the burned-over district. They agreed with Scott that congregations could voluntarily "enter into an association, and form themselves into a general connexion," in order to promote "greater uniformity and efficiency" in the task of social reform. However, they quickly qualified their support for these translocal religious associations, insisting that each abolitionist congregation was not to allow its "personal identity and rights to be swallowed up in the power and general government of a connexion thus formed."[69]

Lee was especially displeased with some of the structures and regulations that the new Wesleyan Methodist Connection carried over from Methodist Episcopacy. At the Wesleyans' organizational convention in Utica, he argued that such rules were inconsistent with God's design for a democratic polity. Burned-over district Wesleyan Methodists wanted a less-dominant denominational authority.[70] Like Goodell, Lee and Prindle thought every local congregation ought to be independent, adhering to a strictly congregational polity; they opposed large organizations and were watchful against any "development of power and undue influence" within the new Wesleyan Methodist structure. Such carefully qualified statements indicate that Lee and Prindle were of a double mind, as were most ecclesiastical abolitionists: They desired a translocal church structure but were fearful of its potential power.[71] Like other rural New York state abolitionists, the Wesleyan Methodists were caught in between their traditional localism and the centralizing culture of the broader society. Although they desired the benefits of the emerging culture, they were threatened by the implied monopolistic consolidation and pluralism that attended it.

Free Baptists

On the northern New England frontier in the 1780s, the Freewill Baptists were founded as a reaction against Baptist doctrines and usages deemed inconsistent with democratic aspirations—specifically, the Calvinist doctrine of predestination, the practice of restricting communion only to members of one's particular sect ("closed communion"), and, later, the mainstream Baptists' complicity with slavery.[72] They remained "Baptist" only in their mode of baptism. Many Freewill Baptists emigrated west from upper New England to New York state in the early national period;[73] in central New York, they encountered an indigenous group, the Free Communion Baptists, that held similar beliefs. By 1840, both of these groups were in close contact with the broader ecclesiastical abolitionist movement in the burned-over district, drawn by their common affinity for democratic reforms. The ecclesiastical abolitionist goal of a Christian union strongly influenced these two religious bodies—so much so that in 1841, the Freewill Baptists and the Free Communion Baptists in New York united into one Free Baptist abolitionist comeouter group.[74] Two years later, at the Syracuse Church Reform Convention, the newly combined Free Baptists (along with the Wesleyan Methodists) considered joining Goodell and his coterie of former Presbygationalists in forming a multidenominational abolitionist alliance.

This union was seriously contemplated as a result of extensive interaction between Free Baptists and other New York state ecclesiastical abolitionists. In the 1840s, a few "proslavery" Freewill Baptists back in New England objected to the firm abolitionist stand taken by the group's leaders. This objection was articulated at the same time that other Free Baptists—especially those in New York state—advocated more radical antislavery measures. Such disparities within the connection caused those with strong abolitionist convictions to establish the Freewill Baptist Anti-Slavery Society in 1842, which most Free Baptists in central and western New York joined. Abolitionist Free Baptists in New York also began to look for support among their local ecclesiastical abolitionist colleagues.[75]

Two leading burned-over district Free Baptists spearheaded this effort, David Marks and Hiram Whitcher. Marks was a zealous revivalist and political abolitionist whose preaching throughout western New York had a great impact on Free Baptist churches in that area. During the early 1840s, he studied at Oberlin; through the persuasive efforts of Marks and other Oberlin-educated Free Baptists, the doctrine of entire sanctification came to have a controlling influence on the connection in western New York.[76] Like the Franckeans, most Free Baptists accepted Finney's interpretation of the doctrine of Christian perfection,[77] affirming that "the attainment of entire sanctification in this life, is both the privilege and duty of every Christian." When individuals completely consecrated themselves to God, they were "cleansed from all the pollutions of sin" and were set apart "for holy service" in the work of social reform. Free Baptists stressed that sanctification was marked both by an individual "inward purity" that would "manifest itself in outward obedience" and by a corporate purity that would reveal itself in perfected religious and political organizations.[78]

The second influential Free Baptist leader was Hiram Whitcher. Like John Lawyer and Luther Lee, Whitcher's earlier participation in antislavery societies introduced him to the broader concerns of ecclesiastical and political abolitionism.[79] Whitcher's revival preaching took him throughout western and central New York, where he helped to spread political and religious reform. As eager promoters of spiritual democracy, he and David Marks had been instrumental in facilitating the union of the Freewill Baptists and the Free Communion Baptists, and Whitcher was one of the initiators (with Goodell) of the Syracuse plan for a General Evangelical Secession. Whitcher was also a leader of the Liberty Party in New York, and because of his campaigning, some of the state's highest Liberty vote totals were recorded in communities where he preached regularly.[80]

Broad support for the Liberty Party was evident among the Free Baptists of the burned-over district. Political abolition was recommended by the connection's General (national) Conference as early as 1841. While there was resistance to this uncompromising antislavery position among Free Baptists in New England and in Ohio,[81] the New York state Free Baptists consistently supported political activity against slavery;[82] David Marks, for example, was an avid Liberty man,[83] as were many prominent Free Baptist preachers in the state.[84] Strong political abolitionist resolutions were issued by the regional Free Baptist representative bodies in St. Lawrence County and in western New York. These assemblies insisted that lay as well as clergy support for the Liberty Party was necessary; the St. Lawrence meeting declared that it was "the duty of every member our churches . . . to remember at the ballot-box the poor slave." Evidently such admonitions worked, for the Freewill Baptist Anti-Slavery Society proudly announced that "a large majority" of the Free Baptist laity voted for abolitionist candidates.[85]

Like other comeouter groups, the Free Baptists took "no extreme ground" on the issue of church reform. They believed that human institutions were necessary—the human counterpart to divine government—but that those institutions were presently evil and needed to be sanctified.[86] Such middle ground was manifest in their anticreedal sentiments. The Free Baptists formulated a "treatise" of doctrines that was "by no means designed to form a new creed for our brethren," claiming that neither they nor any religious authority had the power "to bind the consciences of men."[87] The open communion stance of the Free Baptists also predisposed them to reject dogmatic denominationalism. Many Free Baptists in New York strived to encourage union among Christians, fraternizing with ecclesiastical abolitionists,[88] cooperating in joint antislavery congregations, and unapologetically claiming a close affinity with fellow comeouters. In Oneonta, for example, Free Baptists and Franckean Lutherans erected a joint meetinghouse for their common abolitionist worship; the Franckeans—formerly adherents to the Augsburg Confession—now considered their perfectionist Free Baptist colleagues to be "similar in doctrine." Even more significantly, the Franckeans recognized that the Free Baptist "form of Church government is the same as our churches."[89]

To be sure, many of the more conservative Free Baptists in New England disliked the growing spirit of spiritual democracy within their own connection, believing that it would lead toward anarchy and disorganization. These conservative Free Baptists felt that it was best for each sect to maintain "distinct organizations" and to prescribe exacting doctrinal membership standards in order to preserve the proper "order in society."[90] Free Baptists from the burned-over district, however, were too imbued with the spirit of ecclesiastical abolitionism to agree to any retentions of old institutional privileges.

Congregational Friends

Quakers were not numerous in upper New York, and even those few were divided into separate Orthodox and Hicksite meetings (the result of an 1828 split in the denomination). The Hicksites were reputedly more liberal, but by the 1840s, some abolitionist Friends felt that the Yearly Meetings (regional judicatories) of the Hicksites held too much authority and did not take consistently strong stands on the slavery question.[91] The result was "quite a spirit of 'come-outerism'" among abolitionist Hicksites of the Genesee Yearly Meeting in western New York. These agitators were convinced that traditional translocal judicatories placed "undue restriction upon individual views" and opened the door "to the exercise of despotic power."[92]

Those who seceded from the Genesee Yearly Meeting tried to remain on a middle road. On the one hand, these "Congregational Friends" had "broken ties of party and sect" as a declaration of their antagonism toward any hierarchical authority. However, rather than abandoning institutionalized politics and religion altogether (as did some anarchistic Quakers), they attempted to reform civil and ecclesiastical structures in order to guarantee "Christian liberty."[93] Politically, that meant support for the Liberty Party;[94] ecclesiastically, it meant establishing comeouter abolitionist Quaker meetings under a "congregational form of religious association." The new Yearly Meetings were carefully limited by certain safeguards; they had "advisory powers only" and could "assume no ecclesiastical authority."[95] The Congregational Friends also developed a comprehensive reform agenda and supported efforts toward broader Christian union.[96] Because Quakers were few and far between in upper New York, most Congregational Friends were isolated individual seceders, but a few were able to gather enough people to reorganize into local congregations.[97]

Antislavery Baptists

Baptists (often referred to as Regular Baptists, to distinguish them from the Free Baptists and others) had a diffused polity, and they cherished their tradition of local church independence. Goodell gave them credit for being "more thoroughly congregational than the Sect known by that name."[98] At least theoretically, their Associations (regional judicatories) lacked binding authority and were viewed only as advisory. Most abolitionist Baptists, therefore, felt no need to withdraw from any Baptist judicatory; this lack of hierarchical authority may explain why comparatively few Baptists shifted from antislavery agitation to the broader ecclesiastical abolitionist movement.

Baptists also had a tradition of noninterference in civil affairs that led many individual Baptist churches to hesitate to commit themselves to the political aspects of abolitionism. The Truxton Baptist Church resolved that "we consider the subject of slavery as it now exists before the Publick to be a Political thing and not proper for us to act upon as a Religious body." When Baptist churches took such indefinite, compromising positions on political antislavery, the perfectionist abolitionists within those churches were faced with a problem. According to evangelical perfectionist reasoning, they were implicated in the sin of compromising with slaveholders by remaining in those churches. Thus, some antislavery advocates in Baptist churches reacted with the standard ecclesiastical abolitionist solution—secession and reorganization.[99]

The abolitionist Baptists who seceded did so in varying ways. In one case, several members of the Baptist church in Shelby withdrew and formed a Free Baptist church.[100] Others became Unionists. The most prominent Regular Baptist to become a Unionist was J. N. T. Tucker, one of Luther Myrick's close associates, a leading Liberty man, and the editor of the *Liberty Almanac*. Like other ecclesiastical abolitionists, he had been a traveling agent for the New York State Anti-Slavery Society; he was also one of the abolitionists who, along with Goodell, proposed the 1843 church reform convention in Syracuse that attempted to unite Wesleyan Methodists, Free Baptists, former Regular Baptists, former Presbygationalists, and others into one "Christian Union."[101]

Most abolitionist Baptists responded in the manner of the other comeouter groups of the region, preferring to retain a measure of their Regular Baptist identity. Consequently, the congregations formed by the comeouters were often called Anti-Slavery Baptist churches, or some similar title.[102] In most cases,

THE
LIBERTY ALMANAC,
FOR
1844.

BEING THE 68TH AND 69TH YEARS OF AMERICAN INDEPENDENCE ; (SO CALLED.)

PROCLAIM LIBERTY THROUGHOUT ALL THE LAND, UNTO ALL THE INHABITANTS THEREOF.—BIBLE.

EDITED BY J. N. T. TUCKER.

CALCULATIONS BY GEO. A. PERKINS, A. M. PROFESSOR OF MATHEMATICS.

DESIGNED FOR NEW YORK, OHIO, MICHIGAN, UPPER CANADA, &c.

SYRACUSE:
PUBLISHED BY I. A. HOPKINS,
AND SOLD WHOLESALE AND RETAIL, AT HIS BOOKSTORE, TOWNSEND BLOCK.

J. BARBER, PRINTER, TOWNSEND BLOCK.

Title page of *The Liberty Almanac for 1844*, edited by J. N. T. Tucker. *Courtesy of the Library of Congress.*

abolitionist Baptist congregations seceded from their Associations one at a time, but in one unusual instance, the abolitionist comeouters in Chautauqua County withdrew from their county Association and formed the Reorganized Chautauqua Baptist Association. The reorganized Association made explicit its "merely advisory" capacity and insisted that ultimate authority rested with each congregation; evidently, the parent Association had not exhibited those practices to the satisfaction of the seceders.[103]

The diversity in comeouter tactics among antislavery Baptists is illustrated in the approaches taken by the two most prominent Baptist abolitionists in New York state, Cyrus Grosvenor and Elon Galusha. In 1844, Grosvenor was bothered that the American Baptist Missionary Society refused to bar slaveholders from missionary service or patronage. Local churches that supported the mission society could thus be accused of complicity with slavery.[104] Consequently, Grosvenor and other abolitionist Baptists set up an alternative agency based in Utica—the American Baptist Free Missionary Society. Although the original intent of this new society was merely to organize mission work untainted by slavery, it eventually operated as a coordinating forum for abolitionist Baptists and took on some of the characteristics common to the other comeouter groups.[105]

Galusha took a very different tack. He had longstanding connections with many of the leading political and ecclesiastical abolitionists in the burned-over district. Galusha's promotion of the Liberty Party was unflagging, and by his preaching many Baptist churches were abolitionized.[106] Like other ecclesiastical abolitionists, he was convinced that the millennial society was imminent; although most abolitionists believed that the perfect state of society would be the catalyst for Christ's return (postmillennialism), Galusha believed that Christ's return would occur cataclysmically before the establishment of the perfected society (premillennialism). Nonetheless, both Galusha and the other ecclesiastical abolitionists agreed that the specifics about how the millennium would occur were less important than the urgency in preparing for it—by converting individuals and by reforming the society.[107] In particular, Galusha became persuaded that sectarian divisions—including the continued perpetuation of the Baptist denomination—would only impede the promised consummation. He despaired at "ever realizing a Baptist millennium."[108] Thus, in 1844, Galusha embraced what seems on the surface to be a rather novel comeouter strategy for a politically minded abolitionist: he seceded from the Baptist church and became an Adventist.

Millerism and the Enthusiasm of 1843-44

Galusha's strategy seems unusual because Adventists (also called Millerites) are often described as pessimistic premillennialists who were too distracted by their obsession with the impending apocalypse to be concerned with ameliorative reform work.[109] Although this description is true of some Millerites, others—such as Galusha—did not fit the pattern; what seems to be more accurate is that a "complex relationship" existed between Millerism and social reforms such as abolitionism.[110] Indeed, Adventists acted out a range of behaviors parallelling the various abolitionist/perfectionist responses described earlier. A few Liberty activists, for example, embraced Millerism as a way of expressing their ecclesiastical abolitionism and as an avenue for coming out of undemocratic institutions.

Millerite ideas were sometimes represented as a manifestation of the doctrine of Christian perfection. When a person accepted Millerite millennial predictions, that new commitment was often described as a second conversion following regeneration. One's dedication to Millerism was viewed as the ultimate entire sanctification experience—a uniting of personal perfection and societal perfection in the conviction that the millennium was truly at hand.[111]

Adventists—like other abolitionists and perfectionists—were found along the entire institutionalization continuum.[112] A large number of anarchistic perfectionists, for instance, were drawn toward Millerism; the promise of a radical annihilation of earthly powers appealed to them. These admirers of Millerite teachings included John Humphrey Noyes, a number of Garrisonians, and many members of the Christian Connection.[113] In contrast, many Millerites, including William Miller himself, were quite conservative. Although they withdrew from their denominations, their secession was caused by the cool reception they received from their churches, not by any anti-institutional scruples. Some of them, in fact, attempted to institutionalize the Adventist movement as soon as possible; these were the Adventists who tend to fit the interpretive stereotype—they were pessimistic about social amelioration and consequently would not work for social or political reform. Miller's own views on the possibility of personal or societal sanctification were extremely cautious; using qualified language similar to that used by Nathaniel W. Taylor, Miller held that "we ought to strive to attain to perfection as much as if it was [possible]."[114]

Finally, there were a few moderate Adventists (particularly in the burned-over district) who seceded from their denominations and political parties to form new abolitionist organizations.[115] In their political affairs, they continued to be zealous Liberty partisans even while advocating an impending end to history, optimistic activists who supported the "practical bearings" of political action even at the height of Millerite frenzy. For example, Elon Galusha eagerly continued his Liberty Party involvement in the mid-1840s, believing that an increase in sanctified reformatory efforts could only speed the Lord's coming.[116]

In their ecclesiastical affairs, the moderate Adventists formed comeouter antislavery congregations, founded on the principles of spiritual democracy. The comeouter Adventists despised hierarchical castes and "denominational pride."[117] Galusha withdrew from the Baptist denomination and started his own Adventist comeouter congregations in Lockport and Perry. At his Advent Hall in Lockport, Galusha hosted multidenominational ecclesiastical abolitionist meetings—even though many of the attendees were not at all favorable to Miller's particular millennial predictions. These meetings were held under the auspices of the Liberty Party for the expressed purpose of advocating ecclesiastical comeouterism and antislavery voting.[118]

Most ecclesiastical abolitionists did not subscribe to the specific cataclysmic chronology of the Millerites, but all of them were favorable to the idea that the establishment of God's perfected society was imminent. A growing sense of fervency and optimism in the early 1840s led many antebellum reformers to believe that God's reign on earth was about to commence. Millerism was only one factor leading to this peak of excitement; an even greater cause was an outburst of evangelical perfectionist religious enthusiasm in the burned-over district from about 1841 to 1845. Hopeful signs of growth in the Liberty Party and among the comeouter churches contributed to the general perception of millennial expectation.[119]

"A Signal Crisis in the History of the Church"

In the early 1840s, ecclesiastical abolitionists were certain that the promised state of continuous revival was upon them. It was during this time that Finney conducted his series of meetings in western New York for those "deeply interested in the doctrine of Entire Sanctification in this life"; many new perfectionist antislavery congregations began as a result of Finney's meetings.[120] The

TABLE 1 **Abolition Churches in Upper New York: Number of Congregations and Approximate Membership Statistics, ca. 1844**

Comeouter Group	Number of Congregations	Approximate Membership
Unionist/independent Congregational	101	5,500
Franckean Lutheran	37	2,500
Wesleyan Methodist	119	6,400
Free Baptist	44*	2,400*
Congregational Friends	4	200
Antislavery Baptist/Adventist	12	600

* These numbers represent only those Free Baptist churches in upper New York identified as being explicitly abolitionist.

half-decade after 1840 was also the high point of influence for church reform activity, when the earliest comeouter congregations (those formed in the 1830s) reported their "greatest prosperity"[121] and when scores of new secessionist churches sprang up and flourished.[122] Over a hundred Wesleyan Methodist congregations were founded in New York within a three-year period, the upstate Free Baptists had their largest increase during these years, and the Franckean Lutherans announced that "revival has succeeded revival."[123] By the mid-1840s, there were over three hundred abolition churches in New York state alone.[124] (See table 1.)[125]

Ecclesiastical abolitionists were elated by this increased interest. They pointed with pride to the proliferation of congregational disruptions caused by evangelical perfectionism, antislavery, and church reform agitation. Goodell observed that "in almost every little village, or neighborhood, there is a church controversy going on" over these issues.[126]

Ecclesiastical abolitionists were most exhilarated by the way in which abolition churches banded together for cooperative social action. An informal but very dynamic network of grassroots ecumenism developed, primarily for the purpose of political mobilization. One result of this networking was a desire to promote a broadly based union among antislavery comeouters; encouraging signs of greater interest in Christian union included the Free Baptist merger of Free Communion Baptists with Freewill Baptists and the conglomeration of former members of several different denominations that joined to become the Wesleyan Methodist Connection. Church reform conventions increased in frequency and size during the 1840s, as more and more political abolitionists became convinced that "the existing church order . . . is the greatest bulwark in the way of the onward progress of the Liberty party."[127] This was exemplified by the participation of Wesleyan Methodist leader Luther Lee, Free Baptist leader Hiram Whitcher, and Unionist leader William Goodell at the Syracuse Church Reform Convention. All three men had long been attracted to the ideals of spiritual democracy and abolitionist unity.[128] Despite the fact that the united General Evangelical Secession never came into being, this high level of interdenominational mutuality based on common social justice commitments was unprecedented.

Unionist pastor Lewis C. Lockwood, reflecting on the Syracuse convention, marvelled at the millennial implications implicit in the newfound popularity of antislavery church reform: "There seems to be a 'turning and overturning,' preparatory to some great events. The curtain of the future is rising, and new scenes in the moral government of God in this world are developing themselves."[129] All of the secession and reorganization activity convinced ecclesiastical abolitionists that they were witnessing "a signal crisis in the history of the church." Surely, Goodell concluded, "another era has dawned."[130]

FIVE

A Political Millennium  *The Imminent*
Inauguration of God's Government

THE MILLENNIUM IS AT HAND," confidently proclaimed the edi
tor of the *Oberlin Evangelist* in 1841. The increase of "practical piety,"
demonstrated by the growing interest in social reforms such as abolition and the democratic reorganizing of churches, convinced him that the
promised perfect state of society would arrive in the near future. He observed
that "the age in which we live is an era of expectation" regarding the religious
and political reformation of the nation. To all appearances, the entire sanctification of America was impending and inevitable.[1]

During the 1840s, ecclesiastical abolitionists seemed ready to explode with
frenzied enthusiasm. Burned-over district reformers had high hopes that the
moral government of God would be established on earth—one community at a
time—as purified civil and religious organizations were established. Contemporary observers were convinced that the Liberty Party was on the verge of acquiring significant political power. It also appeared that abolition churches had
gained enough influence to threaten the entire religious establishment of the
nation—a prospect made more imaginable after the Methodist Episcopal
Church and the Baptist General Convention, the two largest Protestant bodies,
both split in the mid-1840s into Northern and Southern branches over the issue of slavery. The declaration of an 1845 Liberty Party convention was typically exuberant: "Tens of thousands have felt it [liberty], and burst the bands,

which united them to pro-slavery ecclesiastical and pro-slavery political parties. . . . Anti-slavery churches exist without number; and . . . we have a political party, whose purpose is, God helping it, to get hold of the reins of
Government, and abolish American slavery."[2]

The uniqueness of this integration of earthly and heavenly concerns was
not lost either on supporters or on critics of ecclesiastical abolitionism. Lewis
Lockwood admiringly declared that the coincidence of ecclesiastical reform
with political antislavery was "a remarkable juncture in the affairs of the church
and of civil society."[3] Proslavery apologist George Fitzhugh agreed with Lockwood's analysis but not with his value judgment, fearing that abolitionists such
as William Goodell and Gerrit Smith had planned "not only to abolish Southern slavery, but to abolish, or greatly modify . . . the institution of Christian
churches as now existing in America."[4] Likewise, Calvin Colton warned his fellow Whigs that the now-numerous abolition churches were clandestine bases
of operation for the advancing Liberty Party.[5]

For ecclesiastical abolitionists, the 1840s became their perfectionist moment. Several encouraging developments occurred within a relatively short period of time, persuading ecclesiastical abolitionists that the immediate
configuration of promising events had eternal consequences. At the beginning
of the decade, they believed that America would be sanctified by the democratic restructuring of individuals and of local institutions; by 1847, the ultraist demands of their theology and the actual experience of working for change
within the national political apparatus led ecclesiastical abolitionists to pro-
pose a more comprehensive and corporate reform of the entire society.

Temporal Events, Divine Activity

From approximately 1841 to 1845, a general revival swept over upper New
York state's religious community.[6] The revival was especially evident among
abolitionist Christians anticipating the imminent initiation of a perfect society.
Some historians have attributed the increased religious interest of these years
to the Millerite excitement,[7] while others have referred to the revival of the early 1840s as "the highwater mark of [Finneyite] New Measures."[8] These two religious explanations would seem to be mutually exclusive, especially if one
holds the generally accepted view that the postmillennialism prevalent among
antebellum revivalistic reformers such as Finney was vastly different from the

premillennialism of the Millerites.[9] However, the millennial fervor of the 1840s should be interpreted in a dynamic fashion, recognizing that the various eschatological views were often conflated, their distinctions blurred;[10] in fact, the religious enthusiasm was evident among activists who adhered to the idea of an imminent millennial society in whatever form.

Such an interpretation helps to explain why some early Adventists such as Elon Galusha insisted that believers continue to struggle for societal transformation right up until Christ's second coming. It also clarifies why many perfectionistically influenced postmillennialists—who had formerly stressed a slow, gradual progression toward the perfected society—came to believe that the millennium was close at hand. Most ecclesiastical abolitionists were postmillennialists of this type, convinced that they had entered into the penultimate time just before the eschaton; the crucial moment had arrived for them to redouble their efforts. Finney often stated that the millennium would come within a few years if Christians would get on with the task of converting persons and sanctifying the society.[11]

The increasing millennial expectations of the early 1840s reached a fevered pitch in the autumn of 1844. More than a decade of urgent revivalistic preaching had conditioned the people of the burned-over district to be particularly receptive to the proposition of an immediate consummation of history. This excitement was partly a result of Millerite predictions of a cataclysmic apocalypse, but even those who did not accept Miller's specific chronology were convinced that the coming reign of God, in some form, was right on the horizon.[12]

Although religious folk agreed that the millennium was just around the corner, they had differing conceptions of how it would begin and what it would look like once it appeared. The Millerites determined that the millennium would commence on Tuesday, October 22, 1844, with the dramatic return of Christ. Ecclesiastical abolitionists were also caught up in the eschatological fervor of that autumn, but they looked for the millennium to begin two weeks later—on the first Tuesday of November—with the election of Liberty candidates. Indeed, on every election day in the 1840s, ecclesiastical abolitionists hoped for the beginning of a spectacular series of events that would lead to what they called "a political millennium."[13]

The political millennium was a phrase and a concept fraught with contradictions, indicating as it did the breaking of the sacred into the secular order. Because ecclesiastical abolitionists perceived that God's will for America (and for the world) was a purified democracy, they were assured that the eventual election of an antislavery slate of candidates was a foregone conclusion; when that took place, the establishment of God's domain on earth would begin. The inauguration of a Liberty Party government (a humanly-constructed, temporal event) would bring about the inauguration of God's moral government (a divinely-ordered, eternal condition).[14]

The forthcoming sanctified society envisioned by the ecclesiastical abolitionists had several characteristics: a state of continuous revival resulting in worldwide conversion to Christ; the extension of universal benevolence; and the destruction of hierarchies of all kinds.[15] The Garrisonians also envisioned the destruction of aristocratic institutions, but they believed that God's sovereign rule would prevail naturally without any "worldly" structures. The ecclesiastical abolitionists differed from Garrisonians on this point, because they believed humans needed to cooperate with divine agency by replacing dismantled institutions with democratically holy organizations. The projected millennial society of the ecclesiastical abolitionists was to be representative of God incarnate—wholly human and wholly divine. It was to be a millennium, hence dependent on God's governance; yet, it was to be political, hence the actual governing was to be accomplished through reorganized human structures.

In practice, it was difficult for Liberty activists to reconcile their experience of hardheaded politics with their perception of the divine will. This difficulty among Liberty advocates—the difficulty of holding together coexistent but diverse ideals—reflected a similar tension inherent in the American democratic experiment. How does a society, they pondered, provide both maximum personal freedom and the maintenance of public order? And how does a democratic government help to produce the "perfect society" when less-than-perfect means are used to effect it?

Compounding their difficulties, an influx of nonperfectionists into the Liberty ranks altered the complexion of the party at the national level. Liberty promoters had been successful in politicizing antislavery, and through the 1840s, the party began to attract a broader constituency, a larger number and a wider cross section of the Northern citizenry. Most of these newer Liberty partisans—such as Salmon P. Chase, Gamaliel Bailey, William Jay, and Edward Beecher—were from outside of the burned-over district. Some were conservative abolitionists influenced by the anti-Garrison sentiments of the American and Foreign Anti-Slavery Society; these conservatives felt uncomfortable with the perfectionist doctrine, antidenominational rhetoric, and women's rights advocacy of the ecclesiastical abolitionists, all of which seemed to align with Garrison's views. Other newcomers to the Liberty Party were seasoned political professionals who eventually grew impatient with the high-flown ideals and moral imperatives of the ecclesiastical abolitionists. They were less interested in radical social programs such as equal rights for African Americans and more interested in securing the economic interests of white laborers.[16]

During the four years prior to 1848, these nonperfectionist Liberty men tried to move the party toward pragmatic compromise and coalition politics. Most of the original ecclesiastical abolitionist Liberty leaders from upper New York fought against the new compromises; some, however, were intrigued by the practicality of a broader base. Observing the embryonic factions developing within the party, Gerrit Smith and other evangelical perfectionists correctly perceived that problems lay ahead, and they attempted to devise a strategy to deal with those problems.[17]

Smith was concerned that an "impatience to multiply numbers" was prompting some Liberty supporters to endorse the party's policies out of expediency rather than principle. He lamented that these pragmatists supported the elimination of slavery because, as they put it, "national prosperity . . . demands its abolition"—not because it was the morally right thing to do. Why were such Liberty members, Smith asked in disbelief, more interested in "Banks and Tariffs and Monopolies" than the immorality of "cling[ing] to a proslavery church?" According to Smith, the pragmatic Liberty members espoused popular political views "on financial and economical questions" merely for the sake of numerical growth in the party. Such a plan would surely backfire, for the endorsement of a particular economic position might repel as many people as it attracted.

Smith had an alternative strategy. He proposed that the perfectionist wing of the party—which he identified as "Birney, Goodell, Green" and about five thousand others—were the Liberty activists most qualified to lead the whole complement of sixty-five thousand Liberty voters in a two-year period of self-study. The party members were to spend these two years thoroughly examining the moral and political implications of the "principle of equal rights." Smith was confident that with such a plan, the entire Liberty Party would eventually harmonize around certain comprehensive campaign issues, such as universal suffrage. Then, with a principled platform in hand, the unified bloc of Liberty voters would "work out the victory" at the polls.[18]

"Our Increasing Party"

The frenzied campaign atmosphere of the 1840s created a "political tempest" of partisan competitiveness.[19] For backcountry communities, the annual electoral contests were sources of entertainment as well as occasions for serious politicking. Candidates took full advantage of new mass communication techniques and voters entered into political debates with keen interest. Voter participation in elections was at record levels; New York's turnout of 92.4% of eligible voters in the presidential election of 1844 was the highest in the state's history.[20] These circumstances lent excitement and anticipation to the political discourse of the era, and in the midst of this partisan whirlwind, Liberty advocates developed their political quest for the end of slavery.

Beyond the frenetic behavior common to electoral campaigning of the period, ecclesiastical abolitionists were driven by the added urgency of bringing about the government of God. Momentous and eternal consequences would result from their political activity, as evidenced especially by the ever expanding influence of the Liberty Party. Believing that God desired their crusade to prevail, they saw the Liberty Party's electoral growth as a confirmation of their inevitable success;[21] in the span of only one quadrennium, beginning in 1840, the Liberty vote had grown from a handful of ballots to a plurality in some upper New York state communities. Liberty candidates were winning local elections,[22] and by 1842 they held the balance of power between the major parties in New York.[23] Liberty supporters were so encouraged by the party's showing in 1843 that they looked forward to a thoroughly abolitionized electorate within five years.[24] Shortly after that, they predicted, the democratic government of God would be instituted.

Ecclesiastical abolitionists were exultant. The Franckean Lutherans boasted of "the brightening prospects of the Liberty party." The "anti-slavery enterprise," they declared, had "advanced beyond the expectations . . . of its most sanguine friends"; Franckean pastors were convinced that success in electing "our candidates" was not far off. Likewise, J. N. T. Tucker, the Unionist editor of the *Liberty Almanac,* exuded the confidence of Liberty members when he described the "rapidly growing cause, and our increasing party."[25]

Ultimate victory was assured not because of any political savvy but because of their "firm basis of principle." The holy ideals nurtured in abolition churches would provide them with a steady increase until the Liberty vote became a national majority; according to Luther Myrick, the party was "destined, at no distant period, to triumph most gloriously." Pending the consummation of their goals, Liberty activists were encouraged to believe that "the cause is onward. There will be a great increase of votes at the ensuing election. Onward, then, ye lovers of liberty."[26]

"The Aggregate Influence of the Church"—Abolition Churches and Liberty Party Strategy

William Goodell was speaking from his own experience when he stated that "the measure of organizing anti-slavery churches commenced with members of the Liberty party and has been chiefly confined to them." In the minds both of proponents and of opponents, "the political and ecclesiastical seceders of central and western New York" were identified together.[27] Ecclesiastical abolitionists were Liberty advocates and, inversely, nearly all of the Liberty Party leaders from upper New York were engaged in the democratic restructuring of churches.[28] In addition to the leaders, rank and file Liberty voters also were members of abolition churches; references to the penchant for church reform among ordinary Liberty supporters filled the party's newspapers. Wesleyan Methodists were confident that most members of their connection voted for the Liberty ticket; similarly, the Free Baptists determined that a majority of their number cast their ballots for antislavery candidates. Some abolitionist congregations declared themselves, one and all, as Liberty Party–supporting antislavery societies. Other comeouter churches advertised their partisan intentions in the Liberty Party papers; the individual members of the churches had their names printed in the advertisements so that there would be no doubt about their sanctified political preference for liberty.[29]

Because Liberty voters were religious comeouters, Liberty Party strategy centered around the influence of abolitionist congregations in their respective communities. The comeouters of the Church of Warsaw, for example, believed that God's sanctifying activity over all of society would begin when "the aggregate influence of the church is wielded" in every town.[30] Purified people would constitute a purified church that would then purify the entire town by the force of its example. Every person, every church, and every reformed community— no matter how remote—could effect a change with millennial implications.[31] According to Goodell, the organization of a New York town (the basic local political subdivision)[32] was equated to the structure of a local church: democratic town government was originally modeled after the concept of self-sufficient New England congregational churches, which was itself modeled after the pattern of New Testament churches. Civil and ecclesiastical polities were intended to function most smoothly at local levels; when operating as they ought, churches and towns were independent, democratic, voluntary organizations, and both could be perfected by the aggregate sanctification of their constituents.[33] In an age in which the commercial values of the larger urbanizing society were beginning to impinge upon the relatively secure world of small New York communities, this identification of rural village life with God's intended order for humanity was very appealing.[34]

Starting with the example of their own sanctified congregations, Liberty members in each village were encouraged to establish a model "perfect community" by abolitionizing their town. This would occur politically when they "secur[ed] control of the town power" by electing local Liberty candidates.[35] Such perfected communities would then set the pace for others to follow. Liberty Party papers extolled the role of the sanctified reformer and of the local comeouter church: "Through the ballot-box, one can exert an influence that is felt through the length and breadth of this mighty nation against oppression."[36] The 1843 national Liberty Party convention encouraged the faithful to "regard the world as their field, and although destined to labor in small portions of it, as laboring nevertheless, for the great end of bringing the whole world to the Savior." Thus, Liberty advocates articulated a reform strategy that was at once localized and worldwide, temporal and eternal, secular and sacred.[37]

Gerrit Smith developed the most comprehensive application of this strategy. He compared his abolitionized home village of Peterboro with the unreformed character of other villages, and urged Liberty activists to emulate the former. Smith also used the example of Peterboro as a model for the reformation of all of the towns in his county. It would only be a matter of time, he was sure, before Madison County was thoroughly abolitionized: "Such success of our dear cause in this County would be the knocking of a stone out of the arch of American slavery. . . . Taught by her success that they can follow her example, other Counties would quickly follow it: and but a few years would pass away ere American slavery would be no more. Such is my hope of the rapid progress of the anti-slavery cause." Through Smith's untiring efforts his wish was partially fulfilled, as Madison County consistently polled the highest percentages of Liberty vote totals in the state.[38]

As the bases of operation for mobilizing the hamlets and crossroads of the burned-over district, abolitionist churches served as a major source of Liberty Party recruitment. Even evangelism had a political function; new members of abolition churches meant more Liberty votes. Liberty leaders often used the pulpits of friendly comeouter churches to read public notices about upcoming abolitionist rallies or to "preach anti-slavery on the Sabbath."[39] In small villages such as Peterboro, Warsaw, and over two hundred and fifty other New York communities, the local comeouter congregation served as the bully pulpit and organizational center for Liberty campaigning.

An analysis of Liberty election returns from the 1844 presidential contest in New York demonstrates that communities with high Liberty vote totals were the same communities that contained antislavery churches (see appendixes A and B). Of the fifty-five upstate towns that polled over sixty Liberty votes, fifty-three (96.4%) contained a comeouter abolition church or demonstrated significant interest in antislavery church reform. Of the 182 towns that polled over thirty Liberty votes, 165 (90.7%) had an abolition church (see map B, page 178). Conversely, of the seventy-nine towns in upper New York that polled no Liberty votes, only one contained a comeouter congregation (1.3%).[40] The villages or hamlets in which abolition churches were established were almost invariably located in towns that polled the highest Liberty tallies in their respective counties, and the more thriving the antislavery congregation in a particular town, the higher the Liberty vote.[41] At least in upper New York state—where Liberty advocates had their greatest success—the party's vital energy was a direct result of political advocacy by antislavery congregations.[42]

Representative Ecclesiastical Abolitionist Communities

Hiram Whitcher's 1844 pastorate of the Free Baptist congregation in the hamlet of Unadilla Forks is a particularly noteworthy instance of the influence of abolition churches on Liberty vote turnout. Just a month before the 1844 national election, Whitcher's church hosted the triennial General Conference of the Free Baptist Connection, along with the annual meeting of the Freewill Baptist Anti-Slavery Society. Considering all of the excitement and interest that must have gripped the community when a national antislavery conference of several hundred people met in their little village, it is not surprising that at the general election the New York Liberty Party received its second highest percentage and eighth highest raw number of votes from Plainfield, the sparsely populated town in which the hamlet of Unadilla Forks lies.[43]

Table 2 lists upper New York towns such as Plainfield that provided the Liberty Party with its greatest support in the 1844 election (over one hundred votes each).[44] Every one of the towns had at least one antislavery church, and many of these particular churches were the most active centers of ecclesiastical abolitionism in the state, including (among others) Luther Myrick's original Union church in Cazenovia; Gerrit Smith's Free Church of Peterboro (town of Smithfield); the prominent Wesleyan Methodist church in Fulton (town of Volney), later pastored by Luther Lee; Wesley Bailey's Wesleyan Methodist church, a hub of antislavery agitation in Utica; the comeouter Congregational church in Cortland, soon to be pastored by Samuel Ringgold Ward; Hiram Whitcher's Free Baptist church in Unadilla Forks; Elon Galusha's Advent Hall in Lockport; and Beriah Green's independent Congregational church in Whitestown.[45]

The activities of the Free Church of Sherburne also demonstrate the close relation between abolition churches and Liberty Party advocacy. In the 1840s,

TABLE 2 **1844 Liberty Vote Totals over 100 in Upper New York State Towns**

Town	County	Liberty Vote	Abolition Church(es)
Cazenovia	Madison	177	Cazenovia Union Church
Smithfield	Madison	174	Free Church of Peterboro
Volney	Oswego	140	Fulton Wesleyan Methodist Church
Sullivan	Madison	140	Chittenango Union Church
			Canaseraga Union Church
Utica	Oneida	120	Utica Church of Christ
			Utica Wesleyan Methodist Church
Brookfield	Madison	116	Brookfield Free Baptist Church
Cortlandville	Cortland	116	Cortland Congregational Church
Plainfield	Otsego	113	Unadilla Forks Free Baptist Church
Lenox	Madison	112	Canastota Independent Church
			Lenox Antislavery Baptist Church
Lockport	Niagara	112	Advent Hall of Lockport
			Lockport Wesleyan Methodist Church
			Lockport Congregational Church
Whitestown	Oneida	107	Whitesboro Congregational Church
			Whitesboro Free Baptist Church
Collins	Erie	104	Lodi Congregational Church
			Collins Congregational Friends
Richland	Oswego	100	Pulaski Congregational Church

Free Church of Sherburne, Sherburne, New York. *Courtesy of Julian D. Button.*

abolitionists in this central New York town were disciplined by their local Presbygational church for attending and publicizing Liberty Party meetings on the
sabbath. Consequently, a number of Sherburne's Liberty men and women
withdrew their membership and with like-minded colleagues from the neighboring town of Smyrna established a comeouter church. The new Free
Church, nicknamed the "Abolition Church," served as the unofficial Liberty
Party headquarters for Chenango County. Jonathan Copeland, one of the
prominent founding members of the Free Church, was a member of the central
committee of the state party, and as in other ecclesiastical abolitionist congregations, the pulpit of the Free Church was always open to preaching on behalf
of the Liberty Party and other reformatory causes. Accordingly, the Liberty
Party vote totals for the town of Sherburne were the highest in the county.[46]

An examination of 1844 voting returns for Chenango County illustrates the
political effect of abolitionist congregations such as Sherburne's Free Church
(see table 3). Each of the towns in Chenango County with an abolition church
had comparatively high Liberty Party vote totals in relation to other towns in

TABLE 3   **1844 Liberty Party Election Return: Chenango County**

Town	Liberty Vote	Total Vote	% Liberty Vote to Total Vote	Abolition Church
Sherburne	52	644	8.1	Union ("Free Church")
Lincklaen	49	244	20.1	Independent Congregational
Pitcher	35	311	11.3	Independent Congregational
Smyrna	27	429	6.3	Union (with Sherburne)
New Berlin	20	624	3.2	none
Guilford	14	635	2.2	none
Otselic	12	329	3.6	none
Norwich	10	960	1.0	none
Bainbridge	8	686	1.2	none
Columbus	6	370	1.6	none
Coventry	5	409	1.2	none
Pharsalia	2	268	0.7	none
Oxford	1	733	0.1	none
Plymouth	1	369	0.3	none
Smithville	1	376	0.3	none
German	0	197	0.0	none
Greene	0	812	0.0	none
MacDonough	0	288	0.0	none
Preston	0	257	0.0	none

the county. To be more specific, the four towns with the largest number of Liberty votes (Sherburne, Lincklaen, Pitcher, and Smyrna) were all influenced by antislavery church reform.[47] In contrast, none of the fifteen towns in Chenango County with comparatively low Liberty vote percentages (3% or lower) had an abolition church. In quantitative terms, the correlation between Liberty votes and the presence of an abolition church in the towns of Chenango County was a significantly high coefficient of +.90.[48]

The Congregational church of Arcade provides another example of the connection between political abolitionism and ecclesiastical abolitionism. During the early 1840s, this church experienced a heightening of spiritual interest, adopted new, non-Calvinist articles of faith that stressed the principles of spiritual democracy, and called a succession of evangelical perfectionist pastors (including Huntington Lyman and John Keep) who were trained at or influenced by Oberlin. Similar to many other abolition churches, the church in Arcade seceded from the presbytery but never changed its name, because the members felt that the church's original "Congregational" title was sufficiently descriptive of their democratic ecclesiology. True to the principles of spiritual democracy, the church refused to join the regional Congregationalist judicatory.

GRAND LIBERTY CONVENTION.

On Wednesday July 31st, and Thursday the

1st of August, 1844,

at the Village of

ARCADE,

Wyoming Co. will be held a Liberty Party Convention for Western New York.

It is intended to make the Convention *large, interesting* and *profitable;* and to this end efforts have been made to secure the attendance of able Speakers from a distance, as well as those near home. There will be no lack on this score. Appropriate

LIBERTY SINGING,

may also be expected by different individuals, in choirs and by single voices.

On *Wednesday* the Convention will open at 10 o'clock A.M. in the Grove and Bower, on the corner opposite the Arcade Temperance House. The evening sessions will be held in one or both the churches,

On *Thursday August* 1st. some exercises commemorative of West India Emancipation will be had. Among other things, an

EMANCIPATION DINNER.

in Pic-nic style, will be served up in an adjacent Bower, at 1 o'clock P.M. under the superintendance of the *Ladies.* Preparations will be made for some hundreds; and all who intend to dine (and who does not ?) are requested to purchase tickets, at the Temperance house, immediately on their arrival in the village, in order that a Table may be set corresponding with the number of tickets sold.

After dinner, at the table, brief remarks and sentiments will be offered, and an *Emancipation Hymn* sung by Ladies. Price of tickets, 50 cents. The proceeds of the dinner to be devoted to the Liberty cause under the direction of the officers of the Convention. This method is adopted instead of the usual one of taking collections. The hospitalities of the village and vicinity, are cheerfully tendered during the Convention.

Among the speakers confidently expected, are

    ALVAN STEWART,
    SAMUEL R. WARD,
    W. L. CHAPLIN,
    A. C. JACKSON,
    C. D. M'KAY,
    G. W. JONSON,
    J. ANDREWS,
    C. GRAY, &c. &c.

It is also quite probable that the *Hon. James* G. Birney and the *Hon. Thomas Morris,* or one of them, will be present—though the's cannot now be ascertained with certainty. They are looked for in this Book, so last or only. Should they arrive at Buffalo in season, they will be at this Convention. In such case, the earliest possible information will be given.

And now, all things are ready for a great gathering of Freedom's friends. Let them come from Chenango, Cattaraugus, Allegany, Livingston, Wyoming, Genesee, Onondaga and Niagara counties, and throng each other on, in the glorious warfare against Slavery, and for Universal Liberty.

"Now's the day, and now's the hour."

Reary and the *Hon. Thomas Morris,* or one of them, will be present—though the's cannot now be ascertained with mission. Let us meet them in the great assembly, with argument, and in November next, with

"A weapon that cannot down its will
As more dishes fall upon the soil,
And crushes a freeman's will,
As lightning does the will of God.
And from its flint—robed tops, not looks
Clan should throw—'tis the Ballot-box."

Clay, Clay, ...

Liberty Convention announcement (1844). Convention held under the sponsorship of Arcade Congregational Church. *From* The Countryman *(July 1844); courtesy of Arcade Historical Society.*

The Congregational church of Arcade hosted two of the largest Liberty Party rallies ever held. One of these rallies, in January 1840, was the assembly that issued the call for the national antislavery nominating convention later held in Albany. Gerrit Smith thus considered the 1840 Arcade convention to be the founding meeting of the third party. Advertisements for the second Liberty convention, in 1844, featured the church's pastor, Calvin Gray, and Samuel Ringgold Ward, who had preached previously at the Arcade church. Charles O. Shepard, one of the luminaries of the church, was twice the state Liberty Party's candidate for lieutenant governor. Several other church members were active in party leadership, and the town of China (Arcade) polled the third highest percentage of Liberty votes in New York in 1844. Due to the church's reputation as an advocate for the rights of African Americans, Arcade acquired the epithet "Niggerville"—certainly an unusual label for a rural village that, according to the State census, had no black residents.[49]

A survey of the Liberty vote totals in Wyoming County (in which Arcade is located) reveals a pattern similar to the one observed in Chenango County (see table 4). The four towns with abolition churches showed the greatest level of Liberty support. In Perry, the political preaching of Elon Galusha broke apart a Baptist church and caused the formation of a new antislavery Adventist church. The abolitionist activities of the (previously described) comeouter Church of Warsaw account for the high Liberty vote there, as do those of the Congregational church in Arcade. The Presbygational church in Castile was also disrupted by antislavery church reform agitation, which helped to influence that town's large Liberty showing. The direct opposite occurred in the nine Wyoming County towns in which there was no abolition church;

TABLE 4 **1844 Liberty Party Election Returns: Wyoming County**

Town	Liberty Vote	Total Vote	% Liberty Vote to Total Vote	Abolition Church
Perry	82	623	13.1	Antislavery Baptist/Adventist
Warsaw	75	534	14.0	Union
China (Arcade)	71	303	23.4	Independent Congregational
Castile	61	480	12.7	Independent Congregational
Gainesville	25	415	6.0	none
Java	21	387	5.4	none
Middlebury	21	432	4.9	none
Wethersfield	21	254	8.3	none
Attica	20	462	4.3	none
Sheldon	16	394	4.1	none
Covington	12	283	4.2	none
Orangeville	12	282	4.3	none
Bennington	5	449	1.1	none

these nine towns had comparatively low Liberty vote totals. Thus, the correlation between a large number of Liberty votes and the presence of an abolition church in the towns of Wyoming County was a coefficient of +.97, indicating an astoundingly high positive relationship.[50]

The interplay between church reform and antislavery politics was well represented by the Seneca Falls Wesleyan Methodist church. Formed in 1843 when antislavery activists seceded from the town's Methodist Episcopal Church, it became the religious haven for comeouter abolitionists from many denominations. As in abolition churches in other communities, the Seneca Falls Wesleyan Methodists were leaders in the Liberty Party; the brothers Jonathan and Joseph Metcalf, for instance, both comeouters from the Methodist Episcopal Church, were well-known Liberty men.[51] Because of the active Liberty campaigning radiating from the Wesleyan Methodist church, Seneca Falls provided the largest tally for antislavery candidates of any town in Seneca County (see table 5).[52]

The Seneca Falls Wesleyan Methodist church was well known locally as a hub of radical politics years before it became famous nationally for its entertainment of the first women's rights convention in 1848. No doubt convenience was one reason Elizabeth Cady Stanton chose the "Wesleyan chapel" in her home town as the place in which to hold the meeting, but the church was not merely the closest available building that would accommodate the convention; in fact, it was a particularly appropriate venue for the beginning of the suffragist

Congregants of Seneca Falls Wesleyan Methodist Church, Seneca Falls, New York (ca. 1850). *Courtesy of Seneca Falls Historical Society.*

TABLE 5   **1844 Liberty Party Election Returns: Seneca County**

Town	Liberty Vote	Total Vote	% Liberty Vote to Total Vote	Abolition Church
Seneca Falls	39	711	5.5	Wesleyan Methodist
Tyre	27	287	9.4	Wesleyan Methodist
Waterloo	25	627	4.0	Congregational Friends
Ovid	15	463	3.2	none
Fayette	7	773	0.9	none
Romulus	4	432	0.9	none
Varick	3	401	0.7	none
Junius	2	318	0.6	none
Lodi	2	504	0.4	none
Covert	0	504	0.0	none

movement. The church's environment of abolitionism and antidenomination-alism offered an especially suitable location from which to promulgate the radically innovative ideas of social and political equality for women.[53] At least ten of the one hundred signers of the declaration that issued from the convention were members of or affiliates with the Seneca Falls Wesleyan Methodist church.[54] In the mid-1840s, the evangelical perfectionist theology and political involvement of the Seneca Falls Wesleyan Methodists led them and other ecclesiastical abolitionists to move beyond the "one idea" of antislavery reform to a more comprehensive advocacy of "universal reform"—including women's rights.

An "All-Comprehensive Reformatory Enterprise"

In their efforts to agitate against the oppression of African Americans, many evangelical perfectionistic abolitionists began to see the correlation between the despotism of slavery and the "encroachments of despotism" upon the liberties of all Americans. They visualized "a political association for the correction of ALL abuses in the government, for the repeal of ALL unjust laws, and for the equal and impartial protection of ALL MEN." Such reasoning had already led the comeouter churches to evolve from advocating antislavery reform alone to the support of an "all-comprehensive reformatory enterprise"; the abolition churches felt that they could not "be indifferent or remain neutral with regard to any moral enterprise truly benevolent." Now Liberty supporters, as members of antislavery congregations, followed their churches' lead in promoting a broader synthesis of reform activities.[55]

Two things led ecclesiastical abolitionists to embrace a more comprehensive agenda. First, by entering into politics, they encountered the multifaceted complexity that accompanies any attempt to legislate social change. By "stepping into the arena of political life, and thus attempting the discharge of the duties growing out of our relations to civil government," Liberty Party members passed beyond the "'one-idea' of abolishing chattel slavery." The reality of partisan campaigning opened the eyes of abolitionists to the limited perspective of single-issue politics and to the shortsightedness of individualistic strategies of social reform.[56]

Because the traditional evangelical approach to social problems was the regeneration of persons, one at a time, until the whole community and nation was transformed, the reformers had tackled one moral cause at a time. Abolitionists learned this method during their earlier work within the temperance movement and other task-specific voluntary benevolent societies.[57] By 1847, however, many politically active ecclesiastical abolitionists developed a more solidaristic strategy, a strategy that stressed the unified nature of all sin. They became persuaded that "social sins" needed to be tackled in their institutional capacities as well as through the reform of persons. Slavery, for instance, was no longer understood as a solitary sin. "Considered in its connections and its affinities," slavery could be "fully seen as it is"—an intricate web of economic and social evils. "Slavery will be abolished," William Goodell wrote, and so will every other "oppression and encroachment upon human rights," as soon as there is *"national* along with *individual* reform" and as soon as reformers include *"political* as a part of *moral* and of *spiritual* renovation." During the early and mid-1840s, direct involvement in partisan politicking over the issue of slavery convinced ecclesiastical abolitionists that God's sanctified government would be effected by a divinely directed yet very worldly political millennium. By the end of the decade, this same political activity encouraged them to enlarge their vision of the millennial society to include many reforms beyond antislavery.[58]

A second factor that led ecclesiastical abolitionists toward universal reform was the logic of their perfectionist theology. The continual striving for entire sanctification among ecclesiastical abolitionists created a sense of obligation to "wage an uncompromising warfare with all sin." In their pursuit of "higher and still higher attainments in holiness," each individual abolitionist was not "content to cease his reformatory labor" until a sanctified society was established.

The more self denying, extensive, and successful his labors, the more will the Christian discover remaining still to be done. The completion of any *one* Christian, reformatory, and benevolent enterprize [*sic*], however it may be described, will be found to involve and require for such completion, the espousal of every kindred Christian enterprise. One reformatory, benevolent, or evangelizing enterprise, whether completed or in progress, is only the Christian laborer's stepping stone to another, and yet another.

According to Liberty activists, the enterprise of antislavery had been the sole appropriate reform endeavor "for a certain time," but by the late 1840s, they believed that the abolition of slavery should no longer be seen as the "panacea for all social ills."[59]

A Universal Reform Party

The perfectionist leanings of many Liberty Party leaders led them to advance a broader social agenda. As early as 1843, Liberty advocates stated that they were obliged by their obedience to the moral law of God to "carry out the principles of Equal Rights, into all their practical consequences and applications."[60] Because of the interconnectedness of various kinds of oppression, Liberty Party members were convinced of their need to be "comprehensive in their views of human rights." Thus, by 1847, a group of Liberty activists gave notice that if they could be shown "any other measure that justice requires" beyond simply the elimination of slavery, they would add it to their platform.[61]

Transforming the Liberty Party from an antislavery party to a "universal reform" party was first broached at a New York state Liberty convention in 1845, but it was not formalized until the establishment of the Liberty League at Macedon Lock, New York, in 1847. The league was a political pressure group, a perfectionist faction of the Liberty Party composed almost exclusively of ecclesiastical abolitionists from the burned-over district. The league's intent was to goad the Liberty Party toward the political millennium by advancing more radical reform measures.[62]

An essential item on the comprehensive agenda of the Liberty Leaguers was their continued commitment to ecclesiastical reform, because they believed that the "existing Church order . . . is the greatest bulwark in the way of the onward progress of the Liberty Party." Political equality for all persons could not be contemplated if people did not already have religious equality. Goodell declared that the Liberty Party was able to maintain its radical principles against the pressures to compromise politically only because "its leading members commonly hold a corresponding ecclesiastical position." Church fellowship among antislavery comeouters provided the support structure needed by perfectionist Liberty men and women; consequently, one of the articles of the national platform of the Liberty League was a specific summons to form abolition churches.[63]

Beyond the democratization of church structures, the evangelical perfectionist Liberty advocates championed various legislative proposals calculated to extend equal rights to all persons residing in the United States. From the beginning of the Liberty Party, the list of such proposals always began with an explicit repudiation of slavery. As the 1840s wore on, Liberty supporters progressively expanded the moral and political implications of their antislavery platform; besides condemning the sin of slaveholding, they also dedicated themselves to demolishing racism and securing the full rights of citizenship for African Americans and others.[64]

Unafraid of charges of racial amalgamation, for example, Liberty leaders encouraged blacks to assume positions of power. Several upstate African Americans held leadership positions within the party, including Henry Highland Garnet, Samuel Ringgold Ward, William Wells Brown, Charles B. Ray, Jermain W. Loguen, and, later, Frederick Douglass.[65] Unlike many other reformers, the perfectionist Liberty activists correctly understood that one of the fundamental antislavery problems to be addressed was racial injustice as well as legal emancipation. They were fearful that once African Americans were emancipated they would be forced into a new servitude because of lingering prejudice, the absence of economic opportunity, and the lack of real political power. The denunciation of racism was also evident in the Liberty League's pacifist proposals to end the Mexican War; the chief problem with the war, according to the Leaguers, was that the war's proponents intended to extend slavery and to oppress Mexicans.[66]

Other equal rights issues captured the interest of perfectionist Liberty men and women. Their comprehensive program included such novel ideas as homesteading, land use reform, a progressive income tax, the abolition of war as an instrument of national policy, and the direct election of all federal officials (including senators, the cabinet, members of the judiciary, and the president—thereby abolishing the electoral college). Along with their advocacy on behalf of African Americans, they also declared their opposition to nativism and to economic exploitation, particularly as directed against Chinese Americans, Native Americans, Irish immigrants, and the industrial working class.[67] This broad agenda indicated a growing understanding of the corporate nature of evil and the need for a structural approach to social reform.[68]

One other noteworthy aspect of the evangelical perfectionist wing of the Liberty Party was its programmatic emphasis on the enfranchisement and empowerment of women, again characteristic of the ecclesiastical abolitionists' attention to universal reform. Gerrit Smith openly recommended women's suffrage as early as 1846. At the National Liberty Convention held in Buffalo in June 1848—one month before the famous Seneca Falls Women's Rights Convention—party members adopted a resolution stating their opposition to the "exclusion of woman" from the right to vote. A sanctified government, they reasoned, must include the political participation of women. This radical assertion was backed up by concrete action: at Liberty conventions in 1847 and in 1848, women received votes for nomination as the party's candidates for president and for vice president of the United States.[69] Thus, on several different public occasions during the year prior to the Seneca Falls convention, the Liberty Party raised the issue of women's suffrage.

Indeed, there is a clear connection between the early women's rights movement and the activities of political and ecclesiastical abolitionists.[70] Liberty Party leaders and women's rights activists were in regular correspondence; the Liberty Party frequently declared its support for the equal social and political rights of women; and women's rights leaders spoke at Liberty Party conventions.[71] Free Baptist reformer Hiram Whitcher was a lauded figure at one of the earliest women's rights conventions,[72] and Antoinette Brown's stint on the National Committee of the Liberty Party occurred simultaneously with her pathbreaking pastorate in the comeouter church of South Butler and with her advocacy for equal rights for women.[73]

Many leaders of the women's rights movement evinced the reforming position toward institutional structures so characteristic of ecclesiastical abolitionism. In language identical to that used by their ecclesiastical abolitionist colleagues—who had "come out" of conventional denominations and political parties in order to organize purified structures in their place—the suffragists stated that their task was to "pull down [the] present worn-out and imperfect human institutions" and to "reconstruct them upon a new and broader foundation."[74] In political matters, such institutional reconstruction meant that from the Seneca Falls convention onward, these women stressed the importance of obtaining the ballot. "The Right of Suffrage," they declared, is "the corner-stone of this enterprise."[75]

Abolitionist historians have often argued that most women's rights activists of the 1840s and 1850s were Garrisonian abolitionists who held heterodox doctrines.[76] Although generally true, this is not the whole story, for another coterie of women's rights activists were Liberty Party supporters who were involved in the restructuring of church organizations. Because involvement in the political process was antithetical to the ideals of the Garrisonians, some early feminists were drawn toward the more practical strategy of the political and ecclesiastical abolitionists.

Liberty Party suffragists faced a dilemma, however. The tangible goals of these women, who desired above all to achieve actual political power, put many of them into a close alignment with pragmatists who urged a broader political alliance in order to be successful.[77] The strategic tension faced by those who wanted to obtain the franchise for women was the sort of dilemma that confronted the entire Liberty Party in the late 1840s. The dilemma was particularly acute for those Liberty leaders who were ecclesiastical abolitionists; the evangelical perfectionist concept of the political millennium encouraged a strategy that was simultaneously practical and idealistic, but it was hard to balance these two emphases. Some reformers sought greater results from their political efforts and tended to drift in the direction of a more open-ended antislavery coalition. Others continued to put their highest priority on the need for a divine government and worked to enhance the radical sanctification of the Liberty Party. By 1848, the factionalism among Liberty supporters resulted in a full-blown division of the party—a phenomenon that did not bode well for the future of perfectionist politics.

SIX

The Burned-Out District

The Fragmenting of Ecclesiastical Abolitionism

C HARLES O. SHEPARD and Huntington Lyman, brothers-in-law from Arcade, New York, entered the 1840s as ecclesiastical abolitionist colleagues, working in tandem to advance the Liberty Party and antislavery church reform. Lyman had trained for the ministry at Oberlin and had briefly preached at his home church in Arcade before accepting a call to become the pastor of the comeouter Congregational church in the neighboring village of Warsaw. In Warsaw and in other towns where he ministered, Lyman combined his interest in democratizing church structures with his work for political abolition. Meanwhile, Shepard managed the family mercantile business, immersed himself in statewide Liberty Party campaigning, and promoted church reform within the Arcade congregation.[1]

By 1850, however, Shepard and Lyman carried out their reform activities from opposing antislavery camps. The critical turn of events for Shepard began when the Arcade church called a new pastor in 1847. To the bewilderment of Shepard and of the other ecclesiastical abolitionists in the congregation, this new minister insisted on returning to the original Calvinistic doctrinal basis for church membership, thus forgoing the anticreedal, ethically based criteria adopted by the evangelical perfectionists. During the pastor's tenure, Shepard was brought before a church trial and was formally accused of spending too much time on his political abolition activities; other perfectionist members

Arcade Congregational Church, Arcade, New York. *Courtesy of Arcade Historical Society.*

were accused of promoting Unionist beliefs. Tensions increased until 1849, when a schism occurred between the church's perfectionist and nonperfectionist factions; seventeen months later, the schism was healed, but not without the resignation of most of the leading perfectionists. For his part, Shepard would never be reconciled to organized religion.[2]

After midcentury, the Arcade Congregational Church—minus all of its leadership and much of its membership—moved to the periphery of community life. Maintenance concerns predominated in church meetings, to the noticeable neglect both of social reform and of revivalistic activity. With ecclesiastical abolitionists removed from the congregation, there was no longer any direct connection between the church and political matters; though the personal holiness of sanctified individuals continued to be emphasized, the ideal of establishing a sanctified society faded away. Moreover, although Shepard and a few other persons in Arcade remained involved in regional politics and finance, neither the church nor the community as a whole retained their earlier evangelical perfectionist vision—a vision in which small towns like theirs had a uniquely momentous role in the unfolding millennial drama of God's government.[3]

At the same time, Shepard also was embroiled in a controversy within the Liberty Party, for the perfectionist vision was no easier to sustain in political matters than in ecclesiastical ones. By 1848, Liberty leaders differed greatly over whether the party should remain a righteous reform organization or should unite with the emerging Free Soil movement to form a more successful force in party politics. Frustrated with the failure of perfectionist ideology to make permanent advances either in church or in state, Shepard chose the more expedient political position and became active in the Free Soil and later the Republican parties.[4]

By contrast, Huntington Lyman took the other route. Following in the footsteps of his friend Gerrit Smith, Lyman continued his support for the radical, post-1848 remnant of the Liberty Party. He also retained his evangelical religious convictions, pastoring several independent Congregational churches into the 1870s.[5]

The strategic parting of the ways experienced by these two brothers-in-law was not unique. Ecclesiastical abolitionism throughout the region had fragmented, its energy diffused and its vitality sapped. Writing a few years later about his contemporaries Gerrit Smith and Beriah Green, a Presbyterian pastor observed that "the fuel in them had burned out." Indeed, in regard to perfectionist reform, the burned-over district had become a "burned out" district by 1860, a victim of external circumstances and of internal contradictions.[6]

As early as 1847, both the Liberty Party and the abolitionist congregations were conscious of "the languishing state of Zion."[7] The party was splitting into competing factions; antislavery churches floundered, some ecclesiastical abolitionists abandoning orthodox Christianity, others preoccupied with entrepreneurial enterprising or with professional politicking. Most of the reformers who remained politically active into the 1850s, such as Charles Shepard, acquiesced in the pragmatic concessions necessary for further electoral success. Other leaders of the movement—especially those who retained their evangelical inclinations—wearied of the struggle and gradually withdrew from active participation in partisan politics. Consumed with the details of denominational organization and of inward spirituality, their perfectionist objective narrowed from achieving societal transformation to obtaining a personal experience of sanctification. In the midst of such disillusionment and factional realignment, only a declining minority of reformers—represented by Huntington Lyman—clung to the goal of a perfected politics leading toward a sanctified society. Except for this small vestige, the religious-political alliance of ecclesiastical abolitionism disintegrated in the 1850s.

The External Challenge: Economic Dislocation and Critical Opposition

After several years of uninterrupted growth in the early to mid-1840s, the political ascent of the Liberty Party peaked with the election of 1846; electoral support for the party began to decline by 1848.[8] Abolition churches reported a similar trend, after 1846, of stabilization and then decline. Alvan Stewart summarized the sentiments of ecclesiastical abolitionists during this period when he wrote that those in the Liberty Party felt "like a man attacked, from *without*, in his own house, who fights for existence, and not for conquest."[9]

One of the external reasons for the demise of ecclesiastical abolitionism was the social transformation of the region.[10] In the two decades that preceded 1845, the agricultural areas of central and western New York expanded greatly, both in population and in productivity. Though the long-term persistence of the expansion seemed tenuous (as illustrated by the panic of 1837), optimism nonetheless ran high during most of the period. Residents of the region believed that their villages could exert a tremendous influence on the nation, and those influenced by perfectionist ideas were convinced that they were on the verge of a new, God-ordained social order.[11]

After the mid-1840s, however, the social fabric of the region began to tear, as the economic condition of rural New York stagnated. By 1845, the region reached its agricultural maturity; almost all of the arable countryside was cultivated. Some land was already depleted, leading to an extensive outmigration to urban areas and to the western territories. Most of the rural towns in New York hit their demographic peak in the 1840s; many communities actually lost population by the 1850s.[12] In the 1845 statewide census, "nearly all the increase [was] in the large towns," while those areas of the state that decreased included "several of the best agricultural counties." In Niagara County, there was a "tendency to growth in Lockport [the county seat] and some of the villages, and a tendency to declension in the country." The abolition churches, most of them rural-based, shared the depopulation, and many struggled merely to survive. One denominational chronicler wrote in 1859 that "for several years there has been some check to the temporal prosperity of this region, from which the churches have suffered, owing to the great emigration to the West."[13]

Ecclesiastical abolitionists had differing views on how to respond to the rapid transitions in their society. On the one hand, quite a few embraced the emerging commercialization—a trend that led the region's entrepreneurs away from localism and toward consolidation with the broader, urbanizing culture. Charles Shepard, for example, left the idealism of religious comeouterism and of the Liberty Party for the cosmopolitan realism of business success and of coalition politics. On the other hand, some ecclesiastical abolitionists were anxious about the direction in which their culture was heading. This was true especially for Huntington Lyman and for those evangelical perfectionists who remained in the Liberty Party after 1848. Canals and railroads, so heralded in their early years as effective means for transmitting revivalism, were now blamed for "divert[ing] trade to other points." The same transportation technology that encouraged regional prosperity and the spread of the gospel also encouraged economic displacement and the spread of unsanctified patterns of behavior. The Wesleyan Methodists in upper New York lamented "the increasing desecration of the Holy Sabbath, especially along canals, railroads, and thoroughfares throughout this nation—thus turning these improvements into curses."[14]

Many ecclesiastical abolitionists after midcentury retained their earlier ambivalence toward translocal institutions. Their political experience opened them up to national concerns and prompted them to promote social reforms that addressed broad structural issues in the society. At the same time, however, those who remained active Liberty advocates into the 1850s were hesitant to commit themselves to any highly centralized political or ecclesiastical institutions—a reflection of their continued allegiance to the locally based organizations characteristic of their small town environment.

Likewise, those still involved in abolition churches had mixed feelings about their connections to cosmopolitan influences. In 1855, when the African American pastor Samuel Ringgold Ward reflected back on the unusual degree of personal affirmation that he had received from his white congregants in South Butler, he was convinced that their unprejudiced behavior was due to the fact that they were "living in the interior of the State, apart from the . . . deceptions of fashion." For Ward and other ecclesiastical abolitionists, relative isolation from the temptations of citified society allowed residents of small towns to live sanctified lives, resisting the worst excesses of materialistic consumption and of bourgeois compromise. Hal Barron has determined that agrarian towns in the latter half of the nineteenth century were "communities against the stream, where local farmers were at once tied to larger national markets and also entwined in a face-to-face local life"; the actions of the ecclesiastical abolitionists indicate that the doubleness among rural Northerners regarding their relationship to the broader culture extended beyond economic concerns to encompass their religious and political lives as well.[15]

Along with the demographic and economic upheaval of the burned-over district, ecclesiastical abolitionism faced another external challenge: increased opposition by powerful critics intent on discrediting the movement. To be sure, this was nothing new for antislavery reformers. In their struggling early years, ecclesiastical abolitionists were regularly vilified by critics who viewed "perfectionism," "unionism," and "abolitionism" as a triple-headed demon.[16] Later, from approximately 1841 to 1846, the influence of political and ecclesiastical abolitionism reached its zenith: preaching on the doctrine of sanctification proliferated rapidly; hundreds of congregations experienced unionist (church reform) disruptions; and both evangelical perfectionism and church reform became leagued with the increasingly successful politicization of abolitionism. In those heady years of the mid-1840s, it seemed to opponents as well as to proponents that the altered society envisioned by the ecclesiastical abolitionists might actually come to pass within the foreseeable future. The politicized "Abolition Church" would be "a fearful power," fretted Calvin Colton, "if it should prevail." In the face of such a perceived threat, the critics of ecclesiastical abolitionism increased their denunciations.[17]

Oberlin College and Oneida Institute, the most conspicuous sources for disseminating evangelical perfectionism and abolitionism, were castigated with particular severity—even by some who had formerly supported the evangelistic efforts of Finney, Green, Myrick, and other revivalists. Many presbyteries, Congregationalist associations, and local Presbygational churches condemned "Oberlin perfectionism" and censured its advocates. Pastors trained at Oberlin or at Oneida were forbidden to take pulpits; the presbytery in Delaware County, New York, implored its member churches "not to employ any preacher" connected with those who "adopt the Oberlin opinions, or the Central Association established [by Luther Myrick] in central New York." Even the New York state legislature considered taking action against Oneida Institute, because it was such a "hot-bed of sedition."[18]

Already in the early 1840s, two specific episodes at Oberlin had discredited that institution and, by implication, its tenets. The first incident involved an eighteen-year-old male student at Oberlin's preparatory school who made sexual advances toward one of the women students. The young man's intentions were discovered by some overly zealous young Oberlin perfectionists, who promptly took it upon themselves to punish the moral perpetrator with twenty-five lashes. The account of this "Oberlin lynching" spread widely. Oberlin's supporters were concerned about the implications of such self-righteous vigilantism. Soon after, an even more serious scandal occurred: H. C. Taylor, editor of the *Oberlin Evangelist* and an avid promoter of political and ecclesiastical abolitionism, confessed to embezzling funds from the *Evangelist* office; he also admitted that he had seduced a young woman and taken "the requisite measures to secure [an] abortion." Oberlin's friends in New York state were aghast. Sherlock Bristol, from Rochester, was "distressed" and "disheartened" on behalf of all "who love the cause of holiness." "It cannot be," Bristol wrote. "The Editor of the *Evangelist!* The preacher of the doctrine of *Entire Sanctification,* & of the way in which it is to be attained, living among the precious revivals of Oberlin." If such immorality and hypocrisy could occur at the very wellspring of evangelical perfectionist beliefs, abolitionists questioned, was the doctrine of entire sanctification still tenable? Instead of representing a model community of the imminent perfect state of society ("what I had never hoped to see but in Heaven," wrote one admirer), perhaps Oberlin more accurately represented the moral frailty of all communities, even those with the holiest of objectives.[19]

The antislavery churches, particularly the independent Congregational and Union churches, shared in the disrepute.[20] The Unionists' noncreedal standard for membership opened them up to charges of "looseness," "Universalism," "fanaticism," and "disorganization." Moreover, because Unionists regularly inveighed against the established denominations, they were often mistakenly identified as Garrisonian-type anarchists, intent on "assaulting the Christian Church" in any organized capacity.[21]

Liberty advocates in the burned-over district were closely aligned with evangelical perfectionists and with church reformers, and they experienced similarly debilitating embarrassments. For the first few years of its existence the Liberty Party's vote was negligible, so the other parties' reactions to it were limited to ridicule or to mild criticism. As the abolitionist tally increased during the 1840s, however, the Liberty Party held the balance of power in several key elections. The Whigs responded to the increase in abolitionist influence with the kind of rough-and-tumble tactics typical of antebellum politics.[22] Most Liberty supporters had little experience with (and even less predilection for) such tactics, however; unlike the arm-twisting machinations, "log cabin" gimmicks, and free liquor distribution characteristic of the major parties, Liberty campaigners did not participate in the standard type of political maneuvering. They had no need to mimic the devices of the Whigs and the Democrats because they developed what they believed to be an effective campaign strategy operating through the agency of the abolition churches. Lest they be accused of unsanctified self-aggrandizement, Liberty nominees for public office did not even campaign directly; rather, they relied on the stump preaching of other Liberty stalwarts to promote their candidacies.[23] Given their disregard for political intrigue, Liberty activists were not prepared for the earthy character of partisan politicking.

The strategic naivete of the Liberty leaders became painfully evident during the presidential race of 1844. During the same campaign season in which James G. Birney was running for president (for the second time) on the Liberty ticket, he allowed his name to be placed in nomination for a Michigan legislative seat on the local Democratic slate. Birney did not see any impropriety in this action. He insisted that if he were elected to the state legislature, he would pursue his abolitionist principles whether or not the Democrats—or anyone else— sponsored him. In effect, Birney accepted nomination to the legislative race but disavowed his connection to the Democratic party that nominated him. The Whigs immediately seized upon Birney's conduct in the matter as evidence of his duplicity and of his "unprincipled" political ambitions.[24] Even so, the aftereffect of the incident might have ended there; although Birney's political shrewdness was open to question, most abolitionists did not doubt his integrity. Another blow soon hit the Liberty Party, however. Just prior to the election, a group of enterprising Whigs circulated a forged letter in which Birney allegedly gave his unqualified support to the Democrats. The letter, later known as the Garland forgery, was cleverly published in several Whig newspapers simultaneously—too late for Birney or for the Liberty Party to print denials.[25] It is uncertain whether the publication of the Garland forgery had any appreciable negative effect on the abolitionist vote in 1844,[26] but the events of the fall campaign did call attention to a quandary faced by the inexperienced Liberty Party: how could they remain pure and succeed politically without becoming immersed in the muddy waters of partisan campaigning?

Liberty promoters with a practical bent were convinced that Birney had become a political liability and should be replaced by a more popular, seasoned candidate. These pragmatists also felt that in order to assure eventual victory at the polls, it would be politically sensible for the Liberty Party to soften its strident moralism, at least temporarily. Conversely, the purists in the party refused to support candidates of questionable moral qualifications or issues of popular interest merely for the sake of expediency.[27] Gerrit Smith, for example, was alarmed by the "immodest self-advancement" demonstrated by the pragmatic Liberty men; he asserted that the "true" Liberty leaders were those who "profess to be conformed to what is right—to what God says is right. With them, expediency is not the rule of right—but right the rule of expediency." Smith and his evangelical perfectionist colleagues were not willing to risk the use of unsanctified means even if those means might result in the possible fulfillment of sanctified ends.[28]

The Internal Challenge: Perfectionist Tensions at the Breaking Point

The external factors of economic transition and of oppositional criticism merely brought to the fore certain tensions within ecclesiastical abolitionism. The central emphasis on an absolute, uncompromising sanctification created an internal challenge for the movement, for the conceptual ideology undergirding ecclesiastical abolitionism—evangelical perfectionism—was intrinsically unstable. This instability was manifested in two ways: first, the revivalistic fervor of evangelical perfectionism and its ever-increasing demands for intense moral rigor were tiring to maintain; and second, the middle course of perfectionist politics was hard to hold without drifting off onto the shoals of institutionalism on the one side or anarchism on the other. That is, those who desired to reform society according to the mediating position of an ordered liberty found that it was a formidable task to support human organization and personal freedom simultaneously—both of which were implicit in the concept of God's government. Given the polemics of the abolitionist debate, the presumed need for social order and the desire for greater democratization became difficult to hold together. This difficulty existed within the broader American culture as well, for evangelical perfectionist tensions mirrored the democratic tensions of the whole society. In the end, the task proved too arduous and the "junction of religion and political power" that was ecclesiastical abolitionism broke apart.[29]

The evangelical perfectionist ethos of ecclesiastical abolitionism meant that antislavery institutions, civil and religious, were placed in a precarious situation. For political comeouters, it was nearly impossible to contend in the partisan arena and to build a successful party organization while maintaining their original revivalistic zeal and unconditional goals; for ecclesiastical comeouters, it became difficult to balance the democratic liberties of each individual believer with the need to establish enduring church structures. Such differences of opinion resulted in the dispersal of ecclesiastical abolitionist efforts, both within the Liberty Party and among the abolition churches.

"Dividing Ourselves Against Ourselves": The Unraveling of the Liberty Party

Despite the damaging "tornado" of the 1844 campaign, most Liberty voters were determined to pick up the political pieces and to try again.[30] After 1846, however, electoral support for Liberty candidates began to deteriorate even further, causing Liberty supporters to question the claim that, given the righteousness of their cause and its foreshadowing of the millennial state of society, Liberty Party growth was divinely ordained. The varying solutions that were suggested to deal with the problem of declension exacerbated the factionalism already present within the party. Although in 1845 there was a "difference of opinion among Liberty men," only two years later the differences had magnified to such a degree that Liberty activists were "dividing ourselves against ourselves."[31]

The perfectionist dilemma within the party was clear: in order to reach their goal of establishing a holy government, it was necessary for Liberty advocates to compromise their own holiness. Ecclesiastical abolitionists stressed pure motives and each individual's inflexible attitude toward personal sin, but they also emphasized practical moral action and the tangible achievement of societal perfection. Eventually the stress on sanctified tactics seemed to preclude the achievement of the party's aims, because political success required concessions to those of dubious religious credentials and of impure political motives. An unpleasant choice faced the perfectionist Liberty leaders: either they could work toward the practical achievement of a reduced goal using impure means, or they could continue to espouse uncompromising means with only the vague hope of an eventual divine consummation—especially with the persistent disappointment of the party at the polls. How does one persevere in the arduous work of establishing a millennial society, they asked themselves, when the promised inevitable outcome does not seem to materialize?

The institutional trappings of authority that were required to develop an effective party structure conflicted with the anti-institutional repudiation of hierarchy implied by one's obligation of entire sanctification. Consequently, the relatively unified Liberty Party of 1844 split into two unequal parts by 1848. The two factions—the coalitionists and the universal reformers—represented the varied views held by abolitionists regarding the degree of institutionalization appropriate for the party. Thus, even within the Liberty Party—which represented only a narrow band on the "institutionalization continuum between the extremes of party and anti-party"[32]—there was a great degree of diversity, a continuum within the continuum.

The coalitionist faction, which received the support of the majority of Liberty voters, intended to institutionalize political abolitionism by widening the movement's appeal. This group believed that political abolitionists should lessen their perfectionist demands; they were willing to disband the Liberty Party in order to form a broad partisan coalition with other Northerners. They hoped that by joining others in a more popular cause, the political abolitionist party structure would become permanent and the goal of emancipation would eventually be achieved. In fact, in 1848, the coalitionist faction of the Liberty Party merged with moderate antislavery Whigs and Democrats into the Free Soil Party.[33] The Free Soilers qualified their stance on the slavery issue by opposing only its expansion into the territories, and they based their opposition on the threat that the Southern slave economy posed to white free labor in the North; they desired "to limit, localize, and discourage slavery" but not to abolish it immediately.[34] Notably, none of the prominent leaders of the coalitionist faction came from the original Liberty Party stronghold of upper New York:

Joshua Leavitt and William Jay were from New York City; Leicester King, Gamaliel Bailey, Samuel Lewis, Stanley Mathews, and Salmon P. Chase were from Ohio; Nathaniel Colver and Elizur Wright were from Massachusetts; and Austin Willey was from Maine.[35]

Some ecclesiastical abolitionists—particularly those influenced by Oberlin—reluctantly aligned themselves with the coalitionist faction. They favored the Free Soil platform on the grounds that it was the most practical way to achieve at least a portion of the millennial goal. The Oberlinites had long been somewhat more institutional on the topics of church reform and of partisan organization than were many other evangelical perfectionists; "[t]he aim at Oberlin in the matter of political action has always been practical"—that is, an abolitionist party should be supported only so far as it is actually effective in electing candidates. Because office seekers from the Liberty Party had achieved very few results, in 1848 the Oberlinites "all voted for Van Buren," the Free Soil presidential candidate.[36] The Free Baptists in New York state (who were also affected to a great degree by Oberlin) agreed with the Oberlinites regarding the wisdom in supporting the pragmatism of the Free Soil Party.[37]

The Oberlinites and their allies gave nominal support to the Free Soil coalition, but they were concerned that too much political activity on the part of sanctified Christians deflected attention away from the essential tasks of revivalism and of reform. Franckean Lutheran and Free Baptist leaders, for example, urged their members to be cautious in their reformatory work; the politically active members of these groups were reminded by their colleagues never to let politics get in the way of spirituality. Finney warned ministers preaching on political topics not to forget "to make the conversion of sinners, and the sanctification of the church the great end at which they aim,—always insisting that right political action will follow . . . from a right state of heart." These abolitionists persisted in the single-minded task of evangelical conversion, believing strongly that right action would necessarily follow regeneration; they still voted for antislavery candidates but they ceased their active campaigning on behalf of political abolitionism.[38]

In direct contrast to the coalitionists was a smaller faction—the universal reformers—composed largely of ecclesiastical abolitionists from central and western New York who were influenced by William Goodell and by Gerrit Smith. The universal reformers endorsed a radicalized and decentralized version of the Liberty Party, remaining committed to the vision of a perfected politics and attempting to balance partisan promotion and moral principle. The universal reformers perceived the "nonextensionist" Free Soil platform as a reduction of their dearest principles; they refused to support the coalitionists because the Free Soil Party highlighted economic issues affecting Northern white men at the expense of human rights issues affecting African Americans and others. These ecclesiastical abolitionists were distressed by the prospect of a diluted antislavery coalition, recommending instead that the Liberty Party embrace a comprehensive agenda of reform measures that included but went beyond the abolition of slavery. They were more interested in expanding evangelical perfectionist ideals than in advancing a particular political organization. The sanctified stress on personal freedom of conscience in response to the perceived demands of God's government took precedence over the pragmatic demands for structuring human government.[39]

The idealized perfectionism of the universal reformers led them to reject the impurity that seemed implicit in the Free Soilers' agenda. Specifically, they repudiated the coalitionists' free labor ideology because it depended on appeals to self-serving economic interests, not to ethical values.[40] Universal reformers, using typical evangelical perfectionist phraseology, demanded "the highest standard of political abolitionism"; Goodell chastised the coalitionists because they supported "new combinations for political effort that shall be less rigid and exclusive." Such latitudinarianism indicated to Goodell that the coalitionists were "abandoning God's method because it does not succeed in their cause," an elevation of pragmatism over idealism.[41]

For the universal reformers, a serious indictment of the coalitionists was their unwillingness to affirm the importance of democratic church reform, since they voted for candidates who belonged to centralized (and therefore "proslavery") denominations.[42] Coalitionists such as Joshua Leavitt and Nathaniel Colver were criticized for wishing to cooperate with the existing established denominations in order to reform them. The coalitionists opposed the retention of controversial measures such as church reform on the political abolitionist platform—measures that might "encumber [the] anti-Slavery enterprise with a crusade against clerical usurpations"; even though church reform was one of the original staples of the Liberty Party, the coalitionists were determined to remove this contentious item from the political abolitionist plate.[43] Goodell, Smith, and their radical associates abhorred the coalitionists' backpedalling on church reform. The universal reformers declared that "secession and re-organization of churches" were "part and parcel of Liberty party ethics." Political abolitionists could not "expect to maintain their political fidelity for any long time, without becoming ecclesiastical abolitionists."[44]

The post-1848 "universal reform" Liberty Party was almost exclusively composed of perfectionistic ecclesiastical abolitionists. An analysis of the identities of the committee members and of the elected officers at the 1848 Liberty Party convention (that is, those few persons who continued to exercise leadership within the Liberty Party after the majority of their colleagues had left to form the Free Soil Party) demonstrates that nearly all of them were active in democratic church reform and were subscribers to Goodell's *Christian Investigator.*[45]

The ecclesiastical abolitionists who opted for universal reform advocated a complete legislative overhaul of society. Like the coalitionists, the universal reform faction wanted to take the Liberty Party agenda beyond the "one-idea" of antislavery; unlike the coalitionists, however, the universal reformers' alteration of the party was designed not to "lower down, but elevate our standard of antislavery political action." The coalitionists sought to change the party's agenda in order to make political antislavery more palatable to a cross section of white Northerners; the universal reform Liberty activists sought to broaden the party's agenda because their belief in entire sanctification led them to strive for the abolition of all types of social evil.[46]

Universal reformers wanted to enlarge the scope of political abolitionism by addressing the multiple oppressions that permeated antebellum society. At the same time that many coalitionists supported the free labor platform with implicitly racist arguments,[47] the universal reformers fought strenuously against inherent racism. The coalitionists did not represent "the heart of the true Liberty Party," according to the universal reformers, "and much less the heart of the true God; but do, on the contrary, betray their insensibility to the highest and holiest claims."[48]

Part of the reason for the formation of the Liberty League in 1847 was an attempt by the universal reform Liberty leaders to preempt the proposed nonextensionist coalition.[49] When the coalitionists were absorbed into the Free Soil Party in 1848, the Leaguers reconstituted (and in their minds purified) the remainder of the Liberty Party. To make clear their intentions, both the Liberty League and its successor, the newly "sanctified" but now much smaller remnant of the Liberty Party, nominated the ultraperfectionist Gerrit Smith as their presidential candidate.[50]

Gerrit Smith (1797–1874). *Courtesy of the Library of Congress.*

The resurrected Liberty Party represented a continuing minority of political abolitionists who still hoped for the establishment of a sanctified society. Increasingly, their hope was based more on the righteousness of their cause than on the real possibility of political victory: "We have learned to estimate the value of political parties less by their numbers, than by the purity of their intentions." According to Smith, "[T]he organization of the Liberty Party was a novel and bold experiment" because of its consistent adherence to "the right and the true." Others might view their principles as "impracticable and fanatical," but such opinions did not matter, for their "experiment was well worth making, even if it had been made in the face of all probability of success . . . for the sake of [God's] enslaved poor."[51]

The factionalism of the Liberty Party in the late 1840s resulted in the dismemberment of political abolitionism. Those who went into the Free Soil Party discovered that the promotion of a less-moralistic platform did in fact result in greater political success; in contrast, smaller and smaller numbers of the Northern electorate supported the increasingly radical proposals of the rump Liberty Party. In 1851, one of the remaining Liberty supporters lamented that most of his formerly high-minded colleagues had "gone home to their farms and their merchandise"—and even, he added with chagrin, to "their politics," by which he meant their unprincipled Free Soil politics.[52] From a high of 74,017 Liberty votes in 1846, only 2646 votes were cast nationwide for the party in 1848, and all but 101 of those were from New York state. Although the New York Liberty tally rose slightly to 3483 votes in the 1850 gubernatorial race, the party was unable to rally any significant electorate outside of a few isolated localities. Seventeen percent (600 votes) of the statewide Liberty total in 1850, for instance, came from one sparsely settled county (Madison), and this relatively good-sized number simply reflected the continued influence of Gerrit Smith in his home region. The party's decline can be seen graphically by comparing the 1844 and 1850 poll results for several formerly strong Liberty vote–granting counties in upper New York (see table 6).[53]

Although the vestigial remainder of the Liberty Party ceased to look for electoral success, it still expected to see the eventual triumph of the government of God. "The present time," declared Samuel Ringgold Ward in 1849, is "a period of transition, revolution, and preparation for the millennium." The attendees at the 1848 Liberty convention were not oblivious to the extent of the party's demise, but they were hopeful nonetheless—for their ultimate victory was assured.

That this Party will be popular, we do not claim. That corrupt men—men, who are more for numbers than principles—for ballot-box victories than for truth—will approve of it, we do not expect . . . That God will be on its side is our firm belief:—and, humbly and fervently, do we pray, that He will condescend to make it a means of hastening the time, when oppression and war shall be unknown, . . . when "the earth shall be filled with the knowledge of the glory of the Lord, as the waters cover the sea."[54]

TABLE 6 **Comparative Liberty Party Returns for Selected Counties: 1844 and 1850**

County	1844	1850
Allegany	435	19
Chenango	243	57
Madison	1341	600
Oneida	1144	98
St. Lawrence	468	56
Saratoga	119	27
Seneca	124	43
Wayne	563	203
Wyoming	442	29

"Seasons of Declension": The Unraveling of Antislavery Church Reform

The perfectionist dilemma also manifested itself within the abolition churches, as illustrated by events that took place at the Seneca Falls Wesleyan Methodist church. The famous Wesleyan chapel in Seneca Falls did not live up to its radical reputation during the decades that followed its moment of glory in 1848; like many comeouter congregations, the church ceased to provide political leadership or to press for structurally challenging social reforms after the 1850s.

Various subgroups developed within the Seneca Falls congregation. Some reformers lapsed from their church involvement and replaced their religious activities with capitalistic enterprising. Others continued active in the church but became preoccupied with "connexional" (denominational) issues and with organizational maintenance—an ironic development, given their earlier commitment to anti-institutional church reform. A third group, led by the pastor, interpreted the renewed interest in institution-building as the reintroduction of moral laxity and of denominational hierarchy; in the mid-1860s, these dissenters voted to sever their ties with the Wesleyan Methodist Connection, building themselves a separate meetinghouse and, fittingly, organizing as an independent Congregational church. The small remainder of the Wesleyan Methodist church that still met in the historic chapel eventually faded into nonexistence.[55]

After 1855, the unified movement for antislavery comeouterism among the churches of the burned-over district disintegrated. Church reform efforts diminished and comeouter congregations closed or retrenched. The situation at the Anti-Slavery Baptist church of Cato was typical, as too much agitation on social reform issues caused "seasons of declension." Many abolition churches, perhaps a majority, folded after their initial burst of enthusiasm; Free Baptist membership declined after the mid-1840s, and the Franckeans reported in 1846 that they were "in the midst of a general spiritual dearth of the land." In a typical description, the antislavery congregation in Yates "had a brief existence and never acquired much stability or prominence." The situation in South Butler was similar, and soon after Antoinette Brown's famous pastorate there in the early 1850s, "the society languished and finally ceased to exist." Even in Madison County—the epicenter of church reform agitation—every single Union church dwindled and then died. The chronicler of Madison County's churches fittingly called these congregations "ecclesiastical sepulchres."[56]

There were several reasons for the decline. As with the Liberty Party, some factors were external. The population shift to the cities and to the west greatly affected the abolition churches. Ecclesiastical abolitionism was centered in rural areas, so antislavery congregations, along with the rest of the churches in the region, lost many people during this time—including some of their most prominent leaders.[57]

The difficulties among antislavery church reformers, however, cannot be attributed merely to economic and demographic changes. Like the struggles within the Liberty Party, part of the problem lay in the evangelical perfectionism that undergirded ecclesiastical abolitionism. It was very hard for persons to maintain the intense religious fervor and unrelenting moral rigor that perfectionism required. According to perfectionist reasoning, an individual reformer could make "progress in holy activity" only by "wrestling, struggling, running, fighting, agonizing to reach the object he has in view." The sanctified come-outers in Warsaw insisted on ever expanding goals "to keep up that degree of feeling which [already] very powerful means . . . had excited, and which must be sustained, or the cause of Christ cannot be expected to prosper." In this never ending spiral of sanctification, each abolitionist "long[ed] more and more after higher and still higher attainments in holiness." Goodell contended that one social reform was "only the Christian laborer's stepping stone to another, and yet another, and never will he be content to cease his reformatory labor while life lasts." Few persons could maintain such religious intensity for very long.[58]

Ecclesiastical abolitionists experienced spiritual exhaustion, a burning out of their energies. Oneida Institute was described as "worn out by its parox-ysms." At Oberlin, the promotion of perfectionist doctrine and radical reforms diminished over time. The editor of the *Oberlin Evangelist* determined that a "chill of spiritual declension" had occurred because Christians were too in-volved in political wrangling; no one, he concluded, can "be strongly excited on two subjects at the same moment." Even William Goodell suspended publi-cation of the *Christian Investigator* in 1848, explaining that the termination of the paper was due to his inability to continue his many responsibilities. Good-ell observed that he "had more 'irons in the fire'—political and ecclesiastical, than falls to the share of most ministers." Such weariness was the fate of many abolitionist comeouters.[59]

The decline among antislavery churches was also due to continuing ten-sions over the appropriate scope of religious democratization. Ecclesiastical abolitionists were unable, for example, to hold together the mutually exclusive concepts of structure and antistructure. They believed that a union of all sanc-tified Christians would occur naturally when "artificial" impediments were removed (such as slavery and denominational hierarchy), because those imped-iments obstructed the relationship that ought to exist between an individual and God. In the actual implementation of this union, however, as was evident at the Syracuse convention of 1843, church reformers could not agree on the kind or amount of structure that would be necessary to maintain a stable and effi-cient organization.[60]

The "liberty versus order" debate engendered other questions for church reformers. Should individuals and local churches have complete freedom of doctrinal expression or should ecclesiastical abolitionists assert certain funda-mental beliefs of Christian orthodoxy? If so, which beliefs? Should church re-formers accept all persons into their congregations as part of their commitment to open-ended church membership or should they insist on ethical purity as the necessary mark of good standing in a sanctified congregation? If so, what degree of ethical purity was to be required of each abolitionist? Among some evangelical perfectionists, there developed a sort of infinite regression of culpa-bility regarding one's acquiescence in the sin of slavery; according to Gerrit Smith, abolition church members were obliged "to hold it infamous to be a slaveholder, or to vote for a slaveholder, or to vote for him who will vote for a slaveholder." These proliferating demands were not accepted uniformly by all ecclesiastical abolitionists, and the differences of opinion regarding perfection-

ist standards created serious "internal divisions" within antislavery congregations; eventually such divisions caused many congregations to dissolve.[61]

Even abolition churches that managed to survive these internal conflicts
were greatly affected by them. Congregations struggled to balance their desires
for freedom from religious restraint and for some organizational structure; consequently, ecclesiastical abolitionists tended to fall off the middle course that
distinguished evangelical perfectionism. On the one side, the anti-institutional
side, they fell off into secularism or heterodox religious beliefs. On the other
side, the institutional side, they fell off into doctrinal rigidity or denominational bureaucratization.[62]

To be more specific, a substantial number of ecclesiastical abolitionists in
the 1850s and 1860s moved in an anti-institutional direction away from the
strictly defined norms characteristic of evangelical perfectionism and toward
the inner-directed personal pursuits characteristic of anarchistic perfectionism. This spiritual wandering was accentuated by the abolitionists' continuing
disgust at the intransigence of the establishment denominations regarding slavery. Some ecclesiastical abolitionists gradually drifted away from traditional
Christian belief toward unitarianism, universalism, spiritualism, freethinking
religious ideas, or various "religions of reason." Considered "unorthodox"
apostasy by the more traditional ecclesiastical abolitionists, this was the track
taken by Unionists Gerrit Smith, James G. Birney, James C. Jackson, and Beriah Green, as well as a few representatives from the other comeouter groups,
such as Franckean John Lawyer and Free Baptist Martin Steere.[63] A longstanding emphasis on the free investigation of ideas gave these ecclesiastical abolitionists permission to experiment with prevailing social, political, and even
theological standards; Antoinette Brown, for instance, called herself a believer
in "limited orthodoxy." Creedal formulae (such as the doctrine of the Trinity)
and external authorities (such as the Bible) became suspect. Ecclesiastical abolitionists who leaned toward religious anti-institutionalism were stretching—
and breaking—the commonly accepted theological boundaries of antebellum
evangelicalism.[64]

A number of abolitionist comeouters gave up on the Christian church altogether. Some of these lapsed church members wanted to spend more time pur-
suing economic gain or political advancement; others were disillusioned by
religious hypocrisy. Charles O. Shepard had to endure a long and arduous
church trial because he participated in activities that he sincerely believed were

the fulfillment of his obligation to live a sanctified life; consequently, after years of frustration, he withdrew his membership from the church. Likewise, after engaging in the difficult task of establishing an independent congregation, the tired and disenchanted members of the Free Church of Sherburne "sold their [meeting]house, and generally remain[ed] isolated from all church relations."[65]

By no means, however, did all antislavery comeouters abandon their evangelical commitments; many ecclesiastical abolitionists and their progeny remained active in organized forms of evangelical Christianity. The tendency of these persons was to move off of the middle course onto the side of greater institutionalization. In theological matters, the institutionally prone ecclesiastical abolitionists were the exact opposite of the anti-institutional freethinkers described above, who rejected the prescriptions of Protestant orthodoxy. Rather, those who were oriented toward theological institutionalization encouraged more precise definitions of what constituted "essential" religious doctrines. Just as evangelical church reformers in the 1840s insisted that sanctified Christians affirm certain "fundamental" beliefs,[66] so too some of their postbellum successors emphasized the need for all believers to adhere to a set of doctrinal standards that were believed to represent the essence of the apostolic faith—a road that eventually led to fundamentalism. In fact, one of the paradoxes of ecclesiastical abolitionism is that some of the descendants of "liberal" mid-nineteenth-century church reformers became thoroughgoing fundamentalists by century's end.[67]

In ecclesiological matters, institutionally oriented church reformers moved toward greater denominational consolidation. After the Civil War, when the issue of slavery was ostensibly settled by the passage of the Thirteenth, Fourteenth and Fifteenth Amendments, abolition churches were left without their primary raison d'etre. Church comeouters had difficulty justifying their continued separation from their old denominations, and many returned to them: Unionists reunited with their former Presbygational churches, and independent Congregational churches and their pastors rejoined their old associations or presbyteries. Five members of one defunct abolitionist congregation "returned, after the lapse of fourteen or fifteen years, to the bosom of the church, which they had repudiated." Elon Galusha went back into the Baptist church.[68] A large number of Wesleyan Methodists returned to the Methodist Episcopal Church in 1866[69]—the same year that the entire Franckean Synod reestablished its ties with the General Synod of the Lutheran church.[70]

Ironically, even the diminishing number of ecclesiastical comeouters who remained steadfastly independent of their former denominations during the post–Civil War period began to consolidate their own institutional structures. Free Baptists became increasingly denominationally conscious. Adventists developed a distinctive organizational authority—after it became clear that the millennium was not quite as imminent as they had supposed. The surviving records of many postbellum abolition churches indicate a stepping back from controversial political action; instead, the churches stressed issues of institutional maintenance and personal holiness, such as the prohibition of tobacco, alcohol, dancing, card playing, theater going, and circus attendance.[71] Some of the remaining ecclesiastical abolitionists interpreted these consolidations as reintroducing "sectarianism" (i.e., denominational hierarchy) and withdrawing from earlier commitments to universal reform. Consequently, there was further splintering among the few remaining antislavery church reformers, as happened when a portion of the Wesleyan Methodist church in Seneca Falls seceded in order to set up its own independent Congregational church.

The specific incident that created trouble in the Seneca Falls church occurred in 1866. That year, representatives from the Wesleyan Methodists, the Methodist Protestants, and several unaffiliated, antihierarchical congregations met together in Cincinnati in an attempt to find common ground for a united church body. Though less ambitious than the church reform conventions of the 1840s in terms of denominational breadth, the ecumenical intent of the Cincinnati gathering was similar to the earlier efforts of Goodell, Lee, and others to establish a sanctified union church. Lee, in fact, was a prominent organizer of this latter-day church reform assembly.[72]

The Rev. W. W. Lyle, pastor of the Seneca Falls Wesleyan Methodist church, was hopeful that ecclesiastical abolitionists would finally be able to establish a perfected church organization. Lyle presented a letter to the Cincinnati convention in which he offered a radical political agenda for the projected union church, exhorting the conference members to embrace legislative efforts in favor of the recently proposed plan of national reconstruction. A sanctified union church, Lyle believed, must take definitive political stands so that the "equal rights and duties of all men" could be thoroughly safeguarded. The conference members, however, rejected Lyle's entreaty. "We may better express our . . . subjection to the 'powers that be,'" the conferees resolved, "by avoiding any expression that could be claimed by political parties." Certainly a great distance had been travelled from the political action of two decades before. "All mere social and political questions," the conference stated, along "with all other non-essentials in faith and practice, shall be left with the individual conscience." Lyle was aghast. He knew that "to deny the colored man the protection and the rights . . . of the laws . . . is virtually to throw him back into the house of bondage." To Lyle, the Wesleyan Methodist Connection had turned an about-face. No wonder he led a group of his congregants out of the denomination and formed an independent church; secession was a strategy that ecclesiastical abolitionists such as Lyle knew well.[73]

Despite Lyle's misgivings, a large number of Wesleyan Methodists and their fellow colleagues did follow through on their earlier commitments. This was especially true in the nascent Holiness movement, a loose grouping of preachers, churches, camp meeting associations, and publications that encouraged the religious experience of entire sanctification.[74] Many evangelical perfectionists continued to be interested in social justice concerns during the post–Civil War period; Wesleyan Methodist founders Lucius Matlack and La Roy Sunderland, for example, were leaders in desegregating churches and public schools in the 1870s.[75] Victor Howard has described how Wesleyan Methodists, Free Baptists, and the newly formed Free Methodists stood in the forefront of postbellum efforts to secure a fully integrated society. Persons from these three antislavery church groups were involved in the political campaigns for prohibition and female suffrage, and in the efforts to secure political and economic equality for African Americans; the judicatories of all of these groups precisely instructed their members how to vote on such issues.[76]

In general, though, the postbellum heirs of ecclesiastical abolitionism did not maintain the magnitude or the dynamism of their earlier social and political activity. In search of a reason to exist, they became preoccupied with individualistic moralism and the pursuit of a highly routinized type of affective religious experience. For example, the language of discourse used by the later nineteenth-century Wesleyan Methodists regarding reform issues was often couched in images that were philanthropic and therapeutic, concerned with the effects rather than with the causes of social problems. Wesleyan Methodist leader Adam Crooks[77] articulated this perceptual change in social reform strategy: "in former times"—that is, before emancipation—God had used the Wesleyan Methodists as "His vanguard in His great battle for the temporal deliverance of his oppressed poor," but because their objective was seemingly

accomplished with the demise of slavery, Crooks believed that God had "in reserve for [the postbellum Wesleyan Methodists] a future of still higher and
more glorious significance." Crooks now wanted the Wesleyan Methodists to
emphasize the experience of entire consecration accompanied by a "Baptism
of power."[78] Among antebellum Wesleyan Methodists, the experience of Christian perfection had been a means to achieve the goal of social reform. For their
postbellum successors, the achievement of the experience itself became the
goal.[79]

Although a considerable amount of social involvement remained from the
optimistic reform activism that characterized their antebellum forebears, the
general trend among the postbellum descendants of ecclesiastical abolitionism
was toward subjectivism and moralism. The Wesleyan Methodists, the Free
Baptists, the few remaining independent Congregational churches, and the
other surviving comeouters in the post–Civil War era were greatly diminished
in size and in influence. The evangelical perfectionist organizations of ecclesiastical abolitionism—both the antislavery churches that continued to be active
and the remnant of the Liberty Party—were only shadows of their former
selves. By 1860, most of the revivalistic fires of sanctified reform had burned
over—and out.

Epilogue  *An Enduring Legacy*

ECCLESIASTICAL ABOLITIONISM operated as a unified enterprise for a short while in the 1840s, and then divided into various factions. Despite the fragmentation of ecclesiastical abolitionism, however, the enduring significance of its constituent components—both the universal reform wing of the Liberty Party and the interconnected network of antislavery churches—lasted far beyond the movement's relatively brief halcyon days. The scattering of ecclesiastical abolitionism helped to seed a number of causes that flowered during the Civil War and postbellum periods.

In regard to political action, the ecclesiastical abolitionists who remained in the Liberty Party after 1848 continued to participate in the contested interchange of ideas that accompanied the partisan realignment of mid-nineteenth-century America. "The old parties are crumbling, and new combinations are forming," declared William Goodell in 1855, just after the organization of the Republican Party; "Radicalism must seize the helm." Liberty activists viewed themselves as a necessary alternative to the political compromising of the day, whether Democratic, Free Soil, or Republican. Though the Liberty organization was a mere skeleton of its earlier size, the perfectionist rump of the party managed to nominate candidates throughout the 1850s. Indeed, Liberty advocates named prominent church reformers as their favorite sons to run for president: Goodell in 1852 and Gerrit Smith in 1856 and in 1860. In order for there to be no mistake about its principled intentions, the Liberty Party remnant renamed itself the Radical Abolitionist Party prior to the 1856 election; these few sanctified stalwarts continued to endorse persons for office as late as 1860. Even after the Civil War, many of them were so convinced of the value of independent, religiously oriented political action that they affiliated with the new Prohibition Party.[1]

During the 1850s, the state organization in New York was the only branch of the Liberty Party with enough political strength to maintain any semblance of a partisan structure. Liberty supporters continued to field candidates in New York for a number of local and statewide contests. It is not surprising, then, that the central part of New York was the scene of the evangelical perfectionists' most significant ballot box victory: in 1852, Gerrit Smith was elected to the House of Representatives from the twenty-second Congressional district.[2]

The influence of Liberty men and women is not to be found, however, in the party's relatively negligible electoral support; rather, it is to be found in the ethical values that, because of their (often annoying) presence, remained a part of the political discourse of the period. Smith, for example, proudly introduced his radical "political creed" to Congress; among other items, Smith's agenda included the unconstitutionality of slavery and the extension of the right of suffrage to "all persons, the black as well as the white, the female as well as the male."[3]

As the decade of the 1850s wore on, the pronouncements and the behavior of the Liberty remnant became ever more demanding. To an even greater degree than before, they promoted an overtly perfectionist agenda. Liberty members established nondiscriminatory abolitionist colleges and "free" missionary societies and continued to support the formation of new abolition churches. They defied the Fugitive Slave Law by assisting escaped slaves and by coordinating the underground railroad. In increasing numbers, women and African Americans served on important committees of the party. Blacks in particular were urged to run for public office: Frederick Douglass and James McCune Smith, for example, were both nominated (in 1855 and 1857 respectively) to run for the position of secretary of state in New York. Samuel Ringgold Ward was nominated for the state assembly, the first African American to campaign actively for a legislative seat; Ward's campaign platform included such novel proposals as property ownership restrictions (no more than two hundred acres), a governmental welfare system, and a tax on liquor dealers for "the maintenance of paupers and the prosecution of criminals."[4]

During this period, the Liberty Party/Radical Abolitionists did not expect to win many elections. They simply hoped to keep their principles alive, and in this they succeeded: While politicians in the Free Soil and Republican parties diluted their earlier antislavery commitments almost beyond recognition, Liberty men and women held forth an uncompromised dream of universal reform and racial equality. This dream was not completely illusory; by stirring up the conscience of the North, political antislavery kept the subject of equal rights before the public.[5] The achievement of the Liberty Party, according to historian Charles Sellers, was that it compelled "a racist white North to confront the great American contradiction" of the existence of chattel slavery in a democratic republic. The fact that African Americans ran for statewide office, for instance, forced whites to become cognizant of racial disparities in the American political system and provided blacks with a visualized goal of true political equality.[6]

Like the Liberty Party, the abolition churches made a lasting contribution that went beyond the immediate difficulties of the late 1840s and 1850s; the multifaceted character of these congregations helped to spawn several post–Civil War religious developments. In the first place, a direct connection can be made between antislavery comeouters (especially the Wesleyan Methodists) and the evolution of the Holiness movement. Like their antebellum abolitionist forebears, for example, postbellum Holiness advocates valued decentralized structures and rejected denominational hierarchy. Later in the nineteenth century, the church reformers' interest in maintaining a noncreedal, localistic form of evangelical ecclesiology found expression in religious organizations such as the Church of God and a number of similar antidenominational Holiness and early Pentecostal groups.[7]

Moreover, the ecclesiastical abolitionists' distinctively ethical articulation of the doctrine of entire sanctification made its mark on the Holiness movement. In the 1840s, the religious vitality of entire sanctification in the lives of ordinary Christians included a stress on affective experience and on volitional ethical action. This dual emphasis of ecclesiastical abolitionism bequeathed to the Holiness folk both a fervor for piety and a passion for advocating broad social concerns. Although it is true that later Holiness preachers placed much of their stress on the specifics of receiving a "second blessing" crisis experience and on the details of practicing a strict personal moral code, many of them continued their involvement in public policy issues as well. The influence of the Salvation Army and of certain other Holiness advocates such as B. T. Roberts constituted a strong force for progressive change among Gilded Age evangelicals and provided a heritage of social transformation that still inspires present-day descendants of the Holiness movement.[8]

Ecclesiastical abolitionism was also a forerunner of another movement, the Social Gospel. Specifically, the plan for a universal reform of society spearheaded by abolition churches prefigured the comprehensive program embraced by the early social gospellers. In this way, ecclesiastical abolitionists were among the first American Protestants to understand the problem of corporate sin and the need for systemic approaches to social issues.[9]

Ecclesiastical abolitionists did not originally hold a corporate view of social reality; rather, they arrived at this understanding gradually. In the 1830s, the ecclesiastical abolitionist conception of the projected millennial society was simply the aggregate composition of perfected persons, a typically individualistic evangelical approach to social change.[10] It became obvious, however, that the attainment of personal holiness could occur only if sanctified persons operated from the foundation of sanctified organizations—purified churches and political parties. In the early 1840s, this determination caused ecclesiastical abolitionists to be involved in the reorganization of local political and ecclesiastical structures; they became convinced that their society would be perfected when the institutions of each community (the town government and the village church) were reformed along with the individuals of that community. Although their emphasis was still on the sanctification of individuals, increased attention was given to the sanctification of the local institutions of which these individuals were a part. They believed that the total effect of many perfected communities would transform society and usher in the millennium.

By the late 1840s, the ecclesiastical abolitionist vision evolved further. Their participation in the political process and their experiences with the power of large, nationally based institutions exposed them to structural evil and to the need for a comprehensive reform that went beyond that of individuals and of local organizations. Their new vision combined the evangelical emphasis on transforming individuals with an emphasis on transforming oppressive structures.

Ecclesiastical abolitionists learned from their political struggle against slavery that they had not fully appreciated the systemic character of the evil they undertook to remove—the "other forms of oppression that cluster around it and support it." "Wrongs are so mutually sustaining, and so much parts of one whole," the 1848 Liberty convention declared, "as to require the war to be against all of them, in order to be successful against any of them." The Wesleyan Methodists joined their fellow ecclesiastical abolitionists in referring to the interrelatedness of oppressions as the "sisterhood of evil."[11] Understanding the unified character of sin led ecclesiastical abolitionists to understand the need for a unified solution to destroy it. Perfectionist Liberty advocates came to view their "one-idea" of antislavery as an "isolated, partial, specific opposition to particular forms and instances of oppression," which ought to be "displaced by the all-comprehensive, generalized idea of opposition to ALL oppression."[12] By the late 1840s, ecclesiastical abolitionists led the way in the transition from the individualized reform of the revivalistic period to the combination of individual reform and corporate reform characteristic of the early Social Gospel era.

Goodell, for example, called both for the sanctification of individuals and for the sanctification of structures in order to perfect the society. As an evangelical, he did not want to neglect the "old remedy of regenerating the man individually, before he can be regenerated socially," but he continued his appeal in more solidaristic terms:

Along with this old truth we must not take the old error that too commonly went with it, the error of forgetting that man individually, is a social being, with a moral nature socially defined, with social relations binding him in every direction, with social responsibilities intertwined with every fibre of his being, with social duties pressing every where upon him, as the condition of his individual existence and well being.

Goodell surmised that social structures such as the family, the church, and the state had to be "fully perfected," because institutions as well as individuals had "wandered from holiness."[13]

Goodell's interest in broad structural reform did not mean that he and other ecclesiastical abolitionists now approved of large institutional organizations. They were still committed to community-based governance and they hoped to avoid the slavery-tainted urbanity that seemed to be associated with the emerging national culture. Nonetheless, ecclesiastical abolitionists made a significant change when they moved from advocating an individually centered reform to a more structurally oriented reform. They were able to make this change by broadening their concept of community. Rather than just the total number of individuals in a locality, the idea of "community" came to refer to the structures of "church" and "state" in the society as a whole; it was as important for these larger "communities" to be reformed as it was for individuals and for local villages.[14]

Ecclesiastical abolitionism, then, needs to be seen as a formative antecedent of two parallel but ultimately divergent religious developments of the postbellum period, the Holiness movement and the Social Gospel movement. This may seem surprising; church historians have often assumed that these later religious expressions existed on opposite ends of the Protestant spectrum. In the 1840s and 1850s, however, some of the prophetic precursors of these two movements were the same sanctified people.

Finally, ecclesiastical abolitionism left an important legacy by providing us with a unique articulation of the democratic paradoxes of antebellum America. These reformers tried to hold together two seemingly contradictory ideals, an anti-institutional, individualistic desire for freedom from all hierarchies and a pragmatic, ordered appreciation for human organization. Although these ideals were clearly in tension with each other, they were both inherited from the democratic ideology of the early republic. Accordingly, antebellum society was faced with a quandary regarding the nature and scope of democracy. Most Americans dealt with that quandary by mitigating the tension between individual liberty and social order or by emphasizing one goal (either personal freedom or institutional structure) more than the other.[15] Ecclesiastical abolitionists, however, challenged the facile way in which Americans seemed to ignore the contradictions inherent in their basic democratic values. Their theology heightened the "liberty versus order" paradox. According to their articulation of the doctrine of entire sanctification, reformers had an immediate obligation to effect a "political millennium" in which the diverse precepts of divine and human government were kept together without compromise and without dilution. Thus, by attempting to embrace both freedom and social order in equal measure, ecclesiastical abolitionists exposed the immense difference that actually existed between the two ideals. A writer to the Franckean's *Lutheran Herald* expressed the tension clearly: "It is obviously a very difficult matter to maintain a purely republican form of government, whether of a civil or ecclesiastical character. However desirable, there seems to be a constant liability to dwindle into anarchy on the one hand, or tapering up [*sic*] to tyranny on the other." Somehow, ecclesiastical abolitionists believed, the extremes of anarchy and tyranny must be avoided. They perceived two equally troublesome pitfalls: "licentiousness and the shoreless ocean of non-governmentism" on the one side, and "domineering and unbounded encroachments upon the rights of the ruled" on the other. The writer concluded that a balance between the individualistic freedom of God's government and the intrinsic authority of human government must be achieved.[16]

Ecclesiastical abolitionists tried to steer clear of the pitfalls and to hold to the middle course of an ordered liberty, but the rigorous demands of their evangelical perfectionist theology left them with unqualified objectives that were nearly impossible to reach. By failing to sustain their principles for very long, they demonstrated how difficult it is for personal freedom and social order to function simultaneously within an increasingly diverse democratic society.

However, ecclesiastical abolitionism should not be viewed as an example of quixotic religious commitment to a futile cause. Despite their relatively short tenure, the abolition churches and the Liberty Party provided institutional models of interracial equality during a time of unrelenting systematic oppression of African Americans both in church and in state. Ecclesiastical abolitionism afforded an opportunity for thousands of rural Northerners, black and white, to take part in the public discourse of pre–Civil War society. An elaborate reform network developed in which democratized antislavery congregations were mobilized for political action. As a result, ecclesiastical abolitionists helped to expand the vision of what American democracy should look like and who should participate in it. They also raised up a hope for the eventual empowerment—both political and spiritual—of all Americans.

When, in 1835, Alexis de Tocqueville analyzed the character of American democracy, he described the close affinity existing between democratic principles and Christian values in the early republic. Tocqueville found that the ideals of religion and American freedom were "intimately linked together in joint reign over the same land." The people of the United States, he remarked, harbored a deeply felt desire "to harmonize earth with heaven." Tocqueville indicated that the American churches of that time were not interested in acquiring actual political power but rather affected the civic culture in an oblique way. Although Christian mores and American democracy were closely connected, the religious influence on U.S. politics was "indirect." The American clergy, he noted, "were careful to keep clear of all parties." Tocqueville believed that Christianity's pervasive impact on U.S. society was attributable to its common practice of wielding power "in one sphere only"—the religious sphere.[17]

Soon after Tocqueville made his observations, however, ecclesiastical abolitionists crossed over the thin line separating "indirect" moral influence from direct political action. They were no longer interested in keeping clear of partisan activity. Ecclesiastical abolitionists insisted that the ethical implications of the Christian gospel needed to be expressed explicitly within all spheres of human activity, including party politics. Because they believed that specific convictional beliefs affected character and that their regenerative religious experiences shaped every aspect of the lives they lived, they refused to compartmentalize civic involvement apart from faith.

Such intermingling has had a long history in the United States, continuing right up to the present. In particular, the religious/political alliance evident among ecclesiastical abolitionists begs comparison to several contemporary political initiatives. Beginning in the 1970s, religiously motivated political action groups became involved anew in legislative lobbying and in other exercises of power. Similar to the ecclesiastical abolitionists before them, the more recent groups affirmed the importance of a religious witness within political structures and attempted to influence American politics through the mobilization of various faith communities. These groups include well-known religious right organizations such as the Moral Majority and the Christian Coalition, as well as lesser-known "religious left" organizations such as the Interfaith Alliance, the Politics of Meaning forum, and several different progressive evangelical groups: the Sojourners community, the Call to Renewal caucus, and Evangelicals for Social Action.

Despite their common commitment to the appropriateness of religious activity in the public square, the recent groups range widely across the political spectrum—some are conservative, some liberal, and some do not fit any standard political designation. Given such an ideological spectrum, it is crucial to differentiate the platform of each of the particular organizations, for they vary significantly in which social policies they consider to be most imperative to address. For instance, while the Christian Coalition deals primarily with issues related to individual morality (abortion, school prayer, and welfare reform), progressive evangelicals are concerned with both personal and systemic issues—the deficiencies of social structures (racism, sexism, and the maldistribution of economic resources) as well as the deficiencies of character.

In light of this distinction between differing types of social concern, ecclesiastical abolitionism can be seen to resemble the political advocacy of progressive evangelicalism more than that of the religious right. This becomes clear when we view the activity of ecclesiastical abolitionism in the mid- to late 1840s. During that heady period of millennial fervor, the Liberty Party advanced an agenda that included both personal holiness and a structural critique of antebellum society.

Ecclesiastical abolitionists embraced a religious vision with radical social implications—implemented by political means. Thus they hoped to "harmonize earth with heaven" by participating in the democratic process. Although the effort to combine divine goals with temporal means was ultimately frustrating for ecclesiastical abolitionists, it was a strategy that was—and is—consistent with the religious and political culture of the American context.

Appendixes

Notes

Bibliography

Index

Appendix A. *Identifying Ecclesiastical Abolitionism in the Towns of Upper New York*

In order to demonstrate the strength of the ecclesiastical abolitionist network—the correspondence of Liberty Party support to antislavery church reform in the burned-over district—I have identified the abolition churches that existed in upper New York state during the two-year period from March 1843 through March 1845 and have compared that data to the Liberty vote totals for 1844. This particular time span was chosen because it was the height of the "perfectionist moment"—the peak period of antislavery church secessions and the highwater mark of Liberty Party electoral success (coinciding with the 1844 presidential election). During this period, 261 towns in upper New York state were demonstrably affected by antislavery church reform. Most of these towns had an established abolition church (or churches) by 1845. A few towns have been included in the compilation in which an abolition church was established after 1845, but only if there is specific evidence that a significant nucleus of antislavery church reformers already existed by 1845, even though a comeouter congregation was not yet formally organized.

The most important sources for identifying towns affected by antislavery church reform are local, county, and regional histories.[1] Local sources, however, are of spotty quality regarding comeouter abolition churches, partly because these churches were generally short-lived and partly because the comeouters challenged the dominant power structures of their communities. Sometimes an abolition church was able to be identified firmly only after it was determined that the pastor or a leading layperson of the congregation in question was known to be a prominent antislavery church reformer.[2]

Another source for the identification of abolition churches was an itemization of the number and the location of congregations from various antislavery church groups (e.g. Union, Free Will Baptist, Adventist ["Second Advent"], and Wesleyan Methodist) listed in the *Census of the State of New-York for 1855*. This work must be used very cautiously, however. In the first place, it is not reliable to use census data from 1855 to determine the identity of congregations existing a decade earlier. (Unfortunately, the state decennial *Census* for 1845 did not identify any congregations other than those associated with the major denominations.) Also, the tabulation of "Union" churches in the 1855 *Census* included many so-called union churches (buildings that housed several denominations) in the same listing as those Union churches that were actually comeouter abolitionists.[3]

In order to establish an accurate listing of abolition churches, the information obtained from the above sources had to be checked and compared with specific data from abolitionist periodicals and from denominational and congregational records, as follows:

Data on the Franckean Lutheran churches was obtained from the journals of their annual meetings and the *Lutheran Herald.* Thirty-seven Franckean churches existing in 1843–45 were located.

Information on the Congregational Friends was obtained from the *Proceedings* of the Waterloo Yearly Meeting of Congregational Friends; an article by Allen C. Thomas (*Bulletin of Friends' Historical Society* 10 [Nov. 1920]); and local histories. Because of the limited Quaker presence in upper New York, very few Congregational Friends churches existed; four have been positively identified.

Antislavery Baptist churches and antislavery Adventist churches were identified through various local histories and abolitionist periodicals. Eight antislavery Baptist and four antislavery Adventist churches were identified.

Information on the identities of abolitionized Free Baptist churches was obtained from the *Morning Star* (the periodical of the Free Baptists); G. A. Burgess and J. T. Ward, the *Free Baptist Cyclopaedia;* and Marilla Marks, ed., *Memoirs of the Life of David Marks.* Forty-four Free Baptist churches were positively identified as abolitionist, including almost all of the former Free Communion Baptist churches. Given the strong antislavery sentiments of burned-over district Free Baptists, it is probable that other Free Baptist churches were Liberty Party–supporting, but it has been impossible to verify this supposition. Only those Free Baptist churches that can be shown to have had abolitionist sentiments were included in the compilation.

Specific information on the identity of Wesleyan Methodist churches was obtained from lists of congregations and circuits (along with the number of members in each congregation or circuit) which were compiled in the original minutes of the various Wesleyan Methodist conferences in New York state. Compilations of the circuits in these conference minutes are not always accurate because the locations listed may have been the name of the regional circuit and not necessarily the name of the specific town where a Wesleyan Methodist congregation or preaching existed. For example, there was an "Olean" circuit that served the region around Olean, but there was never actually a Wesleyan Methodist church in the town of Olean; the "Allegany," "Cayuga," "Essex," and "Orleans" circuits consisted of various preaching stations throughout each of these counties. Also, the names of a few congregations and circuits were listed with no numerical membership, probably indicating that a church was planned for that location but never established.[4] In order to develop an accurate list of the Wesleyan Methodist churches that actually existed in 1843–45, the compilations from the conference minutes had to be crosschecked with conference histories, local histories, and various papers, particularly the *Liberty Press* (edited by Wesley Bailey, a Wesleyan Methodist) and the *True Wesleyan*. As a result of this process, 119 active Wesleyan Methodist churches were identified in upper New York in 1843–45.

Information on the identities of Unionist and Free or independent Congregational (comeouter Presbygationalist) churches was obtained from various abolitionist papers, especially the *Union Herald,* the *Christian Investigator,* the *Liberty Press,* and the *Liberty Party Paper,* as well as from local histories and (very carefully and selectively) from the 1855 New York *Census.* Also helpful was Silas E. Persons, *A Historical Sketch of the Religious Denominations of Madison County, New York* (1906) and James H. Hotchkin, *A History of the Purchase and Settlement of Western New York, and . . . of the Presbyterian Church in That Section* (1848). Hotchkin listed nearly every Presbygational church in western New York and described in considerable detail the ultraist agitations within these churches. Most of the Congregational churches that belonged to the abolitionist Genesee Consociation, for example, were antislavery comeouters. One hundred and one Unionist or independent abolitionist Congregational churches have been identified as existing in 1843–45, often called by various names.

The multiplicity of names for the various abolition churches (particularly comeouter Presbygational churches) is a researcher's nightmare. The anecdotal town and county histories that describe local ecclesiastical affairs inconsistently use any one of several terms to denote particular antislavery churches. The situation is made even more difficult by the fact that the appellations used by comeouter antislavery churches were often very similar to those used by nonabolitionist churches. Thus, when reading local history, it is not appropriate to take certain names (e.g. "Union church") at face value and to assume automatically that they refer to abolitionist congregations.

For instance, a "Church of Christ" could refer to a Unionist congregation, but it also could refer to a congregation of the nonabolitionist Christian Connection (although those congregations usually were called "Christian churches").[5] A so-called Union church could have been simply a common meetinghouse for several denominations rather than a comeouter abolitionist congregation.[6] The title "Free Church" could refer to a Union Church or it could refer to a church that eliminated pew rentals.[7] The designation "Congregational" is particularly confusing. Some Congregational churches were churches with an independent congregational polity that had seceded from the accommodation plan presbyteries to become abolitionist churches, as described in chapter 2.[8] Other Congregational churches, however, were not abolitionist seceders—that is, they were merely Presbygational churches that, in their local polity, had opted for the Congregational form instead of the Presbyterian form during the years in which the accommodation plan was in effect. These latter Congregationalists were not abolitionist comeouters at all; they still belonged to their "proslavery" presbyteries or Congregationalist associations (regional accommodation plan judicatories).

Thus, in order to identify abolition churches correctly, it is essential to be able to distinguish whether a particular "Church of Christ" was Unionist or "Christian"; whether a "Union" church was a comeouter church or simply a building used by more than one denomination; whether a "Free Church" was Unionist or merely a name for a church that had free seats; and whether a "Congregational Church" was an independent abolitionist church with a congregational polity or actually an accommodation plan Congregationalist church. Some local histories clearly identify churches as abolitionist comeouters, and a few of the comeouter Union churches have surviving records. More often, however, corroborative evidence from ecclesiastical abolitionist periodicals is required for the positive identification of an abolition church. The *Liberty Press,* the papers of the Unionists (the *Union Herald* and the *Christian Investigator*), and the papers of the other comeouter groups were particularly useful for this purpose, because the formation of abolition churches was usually noted in these publications.

There are three further complications in locating abolition churches. First, some town and county boundaries have been altered since the 1840s; it is important to recognize the older boundaries for the purpose of accurate placement. Second, the name of the hamlet or village in which a particular church was located may have been different from the name of the surrounding town that encompassed that village. For example, the Free Church of Peterboro was in the town of Smithfield; the Wesleyan Methodist church in the village of Fulton was located in the town of Volney; and the Free Baptist church in the hamlet of Unadilla Forks was in the town of Plainfield. Voting data was listed by town, so it is essential to know the name of the town as well as the village in which an abolition church was located. Third, because some towns contained several hamlets or villages—with each village having its own abolition church—such towns may have had more than one abolition church (see e.g. table 2).

A few towns have been included in the compilation in which there is no evidence of a formally organized abolition church, but nonetheless there was exhibited a significant level of church reform sentiment. These were often very rural or remotely settled communities in which scattered individual ecclesiastical abolitionists had little opportunity to congregate with others of like mind.[9] Towns were identified as having a significant level of church reform sentiment if there were ten or more paid subscriptions to the *Christian Investigator* (the leading ecclesiastical abolitionist paper) from that town in 1843–45, or if there were ten or more participants from that community who attended a church reform convention (these participants were also listed in the *Christian Investigator*). Twelve such towns were identified.

The result of this entire process is a comprehensive list of 317 abolition churches located in 249 upper New York towns.[10] In addition, twelve more towns demonstrated significant church reform sentiment but did not have an organized abolition church—bringing the total to 261 towns. That is, 261 (36.9%) of the 708 towns in upper New York were affected by antislavery church reform in 1843–45.[11]

Further, the data on these 261 towns has been compared to the Liberty votes in that same area of upper New York. Liberty vote totals for the 1844 presidential election in upper New York state have been compiled by town and county. Approximately 15,400 Liberty votes were cast in upper New York in 1844; this number represented ninety-seven percent of the state total and just under one-quarter of the national total.[12] Two upstate counties (Schenectady and Tompkins) did not itemize their electoral results by town; consequently, neither voting data nor information regarding the abolition churches from these coun-

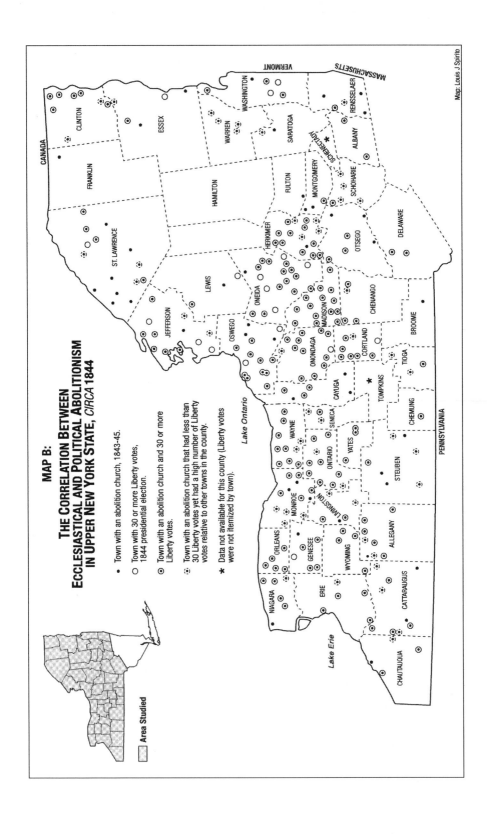

MAP B:
THE CORRELATION BETWEEN
ECCLESIASTICAL AND POLITICAL ABOLITIONISM
IN UPPER NEW YORK STATE, *CIRCA* 1844

• Town with an abolition church, 1843-45.

○ Town with 30 or more Liberty votes, 1844 presidential election.

⊙ Town with an abolition church and 30 or more Liberty votes.

⊙ Town with an abolition church that had less than 30 Liberty votes yet had a high number of Liberty votes relative to other towns in the county.

★ Data not available for this county (Liberty votes were not itemized by town).

Area Studied

Map: Louis J Spirito

ties can be included in this town-by-town analysis. Included in the statistical analysis, therefore, is data from the forty-three upstate counties (comprising 692 towns) that did itemize.

Appendix B displays some of the results of these compilations. It records all Liberty vote totals over thirty, sorted by town in descending order. Abolition churches have also been identified and listed according to the town in which they were located. If the village or hamlet in which the abolition church was located had a different name than its surrounding town, the village or hamlet name is placed in parentheses. The specific abolition church group with which each antislavery congregation was associated is indicated in the right hand column of the table by a letter code. The key for the code is as follows:

AA   Antislavery Adventist
AB   Antislavery Baptist
CF   Congregational Friends
CRS significant church reform sentiment
FB   Free Baptist
FL   Franckean Lutheran
U   Unionist or independent Congregational
WM   Wesleyan Methodist

In the 1844 election, 182 towns in upper New York had thirty or more Liberty Party votes. One hundred sixty-five (90.7%) of the 182 towns have been identified as having an abolition church or a significant level of antislavery church reform sentiment; only seventeen towns did not (these seventeen are indicated in the right hand column of the table by the word "none").

The results of these compilations are displayed in map B. This map provides a visual demonstration of the correlation between Liberty Party support and antislavery church reform. The 261 identified towns that contained an abolition church or significant church reform sentiment have been located (indicated by a single dot) and the 182 towns that polled thirty or more Liberty votes have been located (indicated by a circle). Also indicated are the fifty towns containing abolition churches that polled less than thirty Liberty votes but nonetheless had high Liberty vote totals relative to other towns in their vicinity; such towns are indicated by a broken circle.

Appendix B. *Occurrence of Antislavery Church Reform in Upper New York Towns with 1844 Liberty Vote Totals over Thirty (in descending order)*

Town (Village or Hamlet)	County	Liberty Vote	Abolition Church
Cazenovia	Madison	177	U
Smithfield (Peterboro)	Madison	174	U
Volney (Fulton)	Oswego	141	WM
Sullivan (Chittenango)	Madison	140	U
Utica	Oneida	120	U/WM
Brookfield	Madison	116	FB
Cortlandville (Cortland)	Cortland	116	U
Plainfield (Unadilla Forks)	Otsego	113	FB
Lenox (Canastota)	Madison	112	U/AB
Lockport	Niagara	112	AA/WM/U
Whitestown (Whitesboro)	Oneida	107	U/FB
Collins (Lodi)	Erie	104	U/CF
Richland (Pulaski)	Oswego	100	U
Virgil (Harford)	Cortland	99	WM/FB
Hamilton	Madison	97	U
Rochester	Monroe	93	WM/U
Eaton	Madison	92	CRS
Cicero	Onondaga	89	U/FB
Champlain	Clinton	88	WM
Alexandria	Jefferson	86	FB
Trenton	Oneida	86	U
Mexico (Colosse)	Oswego	85	FL/WM
Madison	Madison	84	CRS
Perry	Wyoming	82	AB/AA
Lawrence	St. Lawrence	81	WM/FB
Salina (Syracuse)	Onondaga	81	WM
Troy	Rensselaer	79	FL/WM/U

Town (Village or Hamlet)	County	Liberty Vote	Abolition Church
Warsaw	Wyoming	75	U/FB
Mooers	Clinton	74	WM
Williamson	Wayne	73	WM/U
Nelson	Madison	73	FB
Clayton (Depauville)	Jefferson	73	WM
Brownville (Perch River)	Jefferson	73	FL
China (Arcade)	Wyoming	71	U
Chazy	Clinton	70	WM
Paris	Oneida	70	none
Homer	Cortland	70	U
Stockbridge	Madison	69	WM
Albany	Albany	68	U/WM
Rose	Wayne	67	WM/U
Manlius (High Bridge)	Onondaga	67	WM/U
Otisco	Onondaga	64	U
Barre	Orleans	64	U
Georgetown	Madison	63	U
Litchfield (Jerusalem)	Herkimer	63	FB/FL/U
Marion	Wayne	63	U
Salisbury	Herkimer	63	FB/FL/U
Camden	Oneida	63	WM
Mentz (Port Byron)	Cayuga	63	U
Buffalo	Erie	63	U/WM
Winfield	Herkimer	62	U
Richmond (Honeoye)	Ontario	62	U
Lebanon	Madison	62	U/AB
Castile	Wyoming	61	U
Theresa	Jefferson	60	none
Perrysburgh (Versailles)	Cattaraugus	59	U
Adams	Jefferson	59	none
Milo (Penn Yan)	Yates	59	WM/U
Orleans (Stone Mills)	Jefferson	58	WM/FL
Macedon	Wayne	57	CF
Westmoreland	Oneida	56	U
Deerfield	Oneida	55	none

Town (Village or Hamlet)	County	Liberty Vote	Abolition Church
Lyme (Cape Vincent)	Jefferson	55	FB/WM
Walworth	Wayne	54	FB
Palermo	Oswego	54	U/WM
Mt. Morris	Livingston	54	AB
Hannibal	Oswego	53	CRS
Franklinville	Cattaraugus	52	U
Leyden	Lewis	52	none
Augusta	Oneida	52	FB
Hebron	Washington	52	AA
Russia (Poland)	Herkimer	52	FB
Sherburne	Chenango	52	U
Plattsburgh	Clinton	52	WM
Spafford	Onondaga	51	CRS
Gaines (Eagle Harbor)	Orleans	51	WM/U
Jerusalem (Penn Yan)	Yates	51	WM/U
Elbridge (Jordan)	Onondaga	51	WM/U
Scriba (Oswego)	Oswego	51	U
Almond	Allegany	50	U
Ontario	Wayne	50	U
Seneca (Geneva)	Ontario	50	WM
Lincklaen	Chenango	49	U/FB
Leon	Cattaraugus	49	WM
Fabius (Apulia)	Onondaga	49	U
Batavia	Genesee	49	FB
Scott	Cortland	48	U
Florence	Oneida	48	U
Otsego	Otsego	48	FB
Cato	Cayuga	47	AB
Ridgeway (Medina)	Orleans	47	FB/U
Fowler	St. Lawrence	46	FB
Portland	Chautauqua	46	WM
Schroeppel (Hinmanville)	Oswego	46	FL/WM
Ellicott (Jamestown)	Chautauqua	46	WM/U
Penfield	Monroe	46	U
Elmira	Chemung	46	WM/U
Oakfield	Genesee	45	none

Town (Village or Hamlet)	County	Liberty Vote	Abolition Church
Aurora	Erie	45	U/FB
Greenwich	Washington	45	U
Danube (Newville)	Herkimer	43	FL
Rushford	Allegany	43	WM
Perrinton	Monroe	43	FB/U
Franklin	Delaware	43	U
Sodus	Wayne	43	U/FL/FB
Canajoharie (Ames)	Montgomery	43	FL/FB
Canandaigua	Ontario	43	CRS
Owego	Tioga	43	WM
Putnam	Washington	42	FB/AA
Randolph	Cattaraugus	42	FB
Fenner	Madison	42	AB
Hartland	Niagara	42	U
Parish	Oswego	41	U/FL/FB
Beekmantown	Clinton	41	WM
Yates (Lyndonville/Ashwood)	Orleans	41	U/WM
Granby (Fulton)	Oswego	41	WM
Oswego	Oswego	41	U
De Ruyter	Madison	40	AB
Bristol	Ontario	40	U
Henrietta	Monroe	40	U
Butler (S. Butler)	Wayne	40	U/WM
Antwerp	Jefferson	40	WM
Mendon (Honeoye Falls)	Monroe	40	U
New Hartford	Oneida	40	U
Little Falls (Bethel)	Herkimer	40	FL
Rome	Oneida	40	WM
New Haven	Oswego	39	none
Walton	Delaware	39	U
Newport	Herkimer	39	FB
Burlington	Otsego	39	FB
Au Sable (Keesville)	Clinton	39	WM
Seneca Falls	Seneca	39	WM
Steuben	Oneida	38	U

Town (Village or Hamlet)	County	Liberty Vote	Abolition Church
Vienna	Oneida	38	none
Onondaga (Onondaga Hill)	Onondaga	38	WM/U
Preble	Cortland	37	U
Sharon	Schoharie	37	FL
Concord (E. Concord)	Erie	37	FB
Argyle	Washington	37	none
Vernon	Oneida	37	CRS
Norway	Herkimer	36	FB
Darien	Genesee	36	U
Prattsburgh	Steuben	36	WM
Pitcher	Chenango	35	U
Remsen	Oneida	35	U/WM
Nunda	Allegany	35	U
Shelby (Chestnut Ridge)	Orleans	35	FB/WM
York	Livingston	35	U
Denmark (Copenhagen)	Lewis	35	U
Frankfort	Herkimer	35	WM
Kirkland (Clinton)	Oneida	35	FB
Stockholm	St. Lawrence	35	WM
West Bloomfield	Ontario	34	U
Hume (Fillmore)	Allegany	34	WM/U
Pembroke	Genesee	34	U
Columbia	Herkimer	34	FB
Moriah	Essex	34	none
Salem	Washington	34	none
De Witt	Onondaga	34	CRS
Marathon	Cortland	33	none
Tully	Onondaga	33	none
Farmington	Ontario	33	WM/CF
Somerset	Niagara	33	WM
Cambria	Niagara	33	U
Phelps	Ontario	33	FB
Jay	Essex	32	WM
Portage	Allegany	32	FB
Madrid	St. Lawrence	32	none

Town (Village or Hamlet)	County	Liberty Vote	Abolition Church
Truxton	Cortland	32	U
Potsdam (Bucksbridge)	St. Lawrence	32	WM
Ellisburgh	Jefferson	32	U
Constantia	Oswego	31	none
Sennett	Cayuga	31	CRS
Bethany	Genesee	31	FB
Victor	Ontario	31	CRS
Rensselaerville	Albany	31	U
Pompey (Oran)	Onondaga	31	WM/U
Middlesex	Yates	30	FB
Fairfield (Middleville)	Herkimer	30	U
Western	Oneida	30	none
Lee	Oneida	30	none
Skaneateles	Onondaga	30	WM/U

Notes

Acknowledgments

1. William Goodell, *Slavery and Anti-Slavery; A History of the Great Struggle in Both Hemispheres; With a View of the Slavery Question in the United States* (New York: William Goodell, 1853), 487.

Introduction

1. Calvin Colton [A northern man, pseud.], *Abolition a Sedition* (Philadelphia: G. W. Donahue, 1839), 114–20; Jonathan Blanchard, *A Perfect State of Society* (Oberlin, Ohio: James Steele, 1839). Colton's Presbyterian pastorate was in LeRoy, New York, in the same presbytery as the neighboring Warsaw church; consequently, Colton had occasion to have regular contact with the perfectionists in Warsaw. Colton eventually became disillusioned with the revivalistic trends within Presbyterianism and converted to Episcopalianism. See Alfred A. Cave, *An American Conservative in the Age of Jackson: The Political and Social Thought of Calvin Colton* (Ft. Worth: Texas Christian Univ. Press, 1969), v–viii, 34–37, 42–43; Andrew W. Young, *History of the Town of Warsaw, New York* (Buffalo: Sage, Sons, 1869), 162, 196–97, 297, 285.

2. Colton, *Abolition a Sedition*, 114–20.

3. For Colton's worries, see Calvin Colton [Junius, pseud.], "Political Abolition," in *The Junius Tracts* (New York: Greeley and McElrath, 1844). As an example of the confidence of the Liberty Party, see "The Right Sort of Politics," *Emancipator Extra* (14 Sept. 1843): 1.

4. The term "ecclesiastical abolitionist" was coined by William Goodell in the *Christian Investigator* 5 (July 1847): 426. Although in contemporary usage the term "ecclesiastical" tends to connote highly structured, institutionalized religion, it was precisely this that Goodell was challenging. For examples of the term "antislavery church reform," see *Christian Investigator* 1 (Dec. 1843): 87; Goodell, *Slavery and Anti-Slavery*, 487. For examples of the term "abolition church," see Sherburne (New York) Free Church, *Organization and Membership of the Free Church of Sherburne, 1847–1856,* typed manuscript, New York State Library, Albany, N.Y., 1; James A. Wright, *Historical Sketches of the Town of Moravia from 1791 to 1918* (Auburn: Cayuga County News, n.d.), 214; C. Peter Ripley, ed., *The Black Abolitionist Papers* (Chapel Hill: Univ. of North Carolina Press, 1985), 3:447.

5. Blanchard, 12.

6. *Christian Union* 1 (Aug. 1841): 61. Unlike the Troeltschian use of the term "sect" to refer to a group that functions outside of the religious mainstream, in the context of mid-nineteenth-century American religion the term referred to one of the established Protestant denominations.

7. See, e.g., *Christian Investigator* 1 (May 1843): 31; ibid., 1 (July 1843): 42; *Union Herald* 6 (20 May 1841): 9; ibid., 6 (23 Sept. 1841): 82; Orange Scott, *The Methodist E. Church and Slavery* (Boston: O. Scott, For the Wesleyan Methodist Connection, 1844), 72–98.

8. The phrase "come out" was derived from Rev. 18.4: "Come out of her [wicked Babylon], my people, that ye partake not of her sins, and that ye receive not of her plagues." See also 2 Cor. 6.17.

9. Colton, "Political Abolition," 77–79.

10. *Christian Investigator* 3 (June 1845): 237–38; ibid., 5 (July 1847): 426.

11. Stephen A. Marini, *Radical Sects of Revolutionary New England* (Cambridge, Mass.: Harvard Univ. Press, 1982), 51, 78, 137, 142–43, 154–55, provides examples of doctrinal perfectionism among several small religious groups in the early Republic; John L. Thomas, "Antislavery and Utopia," in *The Antislavery Vanguard,* ed. Martin Duberman (Princeton, N.J.: Princeton Univ. Press, 1965), 246–49, and Ronald G. Walters, *American Reformers, 1815–1860* (New York: Hill and Wang, 1978), 18–19, 28, 39ff., 72–75, 115, describe the general current of perfectionism in antebellum society. See also Alexis de Tocqueville, *Democracy in America,* ed. J. P. Mayer and Max Lerner (New York: Harper and Row, 1966), 452–54. For the specific development of evangelical perfectionism and the doctrine of entire sanctification, see Merrill E. Gaddis, "Christian Perfection in America" (Ph.D. diss., Univ. of Chicago, 1929); John L. Peters, *Christian Perfection and American Methodism* (New York: Abingdon, 1956); Timothy L. Smith, *Revivalism and Social Reform: American Protestantism on the Eve of the Civil War* (Baltimore: Johns Hopkins Univ. Press, 1980), 103–23; Melvin E. Dieter, *The Holiness Revival of the Nineteenth Century* (Metuchen, N.J.: Scarecrow, 1980).

12. Gilbert H. Barnes, *The Antislavery Impulse, 1830–1844* (New York: Appleton-Century, 1933); David Brion Davis, "The Emergence of Immediatism in British and American Antislavery Thought," *Mississippi Valley Historical Review* 49 (Sept. 1962): 209–30; Anne C. Loveland, "Evangelicalism and Immediate Emancipation in American Antislavery Thought," *Journal of Southern History* 32 (May 1966): 172–88; Donald M. Scott, "Abolition as a Sacred Vocation," in *Antislavery Reconsidered: New Essays on the Abolitionists,* ed. Lewis Perry and Michael Fellman (Baton Rouge: Louisiana State Univ. Press, 1979), 51–74; idem, *From Office to Profession: The New England Ministry, 1750–1850* (Philadelphia: Univ. of Pennsylvania Press, 1978), 76–77, 84–94; John L. Hammond, *The Politics of Benevolence: Revival Religion and American Voting Behavior* (Norwood, N.J.: Ablex, 1979), 1–19.

13. *Christian Investigator* 7 (July 1847): 426.

14. See e.g. Aileen S. Kraditor, *Means and Ends in American Abolitionism: Garrison and His Critics on Strategy and Tactics, 1834–1850* (New York: Pantheon, 1967), 103, 142; John L. Thomas, *The Liberator: William Lloyd Garrison, a Biography* (Boston: Little, Brown, 1963), 251; Clifford S. Griffin, *Their Brothers' Keepers: Moral Stewardship in the United States, 1800–1865* (New Brunswick, N.J.: Rutgers Univ. Press, 1960), 154–59; Louis Filler, *The Crusade Against Slavery, 1830–1860* (New York: Harper, 1960), 130–31, 134–35; Lori D. Ginzberg, *Women and the Work of Benevolence: Morality, Politics, and Class in the Nineteenth-Century United States* (New Haven, Conn.: Yale Univ. Press, 1990), 87.

15. Theodore Clarke Smith, *The Liberty and Free Soil Parties in the Northwest* (New York: Longmans, Green, 1897), 1, 298ff.; William Birney, *James G. Birney and His Times: The Genesis of the Republican Party* (New York: Appleton, 1890), 201–2, 332–33. See also Dwight L. Dumond, *Antislavery Origins of the Civil War in the United States* (Ann Arbor: Univ. of Michigan Press, 1939), 83; John Mayfield, *Rehearsal for Republicanism: Free Soil and the Politics of Antislavery* (Port Washington, N.Y.: Kennikat, 1980), 5–7.

16. Kraditor, 78–79, 100–101, 118; Margaret Louise Plunkett, "A History of the Liberty Party With Emphasis Upon its Activity in the Northeastern States" (Ph.D. diss., Cornell Univ., 1930);

John L. Hendricks, "The Liberty Party in New York State, 1836–1848" (Ph.D. diss., Fordham Univ., 1959), 78–81. Bertram Wyatt-Brown, *Lewis Tappan and the Evangelical War against Slavery* (Cleveland: Case Western Reserve Univ. Press, 1969), 310, 313, agrees in substance with Kraditor, stating that Garrison and Lewis Tappan "shared the leadership of the antislavery crusade" in the 1840s, with Garrison leading the radical wing and Tappan leading the "conservative" or "evangelical" wing.

17. G. Barnes, 76–77.

18. Cincinnati, in particular, was a center of "conservative" abolitionists, who hoped that slavery could be ended with only a minimal modification of the existing civil and ecclesiastical institutional structures. See Robert Merideth, "Edward Beecher: A Conservative Abolitionist at Alton," *Journal of Presbyterian History* 42 (June 1964): 101; Lawrence J. Friedman, *Gregarious Saints: Self and Community in American Abolitionism, 1830–1870* (Cambridge: Cambridge Univ. Press, 1982), 68–70; Joseph G. Rayback, *Free Soil: The Election of 1848* (Lexington: Univ. Press of Kentucky, 1970), 103–6; Stanley Harrold, *Gamaliel Bailey and Antislavery Union* (Kent, Ohio: Kent State Univ. Press, 1986), 64; Filler, 150–51; Mayfield, 67ff.; James Brewer Stewart, *Holy Warriors: The Abolitionists and American Slavery* (New York: Hill and Wang, 1976), 92–96, 100ff.; Wyatt-Brown, 272–79.

19. See Douglas M. Strong, "The Crusade for Women's Rights and the Formative Antecedents of the Holiness Movement," *Wesleyan Theological Journal* 27 (1992): 131–60. For the evangelical convictions of burned-over district Liberty leaders, see Goodell, *Slavery and Anti-Slavery,* 458–61, 466–67; *Christian Investigator* 1 (Jan. 1844): 97.

20. Lawrence J. Friedman, "'Historical Topics Sometimes Run Dry': The State of Abolitionist Studies," *The Historian* 43 (Feb. 1981): 188–90, 194. For examples of the traditional concentration on prominent establishment figures, see Charles C. Cole, Jr., *The Social Ideas of the Northern Evangelists, 1826–1860* (New York: Columbia Univ. Press, 1954); John R. Bodo, *The Protestant Clergy and Public Issues, 1812–1848* (Princeton, N.J.: Princeton Univ. Press, 1954); Griffin. For an early critique of this traditional approach, see Lois Banner, "Religious Benevolence as Social Control: A Critique of an Interpretation," *Journal of American History* 60 (June 1973): 23–41.

21. For descriptions of the range of abolitionist viewpoints, see Ronald C. Walters, "The Boundaries of Abolitionism," in *Antislavery Reconsidered: New Essays on the Abolitionists,* eds. Lewis Perry and Michael Fellman (Baton Rouge: Louisiana State Univ. Press, 1979), 14–19; James M. McPherson, *The Struggle for Equality: Abolitionists and the Negro in the Civil War and Reconstruction* (Princeton, N.J.: Princeton Univ. Press, 1964), 4–5; Lewis Perry, *Radical Abolitionism: Anarchy and the Government of God in Antislavery Thought* (Ithaca, N.Y.: Cornell Univ. Press, 1973), 158ff. Perry observes that political abolitionism and Garrisonian abolitionism shared certain anti-institutionalist and perfectionistic ideas, concluding that in many respects the Garrisonians and the political abolitionists were not as far apart as either they or subsequent historians have made them out to be.

22. Nathan O. Hatch, *The Democratization of American Christianity (New Haven, Conn.: Yale Univ. Press, 1989),* 5–22, 44–46. *See also* Randolph A. Roth, *The Democratic Dilemma: Religion, Reform, and the Social Order in the Connecticut River Valley of Vermont, 1791–1850* (Cambridge: Cambridge Univ. Press, 1987), 1–7, 299–300.

23. *Christian Investigator* 1 (30 Dec. 1843): 96.

24. For examples of the holistic understanding of ecclesiastical abolitionists, see *Friend of Man* 3 (6 Feb. 1839): 34; *Lutheran Herald* n.s. 1 (16 Oct. 1844): n.p.

25. For an example of the ecclesiastical abolitionist conception of the paradoxes within American democracy, see *Lutheran Herald* o.s. 2 (16 Sept. 1840): 69.

26. See e.g. T. L. Smith, *Revivalism and Social Reform;* Donald W. Dayton, *Discovering an Evangelical Heritage* (New York: Harper and Row, 1976); Nancy Hardesty, *Women Called to Witness: Evangelical Feminism in the Nineteenth Century* (Nashville: Abingdon, 1984).

27. Lee Benson, *The Concept of Jacksonian Democracy: New York as a Test Case* (Princeton, N.J.: Princeton Univ. Press, 1961), 208–13.

28. Cole, 100–101, 110–11, 240; Bodo, 11–48, 253–57; Griffin, 23–60, 152–76; David H. Donald, "Toward a Reconsideration of the Abolitionists," in *Lincoln Reconsidered: Essays on the Civil War Era,* ed. David. H. Donald (New York: Knopf, 1956), 19–36.

29. George M. Thomas, *Revivalism and Cultural Change: Christianity, Nation Building, and the Market in the Nineteenth-Century United States* (Chicago: Univ. of Chicago Press, 1989), 67, 82, 84ff.; Paul E. Johnson, *A Shopkeeper's Millennium: Society and Revivals in Rochester, New York, 1815–1837* (New York: Hill and Wang, 1978); Harry L. Watson, *Liberty and Power: The Politics of Jacksonian America* (New York: Hill and Wang, 1990), 178–79.

30. For classic statements of this integrative approach, see Whitney R. Cross, *The Burned-Over District: The Social and Intellectual History of Enthusiastic Religion in Western New York, 1800–1850* (Ithaca, N.Y.: Cornell Univ. Press, 1950), 3–13; Daniel Walker Howe, "The Evangelical Movement and Political Culture in the North during the Second Party System," *Journal of American History* 77, no. 4 (Mar. 1991): 1235.

31. Although Whitney Cross was responsible for popularizing the term "burned-over district" among twentieth-century historians, the phrase was also used regularly by nineteenth-century writers, including Finney himself; see e.g. Charles G. Finney, *Memoirs of Rev. Charles G. Finney: Written by Himself* (New York: A. S. Barnes, 1876), 78. See also Philemon H. Fowler, *Historical Sketch of Presbyterianism within the Bounds of the Synod of Central New York* (Utica, N.Y.: Curtiss and Childs, 1877), 138, 276.

32. Cross, 4, determined an "arbitrary boundary" that established the burned-over district as those parts of New York state lying west of the Catskills and of the Adirondacks; however, almost all of New York state north of the Catskills would fit Cross's description of a region pervaded by enthusiastic religious reform. Moreover, several historians have recognized that the "boundaries" of the burned-over district should be widened to include areas beyond New York state. See David L. Rowe, "A New Perspective on the Burned-Over District: The Millerites in Upstate New York," *Church History* 47 (Dec. 1978): 412; Roth, 2–5; P. Jeffrey Potash, *Vermont's Burned-Over District: Patterns of Community Development and Religious Activity, 1761–1850* (Brooklyn, N.Y.: Carlson, 1991); Robert R. Dykstra, *Bright Radical Star: Black Freedom and White Supremacy on the Hawkeye Frontier* (Cambridge, Mass.: Harvard Univ. Press, 1993), 28–29, 73. Among earlier observers of the region, Benjamin B. Warfield described a broad area of religious enthusiasm without using the specific "burned-over" designation: "Oberlin was only an extension of Western New York into the wilds of Northern Ohio, and it repeated its religious history" (*Perfectionism* [New York: Oxford Univ. Press, 1931], 8). For an overview of the burned-over milieu, see Michael Barkun, *Crucible of the Millennium: The Burned-Over District of New York in the 1840s* (Syracuse, N.Y.: Syracuse Univ. Press, 1986), 2–6.

33. For the purposes of my analysis, upper New York is defined as that portion of the state lying north of and including the counties of Delaware, Schoharie, Albany, and Rensselaer. (Note that Schuyler County was not yet established.) For Liberty vote totals, see T. C. Smith, 96–97; Hendricks, 194ff.; W. Dean Burnham, *Presidential Ballots, 1836–1892* (Baltimore: Johns

Hopkins Univ. Press, 1955). Approximately 25% of Free Baptists, 35% of Wesleyan Methodists, and over 80% of Franckean Lutherans hailed from upper New York; see appendix A for more detail.

34. Hal Barron contends that rural Northerners during this period were "hybrids" between traditional peasantry and modern entrepreneurialism, who both endorsed and circumscribed the influence of broader markets (Hal S. Barron, *Those Who Stayed Behind: Rural Society in Nineteenth-Century New England* [Cambridge: Cambridge Univ. Press, 1984], 5, 135, 136). For background on these economic developments, see David Brion Davis, *The Problem of Slavery in the Age of Revolution, 1770–1823* (Ithaca, N.Y.: Cornell Univ. Press, 1975), 349–85; Daniel J. McInerney, "'A State of Commerce': Market Power and Slave Power in Abolitionist Political Economy," *Civil War History* 37, no. 2 (June 1991): 101–19; Jonathan A. Glickstein, "'Poverty is not Slavery': American Abolitionists and the Competitive Labor Market," in *Antislavery Reconsidered: New Essays on the Abolitionists,* eds. Lewis Perry and Michael Fellman (Baton Rouge: Louisiana State Univ. Press, 1979), 195–218.

35. Perry, 90ff.; John R. McKivigan, *The War Against Proslavery Religion: Abolitionism and the Northern Churches, 1830–1865* (Ithaca, N.Y.: Cornell Univ. Press, 1984), 143ff.; idem, "Vote As You Pray and Pray As You Vote: Church-Oriented Abolitionism and Antislavery Politics," in *Crusaders and Compromisers: Essays on the Relationship of the Antislavery Struggle to the Antebellum Party System,* ed. Alan M. Kraut (Westport, Conn.: Greenwood, 1983), 181–91; Richard J. Carwardine, *Evangelicals and Politics in Antebellum America* (New Haven, Conn.: Yale Univ. Press, 1993), 135–39. See also Alan M. Kraut, "The Forgotten Reformers: A Profile of Third Party Abolitionists in Antebellum New York," in *Antislavery Reconsidered: New Essays on the Abolitionists,* ed. Lewis Perry and Michael Fellman (Baton Rouge: Louisiana State Univ. Press, 1979), 119–45; Hammond, 68–105; Vernon L. Volpe, *Forlorn Hope of Freedom: The Liberty Party in the Old Northwest, 1838–1848* (Kent, Ohio: Kent State Univ. Press, 1990), 66–79, 120ff.

36. Hammond, 89–105, discusses revivalism; Volpe, 71, and John R. McKivigan, "The Antislavery 'Comeouter' Sects: A Neglected Dimension of the Abolitionist Movement," *Civil War History* 26, no. 2 (June 1980): 149, 158, mention perfectionism but do not discuss the specific content of the doctrine of entire sanctification or the significance of the experience of evangelical perfection as a motivation for political action.

1. A Middle Course

1. See Lewis H. Bishop, "Our Historical Heritage: An Address Delivered at the 150th Anniversary Service in the United Church, Sunday, July 13, 1958," typed manuscript in church office, United Church, Warsaw, N.Y.

2. "Ultraism" was a generally pejorative term employed to describe extreme efforts and measures used to produce evangelistic results or social reform. See e.g. William B. Sprague, *Religious Ultraism: A Sermon Delivered August 25, 1835, at the Installation of the Rev. John H. Hunter, as Pastor of the First Congregational Church in West Springfield, Massachusetts* (Albany, N.Y.: Packard and Van Benthuysen, 1835).

3. See Laura Bristol Robinson, ed., *History of the Centennial Celebration, Warsaw, Wyoming County, New York, June 28–July 2, 1903* (Warsaw, N.Y.: Western New Yorker, 1903), 20, 46–51; Wyoming County (New York), *History of Wyoming County, New York* (New York: F.

W. Beers, 1880), 103–4, 202, 204; Warsaw Presbyterian Church, *Schism the Offspring of Error, Illustrated in Historical Sketches of the Presbyterian Church of Warsaw, Genesee County, N.Y.* (Buffalo: Robert D. Foy, 1841); Joseph E. Nassau, *Seventy-Fifth Anniversary of the Presbyterian Church of Warsaw, N.Y.* (Warsaw, N.Y.: H. A. Dudley, 1885); Young, 162, 196–97, 297, 285; Warsaw (New York) Congregational Church, "The Story of One Hundred Years: The First Congregational Church, Warsaw, N.Y.," typed manuscript in church office, United Church, Warsaw, N.Y., 8–9; idem, "Warsaw Congregational Church," typed manuscript in Wyoming County Historian's Office, Warsaw, N.Y.; idem, *Year Book and Church Directory of the First Congregational Church, Warsaw, New York* (Warsaw, N.Y.: 1932).

4. See George Peck, *Early Methodism within the Bounds of the Old Genesee Conference from 1788 to 1828; or, The First Forty Years of Wesleyan Evangelism in Northern Pennsylvania, Central and Western New York, and Canada* (New York: Carlton and Porter, 1860), 175; Fowler, 37; Dixon Ryan Fox, *Yankees and Yorkers* (New York: New York Univ. Press, 1940), 199ff.; Lois Kimball Matthews, *The Expansion of New England* (Boston: Houghton Mifflin, 1909), 139–69.

5. Oswego County (New York), *History of Oswego County, New York* (Philadelphia: L. H. Everts, 1877), 217; G. Peck, 462.

6. Clara K. Trump, *First Presbyterian Church of Westfield, New York, 1808–1968: A History* (Westfield, N.Y.: Westfield Republican, 1968), 10. See James H. Hotchkin, *A History of the Purchase and Settlement of Western New York, and of the Rise, Progress, and Present State of the Presbyterian Church in that Section* (New York: M. W. Dodd, 1848), 422; *New England Quarterly* 10 (1837): 759, cited in Fox, 211; G. Peck, 258, 370.

7. Robert Hastings Nichols, *Presbyterianism in New York State* (Philadelphia: Westminster, 1963), 114. See China (New York) First Congregational Church records, vol. 2, 1836–1858, archives, United Church of Christ, Congregational, Arcade, N.Y.

8. Hotchkin, 24, 50; Fowler, 167, 240.

9. Nichols, *Presbyterianism*, 78. See also Hotchkin, *A History of Western New York*, 422, 464–65; David G. Hackett, *The Rude Hand of Innovation: Religion and Social Order in Albany, New York, 1652–1836* (New York: Oxford Univ. Press, 1991).

10. Robert Hastings Nichols, "The Plan of Union in New York," *Church History* 5 (Mar. 1936): 29–51, esp. 42.

11. Fowler, 45, 56.

12. Fowler, 67. See also Nichols, *Presbyterianism*, 78–87. The term "Lebanon" referred to that country's traditional reputation as a gardenlike land noted for prosperity and luxuriant growth.

13. James Wood, *Facts and Observations concerning The Organization and State of the Churches in the Three Synods of Western New-York and the Synod of Western Reserve* (Saratoga Springs, N.Y.: G. M. Davison, 1837). See also Fowler, 66, 68; Nichols, *Presbyterianism*, 85; Isaac S. Signor, ed., *Landmarks of Orleans County* (Syracuse, N.Y.: D. Mason, 1894), 552.

14. G. Peck, 197, 244–45, 351, 356–57, 402, 404, 461; Nichols, "The Plan of Union in New York," 39.

15. On the Methodists, see Francis W. Conable, *History of the Genesee Annual Conference of the Methodist Episcopal Church, from its Organization by Bishops Asbury and M'Kendree in 1810 to the year 1872* (New York: Nelson and Phillips, 1876), 50–53, 93–105, 120–38. On the Baptists, see Charles Wesley Brooks, *A Century of Missions in the Empire State, as Exemplified by the Work and Growth of the Baptist Missionary Convention of the State of New York* (Philadelphia: American Baptist Publishing Society, 1909). In the forty-five counties of upper New York

(north of the Catskills) in the 1845 census, 81% of the enumerated churches (2222 out of 2752) were listed as Baptist, Methodist, Presbyterian, or Congregational. New York (State), Secretary of State, *Census of the State of New-York, for 1845* (Albany, N.Y.: Carroll and Cook, 1846), Recapitulation, no. 6 and no. 7.

16. On Methodist growth on the New York frontier, see G. Peck, 356, 362, 368, 460; on Methodist theological emphases in New York, see ibid., 176, 181, 266–67, 482–83.

17. Ibid., 180, 185, 265, 276, 279, 394, 420, 443, 462.

18. See Hotchkin, 322, 477, 545; G. Peck, 459, 466.

19. Presbyterians did not officially recognize Methodists until 1849, when the New York synods began exchanging fraternal delegates with the upstate Methodist conferences (Nichols, *Presbyterianism,* 144), but informal relations occurred much earlier, especially on the local level. See Hotchkin, 435; G. Peck, 364, 435; Henry L. Dox, *Memoir of Rev. Philip Wieting, A Pastor Forty Years in The Same Field* (Philadelphia: Lutheran Publication Society, 1870), 142ff.

20. See G. Peck, 96–97, 469; Robert Baird, *Religion in the United States of America. Or an Account of the Origin, Progress, Relations to the State, and Present Condition of the Evangelical Churches in the United States. With Notices of the Unevangelical Denominations* (Glasgow: Blackie and Son, 1844), 605.

21. See Fowler, *Historical Sketch of Presbyterianism,* 141, 236. Marini, 25–39, demonstrates that by the time of the Yankee emigration to New York state, a degree of religious radicalism had already been present in the settlers' home region of upper New England. See also David M. Ludlum, *Social Ferment in Vermont, 1791–1850* (New York: Columbia Univ. Press, 1939), 25–62.

22. Ancel H. Bassett, *A Concise History of the Methodist Protestant Church, from its Origin: Embracing the Circumstances of the Suspension of the Northern and Western Conferences in 1858, the Entire Career of the Methodist Church, and the Reunion of the two Branches in 1877* (Pittsburgh: James Robison, 1877), 309. Methodist Protestant polity was not strictly congregational, but it was much less hierarchical than the Methodist Episcopal system. See also Rick Nutt, "'The Advantages of Liberty': Democratic Thought in the Formation of the Methodist Protestant Church," *Methodist History* 31 (Oct. 1992): 16–25. There were other schisms within the Methodist Episcopal Church over the issue of polity—James O'Kelly's Republican Methodist church, the African Union church, and the "Methodist Society" (or Stillwellites) of New York city—but these offshoots were not active in upper New York state. See e.g. Lewis V. Baldwin, *"Invisible" Strands in African Methodism: A History of the African Union Methodist Protestant and Union American Methodist Episcopal Churches, 1805–1980* (Metuchen, N.J.: Scarecrow, 1983).

23. See N. Hatch, *Democratization,* 68–81. The Christian Connection of New England and New York was a different group from Barton W. Stone's "Christians" in the mid-South region, although there were similarities in their emphases (see e.g. *Christian Union* 1 [June 1841]: 23). The former group eventually joined with the Congregationalists, and the latter group joined with the Campbellites (Disciples of Christ). There was no significant Disciples presence in New York state before the Civil War (see New York [State], Secretary of State, *Census for the State of New-York for 1855* [Albany, N.Y.: Charles Van Benthuysen, 1857], 478).

24. Baird, 269. See also Tocqueville, 292–94; Samuel Ringgold Ward, *Autobiography of a Fugitive Negro: His Anti-Slavery Labours in the United States, Canada, and England* (London: John Snow, 1855), 41.

25. *Friend of Man* 1 (23 June 1836): 1. The correlation between democracy and Christianity

was regularly asserted by religious Americans in the early to mid–nineteenth century. See, for example, *Union Herald* 6 (11 Aug. 1841): 64; Gerrit Smith, *Abstract of the Argument, on the Public Discussion of the Question, "Are the Christians of a Given Community the Church of Such Community?"* (Albany, N.Y.: S. W. Green, 1847), 10; William Goodell, *The Democracy of Christianity; or An Analysis of the Bible and Its Doctrines, in Their Relation to the Principle of Democracy,* 2 vols. (New York: Cady and Burgess, 1852).

26. *Christian Palladium* 8 (15 May 1839): 2, 25.

27. Colton, *Abolition a Sedition,* 119, 121; idem, *A Voice From America to England,* cited in Cave, 21; idem, *Protestant Jesuitism* (New York: Harper and Brothers, 1836).

28. G. Peck, 497. See also *Christian Investigator* 1 (30 Dec. 1843): 96.

29. Calvin Colton, *Thoughts on the Religious State of the Country; with Reasons for Preferring Episcopacy* (New York: Harper, 1836).

30. John William Ward, *Andrew Jackson: Symbol For an Age* (London: Oxford Univ. Press, 1953).

31. Silas E. Persons, *A Historical Sketch of the Religious Denominations of Madison County, New York* (Cazenovia, N.Y.: Madison County Historical Society, 1906), 19. See also G. Peck, 465ff.

32. Warsaw (New York) Presbyterian Church, 3, 6. See J. I. Root et al. [pseud.?], *An Account of the Trial of Luther Myrick, Before the Oneida Presbytery* (Syracuse, N.Y.: J. P. Patterson, 1834), iii.

33. *Morning Star* (10 May 1837): 7; Nicholas Van Alstine et al., *A Reunion of Ministers and Churches, Held at Gardnersville, May 14–17, 1881* (Philadelphia: Lutheran Publication Society, 1881), 33; Fowler, 138, 276.

34. L. Mathews, 139–69; Glenn C. Altschuler and Jan M. Saltzgaber, *Revivalism, Social Conscience, and Community in the Burned-Over District: The Trial of Rhoda Bement* (Ithaca, N.Y.: Cornell Univ. Press, 1983), 29, 77, 149.

35. Cross, 173–84, 198–208; Warfield, 8; Hammond, 1–19, 89–105.

36. P. Johnson, 79–94, 137. See also Charles Sellers, *The Market Revolution: Jacksonian America, 1815–1846* (New York: Oxford Univ. Press, 1991), 210.

37. G. Thomas, 36–37; Christopher Clark, *The Roots of Rural Capitalism: Western Massachusetts, 1780–1860* (Ithaca, N.Y.: Cornell Univ. Press, 1990), 320–24.

38. *Morning Star* 12 (3 May 1837): 2; ibid., 18 (18 Oct. 1843): 102. See also *Methodist Quarterly Review* (July 1850): 431–32.

39. "Horatio Nelson Waldo," obituary in *Western New Yorker* (Sept. 1895), cited in Harry S. Douglass to Jeffrey Mason, 1 Aug. 1992, memo in records of Arcade (New York) Historical Society; Harry S. Douglass, *Progress With a Past: Arcade, New York, 1807–1957* (Arcade: Arcade Sesquicentennial and Historical Society, 1957), 141; Vaughn Polmenteer, "Reynolds Arcade was the City's Classic: An Address of Distinction," *Rochester Museum and Science Center Focus* 23 (Spring 1989): 22–23; Jeffrey C. Mason and Harry S. Douglass, *Alive in the Spirit Since 1813: The Arcade United Church of Christ, Congregational* (Interlaken, N.Y.: Heart of the Lakes, 1990), 59–69.

40. Howe, "Evangelical Movement," 1225.

41. John Keep, *Congregationalism and Church Action: with the Principles of Christian Union, etc.* (New York: S. W. Benedict, 1845), 19. See also e.g. H. O. Bunnell, *Dansville: 1789–1802: Historical, Biographical, Descriptive* (Dansville, N.Y.: Instructor, 1902), preface, 2; S. Ward, 82.

42. Gerrit Smith, *Substance of the Address, Delivered by Gerrit Smith, Before the Annual Meeting of the American Temperance Society, In the City of New-York, May 7, 1833* (Utica, N.Y.: Gardiner Tracy, 1833).

43. Huntington Lyman, *Address Delivered Before the Temperance Society of Franklinville [N.Y.], at Their Annual Meeting, in Sept., 1830* (Utica, N.Y.: Gardiner Tracy, 1833), 14.

44. Lyman was one of the abolitionist "rebels" who withdrew from Lane Seminary in 1834 (due to the seminary's equivocation on the slavery issue) and enrolled at Finney's new school in Oberlin. See Lane Theological Seminary, *Lane Theological Seminary, General Catalogue of 1828–1881* (Cincinnati: Elm Street, 1881); Oberlin College, *General Catalogue of Oberlin College, 1833–1908* (Cleveland: O. S. Hubbell, 1909); Lawrence T. Lesick, *The Lane Rebels: Evangelicalism and Antislavery in Antebellum America* (Metuchen, N.J.: Scarecrow, 1980), 132, 180; John L. Myers, "The Beginnings of Anti-Slavery Agencies in New York State, 1833–1836," *New York History* 43 (Apr. 1962): 167–68.

45. Lyman Beecher, *A Plea For the West* (Cincinnati: Truman and Smith, 1835), 10–11.

46. *Oberlin Evangelist* 2 (7 July 1841): 110; *Union Herald* 6 (23 Sept. 1841): 85–86.

47. On Taylor and the impact of his theological system, see Sidney E. Mead, *Nathaniel William Taylor, 1786–1858: A Connecticut Liberal* (Chicago: Univ. of Chicago Press, 1942); William R. Sutton, "Benevolent Calvinism and the Moral Government of God: The Influence of Nathaniel William Taylor on Revivalism in the Second Great Awakening," *Religion and American Culture* 2, no. 1 (Winter 1992): 23–47; and Earl A. Pope, *New England Calvinism and the Disruption of the Presbyterian Church* (New York: Garland, 1987), 62–106.

48. Finney's colleagues John and Henry Cowles came directly from Taylor's lectures to their classrooms at Oberlin. On the pervasive influence of Taylor's theology in the Presbygationalist churches of the burned-over district, see Wood, 11–13, 20; Nichols, *Presbyterianism,* 112–13; John Terrill Wayland, "The Theological Department in Yale College, 1822–1858" (Ph.D. diss., Yale Univ., 1933), 125–26, 139–40, 341–44, 430–34; Mead, 202, 204n.; Warfield, 18–19.

49. Taylor's use of the idea of the "moral government of God" was a specific example of his adopting of theological concepts that were derived from common sense realism; see Donald M. Meyer, *The Instructed Conscience: The Shaping of the American National Ethic* (Philadelphia: Univ. of Pennsylvania Press, 1972), 89–107.

50. See e.g. Charles G. Finney, *Lectures on Systematic Theology; Embracing Lectures on Moral Government* (Oberlin, Ohio: James M. Fitch, 1846).

51. Joseph Haroutunian, *Piety Versus Moralism: The Passing of the New England Theology* (New York: Henry Holt, 1932), 266.

52. For Taylor's formulation of these ideas, see Nathaniel W. Taylor, *Concio ad Clerum: A Sermon Delivered in the Chapel of Yale College* (New Haven, Conn.: Hezekiah Howe, 1828).

53. William Goodell, "Entire Sanctification" (manuscript sermon, Apr. 7, 1850), 11, William Goodell Papers, Berea College Archives, Berea, Ky. (hereafter cited as Goodell Papers). See also Fowler, 45–48.

54. *Union Herald* 6 (11 Aug. 1841): 59.

55. Nichols, *Presbyterianism,* 112–13; Mead, 202, 204n.; Wayland, 139–40, 341–44, 430–34.

56. *Friend of Man* 1 (5 May 1837): 182; *Lutheran Herald* n.s. 1 (8 Jan. 1845): n.p.; Blanchard, 12. See D. Scott, "Sacred Vocation," 69; idem, *From Office to Profession,* 76ff.; D. Davis, "Emergence of Immediatism"; Loveland.

57. Amos A. Phelps, *Lectures on Slavery and Its Remedy* (Boston: New-England Anti-Slavery Society, 1834), 179.

58. *Friend of Man* 1 (5 May 1837): 182.

59. George Wallingford Noyes, *Religious Experience of John Humphrey Noyes* (New York: MacMillan, 1923), 187; Cross, 240.

60. The religious concept of the millennium is derived from Rev. 20.1–6. For the prevalence of millennial ideas in early American society, see Nathan O. Hatch, *Sacred Cause of Liberty: Republican Thought and the Millennium in Revolutionary New England* (New Haven, Conn.: Yale Univ. Press, 1977); James West Davidson, *The Logic of Millennial Thought: Eighteenth Century New England* (New Haven, Conn.: Yale Univ. Press, 1977); Ernest Lee Tuveson, *Redeemer Nation: The Idea of America's Millennial Role* (Chicago: Univ. of Chicago Press, 1968); Ruth H. Bloch, *Visionary Republic: Millennial Themes in American Thought, 1756–1800* (New York: Cambridge Univ. Press, 1985).

61. Blanchard, 15. See also James H. Moorhead, "Between Progress and Apocalypse," *Journal of American History* 71 (Dec. 1984): 538; Donald W. Dayton, "Millennial Views and Social Reform in Nineteenth Century America," in *The Coming Kingdom: Essays in American Millennialism and Eschatology,* ed. M. Darrol Bryant and Donald W. Dayton (Barrytown, N.Y.: International Religious Foundation, 1983), 131–38.

62. For the impact of common sense realism on American culture, see N. Hatch, *Democratization,* 173–75; Meyer, 89–107; George M. Marsden, *The Evangelical Mind and the New School Presbyterian Experience: A Case Study of Thought and Theology in Nineteenth-Century America* (New Haven, Conn.: Yale Univ. Press, 1970); Theodore Dwight Bozeman, *Protestants in an Age of Science: The Baconian Ideal and Antebellum American Religious Thought* (Chapel Hill: Univ. of North Carolina Press, 1977); and Mark Noll, "Common Sense Traditions and American Evangelical Thought," *American Quarterly* 37 (1985): 216–38.

63. Cross, 215, 268–71. Other burned-over areas experienced the panic and its results (Potash, 108–9; Volpe, 16–18), but because upper New York was somewhat more prosperous than other areas, it also suffered more greatly when the panic hit.

64. John Humphrey Noyes to Polly Noyes, 30 Mar. 1837, cited in G. Noyes, 330; *Morning Star* 12 (17 May 1837): 16.

65. See John Wesley, "A Plain Account of Christian Perfection" and "The Scripture Way of Salvation," in *The Works of John Wesley,* 3rd ed., ed. Thomas Jackson (London: Wesleyan Book Room, 1872), 11:366–446 and 6:53–54.

66. Peters, 85–86, 217–19.

67. Methodist chronicler George Peck records almost no instances of persons professing "perfect love" in upper New York state after 1811; see G. Peck, 176, 299–300, 371, 469.

68. See Peters, 90–109, 121. Allan Coppedge, "Entire Sanctification in Early American Methodism: 1812–1835," *Wesleyan Theological Journal* 13 (Spring 1978), 34–50, disagrees with Peters's contention that holiness doctrine suffered benign neglect within Methodism in the early decades of the nineteenth century. However, Coppedge does admit to "an increased accent" of Christian perfection as midcentury approached. It is perhaps most accurate to recognize that perfection was a respected but not predominating doctrine from 1815 to 1835, and it continued to be preached sporadically within Methodism during this period. It did not find favor outside of Methodism until the mid-1830s.

69. Lee M. Haines and Paul William Thomas, *History of the Wesleyan Church* (Marion, Ind.: Wesley, 1985), 32; Colton, *Abolition a Sedition,* 114.

70. G. Noyes, 91–92, 186–87.

71. Root, *Trial of Luther Myrick,* 37, 48, 63.

72. Ibid., 58–62. See Joseph I. Foot, *Discourses on Modern Antinomianism, Commonly Called Perfectionism* (Syracuse, N.Y.: J. P. Patterson, 1834).

73. Root, *Trial of Luther Myrick,* i, 43.

74. Ibid., 69.

75. Ibid., 6, 50, 58.

76. Myrick's influence on local Presbygationalist churches is described in Hotchkin, 173, 313, 314, 315, 328, 360.

77. Root, *Trial of Luther Myrick,* iii, i, 38, 70.

78. On the early history of Oberlin College, see James H. Fairchild, *Oberlin: The Colony and the College, 1833–1883* (Oberlin, Ohio: E. J. Goodrich, 1883); Robert Samuel Fletcher, *A History of Oberlin College From Its Foundation Through the Civil War,* 2 vols. (Oberlin, Ohio: Oberlin College, 1943).

79. Fairchild, *Oberlin,* 90; Fletcher, 1:13; G. Noyes, 333; Warfield, 28n., 48–49. Mahan's initial religious experience was in the Sunday School of Warsaw Presbyterian Church; see Robinson, 49.

80. *New York Evangelist* (13 Feb. 1836).

81. *Union Herald* 6 (11 Aug. 1841): 59; James H. Fairchild, "The Doctrine of Sanctification at Oberlin," *Congregational Quarterly* 28 (Apr. 1876): 237–59; Timothy L. Smith, "The Doctrine of the Sanctifying Spirit: Charles G. Finney's Synthesis of Wesleyan and Covenant Theology," *Wesleyan Theological Journal* 13 (Spring 1978): 92–113; Warfield, 66, 68n. In the 1840s, Finney modified his views on holiness away from Wesleyan conceptions, preaching that one's entire consecration was simultaneous with one's conversion. Mahan, however, remained quite Wesleyan in his theology. For the evolving views on Christian perfection among Oberlinites, see Asa Mahan, *Scripture Doctrine of Christian Perfection; With Other Kindred Subjects, Illustrated and Confirmed in a Series of Discourses Designed to Throw Light on the Way of Holiness* (Boston: D. S. King, 1839); Henry Cowles, *The Holiness of Christians in the Present Life* (Oberlin, Ohio: J. Steele, 1840); Charles G. Finney, *Views of Sanctification* (Oberlin, Ohio: J. Steele, 1840); idem, *Lectures on Systematic Theology;* Asa Mahan, *Out of Darkness into Light* (Boston: Willard Tract Repository, 1876).

82. See e.g. *Oberlin Evangelist* (30 Jan. 1839); ibid. (1 Jan. 1839); ibid. (13 Feb. 1839); *Union Herald* 1 (26 Aug. 1841): 70.

83. See Wendell Phillips Garrison and Francis Jackson Garrison, *William Lloyd Garrison, 1805–1879: The Story of His Life Told by His Children* (New York: Century, 1885), 144–45; John H. Noyes, *The Way of Holiness* (Putney, Vt.: J. H. Noyes, 1838).

84. Perry, 52–54.

85. Garrison and Garrison, 145–53, 172.

86. Perry, 66; Kraditor, 91, 105–6.

87. See e.g. Colton, *Abolition a Sedition,* 116–17. Because in the antebellum period perfectionism was leagued with anti-institutionalism, it could only have been popularized *within* an established institution if it were a doctrine that was enshrined as part of the traditional confessional orthodoxy of that institution. In fact, Methodists did have a traditional authority for the doctrine of Christian perfection to which they could refer, namely the corpus of Wesley's writings; thus, some Methodist perfectionists appealed to their doctrinal heritage and stayed within the denomination, not challenging its institutional prerogatives. This was particularly evident in the holiness preaching of lay Methodist evangelist Phoebe Palmer. Palmer considered her continuing friendship with the denominational leadership to be vitally important; consequent-

ly, she steered clear of subjects that might have been divisive. Unlike other early perfectionists, Palmer and her circle "were laggards," according to Timothy L. Smith, "in whatever demanded stern attacks on persons and institutions." T. L. Smith, *Revivalism and Social Reform*, 212. See Charles E. White, *The Beauty of Holiness: Phoebe Palmer as Theologian, Revivalist, Feminist, and Humanitarian* (Grand Rapids, Mich.: Francis Asbury, 1986), 163, 228; Harold E. Raser, *Phoebe Palmer: Her Life and Thought* (Lewiston, N.Y.: Edwin Mellen, 1987), 222ff.; Haines and Thomas, 41; T. L. Smith, "Sanctifying Spirit," 96.

88. G. Noyes, 206.

89. John L. Thomas, "Antislavery and Utopia," 246–47, 249; Robert David Thomas, *The Man Who Would Be Perfect: John Humphrey Noyes and the Utopian Impulse* (Philadelphia: Univ. of Pennsylvania Press, 1977), 33.

90. Alan M. Kraut, "Partisanship and Principles: The Liberty Party in Antebellum Political Culture," in *Crusaders and Compromisers: Essays on the Relationship of the Antislavery Struggle to the Antebellum Party System*, ed. Alan M. Kraut (Westport, Conn.: Greenwood, 1983), 79; Friedman, *Gregarious Saints*, 43–126; McPherson, *Struggle for Equality*, 4–5.

91. Perry, x, 104.

92. *Union Herald* 6 (24 Mar. 1842): 188; ibid., 6 (9 Sept. 1841): 76. Some abolitionist historians have defined "perfectionism" in such a way that the term refers exclusively to the nonresistant, anarchistic ideology represented by the Garrisonians. Among such interpretations of perfectionism, all anti-Garrisonians are perceived to be nonperfectionists. See Robert Abzug, *Passionate Liberator: Theodore Dwight Weld and the Dilemma of Reform* (New York: Oxford Univ. Press, 1980), 175; Kraditor, 100–105; J. Thomas, *The Liberator*, 257, 274, 276. In truth, the politically minded ecclesiastical abolitionists were perfectionists, but of an evangelical variety that was different from that of the Garrisonians.

93. Warsaw (New York) Presbyterian Church, *Schism the Offspring of Error*, 7, 22–24.

94. For a classic presentation, see William Lloyd Garrison, *Principles of the Non-Resistant Society* (Boston, 1839).

95. Because anarchistic perfectionists were against coercion, they rejected force or violence in their measures for eliminating human institutions; thus, they must be distinguished from any type of secular anarchism that encouraged violent means.

96. Blanchard, 3.

97. *Declaration of Boston Peace Convention* (20 Sept. 1838), cited in Blanchard, 3.

98. *Christian Investigator* 1 (Apr. 1843): 24.

99. James Brewer Stewart, *Joshua P. Giddings and the Tactics of Radical Politics* (Cleveland: Case Western Reserve Univ. Press, 1970), 86–87.

100. *Christian Investigator* 1 (Dec. 1843): 87. See also James Brewer Stewart, "Peaceful Hopes and Violent Experiences: The Evolution of Reforming and Radical Abolitionism, 1831–1837," *Civil War History* 17 (Dec. 1971): 293–309.

101. "Disorganization" was a common caricatured term applied to anarchistic perfectionism, while "despotism" was a common term applied to those who supported traditional institutions.

102. *Union Herald* 6 (9 Sept. 1841): 76; *Christian Investigator* 1 (Apr. 1843): 18; ibid. (30 Dec. 1843): 96; Blanchard, 10–11.

103. See e.g. Root, *Trial of Luther Myrick*, 59; Blanchard.

104. *Friend of Man* 4 (19 June 1839): 3. Goodell, as an evangelical perfectionist, specifically called his strategic parameter a "Bible line" to contrast it with anarchistic emphases; anarchistic

perfectionists stressed that God's law should be unmediated by any external authorities, including the Bible.

105. Ibid.; Blanchard, 7.

2. Spiritual Democracy

1. W. H. McIntosh, *History of Wayne County, New York* (Philadelphia: Everts, Ensign, and Everts, 1877), 79. See S. Ward, 31–33, 70–75, 79–86; *Impartial Citizen* (24 Oct. 1849) and (13 Feb. 1850), in *Black Abolitionist Papers* (Sanford, N.C.: Microfilming Corp. of America, 1981), 6:0198, 6:0397; *Christian Investigator* 3 (Mar. 1845): 216; ibid. 4 (Apr. 1846): 318; Antoinette Brown to Gerrit Smith, 13 Oct. 1853, Gerrit Smith Papers, George Arents Research Library, Syracuse Univ., Syracuse, N.Y. Ward was the first pastor of the independent Congregational church in South Butler; during his tenure, the church trebled in membership. Ward's perfectionism may have been at least partially derived from the teachings of his devout Methodist mother. On the life and ministry of Samuel Ringgold Ward, see also Ronald K. Burke, "Samuel Ringgold Ward: Christian Abolitionist" (Ph.D. diss., Syracuse Univ., 1975).

2. *Christian Investigator* 3 (Mar. 1845): 216; ibid. 4 (Apr. 1846): 318; McIntosh, 79; George W. Cowles, ed., *Landmarks of Wayne County, New York* (Syracuse, N.Y.: D. Mason, 1895), 436. In the mid-1840s, the pastor of the South Butler church was Lewis Lockwood, a close associate of church reform leader William Goodell. On Brown's pastorate in South Butler, see Marjorie Allen, "First United States woman minister ordained in S. Butler," *Wayne County Star* (26 Sept. 1973); *National Era* (9 Sept. 1852), cited in M. Leon Perkal, "William Goodell: A Life of Reform" (Ph.D. diss., City Univ. of New York, 1972), 233; Elizabeth Cazden, *Antoinette Brown Blackwell: A Biography* (Old Westbury, N.Y.: Feminist Press, 1983), 31, 42, 56, 67–68, 70–71, 84–85; Carol Lasser and Marlene Deahl Merrill, eds., *Friends and Sisters: Letters between Lucy Stone and Antoinette Brown Blackwell, 1846–93* (Urbana: Univ. of Illinois Press, 1987), 108, 123, 133.

3. Much of the literature on antebellum reform does not mention church reform at all. Those few historians who do mention it view it only as a secondary derivative of abolitionism: see T. L. Smith, *Revivalism and Social Reform*, 25; Stewart, *Holy Warriors*, 114; Ronald G. Walters, *The Antislavery Appeal: American Abolitionism after 1830* (Baltimore: Johns Hopkins Univ. Press, 1976), 47; Dwight L. Dumond, *Antislavery: The Crusade for Freedom in America* (Ann Arbor: Univ. of Michigan Press, 1961), 349; Filler, 116, 122–26; McKivigan, *War Against Proslavery Religion*, 93–110; idem, "Antislavery 'Comeouter' Sects." Only Cross (257–67) views ecclesiastical reform as an independently important benevolent enterprise.

4. Goodell, *Slavery and Anti-Slavery*, 543–44.

5. See, for example, *Union Herald* 6 (23 Sept. 1841): 82, 85; ibid. (24 Feb. 1842): 170, 171.

6. *Union Herald* 6 (6 May 1841): 7.

7. See Nathan O. Hatch, "The Christian Movement and the Demand for a Theology of the People," *Journal of American History* 67 (Dec. 1980): 545–67; idem, *Democratization*, 68–81.

8. Both the Christian Connection and the Methodist Protestant Church, desiring not to offend their Southern members, took a neutral position on abolition. See *Christian Palladium* 5 (1 Apr. 1837): 361; ibid. 8 (15 May 1839): 25; ibid. (15 Apr. 1840): 377.

9. See e.g. Gerrit Smith, *An Address, Reported By Gerrit Smith to the "Christian Union Convention" Held in Syracuse, August 21st, 1838* (N.p.: n.d.), 1; *Christian Investigator* 1 (30

Dec. 1843): 94; S. Ward, 66–72; *Impartial Citizen* (24 Oct. 1849), in *Black Abolitionist Papers* (microfilm), 6:0198.

10. *Friend of Man* 1 (23 June 1836): 1.

11. S. Ward, 66–67; Fowler, 154, 158.

12. Seneca Falls (New York) Methodist Episcopal Church, Minutes, July 1839, archives, United Methodist Church, Seneca Falls, N.Y. (hereafter cited as Seneca Falls ME Church, Minutes).

13. *Friend of Man* 1 (26 Apr. 1837): 178; ibid. 2 (8 Nov. 1837): 81; ibid. 2 (14 Mar. 1838): 151.

14. See Samuel J. Baird, *A History of the New School, and of the Questions Involved in the Disruptions of the Presbyterian Church in 1838* (Philadelphia: Claxton, Remsen, and Haffelfinger, 1868); Marsden, 66–87.

15. C. Bruce Staiger, "Abolitionism and the Presbyterian Schism of 1837–1838," *Mississippi Valley Historical Review* 36 (Dec. 1949): 391–414; C. C. Goen, *Broken Churches, Broken Nation: Denominational Schisms and the Coming of the American Civil War* (Macon, Ga.: Mercer Univ. Press, 1985), 68–78.

16. Pope, 348, 357–59.

17. See e.g. Wood, 8–13, 20–21, 26–28, 34; Sprague, 26–27; Warsaw (New York) Presbyterian Church, *Schism the Offspring of Error,* 12–15; Root, *Trial of Luther Myrick,* 37, 63ff.; Franklin (New York) Congregational Church, *A Statement of Facts connected with the late difficulties in the Congregational Church in Franklin, N.Y.* (N.p.: 1841?), 4ff.; Colton, *Abolition a Sedition,* 114ff.

18. Sprague, 26–27; Wood, 9, 26; G. Noyes, 122.

19. Warsaw (New York) Presbyterian Church, *Schism the Offspring of Error;* Fowler, 69ff., 136–37; Wood, 10–11, 20–21, 27, 34.

20. Wood, 34ff.; Warfield, 36–37; Hotchkin, 316; Root, *Trial of Luther Myrick,* 57.

21. Root, *Trial of Luther Myrick,* 48. See Fowler, 137; *Oberlin Evangelist* (15 Sept. 1841).

22. *Christian Investigator* 1 (Apr. 1843): 18, 24; ibid. (July 1843): 42; Hotchkin, 313, 314, 370, 397–98, 493, 579.

23. Seneca Falls ME Church, Minutes, 12 Oct. 1840; *Friend of Man* 3 (17 Oct. 1838): 279.

24. Franckean Evangelic Lutheran Synod, *Journal of the Fourth Annual Session of the Franckean Evangelic Lutheran Synod, Convened at Seward, Schoharie County, N.Y., June 3d 1841* (Fort Plain, N.Y.: Lutheran Press Association, 1841), 25; *Christian Investigator* 1 (30 Dec. 1843): 94.

25. See G. Smith, *Christian Union Convention,* 1; *Union Herald* 6 (6 May 1841): 2.

26. Hotchkin, 169, 173; Warsaw (New York) Presbyterian Church, *Schism the Offspring of Error,* 14; *Union Herald* 1 (May 1836); *New-York Evangelist* 6 (3 Oct. 1835): 249; *Christian Union* 1 (May 1841): 10; *Christian Palladium* 7 (1 Oct. 1838): 161; ibid. 7 (1 Nov. 1838): 201; ibid. 8 (2 Sept. 1839): 138; ibid. 8 (1 Oct. 1839): 169–70.

27. A case can be made that some independent African American churches, such as the African Union Church and various African Baptist churches, were the first ecclesiastical abolitionist congregations, though they were not located in the burned-over district. See Baldwin, 48.

28. *New-York Evangelist* 6 (3 Oct. 1835): 249. See also appendix A.

29. *Union Herald* 6 (3 June 1841): 19; ibid. (29 July 1841): 53; Persons, 14; *Liberty Press* 3 (8 Mar. 1845): 69; ibid. 4 (13 Dec. 1845): 23; J. Wright, 214; Norman Williams et al., *Vermont Townscape* (New Brunswick, N.J.: Center for Urban Policy Research, 1987), 41. All of these churches were in New York state except for the Randolph Center church, which was in neighboring Vermont.

30. Similar to the Warsaw church, Gerrit Smith's Union Church was called simply The Church of Peterboro. "We would have the Church of [a] village derive its name simply from its locality"; G. Smith, *Christian Union Convention,* [2]. Within a few years of its founding, The Church of Warsaw was referred to as a Congregational church; Warsaw (New York) Congregational Church, "Story of One Hundred Years," 9.

31. *Christian Palladium* 8 (2 Sept. 1839): 138; ibid. (1 Oct. 1839): 169. For the difficulty in identifying abolition churches due to the diverse nomenclature that they used, see appendix A.

32. Samuel C. Pearson, "From Church to Denomination: American Congregationalism in the Nineteenth Century," *Church History* 38 (Mar. 1969): 85; Hotchkin, 246–48; Hugh Davis, *Joshua Leavitt: Evangelical Abolitionist* (Baton Rouge: Louisiana State Univ. Press, 1990), 121, 127–28, 259; Wayland, 141.

33. Hotchkin, 360, 397–98, 521; G. Cowles, 219; S. Ward, 66.

34. Often, Brown's experience in South Butler is used to demonstrate that the first ordination of a woman was in the Congregationalist denomination (which is now part of the United Church of Christ). This contention is problematic because her "Congregational" church was actually an independent abolitionist church that repudiated the Congregationalist denomination. Due to Brown's affinity for antislavery church reform, neither of the two guest participants at her ordination service were Congregationalists; instead, she invited a Unionist, Gerrit Smith, and a Wesleyan Methodist, Luther Lee. Brown to Smith, 23 Aug. 1853, Gerrit Smith Papers; McIntosh, 79; Cazden, 77–78.

35. *Christian Palladium* 7 (1 Oct. 1838): 161; ibid. 7 (1 Nov. 1838): 202; *Christian Union* 1 (July 1841): 47.

36. *Union Herald* 6 (26 Aug. 1841): 68.

37. Ecclesiastical abolitionism had its greatest support in the burned-over district of New York. Besides the African Union Church, only two other comeouter sects existed that were not located primarily in upper New York state: the Indiana Yearly Meeting of Anti-Slavery Friends and the Free Presbyterian Church (located in Ohio and Pennsylvania). These groups behaved like the church reformers in New York; indeed, they could be described simply as extensions of burned-over district ecclesiastical abolitionism into the Northwest. On the Indiana Anti-Slavery Friends, see Walter Edgerton, *A History of the Separation in Indiana Yearly Meeting of Friends; Which Took Place in the Winter of 1842 and 1843, on the Anti-Slavery Question, etc.* (Cincinnati: Achilles Pugh, 1856), 196, 204–5, 264, 295; Lucius C. Matlack, *The Life of Rev. Orange Scott* (New York: C. Prindle and L. C. Matlack, 1851), 228. On the Free Presbyterians, see Free Presbyterian Church, *Distinctive Principles of the Free Presbyterian Church of the United States* (Mercer, Pa.: Wm. F. Clark, 1851); Joseph Gordon, *The Life and Writings of Rev. Joseph Gordon* (Cincinnati: Free Presbyterian Synod, 1860).

38. Keep, 19; *Christian Investigator* 2 (30 Dec. 1843): 89–90.

39. *Christian Palladium* 8 (1 Aug. 1839): 104.

40. McIntosh, 79. Brown was confident that she was actually "ordained"; Antoinette Brown to Gerrit Smith, 16 Aug. 1853; ibid., 23 Aug. 1853, Gerrit Smith Papers. Brown's biographer asserts that those persons who denied that Brown was ordained were participating in a patriarchal maneuver to limit the significance of her new status; Cazden, 84. However, the statements about the specific nature of Brown's clerical status—by her supporters, no less—reflected the perfectionistic repudiation of all authorities, including the authority of the clergy. See Luther Lee, "Woman's Right to Preach the Gospel," 99, in *Five Sermons and a Tract by Luther Lee,* ed. Donald W. Dayton (Chicago: Holrad, 1975).

41. *Union Herald* 6 (11 Aug. 1841): 60; *Christian Palladium* 8 (1 Oct. 1839): 170; G. Smith, *Christian Union Convention*, 1, 2.

42. Myrick consistently affirmed the doctrine of the Trinity, but he conceded that a person who believed in unitarian ideas could still be a Christian. Only a small minority of Unionists actually held unitarian views; see *Union Herald* 6 (1 July 1841): 39; *Christian Palladium* 7 (1 Feb. 1839): 314; 8 (1 Nov. 1839): 205; (16 Dec. 1839): 249; (15 Feb. 1840): 315. Nonetheless, ecclesiastical abolitionists preached and wrote tracts to counteract the impression that there might be incipient unitarianism within their ranks. See e.g. Luther Lee, *Discussion on the Doctrine of the Trinity between Luther Lee, Wesleyan Minister, and Samuel J. May, Unitarian Minister. Reported by Lucius C. Matlack* (Syracuse, N.Y.: Wesleyan Book Room, 1854); Henry L. Dox, *Christ the Foundation* (Albany, N.Y.: J. Munsell, 1849).

43. *Union Herald* 6 (13 Jan. 1842): 146–47, 150; *Christian Palladium* 8 (1 Jan. 1840): 267.

44. *Union Herald* 6 (11 Aug. 1841): 60; ibid. (23 Sept. 1841): 82; *Christian Palladium* 7 (15 Sept. 1838): 154; ibid. (1 Nov. 1838): 200; ibid. 8 (15 Oct. 1839): 185–87.

45. *Union Herald* 6 (11 Aug. 1841): 60; ibid. 6 (5 May 1841): 3; *Christian Palladium* 8 (1 Oct. 1839): 170; *Liberty Leaguer* 1 (May 1849): 9, 12, 14.

46. *Union Herald* 6 (5 May 1841): 3. See also G. Smith, *Christian Union Convention*, 1–2; idem, *Abstract of the Argument*, 10.

47. *Union Herald* (11 Nov. 1841): 107; *Christian Investigator* 2 (Aug. 1844): 152; Garrison and Garrison, 176.

48. See e.g. *Union Herald* 6 (17 July 1841): 29; *Christian Palladium* 7 (15 Oct. 1838): 186; G. Smith, *Abstract of the Argument*, 10.

49. *Union Herald* 6 (29 July 1841): 51; ibid. (2 Dec. 1841); G. Smith, *Christian Union Convention*, 2.

50. *Lutheran Herald* 4 (1 June 1842): 74; ibid. n.s. 1 (13 Aug. 1844): n.p.; ibid. (4 Sept. 1844): n.p.; ibid. (8 Jan. 1845): n.p.; Luther Lee and E. Smith, *The Debates of the General Conference, of the M. E. Church, May, 1844* (New York: O. Scott, 1845), 476–77; *Christian Investigator* 2 (July 1844): 151; ibid. 6 (Aug. 1848): 528.

51. *Christian Investigator* (Feb. 1845): 205. See also *Union Herald* 6 (1 July 1841): 38; ibid. (5 May 1841): 3; G. Smith, *Christian Union Convention*, 2.

52. *Christian Investigator* 1 (Apr. 1843): 17.

53. G. Smith, *Christian Union Convention*, 1, 2; idem, *Abstract of the Argument*, 28, 33, 37.

54. See e.g. *Union Herald* 6 (23 Sept. 1841): 86; ibid. (16 Dec. 1841): 133; ibid. (24 Mar. 1842): 189; ibid. (24 Feb. 1842): 171; ibid. (11 Aug. 1841): 61; *Christian Palladium* 7 (1 Mar. 1839): 330; ibid. (1 Oct. 1838): 161; ibid. (1 Nov. 1838): 200; ibid. 8 (1 Feb. 1840): 297.

55. Goodell, "Entire Sanctification," 23, 25, Goodell Papers.

56. Ibid., 8; *Union Herald* 6 (26 Aug. 1841): 70. See also Freewill Baptist General Conference, *A Treatise on the Faith of the Free-Will Baptists: With an Appendix, Containing A Summary of Their Usages in Church Government*, 4th ed. (Dover, N.H.: Free-Will Baptist Printing Establishment, 1848), 70–72.

57. John Keep to Lydia Keep, 18 May 1839, cited in Fletcher, 229; Mason and Douglass, 165.

58. See e.g. Asa Mahan, *Principles of Christian Union, and Church Fellowship* (Elyria, Ohio: A. Burrell, 1836); Silas Hawley, *"A Declaration of Sentiments," reported by S. Hawley to the "Christian Union Convention," held in Syracuse, Aug. 21, 1838* (Cazenovia, N.Y.: Luther Myrick, 1839); G. Smith, *Christian Union Convention;* idem, *Union of Christians* (Peterboro, N.Y.: 1841?); idem, *Abstract of the Argument;* Cyrus Prindle, "The Methodist Episcopal

Church and the Primitive Church Compared," in Orange Scott, *Church Government* (Boston: O. Scott, for the Wesleyan Methodist Connection, 1844); Keep. See also the regular discussions on church reform in the *Union Herald,* the *Christian Investigator,* the *Oberlin Evangelist,* the *Liberty Press,* the *Lutheran Herald,* and the *True Wesleyan.*

59. On the Oberlinite interest in church reform, see Fletcher, 13, 223–28, 233–35, 254–57. Myrick influenced Finney on this issue; Myrick to Finney, 19 Sept. 1833, Finney Papers, Mudd Library, Oberlin College, Oberlin, Ohio.

60. Finney to T. D. Weld, 21 July 1836, in Gilbert H. Barnes and Dwight L. Dumond, eds., *Letters of Theodore Dwight Weld, Angelina Grimke Weld, and Sarah Grimke, 1822–1844* (New York: D. Appleton-Century, 1934), 1:318.

61. General Association of New York, *Minutes of the General Association of New York, at Their Meeting in Champion, Jefferson County, August 25th, 1842; with an Appendix* (Utica, N.Y.: R. W. Roberts, 1842), 8; Mason and Douglass, 165.

62. On the career of Green and the history of the Oneida Institute, see Milton C. Sernett, *Abolition's Axe: Beriah Green, Oneida Institute, and the Black Freedom Struggle* (Syracuse, N.Y.: Syracuse Univ. Press, 1976).

63. G. Smith, *Union of Christians;* Peterboro (New York), Church of Peterboro, *Church of Peterboro* (Peterboro, N.Y.: Gerrit Smith, 1843?); John E. Smith, *Our County and Its People: A Description and Biographical Record of Madison County, New York* (Boston: 1899), 395–96. An example of Smith's influence was the African American congregation in North Elba, New York, which established a "church on the Peterboro Platform"; see James McCune Smith to Gerrit Smith, 6 Feb. 1850, in Ripley, 4:44. On Smith's life, see Octavius Brooks Frothingham, *Gerrit Smith: A Biography* (New York: G. P. Putnam's Sons, 1878), and Ralph Volney Harlow, *Gerrit Smith: Philanthropist and Reformer* (New York: Henry Holt, 1939).

64. *Impartial Citizen* (24 Oct. 1849), cited in *Black Abolitionist Papers* (microfilm), 6:0198; Franckean Evangelic Lutheran Synod, *Journal of the First Annual Session* (1838), 5; Leslie D. Wilcox, *Wesleyan Methodism in Ohio* (N.p.: n.d.), 23, 66, 69, 77; McIntosh, 79, 173; G. Cowles, 219, 436; S. Ward, 31–32, 56–57, 70–72, 79–83, 85–86; Willis A. Hodges, *Free Man of Color: The Autobiography of Willis Augustus Hodges,* ed. Willard B. Gatewood, Jr. (Knoxville: Univ. of Tennessee Press, 1982), xl–xlii, xlvii–xlviii.

65. On Goodell, see Perkal; Douglas M. Strong, *They Walked in the Spirit: Personal Faith and Social Action in America* (Louisville, Ky.: Westminster John Knox, 1997), 1–15.

66. *Christian Palladium* 8 (1 Jan. 1840): 267; *Christian Investigator* 1 (Jan. 1844): 97, 100; Goodell, *Slavery and Anti-Slavery,* 460, 552; *Liberty Leaguer* 1 (May 1849): 12, 14.

67. Myrick was ambivalent about political abolition when it was first proposed in the late 1830s and was somewhat fearful that political activity would eclipse the interest that ecclesiastical abolitionists had in church reform. By 1841, however, Myrick was supporting the Liberty Party, and he even published a Liberty Party paper (the *Madison County Abolitionist,* later called the *Abolitionist*). See *Union Herald* 6 (2 Dec. 1841): 126; *Madison County Abolitionist* 1 (7 Dec. 1841): 46–47; *Morning Star* 16 (10 Nov. 1841): 115.

68. See Walters, *Antislavery Appeal,* 48; Perkal, 4, 134–35, 180–82, 254, 293–94.

69. *Christian Palladium* 8 (1 Jan. 1840): 267; Fairchild, *Oberlin,* 111; *Christian Investigator* 5 (Oct. 1847): 457; *Liberty Leaguer* 1 (May 1849): 14.

70. Goodell, "Wesley's Plain Account of Christian Perfection," "Discussions on Perfection," "Entire Sanctification," "Relation of Holiness to Happiness," all in Goodell Papers. See Perkal, 9–10; *Christian Investigator* 2 (Dec. 1844): 190–91.

71. Goodell, "Entire Sanctification," "Discussions on Perfection," 14, Goodell Papers. See also *Christian Investigator* 1 (June 1843): 47–48; ibid. (Sept. 1843): 60; ibid. 2 (July 1844): 149.

3. Liberty Party Theology

1. The "Big Tent" was used for large events at Oberlin such as commencement; it was also used throughout the North for purposes aligned with Oberlin's goals. Fletcher, 182, 210, 387, 829.

2. Liberty Party, "The National Liberty Convention," *Emancipator* Extra (tract No. 1) (Sept. 1843), 1–8; "The Right Sort of Politics," *Emancipator* Extra (tract No. 2) (14 Sept. 1843), 1–4.

3. The Big Tent was furnished free of charge for at least two Liberty Party conventions. Fletcher, 387.

4. *Friend of Man* 3 (6 Feb. 1839): 34; *Liberty Press* 4 (13 Dec. 1845): 21.

5. Some of the ecclesiastical abolitionists at the 1843 Liberty convention in Buffalo included William L. Chaplin, G. W. Clark, Elon Galusha, William Goodell, James C. Jackson, John Keep, Charles O. Shepard, Alvan Stewart, H. C. Taylor, Charles T. Torrey, and Samuel Ringgold Ward. Liberty Party, "The National Liberty Convention (1843)," 1–2.

6. David Christy, *Pulpit Politics; or, Ecclesiastical Legislation on Slavery, In Its Disturbing Influences on the American Union* (Cincinnati: Faran and McLean, 1862), 426. For an example of the path from antislavery church reform to politics, see S. Ward, 70–78.

7. Goodell, *Slavery and Anti-Slavery*, 451, 461.

8. *Friend of Man* 3 (17 Oct. 1838): 278; Colton, *Abolition a Sedition*, 114, 120.

9. Colton, "Political Abolition," 8.

10. *Morning Star* 12 (17 May 1837): 15.

11. Numerous examples can be given of local antislavery societies being established during the late 1830s, noted especially in the pages of the *Friend of Man,* the official organ of the New York State Anti-Slavery Society; see e.g. 1 (21 Aug. 1836): 19; (5 Apr. 1837): 160; (26 Apr. 1837): 178.

12. *Friend of Man* 1 (26 Apr. 1837): 178; ibid. 3 (29 Nov. 1838): 201; ibid. 1 (7 June 1837): 201, 202; ibid. 2 (21 Mar. 1838): 151; ibid. 1 (22 Feb. 1837): 141.

13. *Friend of Man* 1 (8 Feb. 1837): 134; Goodell, *Slavery and Anti-Slavery,* 453. Paul Kleppner, *The Cross of Culture: A Social Analysis of Midwestern Politics, 1850–1900* (New York: Free Press, 1970), has argued that party involvement in the antebellum period was crucial for one's self-identification.

14. Seneca Falls ME Church, Minutes, 12 Oct. 1840; *Friend of Man* 3 (29 Nov. 1838): 201; ibid. (17 Oct. 1838): 278. See also "Minutes of the Albany Anti-Slavery Convention," ibid. 2 (14 Mar. 1838).

15. Warsaw (New York) Presbyterian Church, *Schism the Offspring of Error,* 7, 22–24; *Friend of Man* 1 (23 June 1836): 2; Goodell, *Slavery and Anti-Slavery,* 452.

16. Blanchard, 13; *Friend of Man* 1 (10 May 1837): 187; *Christian Palladium* 8 (1 Jan. 1840): 267.

17. *Friend of Man* 1 (30 June 1836): 7; ibid. (3 May 1837): 182; Phelps, 179; D. Scott, "Sacred Vocation," 72; Luther Rawson Marsh, ed., *Writings and Speeches of Alvan Stewart on Slavery* (New York: A. B. Burdick, 1860), 399.

18. Seneca Falls ME Church, Minutes, 1838.

19. *Friend of Man* 1 (5 May 1837): 182; Goodell, *Slavery and Anti-Slavery*, 448, 472–73.

20. Goodell, "Discussions on Perfection" and "Entire Sanctification," Goodell Papers; Colton, *Abolition a Sedition*, 116–17; idem, "Political Abolition." On the connection between entire sanctification and the strategic move to abolitionist political action, see Warsaw (New York) Presbyterian Church, *Schism the Offspring of Error*, 22–24; Wyoming County (New York), 103, 284; Fowler, 69ff., 136–37; Wood, 9–11, 26–27; Sprague, 26–27.

21. Franckean Evangelic Lutheran Synod, *Journal of the Third Annual Session of the Franckean Evangelic Lutheran Synod, Convened at Stone Mills, Jefferson Co., June 4, 1840* (Fort Plain, N.Y.: David Smith, 1840), 23. See also *Lutheran Herald* 2 (1 Dec. 1840): 91; ibid. (16 Dec. 1840): 93, 95; ibid. 3 (1 Nov. 1841): 162, 165.

22. *Morning Star* 12 (17 May 1837): 9. On the political history of the 1840s, see Joel H. Silbey, *The American Political Nation, 1838–1893* (Stanford, Calif.: Stanford Univ. Press, 1991), 125–27; Ronald P. Formisano, *The Birth of Mass Political Parties: Michigan, 1827–1861* (Princeton, N.J.: Princeton Univ. Press, 1971), 133; Benson, *Concept of Jacksonian Democracy*, 22; Carwardine, 50–54. For the specific political situation in New York state, see Richard P. McCormick, *The Second American Party System: Party Formation in the Jacksonian Era* (New York: Norton, 1973), 104–5, 123–24.

23. *Friend of Man* 2 (22 Mar. 1838); *Christian Investigator* 5 (Mar. 1848): 487; *Oberlin Evangelist* 3 (1 Sept. 1841): 138. On the cultural history of the Whig Party, see Daniel Walker Howe, *The Political Culture of American Whigs* (Chicago: Univ. of Chicago Press, 1979), 150ff.; Robert Kelley, *The Cultural Pattern in American Politics: The First Century* (Washington, D.C.: Univ. Press of America, 1979), 166ff.

24. *Friend of Man* 1 (1 Mar. 1837): 146; ibid. (29 Mar. 1837): 156; Fairchild, *Oberlin*, 109–11; Colton, *Abolition a Sedition*, 119–20; idem, "Political Abolition," 6; John J. Butler, *Natural and Revealed Theology* (Dover, N.H.: Freewill Baptist Printing Establishment, 1861), 134; S. Ward, 74.

25. *Friend of Man* 3 (6 Feb. 1839); Blanchard, 13.

26. *Friend of Man* 2 (14 Mar. 1838); ibid. 3 (6 Feb. 1839); *Emancipator* (10 May 1838); ibid. (6 Sept. 1838); ibid. (20 Sept. 1838); ibid. (25 Oct. 1838); "Political Action Against Slavery," *Union Herald, Extra* (22 Oct. 1838), Gerrit Smith Papers.

27. S. Ward, 73–75.

28. [Liberty Party], *History of the Erection of the Monument on the Grave of Myron Holley* (Utica, N.Y.: H. H. Curtiss, 1844); *Friend of Man* 2 (14 Mar. 1838). Although a few individuals had proposed the establishment of a specifically Christian political party (such as Ezra Stiles Ely's sermon on that subject in 1827), the Liberty Party was the first attempt by abolitionists to form a Christian party.

29. Goodell, *Slavery and Anti-Slavery*, 468–71, 515; *Emancipator* (22 Aug. 1839); ibid. (3 Oct. 1839); ibid. (17 Oct. 1839); ibid. (9 Apr. 1840). On the life of Birney, see W. Birney; Betty Fladeland, *James Gillespie Birney: Slaveholder to Abolitionist* (Ithaca, N.Y.: Cornell Univ. Press, 1955).

30. H. Davis, 235–42, 265; Lawrence B. Goodheart, *Elizur Wright and the Reform Impulse: Abolitionist, Actuary, Atheist* (Kent, Ohio: Kent State Univ. Press, 1990), 126–28, 133.

31. Tocqueville, 445; Colton, "Political Abolition," 13, 16; James Birney, *A Letter on the Political Obligations of Abolitionists, By James G. Birney: With a Reply By William Lloyd Garrison* (Boston: Dow and Jackson, 1839), 33. The specialization of roles developed in conjunction

with the differentiation of labor associated with the growth of a market economy. For the development of a prescribed "women's sphere," for instance, see Mary P. Ryan, *Cradle of the Middle Class: The Family in Oneida County, New York, 1790–1865* (Cambridge: Cambridge Univ. Press, 1981), 218; for antebellum clergy roles, see D. Scott, *From Office to Profession*, 22–24.

32. Colton, "Political Abolition," 13–16.

33. Charles G. Finney to Gerrit Smith, 22 July 1840, Gerrit Smith Papers; Goodell, *Slavery and Anti-Slavery*, 453, 521; Gerrit Smith, "To Those Ministers in the County of Madison, Who Refuse to Preach Politics" (Peterboro: 1845), 2.

34. See J. Birney, *Political Obligations*, 4; Blanchard, 13.

35. Charles G. Finney to Gerrit Smith, 22 July 1840, Gerrit Smith Papers; S. Ward, 74–75.

36. J. Birney, *Political Obligations*, 6; Goodell, *Slavery and Anti-Slavery*, 521.

37. J. Birney, *Political Obligations*, 23, 30, 32; see Goodell, *Slavery and Anti-Slavery*, 458, 521.

38. Samuel Porter to Gerrit Smith, 14 Mar. 1845, Gerrit Smith Papers.

39. Goodell, *Slavery and Anti-Slavery*, 469.

40. J. Birney, *Political Obligations*, 4, 5–6, 10–11, 12; *Friend of Man* 2 (22 Mar. 1838); ibid. 3 (6 Feb. 1839).

41. Kraditor, 103; J. Thomas, *The Liberator*, 251; Abzug, 175; Walters, *Antislavery Appeal*, 93; Griffin, 154–59; Filler, 130–31, 134–35; Nancy Hewitt, "The Social Origins of Women's Antislavery Politics in Western New York," in *Crusaders and Compromisers: Essays on the Relationship of the Antislavery Struggle to the Antebellum Party System*, ed. Alan M. Kraut (Westport, Conn.: Greenwood, 1983), 206; Ginzberg, 87.

42. Goodell, *Slavery and Anti-Slavery*, 511–12, 522, 541–44. See also G. Barnes, 175. Cf. Kraditor, 142.

43. Lewis Tappan is a prime example of an AFASS leader who opposed both comeouter churches and the comeouter political party, at least at first. Richard H. Sewell, *Ballots for Freedom: Antislavery Politics in the United States, 1837–1860* (New York: Oxford Univ. Press, 1976), 75.

44. Luther Myrick and James C. Jackson were two of the most conspicuous Liberty advocates in New York who continued to back Garrison. Because of their support for Garrison, these men have been consistently misidentified as opposers of the Liberty Party. Sewell, for example (69, 76, 117), states that all AASS members were nonpolitical and that Jackson was not recruited to the Liberty Party until 1845. In truth, by at least 1841, AASS member Jackson was a fervent Liberty man; see *Madison County Abolitionist* 1 (7 Dec. 1841): 45, 46; *Morning Star* 16 (10 Nov. 1841): 115.

45. S. Ward, 53, 66; Goodell, *Slavery and Anti-Slavery*, 457, 465–67, 545, 552; *Madison County Abolitionist* 1 (7 Dec. 1841): 46; Liberty Party, "The National Liberty Convention" (1843), 3.

46. Liberty leaders involved in women's rights advocacy include Alvan Stewart, Gerrit Smith, William L. Chaplin, Cyrus P. Grosvenor, and Francis Hawley. See Goodell, *Slavery and Anti-Slavery*, 463; J. Thomas, *The Liberator*, 272–73. See also page 225, note 71.

47. *Madison County Abolitionist* 1 (7 Dec. 1841): 46. See Goodell, *Slavery and Anti-Slavery*, 450; Liberty Party, *Proceedings of the National Liberty Convention Held at Buffalo, N.Y., June 14th & 15th, 1848; Including the Resolutions and Addresses Adopted By That Body, and Speeches of Beriah Green and Gerrit Smith On That Occasion* (Utica, N.Y.: S. W. Green, 1848), 5, 14. See also Strong, "Crusade for Women's Rights."

48. *Madison County Abolitionist* 1 (7 Dec. 1841): 45, 46.

49. *The Abolitionist* 2 (11 Oct. 1842): 223; Beriah Green, *Sketches of the Life and Writings of James Gillespie Birney* (Utica, N.Y.: Jackson and Chaplin, 1844), 2.

50. *Oberlin Evangelist* (9 June 1841): 90; *Lutheran Herald* (1 Dec. 1840): 91; J. Birney, *Political Obligations*, 13, 26.

51. *Oberlin Evangelist* (3 Feb. 1841); ibid. (9 June 1841): 90–92.

52. Stewart, *Holy Warriors*, 97, 115, 120. See also Kraut, "Partisanship and Principles," 79; Walters, *Antislavery Appeal*, 15–16; Formisano, *Mass Political Parties*, 74–76; Carwardine, 136–38.

53. *Liberty Press* 4 (13 Dec. 1845): 21.

54. One report described the Liberty Party's state convention in this manner: "It was indeed a revival meeting" (*Liberty Party Paper* 1 [1 Aug. 1849]).

55. S. Ward, 33, 75; *Black Abolitionist Papers* (microfilm), 6:0199; *Historical Wyoming* [New York] 26 (Oct. 1980): 45–47; H. Douglass, *Progress With A Past*, 144.

56. Kraut, "The Forgotten Reformers," 142–44; Benson, *Concept of Jacksonian Democracy*, 210–11; Hammond, 89–105, 185; Volpe, xi–xv; McKivigan, *War Against Proslavery Religion*, 20, 51, 85, 95.

57. Liberty Party, *Proceedings of the Great Convention of the Friends of Freedom . . . 1845* (Lowell, Mass.: Pillsbury and Knapp, 1845), 15; *Christian Investigator* 2 (Oct. 1844): 171; ibid. 5 (May 1847): 410; William Goodell, *Address of the Macedon Convention By William Goodell; And Letters of Gerrit Smith* (Albany, N.Y.: S. W. Green, Patriot Office, 1847), 15. See also *Lutheran Herald* n.s. 1 (11 Dec. 1844): n.p.; Gerrit Smith and Cassius M. Clay, *Cassius M. Clay, of Lexington, Ky., to the Mayor of Dayton, O., with a Review of it by Gerrit Smith, of Peterboro, N.Y.* (Utica, N.Y.: Jackson and Chaplin, 1844), 7; and Liberty Party, *Proceedings of the National Liberty Convention . . . 1848*, 31. See also Ripley, 3:43.

58. *Oberlin Evangelist* 2 (4 Aug. 1841): 127.

59. J. N. T. Tucker, ed., *Liberty Almanac, For 1844* (Syracuse, N.Y.: I. A. Hopkins), 15. Cf. Orange Scott, *The Methodist E[piscopal] Church and Slavery* (Boston: O. Scott, 1844), 72–98, 126; *Morning Star* 18 (8 Nov. 1843): 114; "Wesleyan Minister's Position Defined by Himself," *Liberty Press* 3 (23 Nov. 1844): 9. According to the Free Baptists, "[W]e have carried out the anti-slavery principle in the church, and now we have got to carry it out politically. . . . We may be accused of meddling with politics, but what is that?" (*Morning Star* 18 [8 Nov. 1843]: 114).

60. *Morning Star* 18 (8 Nov. 1843): 114; "The National Liberty Convention" (1843), *Emancipator Extra* (Sept. 1843): 5–6; *Madison County Abolitionist* 1 (7 Dec. 1841): 46; *Lutheran Herald* 2 (1 Dec. 1840): 91; ibid. 3 (1 Nov. 1841): 162; *The Abolitionist* 2 (11 Oct. 1842): 222; ibid. (25 Oct. 1842): 229; Gerrit Smith, *To the Liberty Party of the County of Madison* (Peterboro, N.Y.: Gerrit Smith, 1846).

61. Goodell, "Entire Sanctification," 10–11, and "Discussions on Perfection," Goodell Papers. See also *Christian Investigator* 1 (Sept. 1843): 60; Luther Lee, "Pastoral Address of the Convention assembled at Utica," cited in Lucius C. Matlack, *The History of American Slavery and Methodism, from 1780 to 1849* (New York: Lucius C. Matlack, 1881), 343.

62. Luther Lee, *Autobiography of Rev. Luther Lee* (New York: Phillips and Hunt, 1882), 281. See also *Lutheran Herald* n.s. 1 (2 Oct. 1844): n.p.; ibid. (30 Oct. 1844): n.p.

63. *Liberty Press* 3 (4 Jan. 1845): 33; *Madison County Abolitionist* 1 (7 Dec. 1841): 47; *The Abolitionist* 2 (25 Oct. 1842): 229; *Lutheran Herald* 2 (1 Dec. 1840): 91; Peterboro (New York), Church of Peterboro.

64. Curtis D. Johnson, *Islands of Holiness: Rural Religion in Upstate New York, 1790–1860* (Ithaca, N.Y.: Cornell Univ. Press, 1989), 22ff.

65. *Madison County Abolitionist* 1 (7 Dec. 1841): 45; *The Abolitionist* 2 (25 Oct. 1842): 229.

66. Central and western New Yorkers dominated the leadership and the rank and file of the party. See Filler, 152.

67. In the 1844 presidential election, 15,812 Liberty votes were cast in New York state. All but 386 of those votes came from upstate—the forty-five counties north and west of the southern boundaries of Rensselaer, Albany, Schoharie, and Delaware counties. Thus 15,426 (24.8%) out of the national total of 62,323 Liberty votes came from New York's burned-over district. See T. C. Smith, 97; O. L. Holley, ed., *The New York State Register, for 1845* (Albany, N.Y.: J. Disturnell, 1845), 102–4.

68. See Ludlum, 177, 186; Roth, 291–97; John Quist, "'The Great Majority of our Subscribers are Farmers': The Michigan Abolitionist Constituency of the 1840s," *Journal of the Early Republic* 14 (Fall 1994): 344, 347–49, 356–57; Volpe, 34; Dykstra, 28–29; T. C. Smith, 326–27.

69. S. Ward, 82.

70. See Clark, 320, 324.

71. See Howe, "Evangelical Movement," 1225, 1228.

72. Judith Wellman, "The Seneca Falls Women's Rights Convention: A Study of Social Networks," *Journal of Women's History* 3, no. 1 (Spring 1991): 14–15.

73. L. Mathews, 139–69; Cross, 55–77.

74. Theodore Foster to James G. Birney, 30 Mar. 1846, in James G. Birney, *Letters of James Gillespie Birney, 1831–1857,* ed. Dwight L. Dumond (New York: D. Appleton-Century, 1938), 2:622–23; G. A. Burgess and J. T. Ward, *Free Baptist Cyclopaedia* (Chicago: Women's Temperance Publication Assoc., 1889), 21; G. Smith, *To the Liberty Party;* Lee, *Autobiography,* 293, 300, 313; S. Ward, 32–34.

75. *Madison County Abolitionist* 1 (7 Dec. 1841): 46; *The Abolitionist* 2 (11 Oct. 1842): 222. See "The National Liberty Convention" (1843), 1–3; G. Smith, *To the Liberty Party;* Charles H. Wesley, "The Participation of Negroes in Anti-Slavery Political Parties," *Journal of Negro History* 24 (Jan. 1944); Benjamin Quarles, *Black Abolitionists* (New York: Oxford Univ. Press, 1969), 184–85.

76. See George S. Conover, ed., *History of Ontario County, New York* (Syracuse, N.Y.: D. Mason, 1894), 429; Erasmus Briggs, *History of the Original Town of Concord, Being the Present Towns of Concord, Collins, North Collins, and Sardinia* (Rochester, N.Y.: Union and Advertiser, 1883), 243, 370. Griffith, a prominent Liberty man, gave money to build a Free Baptist church in East Concord and the first public high school in the town of Concord (still named Griffith Institute). Interview with Archibald Smith (grandson of Archibald Griffith), Springville, N.Y., Mar. 1988.

77. S. Ward, 53–60; Keep, 13, 19; Charles G. Finney to Smith, 7 May 1839; Ward to Smith, 26 July 1849, Gerrit Smith Papers; Ward to Nathaniel P. Rogers, 27 June 1840, in Ripley, 3:341.

78. Warsaw (New York) Presbyterian Church, *Schism the Offspring of Error,* 25; *Morning Star* 12 (2 May 1837): 2.

79. S. Ward, 74–75; C. G. Finney to Gerrit Smith, 22 July 1840, Gerrit Smith Papers.

80. S. Ward, 100; Friedman, *Gregarious Saints,* 110.

81. *Union Herald* 6 (24 Mar. 1842): 189; *Christian Investigator* 1 (June 1843): 36. Liberty leaders wanted to "hold [their] conventions in small villages" because of the enthusiastic re-

sponse which they received there. *Union Herald* 6 (27 Jan. 1842): 158. Likewise, African American ecclesiastical abolitionists encouraged their fellows to "forsake the cities and their employments of dependency." *Black Abolitionist Papers* (microfilm), 5:0498. The electoral support for the Liberty Party from large urban areas was low; see *Friend of Man* 6 (9 Nov. 1841): 24.

82. *Christian Investigator* 4 (Oct. 1846): 366; Gerrit Smith, "To the Proslavery Ministers of the County of Madison," Gerrit Smith Papers.

4. The Abolition Church

1. *Christian Investigator* 1 (30 Dec. 1843): 89–90, 96.

2. Ibid.; idem, 2 (Dec. 1843): 88. Some of the participants at the Syracuse convention included: Unionists Gerrit Smith, Beriah Green, Alvan Stewart, William Goodell, Washington Stickney, Joseph Plumb, John Truair, and J. N. T. Tucker; Wesleyan Methodists James C. DeLong and Luther Lee; Free Baptist Hiram Whitcher; and other Liberty Party leaders Charles T. Torrey, G. W. Clark, and William L. Chaplin. This list includes the leading editors and financial backers of the Liberty Party in upper New York state as well as the leaders of each of the three largest ecclesiastical abolitionist groups.

3. Goodell wrote in his personal notes on the convention that there was "general unanimity" among the participants on all points discussed. Goodell, "Syracuse Convention," Goodell Papers.

4. *Liberty Leaguer* 1 (May 1849): 16; *Christian Investigator* 6 (Aug. 1848): 528; Goodell, "Syracuse Convention," Goodell Papers; Matlack, *American Slavery and Methodism,* 337. The Wesleyan Methodists (the largest comeouter group) remained unconvinced that the Unionists would give up their Presbyterian practices.

5. *Impartial Citizen* (7 Sept. 1850), in *Black Abolitionist Papers* (microfilm), 6:0573.

6. Colton, "Political Abolition," 77–78.

7. *Niles' Register* 60 (20 Mar. 1841): 40; *Union Herald* 6 (3 June 1841): 19; ibid. (10 Feb. 1842): 163; *Christian Investigator* 1 (Feb. 1843): 8; ibid. (30 Dec. 1843): 88ff.; ibid. (Mar. 1845): 214; *Liberty Press* 4 (8 Nov. 1845): 1–2; ibid. (15 Nov. 1845): 7; *Impartial Citizen* (24 Oct. 1849), in *Black Abolitionist Papers* (microfilm), 6:0198; Antoinette Brown to Gerrit Smith, 13 Oct. 1853, Gerrit Smith Papers.

8. Historians' use of the term "sect" in referring to abolitionist comeouter groups is in accordance with today's common understanding of the word as a dissenting or schismatic religious body. The antislavery comeouters, however, repudiated the use of the term as a reference to themselves, because in nineteenth-century America the word "sect" connoted a large denominational structure (such as "the Methodist sect" or "the Lutheran sect").

9. Goen, 81–82, 146; Norman Allen Baxter, *History of the Freewill Baptists: A Study in New England Separatism* (Rochester, N.Y.: American Baptist Historical Society, 1957), 102–9; Paul Phillip Kuenning, *The Rise and Fall of American Lutheran Pietism* (Macon, Ga.: Mercer Univ. Press, 1988), 179–219; Douglas C. Stange, *Radicalism for Humanity: A Study of Lutheran Abolitionism* (St. Louis: Oliver Slave, 1970); Allen C. Thomas, "Congregational or Progressive Friends," *Bulletin of Friends' Historical Society of Philadelphia* 10 (Nov. 1920): 21–32; Donald G. Mathews, *Slavery and Methodism: A Chapter in American Morality, 1780–1845* (Princeton, N.J.: Princeton Univ. Press, 1965), 229–32; Charles Baumer Swaney, *Episcopal Methodism and Slavery, With Sidelights on Ecclesiastical Politics* (Boston: Richard G. Badger, 1926), 106–9;

Haines and Thomas, 56–59; Ira Ford McLeister and Roy Stephen Nicholson, *Conscience and Commitment: History of the Wesleyan Methodist Church of America,* 4th ed. (Marion, Ind.: Wesley, 1976), 26–51; Ludlum, 162–63.

10. After many years of interdenominational coalition building around the work of the voluntary benevolent societies, the period from 1835 through the 1850s was an era of renewed denominational parochialism. See Nichols, "Plan of Union," 29. Even during this later period, though, some religious leaders favored denominational cooperation and suggested that the existing denominations join together into an "Evangelical Alliance." Myrick and other antislavery church reformers were not impressed by this proposal; in Myrick's view, such an alliance of denominations would only compound the problem of hierarchical authoritarianism. *Christian Palladium* 8 (1 Aug. 1839): 104.

11. Keep, 19; *Lutheran Herald* 4 (15 Aug. 1842): 95.

12. *Lutheran Herald* 4 (1 June 1842): 74; ibid. n.s. 1 (13 Aug. 1844): n.p.; ibid. (4 Sept. 1844): n.p.; ibid. (8 Jan. 1845): n.p. The term "evangelic" was a synonym for "evangelical."

13. Franckean Evangelic Lutheran Synod, *Journal of the Special Meeting of the Franckean Synod of the Evangelic Lutheran Church* (Albany, N.Y.: Hoffman and White, 1837), 11, 28, 33–35; idem, *Journal of the Second Annual Session of the Franckean Evangelic Lutheran Synod, Convened at Fordsboro, Montgomery Co., June 6, 1839* (Fort Plain, N.Y.: Wm. L. Fish, 1839), 4, 6; Nicholas Van Alstine, *Historical Review of the Franckean Evangelic Lutheran Synod of New York* (Philadelphia: Lutheran Publication Society, 1893), 7, 9; Dox, *Rev. Philip Wieting,* 174.

14. Harry J. Kreider, *History of the United Lutheran Synod of New York and New England* (Philadelphia: Muhlenberg, 1954), 105ff.

15. *Lutheran Herald* 4 (1842): 42, cited in Stange, 27.

16. Much of the historiography on the Franckean Synod has emphasized their capitulation to the evangelical ideas and values of their surroundings: Wentz, 149; Stange, 1–2; Robert Fortenbaugh, "American Lutheran Synods and Slavery, 1830–1860," *Journal of Religion* 13 (Jan. 1933); idem, "The Representative Lutheran Periodical Press and Slavery, 1831–1860," *Lutheran Church Quarterly* 8 (Apr. 1935): 154ff. In contrast, Paul P. Kuenning, "New York Lutheran Abolitionists: Seeking a Solution to a Historical Enigma," *Church History* 58 (Mar. 1989): 53, contends "that the clue to the Franckeans' intense moral activism and abolitionism may have resided more in their Lutheran Pietest antecedents than in the contemporary influences of other Protestant denominations." In attempting to reclaim the Franckean's reform activities as validly Lutheran, Kuenning overemphasized the continuity of their Lutheran particularity. The Franckeans' intense moral activism was due more to their affiliation with the evangelical perfectionist church reform of the ecclesiastical abolitionist movement than it was to their pietist Lutheran heritage.

17. Dox, *Rev. Philip Wieting,* 56, 135, 142, 148ff. See Franckean Evangelic Lutheran Synod, *Journal of the Second Annual Session* (1839), 21; idem, *Journal of the Third Annual Session of the Franckean Evangelic Lutheran Synod, Convened at Stone Mills, Jefferson County, June 4, 1840* (Fort Plain, N.Y.: David Smith, 1840), 7; idem, *Journal of the First Annual Session of the Franckean Synod of the Evangelic Lutheran Church, convened at Clay, Onondaga Co., June 7, 1838* (Albany, N.Y.: Hoffman and White, 1838), 5; *Morning Star* (7 Oct. 1840): 94. The Franckeans embraced the full range of evangelical new measures, including protracted meetings, prayer meetings, extemporaneous preaching, and the "anxious seat." They were proud to call themselves "new measures Lutherans" (*Lutheran Herald* 4 [16 May 1842]: 80).

18. *Friend of Man* 3 (5 June 1839): 96. Despite his first name, Lee was a Methodist—a leader among New York state Wesleyan Methodists.

19. *Friend of Man* 2 (14 Mar. 1838): 151.

20. Franckean Evangelic Lutheran Synod, *Journal of the Third Annual Session* (1840), 8; idem, *Journal of the Sixth Annual Meeting* (1843), 4, 15; idem, *Journal of the Seventh Annual Session of the Franckean Evangelic Lutheran Synod. Convened at Parishville, Oswego Co., N.Y. June 6, 1844* (West Sandlake, N.Y.: Herald Office, 1844), 5, 24; idem, *Constitution and Standing Ordinances of the Franckean Evangelic Lutheran Synod. Together with a Discipline, Recommended as a Guide for the government of Churches* (Cooperstown, N.Y.: H. and E. Phinney, 1839), 6, 12, 19, 35, 55.

21. *Lutheran Herald* 3 (15 Apr. 1841): 61–62; ibid. (1 Oct. 1841): 145; ibid. 4 (15 Oct. 1842): 110; ibid. n.s. 1 (13 Nov. 1844): n.p.; ibid. (11 Dec. 1844): n.p.; ibid. (11 June 1845): n.p.

22. *Lutheran Herald* 2 (16 Dec. 1840): 93; ibid. 3 (1 Apr. 1841): 49; ibid. (15 July 1841): 110; ibid. (1 Nov. 1841): 165; ibid. 4 (1 Dec. 1842): 122. The Franckeans followed Finney's theological evolution concerning the doctrine of entire sanctification. During their "Wesleyan" phase in the early 1840s, they believed in two works of God's grace—justification and entire sanctification (ibid. 2 [16 Dec. 1840]: 95). A few years later (along with Finney), they continued to affirm the doctrine of Christian perfection, but they were less confident that the "theory of our Methodist brethren" regarding two separate soteriological events was the best interpretation of holiness (ibid. n.s. 1 [2 Oct. 1844]: n.p.; ibid. [30 Oct. 1844]: n.p.).

23. Franckean Evangelic Lutheran Synod, *Journal of the Third Annual Session* (1840), 23; idem, *Constitution and Standing Ordinances,* 18–19.

24. Franckean Evangelic Lutheran Synod, *Journal of the First Annual Session* (1838), 5, 10, 15, 16–18, 30–31; idem, *Journal of the Second Annual Session* (1839), 13; idem, *Journal of the Third Annual Session* (1840), 18–19; idem, *Journal of the Sixth Annual Meeting* (1843), 6, 15; idem, *Journal of the Eighth Annual Session of the Franckean Evangelic Lutheran Synod, Convened at Argusville, Schoharie Co., N.Y., On the 5th day of June, 1845* (West Sandlake, N.Y.: Lutheran Herald Office, 1845), 9, 16–19, 23; idem, *Journal of the Ninth Annual Session of the Franckean Evangelic Lutheran Synod, Convened at Fordsboro, Montgomery Co., N.Y., June 4th, 1846* (Albany, N.Y.: J. Munsell, 1846), 16, 26, 28; idem, *Journal of the Eleventh Annual Session of the Franckean Evangelic Lutheran Synod, Convened at Rush, Monroe Co., N.Y. On the 1st day of June, 1848* (Leesville, N.Y.: American Christian Office, 1848), 18; idem, *Constitution and Standing Ordinances,* 51–56.

25. Franckean Evangelic Lutheran Synod, *Journal of the Sixth Annual Meeting* (1843), 9; Sernett, 46; *Lutheran Herald* 4 (15 Oct. 1842): 110. Franckeans agreed to "patronize abolition schools and none other" and "vote for abolition candidates for law-maker and none other" (ibid. [15 Aug. 1842]: 95).

26. Franckean Evangelic Lutheran Synod, *Journal of the Third Annual Session* (1840), 9; idem, *Journal of the Sixth Annual Meeting* (1843), 20; idem, *Journal of the Eighth Annual Session* (1845), 10, 18; idem, *Constitution and Standing Ordinances,* 53. The Franckeans' secessionist slogan—that they would rather be "first pure and then peaceable"—was identical language to the slogans used by the Unionists and by the Wesleyan Methodists. See idem, *Journal of the Seventh Annual Session* (1844), 8.

27. Franckean Evangelic Lutheran Synod, *Journal of the Third Annual Session* (1840), 4, 9, 21–22. Like Myrick, the Franckeans were among "those who prefer[red] Religious liberty to Ecclesiastical slavery" (*Union Herald* 6 [6 May 1841]: 5).

28. Franckean Evangelic Lutheran Synod, *Journal of the Second Annual Session* (1839), 4; John D. Lawyer, "President's Address," idem, *Journal of the Special Meeting* (1837), 33–35;

idem, *Journal of the Second Annual Session* (1839), 21; idem, *Journal of the Third Annual Session* (1840), 23; idem, *Journal of the Fourth Annual Session* (1841), 16; idem, *Constitution and Standing Ordinances*, 2; *Lutheran Herald* 2 (16 Sept. 1840): 69. The Franckeans expunged all parts of the Lutheran Discipline that indicated that a synod had legislative force over its congregations (idem, *Journal of the Special Meeting*, 11). The "spiritual democracy" language that the Franckeans used in their *Constitution* (8) to describe their congregational polity was the same as that used by other comeouters. Cf. Arcade Congregational Church, Declaration of Sentiments, China (New York) Congregationalist Church records, vol. 2, 11 Aug. 1849; *Christian Investigator* 1 (30 Dec. 1843): 90ff.

29. Franckean Evangelic Lutheran Synod, *Journal of the Second Annual Session* (1839), 16; *Christian Investigator* 1 (Mar. 1843): 10; ibid. (Apr. 1843): 24.

30. Franckean Evangelic Lutheran Synod, *Journal of the Third Annual Session* (1840), 15–16; idem, *Journal of the Tenth Annual Session* (1847), 5, 16. The Franckeans drew up a *Constitution* for doctrine and polity, but it was never called a creed, and it was justified as being simply a "summary statement" of biblical doctrines "arranged in a conspicuous and regular order" (idem, *Constitution and Standing Ordinances*, 2; *Union Herald* 6 [11 Aug. 1841]: 60).

31. *Lutheran Herald* n.s. 1 (13 Nov. 1844): n.p.; Van Alstine, *Historical Review*, 16–17; Dox, *Rev. Philip Wieting*, 172; Franckean Evangelic Lutheran Synod, *Journal of the Special Meeting* (1837), 29–30; idem, *Journal of the Tenth Annual Session* (1847), 5.

32. Franckean Evangelic Lutheran Synod, *Journal of the Special Meeting* (1837), 12, 24, 29ff.; Van Alstine, *Historical Review*, 16–17. See also Lewis H. Sanford, *State of New-York. In Chancery. Philip Kniskern and others, v. Philip Wieting, The Evangelical Lutheran Churches of St. John's at Durlach, and St. Peter's at New Rhinebeck in Sharon; and others. Opinion of the Honorable Lewis H. Sandford, Assistant Vice-Chancellor, July 17th, 1844* (New York: William Osborn, 1845); John D. Lawyer, *Letter to the Hon. Lewis H. Sandford, Assistant Vice Chancellor* (Albany, N.Y.: E. H. Pease, 1846). Kuenning asserts that the "alleged" doctrinal aberrations of the Franckeans were "only connected to their abolitionism in an oblique manner, if at all" (*Rise and Fall*, 219). In fact, the Franckeans' perfectionist doctrinal stance was central to their political abolitionism and to their antislavery church reform endeavors, just as it was for the other abolitionist comeouters of the burned-over district.

33. Franckean Evangelic Lutheran Synod, *Journal of the Special Meeting* (1837), 11, 32–36; idem, *Journal of the Second Annual Session* (1839), 4, 6, 21; idem, *Journal of the Third Annual Session* (1840), 4, 14–16, 22, 31; idem, *Journal of the Fourth Annual Session* (1841), 16, 24–25; idem, *Journal of the Fifth Annual Session* (1842), 12–14, 24, 28; idem, *Journal of the Seventh Annual Session* (1844), 4; idem, *Journal of the Ninth Annual Session* (1846), 7, 27; idem, *Journal of the Tenth Annual Session* (1847), 16.

34. Van Alstine, *Historical Review*, 12; James A. Miller, *The History of the Presbytery of Steuben* (Angelica, N.Y.: Allegany County Republican, 1897), 92; *Lutheran Herald* 4 (1 Dec. 1842): 123; Oswego County (New York), 217, 432; Franckean Evangelic Lutheran Synod, *Journal of the Third Annual Session* (1840), 7; idem, *Journal of the Fourth Annual Session* (1841), 10, 12, 19; idem, *Journal of the Sixth Annual Meeting* (1843), 4; idem, *Journal of the Ninth Annual Session* (1846), 6; *Morning Star* 15 (7 Oct. 1840): 94; *Lutheran Herald* 2 (16 Oct. 1840): 79 [incorrectly paginated 83]; ibid. (2 Nov. 1840): 81; ibid. 4 (15 Dec. 1842): 125. Beriah Green was a close friend of the synod (*Lutheran Herald* n.s. 1 [13 Nov. 1844]: n.p.; ibid. [11 Dec. 1844]: n.p.; ibid. [11 June 1845]: n.p.) and several Franckean leaders were directly influenced by William Goodell (*Friend of Man* 2 [14 Mar. 1838]: 151; ibid. 3 [24 July 1839]: 23; *Christian Investigator* 1 [Feb. 1843]: 8; ibid. 5 [May 1847]: 410).

35. *Liberty Press* 4 (15 Nov. 1845): 7.

36. *Lutheran Herald* 3 (1 Nov. 1841): 162; ibid. 4 (15 Aug. 1842): 95; ibid. (1 Nov. 1842): 115; ibid. n.s. 1 (4 Sept. 1844): n.p.; ibid. (18 Sept. 1844): n.p.; ibid. (2 Oct. 1844): n.p.; ibid. (16 Oct. 1844): n.p.; ibid. (30 Oct. 1844): n.p.; ibid. (11 Dec. 1844): n.p.; ibid. (11 June 1845): n.p.

37. If one compares the Liberty vote totals within each county, the Liberty vote totals in towns with Franckean churches were higher than the Liberty vote totals for neighboring towns without Franckean churches. See Douglas M. Strong, "Organized Liberty: Evangelical Perfectionism, Political Abolitionism, and Ecclesiastical Reform in the Burned-Over District" (Ph.D. diss., Princeton Theological Seminary, 1990), 339–82.

38. *Lutheran Herald* n.s. 1 (2 Oct. 1844): n.p.; Franckean Evangelic Lutheran Synod, *Journal of the Eighth Annual Session* (1845), 18–19. One resolution urged the entire Franckean Synod to attend the national antislavery convention that first recommended political action. Idem, *Journal of the Second Annual Session* (1839), 22.

39. *Liberty Press* 4 (15 Nov. 1845): 7. The hamlet of Ames is in the town of Canajoharie. There was also a Franckean congregation in that small hamlet. Canajoharie had the highest Liberty vote of any town in Montgomery County.

40. Nicholas Van Alstine et al., *A Reunion of Ministers and Churches* (Philadelphia: Lutheran Publication Society, 1881), 14–15; Franckean Evangelic Lutheran Synod, *Journal of the Eleventh Annual Session* (1847), 16, 18; idem, *Journal of the Fourth Annual Session* (1841), 8.

41. Franckean Evangelic Lutheran Synod, *Journal of the Fourth Annual Session* (1841), 8; idem, *Journal of the Sixth Annual Meeting* (1843), 5, 6–7; Dox, *Rev. Philip Wieting*, 177–81.

42. Franckean Evangelic Lutheran Synod, *Journal of the Twelfth Annual Session of the Franckean Evangelic Lutheran Synod, Convened at Gardnersville, Schoharie Co., N.Y. On The 7th day of June, 1849* (Rochester, N.Y.: Rochester Daily Advertiser and Republican, 1849), 6.

43. The story of the antislavery crusade within Methodism is told in Matlack, *American Slavery and Methodism;* idem, *The Antislavery Struggle and Triumph in the Methodist Episcopal Church* (New York: Phillips and Hunt, 1887); La Roy Sunderland, *The Testimony of God Against Slavery: A Collection of Passages from the Bible Which Show the Sin of Holding and Treating The Human Species As Property* (Boston: Isaac Knapp, 1836); Orange Scott, *An Appeal to the Methodist Episcopal Church* (Boston: David H. Ela, 1838); idem, *Methodist E[piscopal] Church and Slavery;* James G. Birney, *Debate on "Modern Abolitionism," in the General Conference of the Methodist Episcopal Church, May, 1836* (Cincinnati: Ohio Anti-Slavery Society, 1836); Swaney; Mathews, *Slavery and Methodism.*

44. Bassett, 309; J. Gordon Melton, "Reformed Methodist Church," in *Encyclopedia of World Methodism,* ed. Nolan B. Harmon (Nashville: United Methodist Publishing House, 1974); Nutt, 16–25. The concerns of the Reformed Methodists and the Methodist Protestants resembled one another; in 1838, a large portion of the former sect joined with the latter sect. The Republican Methodists (led by James O'Kelly) and the African Union Church (based in Wilmington, Delaware) were also similar in regard to their interest in spiritual democracy, but neither of these groups had a significant presence in upper New York state.

45. Accounts of the formation and development of the Wesleyan Methodist Connection are found in Matlack, *Antislavery Struggle;* idem, *American Slavery and Methodism;* idem, *Orange Scott.* See also Dayton, *Discovering;* Lee, *Five Sermons;* idem, *Autobiography;* Lee and Smith; McLeister and Nicholson, 4th ed., 26–51; Chris Padgett, "Hearing the Antislavery Rank-and-File: The Wesleyan Methodist Schism of 1843," *Journal of the Early Republic* 12 (Spring 1992): 63–84.

46. *Union Herald* 6 (15 July 1841): 47; ibid. 6 (30 Dec. 1841): 141; *Liberty Press* 3 (1 Mar. 1845): 66; Matlack, *American Slavery and Methodism*, 303; Daniel E. Wager, ed., *Our County and Its People: A Descriptive Work on Oneida County, New York* (Boston: Boston History, 1896), 186–87; Bassett, 309, 522. High Bridge is near Fayetteville, town of Manlius, Onondaga County; here, Bailey published the *Fayetteville Luminary* (beginning in 1839) and the *Methodist Reformer* (1841–42). Harmon, 2:1997.

47. "Wesley Bailey" [Obituary], *Utica Sunday Times* 14 (1 Mar. 1891): 2; *Friend of Man* 6 (28 July 1836): 23; *Christian Investigator* 1 (Dec. 1843): 88. The *Liberty Press* was the successor to two papers, Bailey and Myrick's *The Abolitionist* and the *Friend of Man* (the organ of the New York State Anti-Slavery Society, edited by William Goodell).

48. Rather than the hierarchical-sounding title "Presiding Elder" used by Methodist Episcopals for their district supervisors, Bailey was designated by the more collegial title of "Chairman." See Ira Ford McLeister and Roy Stephen Nicholson, *History of the Wesleyan Methodist Church,* 3rd ed. (Marion, Ind.: Wesley, 1959), 30–31, 33, 41, 380; Stanley W. Wright et al., *One Hundred Years of Service for Christ in the Wesleyan Methodist Church, 1844–1944* [Rochester Conference] (N.p.: n.d. [1944?]), 46; Aldis M. Lamos, ed., *One Hundred and Twenty-Five Years For Christ, 1843–1968: History of the Champlain Conference of the Wesleyan Methodist Church of America* (N.p.: n.d. [1968?]), 5; Wesleyan Methodist Connection, "Record of the Rochester or Western New York Conference, Held in Seneca Falls, April 30–May 5, 1845," manuscript in Wesleyan Church Archives, Indianapolis, Ind.; George Pegler, *Autobiography of the Life and Times of the Rev. George Pegler. Written by Himself* (Syracuse, N.Y.: Wesleyan Methodist Publishing House, 1879). For the important role played by the Reformed Methodists in the formation of the Wesleyan Methodist Connection, especially in New York state, see Matlack, *American Slavery and Methodism,* 334, 344, 348.

49. T. L. Smith, *Revivalism and Social Reform,* 212, indicates that it was Phoebe Palmer's articulation of perfectionism in the late 1840s that was "politically explosive" when combined with the Wesleyan Methodists' reformist persuasion. In fact, the Wesleyan Methodists' politically explosive positions were already well developed in the early 1840s, built upon the evangelical perfectionism of burned-over district ecclesiastical abolitionists such as William Goodell, Beriah Green, Gerrit Smith, Wesley Bailey, and Charles Finney. See Fletcher, 256; Wilcox, 127.

50. Wesleyan Methodist Connection, *The Discipline of the Wesleyan Methodist Connection of America* (Boston: O. Scott, 1843); idem, "Minutes of the Rochester or Western New York Conference," Wesleyan Church Archives. Cf. Franckean Evangelic Lutheran Synod, *Constitution and Standing Ordinances,* 18–19; idem, *Journal of the Third Annual Session* (1840), 23.

51. Haines and Thomas, 34, 60.

52. Lee, *Five Sermons,* 11. See also "Pastoral Address Of the Convention assembled at Utica, N.Y., May 31, 1843, for the purpose of organizing the Wesleyan Methodist Church," in Matlack, *American Slavery and Methodism,* 343; idem, *Orange Scott,* 248–50.

53. Lucille Sider Dayton and Donald W. Dayton, "'Your Daughters Shall Prophecy': Feminism in the Holiness Movement," *Methodist History* 14 (Jan. 1976): 85–86; Strong, "Crusade for Women's Rights," 132–60; William H. Brackney, "The Fruits of a Crusade: Wesleyan Opposition to Secret Societies," *Methodist History* 17 (July 1979): 239–52; Lee and Smith; Wesleyan Methodist Connection, "Minutes of the Champlain Annual Conference, June 26, 1844, meeting in Keeseville, N.Y.," Wesleyan Church Archives; Carol M. Hunter, *To Set the Captives Free: Reverend Jermain Wesley Loguen and the Struggle for Freedom in Central New York, 1835–1872* (New York: Garland, 1993), 216.

54. Wesleyan Methodist Connection, "Minutes of the Champlain Annual Conference," Wesleyan Church Archives; O. Scott, *Methodist E[piscopal] Church and Slavery,* 76–79, 86–88, 93, 98, 111–12, 126.

55. See Douglas M. Strong, "Partners in Political Abolitionism: The Liberty Party and the Wesleyan Methodist Connection," *Methodist History* 23 (Jan. 1985): 99–115.

56. *Liberty Press* 3 (16 Nov. 1844): 3, 6; ibid. (23 Nov. 1844): 9; ibid. (11 Jan. 1845): 37; ibid. 4 (29 Nov. 1845): 15; ibid. (17 Jan. 1846): 41; Swaney, 107.

57. Ludlum, 177, 186. See Wesleyan Methodist Connection, "Record of the First Meeting of the New York Conference of the Wesleyan Methodist Connection of America, held in Syracuse, June 1844," "Minutes of the Champlain Conference," 1844, 36–37, and "Minutes of the Rochester or Western New York Conference," 1845, Wesleyan Church Archives; Short Tract, New York, Wesleyan Methodist Church, "Minutes of Quarterly Meetings, 1850–1906," Houghton College Archives, Houghton, N.Y.; S. Wright et al., 11; *Christian Investigator* 3 (Aug. 1845): 255; *True Wesleyan* 1 (8 Apr. 1843): 155; ibid. (23 Dec. 1843): 203; *American Jubilee* 1 (Feb. 1855): 74. See also Strong, "Partners in Political Abolitionism," 109–11; Swaney, 36n, 115.

58. On Lee, see his *Autobiography;* Paul Leslie Kaufman, "'Logical' Luther Lee and the Methodist War Against Slavery" (Ph.D. diss., Kent State Univ., 1994); William C. Kostlevy, "Luther Lee and Methodist Abolitionism," *Methodist History* 20 (Jan. 1982): 90–103.

59. Lee, *Autobiography,* 217, 227, 281; *Liberty Press* 3 (23 Nov. 1844): 9.

60. Matlack, *American Slavery and Methodism,* 10, 303, 309, 312ff., 340; *True Wesleyan* 1 (8 Apr. 1843): 155; O. Scott, *Methodist E[piscopal] Church and Slavery,* 72; *Union Herald* 6 (20 May 1841): 11; Wesleyan Methodist Connection, *Discipline* (1843). See also *True Wesleyan* 1 (8 Nov. 1842): 1.

61. *Liberty Press* 4 (29 Nov. 1845): 15; William Adams, ed., *Historical Gazateer and Biographical Memorial of Cattaraugus County, N.Y.* (Syracuse, N.Y.: Lyman, Horton, 1893), 451–52, 750–51; Lee and Smith, 458–61; Wesleyan Methodist Connection, "Minutes of the Champlain Annual Conference, Meeting in West Chazy, N.Y., 1843," Wesleyan Church Archives.

62. *Friend of Man* 2 (21 Mar. 1838): 151; ibid. 3 (5 June 1839): 196, 197; Matlack, *American Slavery and Methodism,* 201; *Lutheran Herald* 3 (1 Oct. 1841): 145; *Christian Investigator* 1 (Aug. 1843): 56; ibid. (Dec. 1843): 88–90; Goodell, "Syracuse Convention," Goodell Papers.

63. *Christian Investigator* 2 (Dec. 1843): 88. See also Goodell, "Syracuse Convention," Goodell Papers. Goodell did not believe that the Unionists had any vestiges of Presbyterianism left, but evidently the Wesleyan Methodists believed that they did.

64. Luther Lee, *Wesleyan Manual: A Defence of the Organization of the Wesleyan Methodist Connection* (Syracuse, N.Y.: Samuel Lee, 1862), 113; *Christian Investigator* 1 (Dec. 1843): 88; Matlack, *Orange Scott,* 163; idem, *American Slavery and Methodism,* 340.

65. See William B. Gravely, *Gilbert Haven, Methodist Abolitionist: A Study of Race, Religion, and Reform, 1850–1880* (Nashville: Abingdon, 1973).

66. *Union Herald* 6 (23 Sept. 1841): 82; ibid. (30 Dec. 1841): 141; Mathews, *Slavery and Methodism,* 230.

67. Lee, *Autobiography,* 217, 248; Matlack, *Orange Scott,* 256; Goodell, *Slavery and Anti-Slavery,* 490.

68. Matlack, *Orange Scott,* 202–3, 255–57; Lee and Smith, 477. Scott's relative conservatism was illustrated in his refusal to work for reform in women's rights, a position in sharp contrast to Lee's fervent feminism. Strong, "Partners in Political Abolitionism," 104; Dayton, *Discover-*

ing an Evangelical Heritage, 91. Scott's institutionalism was also indicated by his hope that the new group would be called the "Wesleyan Methodist *Church*" and not a looser "*Connection*" (McLeister and Nicholson, *History,* 3rd ed., 37–38). On the career of Orange Scott, see Donald G. Mathews, "Orange Scott: The Methodist Evangelist as Revolutionary," in *The Antislavery Vanguard: New Essays on the Abolitionists,* ed. Martin Duberman (Princeton, N.J.: Princeton Univ. Press, 1965), 71–101.

69. Lee and Smith, 476–77; McLeister and Nicholson, *History,* 3rd ed., 38; Swaney, 106; *Christian Investigator* 2 (July 1844): 151; ibid. 6 (Aug. 1848): 528.

70. *Christian Investigator* 2 (Dec. 1843): 88; ibid. 2 (Aug. 1844): 152; ibid. 6 (Aug. 1848): 528; Goodell, "Syracuse Convention," Goodell Papers; Matlack, *American Slavery and Methodism,* 337; McLeister and Nicholson, *History,* 3rd ed., 38, 77.

71. Goodell ridiculed Lee's "connexional principle" as inevitably leading toward unwarranted denominational control over congregations. Lee, on the other hand, was displeased with the lack of any regularly constituted coordinating body in the Unionists' polity. See *Christian Investigator* 6 (Aug. 1848): 512, 528; Goodell, "Syracuse Convention," Goodell Papers; Matlack, *American Slavery and Methodism,* 337.

72. J. M. Brewster, *Fidelity and Usefulness. Life of William Burr* (Dover, N.H.: F. Baptist Printing Establishment, 1871), 41, 122; Butler, *Natural and Revealed Theology,* 159ff.; Freewill Baptist General Conference, *Treatise on the Faith,* 7–8, 57–65, 94–95; *Morning Star* 18 (21 Nov. 1843): 122; Marini, 64–67.

73. Many emigrants who had been Congregationalists in New England, such as Ezra Brewster Strong, became Free Baptists after their arrival in the burned-over district.

74. Since the Free Communion Baptists existed only in New York state, the merger of the two groups affected only those Freewill Baptists who were in New York. In New England, the sect continued to be called "Freewill Baptist," while in New York the congregations of the newly merged organization tended to be called "Free Baptists." See Baxter, 1n.; Freewill Baptist Connection, *The Centennial Record of Freewill Baptists, 1780–1880* (Dover, N.H.: Printing Establishment, 1881), 31–32.

75. "The Anniversary of the Freewill Baptist Anti-Slavery Society, Great Falls, N.H., October 18, 1843," *Morning Star* 18 (8 Nov. 1843): 114; Freewill Baptist Anti-Slavery Society, *Fifth Annual Report of the Free-Will Baptist Anti-Slavery Society, Read at Lebanon, Maine, October 9, 1851* (Dover, N.H.: Wm. Burr, 1851), 6–10, 21.

76. Selah Hibbard Barrett, ed., *Memoirs of Eminent Preachers in the Freewill Baptist Denomination* (Rutland, Ohio: 1874), 180–81; *Morning Star* 16 (6 Oct. 1841): 94; ibid. 19 (16 Oct. 1844): 101; ibid. (30 Oct. 1844): 110; Burgess and Ward, 383–84; Fletcher, 255–56.

77. *Morning Star* 18 (16 Aug. 1843): 66; Freewill Baptist General Conference, *Treatise on the Faith,* 70–71.

78. Freewill Baptist General Conference, *Treatise on the Faith,* 68–72. See Butler, *Natural and Revealed Theology,* 191–94, 276–84; idem, *Thoughts on the Benevolent Enterprises, Embracing the Subjects of Missions, Sabbath Schools, Temperance, Abolition of Slavery, and Peace* (Dover, N.H.: Trustees of the Freewill Baptist Connection, 1840), 78, 172; *Morning Star* 16 (23 June 1841): 33; ibid. (1 Dec. 1841): 127; ibid. 18 (23 Aug. 1843): 69; Brewster, 123.

79. *Friend of Man* 3 (21 Mar. 1838): 151.

80. See appendix A.

81. Freewill Baptist Anti-Slavery Society, 23; *Morning Star* 18 (8 Nov. 1843): 114.

82. *Morning Star* 16 (10 Nov. 1841): 115.

83. Marilla Marks, ed., *Memoirs of the Life of David Marks, Minister of the Gospel* (Dover, N.H.: Free-Will Baptist Printing Establishment, 1846), 408–10; J. Woodbury Scribner, "Centennial Paper for the New Hampshire Yearly Meeting, 1892," manuscript, American Baptist Historical Society, Rochester, N.Y.; *Morning Star* 18 (18 Oct. 1843): 103.

84. Besides Whitcher and Marks, other Free Baptist Liberty advocates included William Dick and Moses M. Smart. Burgess and Ward, 162, 601; *Morning Star* 18 (8 Nov. 1843): 114.

85. "St. Lawrence Quarterly Meeting, September 1843," in *Morning Star* 18 (18 Oct. 1843): 103; Freewill Baptist Anti-Slavery Society, 24, 28. See also "Holland Purchase Yearly Meeting, June 1841," in *Morning Star* 16 (14 July 1841): 46.

86. Freewill Baptist Anti-Slavery Society, 23.

87. Freewill Baptist General Conference, *Treatise on the Faith,* 14.

88. Marks, 408; *Morning Star* 16 (14 July 1841): 46; ibid. 12 (17 May 1837): 11; ibid. 15 (28 Oct. 1840): 106; Freewill Baptist Connection, *Centennial Record,* 217; Burgess and Ward, 91, 601; Sernett, 61, 105–6.

89. Franckean Evangelic Lutheran Synod, *Journal of the Third Annual Session* (1840), 7; *Journal of the Fourth Annual Session* (1841), 12. See *Morning Star* 18 (6 Sept. 1843): 80; ibid. 15 (7 Oct. 1840): 94.

90. *Union Herald* 6 (24 Feb. 1842): 170–71; *Morning Star* 16 (3 Nov. 1841): 112; ibid. 19 (6 Nov. 1844): 116.

91. Quaker factionalism and attitudes toward slavery are discussed in William Hodgson, *The Society of Friends in the Nineteenth Century: A Historical View of the Successive Convulsions and Schisms Therein During That Period,* 2 vols. (Philadelphia: Smith, English, 1876); Thomas E. Drake, *Quakers and Slavery in America* (New Haven, Conn.: Yale Univ. Press, 1950), 174–75; H. Larry Ingle, *Quakers in Conflict: The Hicksite Reformation* (Knoxville: Univ. of Tennessee Press, 1986); and Thomas D. Hamm, *The Transformation of American Quakerism: Orthodox Friends, 1800–1907* (Bloomington: Indiana Univ. Press, 1988), 15–35.

92. James and Lucretia Mott, *James and Lucretia Mott, Life and Letters,* 278, cited in A. Thomas, 22; *Friends' Intelligencer* 5 (16 Dec. 1848): 300–301, cited in A. Thomas, 27; Goodell, *Slavery and Anti-Slavery,* 551.

93. Waterloo (New York) Yearly Meeting of Congregational Friends, *Earnest and Affectionate Address to all people, and especially religious professors of every name, and an address to reformers: from the Yearly Meeting of Congregational Friends, held at Waterloo, N.Y.* (Auburn, N.Y.: Oliphant's Press, 1849), 13, 16; idem, *Proceedings of the Yearly Meeting of Congregational Friends, Held at Waterloo, N.Y., From the 4th to the 6th of Sixth Month, inclusive, 1849* (Auburn, N.Y.: Oliphant's Press, 1849), 6, 10–11, 12; James and Lucretia Mott, cited in A. Thomas, 22.

94. Many of the Congregational Friends were closely affiliated with the Garrison wing of the abolitionist movement. Wellman, "Seneca Falls," 24; Nancy Hewitt, "The Perimeters of Women's Power in American Religion," in *The Evangelical Tradition in America,* ed. Leonard I. Sweet (Macon, Ga.: Mercer Univ. Press, 1984), 235. Nonetheless, there is evidence of Congregational Friends' support for the Liberty Party: *Liberty Party Paper* 2 (21 May 1851); A. Thomas, 25. Given the ability of some upper New York Liberty supporters (such as Luther Myrick and James C. Jackson) to remain associated with the Garrisonians at the same time that they were active political abolitionists, it would not be surprising if other Garrisonians in New York state were willing to vote for Liberty. Nancy A. Hewitt, *Women's Activism and Social Change: Rochester, New York, 1822–1872* (Ithaca, N.Y.: Cornell Univ. Press, 1984), 149.

95. Waterloo (New York) Yearly Meeting of Congregational Friends, *Earnest and Affectionate Address,* 16; A. Thomas, 28; Wellman, "Seneca Falls," 25; Hewitt, *Women's Activism,* 135.

96. Waterloo (New York) Yearly Meeting of Congregational Friends, *Proceedings,* 4; idem, *Earnest and Affectionate Address,* 13; A. Thomas, 25, 28.

97. Waterloo (New York) Yearly Meeting of Congregational Friends, *Proceedings,* 13–14; idem, *Earnest and Affectionate Address,* 1; Levinus K. Painter, *The Collins Story* (Gowanda, N.Y.: Niagara Frontier, 1962), 70; A. Thomas, 28. Only two regional Yearly Meetings have been identified (Waterloo, in central New York, and Collins, in western New York). Neither Yearly Meeting could have consisted of more than just a few small congregations.

98. *Christian Investigator* 5 (May 1847): 409. See also ibid. 2 (Oct. 1844): 174.

99. C. D. Johnson, *Islands of Holiness,* 125; *Liberty Press* 3 (8 Mar. 1845): 69.

100. Signor, 550–51.

101. *Friend of Man* 2 (21 Mar. 1838): 151; ibid. (5 June 1839): 197; *Christian Investigator* 1 (Dec. 1843): 88.

102. *Liberty Press* 3 (8 Mar. 1845): 69; ibid. 4 (13 Dec. 1845): 23; Elliot G. Storke, *History of Cayuga County, New York* (Syracuse, N.Y.: D. Mason, 1879), 294.

103. *Chautauqua Baptist Association, Reorganized, Minutes, 1845,* cited in Rowe, "New Perspective," 417–18; S. S. Crissey, *Centennial History of the Fredonia Baptist Church, 1808–1908* (Buffalo: Matthews-Northrup, 1908), 52; *Christian Investigator* 2 (Mar. 1844): 120.

104. *Christian Investigator* (May 1844): 136.

105. American Baptist Free Mission Society, *Review of the Operations of the American Baptist Free Mission Society, For The Past Year* (Bristol, England: Mathews, 1851), 2–3.

106. Frank D. Roberts, *History of the Town of Perry, New York* (Perry: C. G. Clark, 1915), 161–62; Levi Parsons, compiler, *Centennial Celebration, Mt. Morris, N.Y., August 15, 1894* (Mt. Morris, N.Y.: Mt. Morris Union, 1894), 145; *Niles' Register* 60 (Mar. 20, 1841): 40; *Christian Investigator* 2 (Mar. 1844): 136.

107. Elon Galusha, *Address of Elder Elon Galusha, with Reasons for Believing Christ's Second Coming, At Hand* (Rochester, N.Y.: Erastus Shepard, 1844), 3–4, 14, 17; David L. Rowe, "Elon Galusha and the Millerite Movement," *Foundations* 18 (July–Sept. 1975): 252–60.

108. *Christian Investigator* 2 (May 1844): 136.

109. During the 1840s, an Adventist was a follower of William Miller's premillennial predictions that Christ's second coming (and the consequent dramatic consummation of human history resulting from that event) was immediately at hand. Adventists differed in their degree of support for Miller's very specific dating of "the Lord's return." Miller dated the second coming in 1843, and later revised the date to October 22, 1844. Earlier interpretations of Millerism (as described in Jonathan M. Butler and Ronald L. Numbers, *The Disappointed: Millerism and Millenarianism in the Nineteenth Century* [Bloomington: Indiana Univ. Press, 1987], xv–xxi]) have been superseded by several recent monographs: Ruth Alden Doan, "Millerism and Evangelical Culture," in Butler and Numbers, 118–38; idem, *The Miller Heresy, Millennialism, and American Culture* (Philadelphia: Temple Univ. Press, 1987); David L. Rowe, *Thunder and Trumpets: Millerites and Dissenting Religion in Upstate New York, 1800–1850* (Chico, Calif.: Scholars Press, 1985); Barkun.

110. Ronald D. Graybill, "The Abolitionist-Millerite Connection," in Butler and Numbers, 139.

111. Galusha, 11, 19; *Union Herald* 6 (4 Nov. 1841): 109; Ruth Alden Doan, "Perfectionism in the Adventist Tradition," paper given at the Wesleyan/Holiness Study Conference, Asbury

Theological Seminary, Wilmore, Ky., 11 June 1988; idem, "Millerism and Evangelical Culture," 127–28.

112. Doan, "Perfectionism in the Adventist Tradition," 18–20.

113. Joshua V. Himes was a Christian Connection itinerant urned Millerite who was closely associated with anarchistic, nonresistant preachers. *Christian Palladium* 8 (1 Aug. 1839): 104; ibid. (15 Aug. 1839): 121, 123; *Union Herald* 6 (4 Nov. 1841); ibid. (18 Nov. 1841); ibid. (30 Dec. 1841); G. Noyes, 143; Graybill, 141–42, 149.

114. Cited in Doan, "Millerism and Evangelical Culture," 132. See also Graybill, 143, 149–50.

115. Rowe ("New Perspective," 412, and "Elon Galusha," 252, 258ff.) makes a distinction between "moderate" and "radical" Adventists.

116. Galusha, 17–19; *Liberty Press* 4 (8 Nov. 1845): 1; "The National Liberty Convention," *Emancipator Extra* (Sept. 1843): 2; Doan, "Millerism and Evangelical Culture," 133.

117. Galusha, 17–19.

118. *Liberty Press* 4 (8 Nov. 1845): 1; Rowe, "Elon Galusha," 255–57.

119. Galusha, 19; Francis D. Nichol, *The Midnight Cry: A Defense of William Miller and the Millerites* (Washington, D.C.: Review and Herald, 1944), 165.

120. *Oberlin Evangelist* 3 (23 June 1841): 102; ibid. (21 July 1841): 120; ibid. (4 Aug. 1841): 125; *Union Herald* 6 (17 June 1841): 26; ibid. (12 Aug. 1841): 59; Edward P. Marvin, *Semi-Centennary Sketch of the Presbytery of Niagara, 1824–1874* (Lockport, N.Y.: Daily Union Office, 1875), 5, 8; Levi Parsons, *History of Rochester Presbytery from the Earliest Settlement of the Country* (Rochester, N.Y.: Democrat-Chronicle, 1889), 136, 227, 256–57; Ferdinand D. Ward, *Churches of Rochester* (Rochester, N.Y.: Erastus Darrow, 1870), 149–50.

121. Parsons, *Rochester Presbytery*, 222, 227, 231, 293; John O. Gordon, *An Historical Sermon Preached in the Presbyterian Church, Rensselaerville, N.Y., July 2nd, 1876* (Albany, N.Y.: Van Benthuysen, 1876); *Union Herald* 6 (10 Feb. 1842): 163.

122. Parsons, *Rochester Presbytery*, 145; John F. Reynolds, *The Almond Story: The Early Years* (Hornell, N.Y.: John F. Reynolds, 1962), 84; Mary R. Root, *History of the Town of York, Livingston County, New York* (Caledonia, N.Y.: Big Springs Historical Society, 1940), 120; Conover, 436, 456, 462; Adams, 451–52, 1038; James H. Smith, *History of Chenango and Madison Counties, New York* (Syracuse, N.Y.: D. Mason, 1880), 436, 485; Sherburne (New York) Free Church, *Organization and Membership of the Free Church of Sherburne (1847–1856)* (N.p.: n.d.); Storke, 294; Westmoreland (New York) First Congregational Church, *Exercises in Commemoration of the Centennial Anniversary of the First Congregational Church of Westmoreland, N.Y., Tuesday, September 20th, 1892* (Clinton, N.Y.: J. B. and H. B. Sykes, 1893), 17; Franklin B. Hough, *History of Lewis County, New York* (Syracuse, N.Y.: D. Mason, 1883), 194; Elizabeth Hagan, ed., *Poland, New York: Past and Present* (Poland, N.Y.: Poland Bicentennial Committee, 1976), 15; Oswego County (New York), 432; Millard F. Roberts, *A Narrative History of Remsen, New York, Including Parts of Adjoining Townships of Steuben and Trenton, 1789–1898* (N.p.: Millard F. Roberts, 1914); John Durant, *History of Oneida County, New York* (Philadelphia: Everts and Fariss, 1878), 434, 443, 448; Franklin (New York) Congregational Church, 2–3; Helen Lane et al., *The Story of Walton, 1785–1975* (Walton, N.Y.: Walton Historical Society, 1975), 208; Gates Curtis, *Our County and Its People: A Memorial Record of St. Lawrence County, New York* (Syracuse, N.Y.: D. Mason, 1894), 582–83; H. P. Smith, *History of Cortland County* (Syracuse, N.Y.: D. Mason, 1885), 412; Signor, 460, 461, 550–51, 622.

123. Wesleyan Methodist Connection, "Minutes of the Champlain Annual Conference," 1843, 1844; idem, "Minutes of the Rochester Conference," 1844, 1845, 1846, Wesleyan Church

Archives; Freewill Baptist Connection, *Centennial Record of the Freewill Baptists,* 239; Burgess and Ward, 211–12; Franckean Evangelic Lutheran Synod, *Journal of the Fourth Annual Session* (1841), 5; idem, *Journal of the Fifth Annual Session* (1842), 8; idem, *Journal of the Seventh Annual Session* (1844), 4–5, 24.

124. Goodell, *Slavery and Anti-Slavery,* 544n. See also appendix A.

125. Approximate membership numbers for antislavery comeouter groups were interpolated on the basis of an average of fifty-four members per congregation. This figure has been derived from the average membership numbers of Wesleyan Methodist and Unionist congregations for which data is available. Franckean Lutheran membership statistics came from their journals (see Franckean Evangelic Lutheran Synod, *Journal of the Seventh Annual Session* [1844], 7; idem, *Journal of the Eighth Annual Session* [1845]). See Wesleyan Methodist Connection, "Minutes of the Champlain Annual Conference," (1843); idem, "Minutes of the Rochester Annual Conference," (1844–47), Wesleyan Church Archives. See also Matlack, *American Slavery and Methodism,* 349; Burgess and Ward, 211–12; *Morning Star* (6 Sept. 1843).

126. *Christian Investigator* 3 (Oct. 1845): 268. See also Hotchkin, 332.

127. *Christian Investigator* 3 (Mar. 1845): 215.

128. Part of Lee's attraction to antislavery unity came from his long experience with other ecclesiastical abolitionists. He preached for Unionist and Franckean Lutheran congregations (*Friend of Man* 3 [5 June 1839]: 196), traveled with leading Unionists when he was an antislavery agent (ibid. 3 [5 June 1839]: 197), and subscribed to Goodell's church reform newspaper (*Christian Investigator* 1 [Aug. 1843]: 56).

129. *Christian Investigator* 2 (Jan. 1844): 97. Lockwood contrasted his optimistic interpretation of religious events with William Miller's pessimistic apocalypticism.

130. Lewis C. Lockwood to the Syracuse convention, Dec. 12, 1843, in *Christian Investigator* 2 (Jan. 1844): 97; ibid. 2 (Mar. 1844): 114.

5. A Political Millennium

1. *Oberlin Evangelist* 3 (17 Feb. 1841): 2; ibid. (9 June 1841): 94; ibid. (23 June 1841): 101; ibid. (7 July 1841): 110; ibid. (21 July 1841): 119. See Blanchard, 1.

2. Liberty Party, *Proceedings of the Great Convention . . . 1845,* 19.

3. *Christian Investigator* 2 (Jan. 1844): 97.

4. George Fitzhugh, *Cannibals All! Or Slaves Without Masters,* ed. C. Vann Woodward (Cambridge, Mass.: Belknap, 1960), 85.

5. Colton, "Political Abolition," 77–78.

6. See, e.g., C. H. Dibble, *Centennial History of the Presbytery of Genesee, 1819–1919* (Batavia, N.Y.: Daily News Job Press, 1919), 18; Parsons, *Rochester Presbytery,* 293; Miller, 53, 63; Hotchkin, 156–57, 298, 301, 304, 315, 324, 338, 342, 344, 357, 372, 378, 384, 394, 403, 407, 422, 435, 442, 455, 502, 504, 514, 534, 565, 583, 586, 591, 595, 596. The Franckean Lutherans reported in 1843 that "this has been a year of revivals—such as the country has not seen since the years '31 and '32." Franckean Evangelic Lutheran Synod, *Journal of the Sixth Annual Meeting* (1843), 6.

7. Cross, 297–98; Fowler, 240.

8. Frank H. Seilhamer, "The New Measure Movement Among Lutherans," *Lutheran Quarterly* 12 (1960): 140. See Nichols, *Presbyterianism,* 142.

9. See Tuveson, 33–35; Howe, "Evangelical Movement," 1227.

10. Samuel Ringgold Ward, *Impartial Citizen* (13 Feb. 1850), in *Black Abolitionist Papers* (microfilm), 6:0400–02; Moorhead, "Between Progress and Apocalypse," 539–40; Doan, "Millerism and Evangelical Culture."

11. See Charles G. Finney, *Lectures on Revivals of Religion* (New York: Fleming H. Revell, 1868), 312.

12. Nichol, 165.

13. *Christian Investigator* 1 (Sept. 1843): 60; *Liberty Press* 4 (7 Feb. 1846): 54; Fletcher, 223.

14. Gerrit Smith, "To the Liberty Party," 7 May 1846, Gerrit Smith Papers.

15. *Christian Investigator* 1 (Sept. 1843): 60.

16. *Christian Investigator* 3 (June 1845): 237–38; ibid. 5 (July 1847): 426. See Eric Foner, *Free Soil, Free Labor, Free Men: The Ideology of the Republican Party Before the Civil War* (New York: Oxford Univ. Press, 1970), 9–13, 79–80, 296–97.

17. "Letter From Gerrit Smith To the President of the National Convention of the Liberty Party, which is to be held in the city of Buffalo, August 30th and 31st, 1843," *Emancipator Extra* (Sept. 1843): 8.

18. G. Smith, "To the Liberty Party," Gerrit Smith Papers.

19. Liberty Party, *Proceedings of the Great Convention . . . 1845,* 19.

20. See Benson, *Concept of Jacksonian Democracy,* 123–24; McCormick, 123.

21. The optimism of Liberty supporters continued until after the election of 1844 and, to some degree, until 1846. After a few years of phenomenal growth, Liberty vote totals stabilized from 1844 to 1846, and declined by 1848. For a county-by-county breakdown of Liberty vote totals in New York, 1840–1845, see Hendricks, 194ff.

22. A number of Liberty Party–nominated supervisors (the chief executive officer of a town) were elected in 1844 (J. N. T. Tucker, *The Liberty Almanac, No. Two, 1845* [Syracuse, N.Y.: Tucker and Kinney, 1845], 17). The citizens of China (Arcade) elected the entire local Liberty Party ticket in 1845 (*Historical Wyoming* 26 [Oct. 1980]: 48) and several towns in Madison County regularly gave a plurality to the Liberty slate.

23. *Union Herald* 6 (2 Dec. 1841): 126; *Liberty Press* 3 (23 Nov. 1844): 10; Benson, *Concept of Jacksonian Democracy,* 133–34; Hendricks, 102–3; Ronald P. Formisano, *The Transformation of Political Culture: Massachusetts Parties, 1790s–1840s* (New York: Oxford Univ. Press, 1983), 36, 329.

24. "Here is a leaven widely diffused and actively at work, which by the rules of arithmetic will leaven the whole lump of dough by the year 1848" ("The Right Sort of Politics," *Emancipator Extra* [14 Sept. 1843]: 1).

25. *Lutheran Herald* n.s. 1 (16 Oct. 1844): n.p.; Franckean Evangelic Lutheran Synod, *Journal of the Fifth Annual Session* (1842), 8; *Lutheran Herald* n.s. 1 (2 Oct. 1844): n.p.; Tucker, *The Liberty Almanac, No. Two, 1845,* 19. See also B. F. Morris, ed., *The Life of Thomas Morris: Pioneer and Long A Legislator of Ohio, and U.S. Senator From 1833 to 1839* (Cincinnati: Moore, Wilstach, Keys, and Overend, 1856), 233.

26. *Madison County Abolitionist* 1 (7 Dec. 1841): 46–47; *The Abolitionist* 2 (11 Oct. 1842): 222.

27. *Christian Investigator* 3 (June 1845): 238; ibid. 5 (July 1847): 426; Goodell, *Slavery and Anti-Slavery,* 551–52. See also Colton, "Political Abolition," 77–78; *American Jubilee* 1 (Feb. 1855): 74.

28. A list of prominent upstate New York Liberty men and women who were also ecclesias-

tical abolitionists (church reformers) includes: Gerrit Smith, Beriah Green, Alvan Stewart, William Goodell, James C. Jackson, J. N. T. Tucker, William L. Chaplin, Charles T. Torrey, Charles O. Shepard, Huntington Lyman, Charles C. Foote, John Keep, Calvin Gray, Antoinette Brown, Rachel Ball, Jonathan Copeland, Oren Cravath, James C. DeLong, Samuel Ringgold Ward, Willis A. Hodges, Wesley Bailey, Jonathan and Joseph Metcalf, F. C. D. McKay, George A. Avery, Michael B. Bateham, David Plumb, Hiram Pitts, E. W. Clark, Samuel Hastings, Archibald Griffith, Joseph Plumb, Elon Galusha, Luther Lee, Cyrus Prindle, John Lawyer, Henry L. Dox, Fayette Shipherd, Hiram Whitcher, William Dick, Moses M. Smart, David Marks, J. J. Butler, John Thomas, Samuel D. Porter, and Avelyn Sedgwick. This list comprises the entire leadership of the party in upper New York (with the possible exception of Henry B. Stanton). The Liberty Party's two-time candidate for president, James G. Birney, was also an ecclesiastical comeouter, although he was not from New York state. Identification has come from local and county histories (listed in bibliography), church records, proceedings of Liberty Party conventions, and the region's political and ecclesiastical abolitionist papers, e.g.: the *Union Herald,* the *Christian Investigator,* the *Friend of Man,* the *Liberty Press, The Abolitionist,* the *Liberty Party Paper,* and the *American Citizen.* See also Tucker, *Liberty Almanac, for 1844,* 29; Fowler, 160ff.; Hodges, xlvii; Fladeland, 271; Albert Bushness Hart, *Salmon Portland Chase* (Boston: Houghton Mifflin, 1899), 85; Harlow, 193ff.; Fletcher, 387; James Logan McElroy, "Social Reform in the Burned-Over District: Rochester, New York, as a Test Case, 1830–1854" (Ph.D. diss., State Univ. of New York at Binghamton, 1974), 222, 225, 229; Burgess and Ward, 162, 601, 692; Parsons, *Rochester Presbytery,* 256–61; F. Ward, 149–50.

29. *True Wesleyan* 1 (23 Dec. 1843): 203; Freewill Baptist Anti-Slavery Society, *Fifth Annual Report of the Free-Will Baptist Anti-Slavery Society,* 28; China (New York) Congregational Church, records; Sherburne (New York) Free Church, 4–8; *Liberty Party Paper* 2 (21 May 1851); *Christian Investigator* 4 (Feb. 1846): 304; ibid. 5 (Mar. 1847): 394; ibid. 3 (Aug. 1845): 255; *Liberty Press* 3 (11 Jan. 1845): 37; ibid. (15 Feb. 1845): 59; ibid. (8 Mar. 1845): 69; ibid. 4 (8 Nov. 1845): 2; ibid. (15 Nov. 1845): 7; ibid. (29 Nov. 1845): 15; *Madison County Abolitionist* 1 (7 Dec. 1841): 45, 46; Coe Smith Hayne, *Baptist Trail-Makers of Michigan* (Philadelphia: Judson, 1936), 106.

30. Warsaw (New York) Presbyterian Church, *Schism the Offspring of Error,* 22.

31. Lyman, 14.

32. The foundational political unit in New York state and in New England is called the town (a subdivision of a county); this term is roughly equivalent to the term "township" as used in some other states, such as Pennsylvania and New Jersey. A populated community within the bounds of a town is called a "hamlet" or (if incorporated) a "village."

33. *Christian Investigator* 2 (July 1844): 146.

34. See Hal S. Barron, "Staying Down on the Farm: Social Processes of Settled Rural Life in the Nineteenth-Century North," in *The Countryside in the Age of Capitalist Transformation: Essays in the Social History of Rural America,* ed. Steven Hahn and Jonathan Prude (Chapel Hill: Univ. of North Carolina Press, 1985), 327–29, 337–40.

35. *Union Herald* 6 (16 Dec. 1841): 136; O. Frothingham, 65.

36. *The Abolitionist* 2 (18 Oct. 1842): 229.

37. "The National Liberty Convention," in *Emancipator Extra* (Sept. 1843): 5, 7–8.

38. Gerrit Smith, "Report From The County Of Madison," 13 Nov. 1843, 2; idem, "To the Ministers in the County of Madison, Who Refuse to Preach Politics," 15 July 1845, 2–3, Gerrit Smith Papers. See [Gerrit] Smith and [A.] Brown, Jr., *Two American villages: Peterboro' and*

Auburn, the one reformed and the other unreformed; the result of a careful visitation (Preston, N.Y.: J. Livesay, n.d.). In the fall of 1842, Smith gave abolitionist lectures in every town in Madison County (see Gerrit Smith to Seth Gates, Jan. 23, 1843, Gerrit Smith Papers). Similarly, Goodell traveled throughout the area around his home in Honeoye and succeeded in abolitionizing "several villages and neighborhoods in the adjacent region" (*Christian Investigator* 1 [July 1843]: 47).

39. See Colton, "Political Abolition," 77; Fowler, 143; James E. Quaw, *The Wolf Detected, or Political Abolition Exposed* (Detroit: Geiger and Christian, 1845), 14–15; *Union Herald* 6 (16 Dec. 1841): 132; *Morning Star* (8 Nov. 1843): 114; *Oberlin Evangelist* (24 Sept. 1845): 155; *Western New Yorker* (18 Oct. 1843); G. Smith, "Report from the County of Madison," 2; idem, "To Those Ministers . . . Who Refuse to Preach Politics," Gerrit Smith Papers.

40. A listing of New York's abolition churches compared to the voting returns for 1844 can be found in Strong, "Organized Liberty," 339–82. Further research has uncovered approximately fifty abolition churches that were not in this 1990 listing; these additional churches have been incorporated in the data provided here and in appendixes A and B.

41. See Alan M. Kraut, "The Liberty Men of New York: Political Abolitionism in New York State, 1840–1848" (Ph.D. diss., Cornell Univ., 1975), 422–23; Strong, "Organized Liberty," 339–82.

42. See Colton, "Political Abolition," 77–79.

43. Freewill Baptist Connection, *Centennial Record*, 241; Burgess and Ward, 692; *Liberty Press* 3 (16 Nov. 1844): 5; ibid. (15 Feb. 1845): 59; *Morning Star* 18 (8 Nov. 1843): 114; *Christian Investigator* 1 (Dec. 1843): 88.

44. Thirteen towns in the burned-over district polled 100 or more Liberty votes. Outside of central and western New York, only New York City polled more than 100 Liberty votes. Holley, 69–103.

45. The hamlet or village in which a particular abolition church was located may have been in a town with a different name. In some cases, towns contained more than one village, each of which had an abolition church.

46. *The Abolitionist* 2 (11 Oct. 1842): 223; *Liberty Press* 3 (15 Feb. 1845): 59; *Liberty Party Paper* 2 (21 May 1851); Hotchkin, 290; Sherburne (New York) Free Church; Joel Hatch, Jr., *Reminiscences, Anecdotes and Statistics of the Early Settlers and the "Olden Time" in the Town of Sherburne, Chenango County, N.Y.* (Utica, N.Y.: Curtiss and White, 1862), 91–93, 98; Holley, 73.

47. Holley, 73; Burgess and Ward; Hotchkin, 417; J. Hatch, 95–96; J. H. Smith, *Chenango and Madison Counties*, 436, 485. In Pitcher and Lincklaen, the local Presbygational churches—prompted by Oberlin perfectionism—withdrew from the presbytery and became independent Congregational churches. Smyrna did not have its own abolition church, but the hamlet of Smyrna is only four miles from the village of Sherburne, and many of Smyrna's citizens were members of the Free Church in Sherburne. See Sherburne (New York) Free Church.

48. The coefficient of correlation is a measure of the strength of the linear relationship between two sets of data. The coefficient varies from +1.0 (indicating an absolute positive relationship) to 0 (indicating no relationship at all) to –1.0 (indicating an absolute negative relationship). In order to determine if the number of Liberty votes received and the presence of an abolition church are correlated in the towns of any particular county, the coefficient of correlation can be determined by simple linear regression analysis. A correlation of +.90 thus demonstrates that those towns in Chenango county that had a relatively large Liberty vote total had a very high positive relationship to the presence of an abolition church in those towns.

49. China (New York) Congregational Church, records, 3 Apr. 1841–23 Sept. 1846; G. Smith, "To the Liberty Party," 7 May 1846, Gerrit Smith Papers; *Christian Investigator* (Sept. 1843); ibid. (Mar. 1845); Mason and Douglass, 59–69, 71, 73–75; *Historical Wyoming* 11 (July 1964): 96–97; ibid. 26 (Oct. 1980): 45–47; H. Douglass, *Progress With A Past*, 70–71, 143–44; Harry S. Douglass, "Antislavery Sentiment" and "The Great Schism," in *United Church of Christ, Congregational, Arcade, New York, 1963* (Arcade, N.Y.: Tri-County Publications, 1963), n.p.; idem, "Origins of Abolitionist Movement," *Historical Wyoming* 16 (Oct. 1959): 22–24; New York (State), Secretary of State, *Census . . . for 1845*, no. 58-1.

50. F. Roberts, 151–52; Rowe, "Elon Galusha," 255–57; Robinson, 46–51; Wyoming County (New York), 125, 284; Katherine Barnes, *A History of the United Community Church, Castile, N.Y.* (N.p.: n.d.), 10–14; *Christian Investigator* 1 (Sept. 1843); Holley, 100.

51. *The Abolitionist* 2 (11 Oct. 1842): 223; ibid (18 Oct. 1842): 227; Seneca Falls (New York) Wesleyan Methodist Church, "Book No. 1. The Property of the First Wesleyan M. Church, Seneca Falls, N.Y.," manuscript at Seneca Falls Historical Society; Seneca County (New York), *Manual of the Churches and Pastors of Seneca County, 1895–1896* (Seneca Falls, N.Y.: Courier, 1896), 171–72; S. Wright et al., 41–42; Seneca Falls ME Church, Minutes; Pegler, 408–16. Joseph Metcalf was the primary financial backer of the new Wesleyan Methodist church.

52. Holley, 94. The correlation coefficient between Liberty votes and the presence of anti-slavery church reform sentiment in the towns of Seneca County was +.90 (another very high positive relationship). For the identity of abolition churches in Seneca county, see Wesleyan Methodist Connection, "Record of the New York Conference of the Wesleyan Methodist Church in America, held in Syracuse, June 1844," Wesleyan Church Archives; Waterloo (New York) Yearly Meeting of Congregational Friends, *Proceedings of the Yearly Meeting . . . 1849;* and subscription lists in the various issues of the *Christian Investigator* (1843–45).

53. S. Wright et al., 41–42; Matlack, *American Slavery and Methodism*, 178; Seneca Falls ME Church, Minutes; Pegler, 408–11. The contention by several historians that the "reluctant [Wesleyan] minister had regretted his rash act in making his premises available for such an occasion" is plainly erroneous. See Eleanor Flexner, *Century of Struggle: The Woman's Rights Movement in the United States* (Cambridge, Mass.: Belknap, 1959), 76; Rheta Childe Dorr, *Susan B. Anthony: The Woman Who Changed the Mind of a Nation* (reprint, New York: AMS, 1970), 49. Indeed, one of the signers of the women's rights "Declaration" was Saron Phillips, the minister of the church. See Seneca County (New York), 171; Theodore Stanton and Harriot Stanton Blatch, eds., *Elizabeth Cady Stanton As Revealed in Her Letters, Diary, and Reminiscences* (New York: Harper, 1922), 1:147.

54. Signers of the "Declaration of Rights and Resolutions" included the following persons: Sophia Taylor, Sarah Whitney, Joel Bunker, and Saron Phillips, who were members of the Wesleyan Methodist church; Sally Pitcher and Jonathan Metcalf, who were probably members of the church; Mary and Elizabeth Conklin, whose parents were members of the church; Mary Martin, whose husband was a member; and Henry Seymour, whose wife was a member. See Seneca Falls (New York) Wesleyan Methodist Church, "Book No. 1"; idem, "Roll of Members," 5, 7, manuscripts at Seneca Falls Historical Society; Stanton and Blatch, 1:147. Judith Wellman provided me with data on the identities of these persons. Other "subscribers" to the Women's Rights Convention included Jeremy and Rhoda Bement, who attended the Wesleyan Methodist church but were not members; see Altschuler and Saltzgaber, 48, 143.

55. Goodell, *Address of the Macedon Convention*, 10; Franckean Evangelic Lutheran Synod, *Journal of the Tenth Annual Session* (1847), 18. See also *Christian Investigator* 6 (Apr. 1848): 497.

56. Goodell, *Address of the Macedon Convention*, 6–8.

57. *Liberty Press* 3 (23 Nov. 1844): 11; ibid. 4 (14 Feb. 1846): 58.

58. Goodell, *Address of the Macedon Convention*, 6–8; *Christian Investigator* 1 (Sept. 1843): 60; Gerrit Smith, *To the Church of Peterboro* (Peterboro, N.Y.: Gerrit Smith, 1849); *Liberty Press* 4 (7 Feb. 1846): 54; ibid. (14 Feb. 1846): 58.

59. *Christian Investigator* 6 (May 1848): 500–501; Goodell, *Address of the Macedon Convention*, 6.

60. "The National Liberty Convention," in *Emancipator Extra* (Sept. 1843): 3 (resolution 4). See also Tucker, *The Liberty Almanac, for 1844*, 15.

61. Goodell, *Address of the Macedon Convention*, 8–14.

62. William Goodell, *Address Read at the New-York State Liberty Convention, Held at Port Byron, on Wednesday and Thursday, July 25 and 26, 1845* (Albany, N.Y.: Albany Patriot ["Extra"], 1845); idem, *Address of the Macedon Convention*, 1, 12; idem, *Slavery and Anti-Slavery*, 474–75, 535; *Impartial Citizen* (15 Aug. 1849), in *Black Abolitionist Papers* (microfilm), 6:0079; *Liberty Leaguer* 1 (May 1849): 12, 16.

63. *Christian Investigator* 3 (Mar. 1845): 215; ibid. 4 (Aug. 1846): 352; ibid. (Sept. 1846): 358–59; G. Smith, "To the Liberty Party," 7 May 1846, Gerrit Smith Papers; Goodell, *Slavery and Anti-Slavery*, 473; Goodell to Birney (1 Apr. 1847), in J. Birney, *Letters*, 2:1047–51.

64. *Liberty Leaguer* 1 (May 1849): 12–13.

65. See Liberty Party, "The National Liberty Convention" (1843), 1–3; Frederick Douglass, *The Life and Writings of Frederick Douglass*, ed. Philip S. Foner (New York: International Publishers, 1950), 2:67–68; Quarles, 184–85, 188.

66. Goodell, *Address of the Macedon Convention*.

67. Gerrit Smith, *To the Liberty Party of the County of Madison* (Peterboro: n.p., 1846); idem, "To the Liberty Party," 7 May 1846, Gerrit Smith Papers; idem, *To the Voters of the Counties of Oswego and Madison* (Peterboro: n.p., 1852); Goodell, *Address of the Macedon Convention*, 3–14; *Liberty Party Paper* 1 (1 Aug. 1849); Liberty Party, *Proceedings of the National Liberty Convention . . . 1848*, 7–9, 14, 32.

68. Goodell, *Slavery and Anti-Slavery*, 474.

69. Gerrit Smith, "To the Liberty Party," 7 May 1846, Gerrit Smith Papers; Liberty Party, *Proceedings of the National Liberty Convention . . . 1848*, 5, 14; Goodell, *Slavery and Anti-Slavery*, 450.

70. Several of the early women's rights advocates (Antoinette Brown, Lucy Stone, and Caroline Maria Seymour Severance, for example) were educated at Oberlin, although they did not always accept Oberlin's teachings in full. Women's rights leaders often used typically perfectionist phraseology in their speeches and writings. Elizabeth Cady Stanton, Susan B. Anthony, and Matilda Joslyn Gage, eds., *History of Woman Suffrage* (New York: Fowler and Wells, 1887), 1:78, 523; Stanton and Blatch, 146.

71. "The Liberty Party of the United States, To the People of the United States," in Liberty Party, *Proceedings of the National Liberty Convention*, 14; *Liberty Party Paper* 2 (12 Feb. 1851); Stanton, Anthony, and Gage, 1:76, 519–20; "Minutes of the State Liberty Party Convention," *Liberty Party Paper* 1 (1 Aug. 1849); Perkal, 233; Hewitt, "Social Origins," 209. Some of the persons who interacted with both political abolitionism and the women's rights movement included Luther Lee, Hiram Whitcher, Antoinette Brown, Rachel Ball, Caroline Maria Seymour Severance, Jonathan Metcalf, Samuel D. Porter, G. W. Johnson (state chairman of the Liberty Party), and Dr. Cutcheon (of New York Central College in McGrawville). *See also* page 206. Charles C. Foote, an Oberlin graduate, a comeouter pastor, and the Liberty Party candidate for

vice president in 1848, was a committed women's rights activist. See C. C. Foote, "Woman's Rights and Duties," *Oberlin Quarterly Review* 3 (Oct. 1849): 383–408.

72. Whitcher (misspelled "Wicher") was invited to open the Rochester Women's Rights Convention (1848) with prayer. Stanton, Anthony, and Gage, 1:76; Burgess and Ward, 692.

73. *National Era* (9 Sept. 1852), cited in Perkal, 233; Lasser and Merrill, 198, 123; Cazden, 67–68; Stanton, Anthony, and Gage, 1:519n., 524–25, 535–40.

74. Stanton, Anthony, and Gage, 1:524; Hewitt, *Women's Activism and Social Change,* 106.

75. Stanton, Anthony, and Gage, 1:527, 825.

76. Blanche Glassman Hersch, *The Slavery of Sex: Feminist-Abolitionists in America* (Urbana: Univ. of Illinois Press, 1978), 25–26; Hewitt, *Women's Activism and Social Change,* 36, 168; Gerda Lerner, "The Political Activities of Antislavery Women," in *The Majority Finds Its Past: Placing Women in History,* ed. Gerda Lerner (New York: Oxford Univ. Press, 1979), 112–28; Ellen DuBois, "Women's Rights and Abolitionism: The Nature of the Connection," in *Antislavery Reconsidered: New Essays on the Abolitionists,* ed. Lewis Perry and Michael Fellman (Baton Rouge: Louisiana State Univ. Press, 1979), 238–51.

77. See Wellman, "Seneca Falls"; Wendy Hamand Venet, *Neither Ballots Nor Bullets: Women Abolitionists and the Civil War* (Charlottesville: Univ. Press of Virginia, 1991), 20. Despite the participation in early women's rights activism by many ecclesiastical abolitionists, not all Liberty Party members nor all evangelical perfectionists supported the expansion of women's rights. The determinative factor was whether or not they were influenced by the more radical reform impulse of the burned-over district, which tended to challenge prevailing social conventions to a greater degree than the reform impulse elsewhere. Those abolitionist come-outers (such as Orange Scott and James Birney) and those institutionally supportive perfectionists (such as Phoebe Palmer) who were from other regions tended to be more conservative concerning women's issues. See J. L. Thomas, *The Liberator,* 261–62; Dumond, *Antislavery,* 160; and Theodore Hovet, "Phoebe Palmer's 'Altar Phraseology' and the Spiritual Dimensions of Woman's Sphere," *Journal of Religion* 63 (July 1983): 264–80.

6. The Burned-Out District

1. Mason and Douglass, 67–69; *Historical Wyoming* 11 (July 1964): 96–97; ibid. 26 (Oct. 1980): 45–47; H. Douglass, *Progress With A Past,* 70–71, 143–44; idem, "Congregationalism in Arcade," *Historical Wyoming* 17 (July 1964): 91–103; list of subscribers, *Christian Investigator* 1 (Sept. 1843) and 3 (Mar. 1845).

2. China (New York) First Congregational Church, records, vol. 2, Apr. 4, 1846–Oct. 31, 1851; Young, 330; H. Douglass, "Great Schism"; Mason and Douglass, 77–93.

3. China (New York) First Congregational Church, records, vol. 2.; Mason and Douglass, 95–98.

4. Harry S. Douglass, *Famous Sons and Daughters of Wyoming County* (N.p.: Wyoming County Newspapers, 1935), 31; idem, *Progress with a Past,* 143–44; Young, 330; Wyoming County (New York), 104. Shepard attended the 1848 Liberty Party convention, but after years of accepting leadership positions with the party, he refused to do so that year; instead, he went over to the Free Soilers. Liberty Party, *Proceedings of the National Liberty Convention . . . 1848,* 3–4.

5. List of Liberty Party Paper subscribers, 1849, Gerrit Smith Papers; Oberlin College,

Semi-Centennial Register of the Officers and Alumni of Oberlin College, 1833–1883 (Chicago: Blakely, Marsh, 1883), 16.

6. Fowler, 160–62.

7. Franckean Evangelic Lutheran Synod, *Journal of the Tenth Annual Session of the Franckean Evangelic Lutheran Synod, Convened at Richmondville, Schoharie Co., N.Y. On the 3rd day of June, 1847* (Leesville, N.Y.: American Christian Office, 1847), 7.

8. The 1846 national Liberty Party vote was 74,017, its highest tally; see T. C. Smith, 96–97. New York Liberty Party election statistics for 1840–45 (county by county) are in Hendricks, 194ff. The 1848 total is provided in Burnham, 933. Liberty Party tabulations for 1850 are listed in "Table of Liberty Party votes cast for William S. Chaplin and others for Governor in 1850," manuscript in Gerrit Smith Papers.

9. *Liberty Press* 3 (4 Jan. 1845): 33.

10. On the social transformation of the burned-over district in the 1840s and 1850s, see Cross, 354–55; G. Thomas, 35–37, 63–75. See also Clark, 320–29; Mark R. Hanley, "The New Infidelity: Northern Protestant Clergymen and the Critique of Progress, 1840–1855," *Religion and American Culture* 1, no. 2 (Summer 1991): 220–21; Barron, "Staying Down on the Farm," 337–40; idem, *Those Who Stayed Behind,* 112–13, 128–36.

11. *Christian Investigator* 1 (Sept. 1843): 60.

12. H. Douglass, *Progress With A Past,* 85–86; Parsons, *History of Rochester Presbytery,* 231; J. Hatch, 62; Young, 390; Hamilton Child, *Gazateer and Business Directory of Wyoming County, New York, for 1870–71* (Syracuse, N.Y.: Journal Office, 1870), 18; Marvin, 6.

13. *Liberty Press* 4 (22 Nov. 1845): 11; Hubbard Winslow, *The Former Days: History of the Presbyterian Church of Geneva* (Boston: Crocker and Brewster, 1859), 22. Numerous ecclesiastical accounts attested to and bemoaned the religious declension in relation to the material declension. Persons, 18; Parsons, *History of Rochester Presbytery,* 156, 296.

14. Parsons, *History of Rochester Presbytery,* 156; S. Wright et al., 17.

15. S. Ward, 82–83; Barron, "Staying Down on the Farm," 340.

16. Warsaw (New York) Presbyterian Church, *Schism the Offspring of Error,* 7, 24; Colton, *Abolition a Sedition,* 114ff.; Sprague, 26–27; Wood, 20–21; Hotchkin, 313, 314, 370, 397–98; Fowler, 136–43; *Union Herald* 6 (12 Aug. 1841): 59 (citing the action of Delaware [County, N.Y.] Presbytery); ibid. (9 Sept. 1841): 76 (citing the action of the Presbytery of Detroit); *Christian Palladium* 8 (1 Feb. 1840): 297–98; Franklin (New York) Congregational Church, 3; Signor, 622.

17. Colton, "Political Abolition," 15. In the *Western New Yorker* (Nov. 8, 1843), the Whigs of Wyoming County admitted that they were "badly scared" after the inroads that the Liberty Party made in their ranks: "The abolitionists have made sad havoc in our party."

18. Fowler, 137, 162, 278, 285; Signor, 622; *Union Herald* 6 (15 July 1841): 43; *New York Evangelist* (9 Oct. 1841) and *Western Monthly Magazine* 5 (Apr. 1836): 224, cited in Fletcher, 226, 441; Franklin (New York) Congregational Church, 3ff.

19. Gerrit Smith to Charles G. Finney, Jan. 12, 1841, Gerrit Smith Papers; *Christian Investigator* 1 (July 1843): 48; "The National Liberty Convention," *Emancipator Extra* (Sept. 1843): 1, 2, 6; *Oberlin Evangelist* (20 Dec. 1843); Sherlock Bristol to Hamilton Hill and others, 14 Dec. 1843, and Catharine E. Beecher to Charles G. Finney, cited in Fletcher, 225, 450; *Christian Investigator* 3 (May 1845): 224; Matlack, *American Slavery and Methodism,* 354–55. The Wesleyan Methodists continued well into the twentieth century to look upon Oberlin as a "model" of holiness for the education of their young people; see Frieda A. Gillette and Katherine W.

Lindley, *And You Shall Remember: A Pictorial History of Houghton College* (Houghton, N.Y.: Houghton College, 1983), 94.

20. Fowler, 137; Franklin (New York) Congregational Church, 3.

21. *Christian Investigator* 2 (Dec. 1844): 189–90; ibid. 3 (Sept. 1845): 261; ibid. (Mar. 1845): 215; ibid. (June 1845): 238; ibid. (July 1845): 247.

22. *Western New Yorker* (18 Oct. 1843); ibid. (8 Nov. 1843). Whigs accused Liberty campaigners of being "desecrators of the Sabbath" for preaching antislavery politics on Sundays (ibid. [18 Oct. 1843]) and "immoral" for slandering slaveholders and advocating that slaves steal and rebel. Critics connected Liberty activists to the perfectionists at Oberlin—both of whom were accused of being "unpatriotic . . . traitors" because they allegedly were financed by foreigners. Quaw, 18, 25.

23. Birney did no campaigning at all during his presidential candidacy in 1840; instead, he traveled in England from May to late November. Fladeland, 188.

24. Quaw, 8, 17; *True Wesleyan* 2 (9 Nov. 1844): 179; Fladeland, 241–44.

25. In the forged letter, Birney supposedly stated that "he was a Democrat in principle and would, if elected, support Democratic men and measures"—the direct opposite of his previous statements. *Western New Yorker* (16 and 30 Oct. 1844). Wesley Bailey, editor of the *Liberty Press,* was livid because of the forgery—and even more so because the Whig papers perpetuated the lie by printing it. *Liberty Press* 3 (Nov. 1844): 2; ibid. (Dec. 1844): 176. Likewise, the *Oberlin Evangelist* "most deeply deplored" the use of such low tactics. *Oberlin Evangelist* (20 Nov. 1844): 191.

26. In spite of the alleged duplicity of Birney, the Wesleyan Methodists chose to believe the best about their candidate: "We do not cast away the noble Birney, much less the liberty party. We shall stand by both the one and the other, and we trust all *true* liberty men will do the same" (*True Wesleyan* 2 [9 Nov. 1844]: 179). Nonetheless, some abolitionists may have been persuaded to vote for Clay instead of Birney. See "Address to Members of the Liberty Party," *Western New Yorker* (30 Oct. 1844).

27. *Liberty Press* 3 (29 Dec. 1844): 30; ibid. (1 Mar. 1845): 65.

28. Gerrit Smith, *Report from the County of Madison* (Peterboro, N.Y.: n.p., 13 Nov. 1843), 2–3, Gerrit Smith Papers.

29. Colton, "Political Abolition," 14.

30. *Liberty Press* 3 (8 Feb. 1845): 55.

31. "Letter From Gerrit Smith. To the President of the National Convention of the Liberty Party, which is to be held in the city of Buffalo, August 30th and 31st, 1843," *Emancipator Extra* (Sept. 1843): 8; S. P. Chase to H. B. Stanton and Elizur Wright, Jr., in Liberty Party, *Proceedings of the Great Convention . . . 1845,* 31; Goodell, *Address of the Macedon Convention,* 7.

32. Kraut, "Partisanship and Principles," 79.

33. The history of the Free Soil Party in relation to the Liberty Party is found in Hart, 95–102; T. C. Smith, 64–65, 120–46; Foner, 81ff.; Sewell, 152–69; Frederick J. Blue, *The Free Soilers: Third Party Politics, 1848–54* (Urbana: Univ. of Illinois Press, 1973).

34. Oliver Dyer, *Oliver Dyer's Phonographic Report of the Proceedings of the National Free Soil Convention At Buffalo, N.Y., August 9th and 10th, 1848* (Philadelphia: Dyer and Webster, 1848), 11, 16–19.

35. *Christian Investigator* 4 (Apr. 1846): 317–18; H. Davis, 235, 240–42, 265; Goodheart, 126–28, 133; Wyatt-Brown, 272–79; Rayback, 103–10; Blue, 1–15; Filler, 150–51; and Harrold, 40, 64–65, 112–13.

36. Fairchild, *Oberlin*, 111; H. C. Taylor to Gerrit Smith, Jan. 15, 1849, Gerrit Smith Papers. Oberlin president Asa Mahan gave an address at the convention of the Free Soil Party, and encouraged Liberty voters to accept the coalitionist platform (Dyer, 22–24).

37. Free Baptist leader and editor of the *Morning Star*, William Burr was "a practical anti-slavery man." He was a strong supporter of his fellow Dover, New Hampshire, resident, John P. Hale; Hale was the original choice of the coalitionist Liberty men for president, before they agreed on Van Buren's candidacy at the Free Soil convention. Hale had close interaction with and admiration for the Free Baptists. J. M. Brewster et al., *Centennial Record of the Freewill Baptists, 1780–1880* (Dover, N.H.: Printing Establishment, 1881), 164; Barrett, 194; T. C. Smith, 120, 132, 143.

38. *Oberlin Evangelist* 6 (24 Sept. 1845): 155. See Franckean Evangelic Lutheran Synod, *Journal of the Sixth Annual Session* (1843), 7; idem, *Journal of the Eighth Annual Session* (1845), 21; *Morning Star* 19 (24 Apr. 1844): 2.

39. Liberty Party, *Proceedings of the National Liberty Convention . . . 1848*, 32.

40. On the free labor argument and its relation to the Liberty Party, see Foner, 79–80, 296–97; Blue, 75, 81, 101–2, 129.

41. Goodell, *Slavery and Anti-Slavery*, 455, 535; *Christian Investigator* 5 (Mar. 1847): 394. See *Liberty Press* 3 (1 Mar. 1845): 65; Samuel Ringgold Ward to Gerrit Smith, 14 Aug. 1848, Gerrit Smith Papers.

42. *Christian Investigator* 3 (Oct. 1845): 268; ibid. 5 (Jan. 1847): 392.

43. *Christian Investigator* 5 (Mar. 1847): 393; ibid. 6 (Mar. 1848): 487; ibid. 3 (Feb. 1845): 208; Goodell, *Slavery and Anti-Slavery*, 542.

44. *Christian Investigator* 3 (June 1845): 237–38; ibid. 4 (Aug. 1846): 352; ibid. 5 (July 1847): 426.

45. See the participants listed in Liberty Party, *Proceedings of the National Liberty Convention . . . 1848*, 3–6, compared to the subscription lists and articles on church reform in the various issues of the *Christian Investigator*.

46. Goodell, *Address of the Macedon Convention*, 13. See *Impartial Citizen* (13 Feb. 1850), in *Black Abolitionist Papers* (microfilm), 6:0400–02; Charles G. Finney to Gerrit Smith, 13 Sept. 1852, Gerrit Smith Papers.

47. See Foner, 296–97; Goen, 156, 186.

48. *Liberty Leaguer* 1 (May 1849): 12–13; Liberty Party, *Proceedings of the National Liberty Convention . . . 1848*, 8.

49. Goodell, *Slavery and Anti-Slavery*, 474. The title, "Liberty League," was designed to be an alternative name to the evasive "Anti-slavery League" that the coalitionists were advancing. The term "liberty" indicated a fuller agenda—the liberty of all persons—as opposed to the more limited term "anti-slavery." *Liberty Leaguer* 1 (May 1849): 12–13; Hart, 97.

50. The Liberty League maintained its separate existence as a political pressure group for the Liberty Party until 1849. *Liberty Leaguer* 1 (May 1849): 12, 16.

51. Goodell, *Address of the Macedon Convention*, 4, 5, 12, 14; Goodell, *Slavery and Anti-Slavery*, 475, 482; Liberty Party, *Proceedings of the National Liberty Convention . . . 1848*, 4–5, 6–9, 13, 31–32; G. Smith, *Report from the County of Madison*, 2–3, Gerrit Smith Papers.

52. *Liberty Party Paper* 2 (12 Feb. 1851).

53. T. C. Smith, 97; Blue, 142n.; "Table of Liberty Party votes cast for William S. Chaplin and others for Governor in 1850," and "The Liberty Party," 28 Nov. 1850, Gerrit Smith Papers; *Liberty Party Paper* 2 (28 Nov. 1850); Holley, 102–3.

54. *Liberty Leaguer* 1 (May 1849); Liberty Party, *Proceedings of the National Liberty Convention . . . 1848, 32.*

55. Seneca County (New York), 172–73; S. Wright et al., 15–17, 42–43; "John A. Rumsey," in Edgar Luderne Welch, *Grip's Historical Souvenir of Seneca Falls* (Syracuse, N.Y.: Grip, 1904), 86–88; Non-Episcopal Methodist Convention, *Minutes of the Non-Episcopal Methodist Convention, Held In Cincinnati, Ohio, May 9–16, 1866* (Springfield, Ohio: Western Methodist Protestant Office, 1866), 29–30, 43. After the 1860s, the Wesleyan Methodist congregation in Seneca Falls gradually declined; the building was sold sometime after 1920. In 1994, the chapel was restored and reopened as part of the Women's Rights National Historic Park.

56. Storke, 294; Adams, 451–52, 750–51, 953; Oswego County (New York), 432; Curtis, 582–83; Mason and Douglass, 129; G. Cowles, 436; Persons, 16, 18; Brewster et al., *Centennial Record of Freewill Baptists,* 239; Franckean Evangelic Lutheran Synod, *Journal of the Ninth Annual Session* (1846), 19; Signor, 622; Conover, 462.

57. Hotchkin, 297, 335, 403, 452, 581, 593; Parsons, *Rochester Presbytery,* 156, 296; *Liberty Press* 4 (22 Nov. 1845): 11; Young, 390; Marvin, 6; Winslow, 22.

58. *Christian Investigator* 6 (Apr. 1848): 497; Warsaw (New York) Presbyterian Church, *Schism the Offspring of Error,* 9.

59. Fowler, 160, 244; Fairchild, "Doctrine of Sanctification"; *Oberlin Evangelist* 6 (4 Dec. 1844): 197; *Christian Investigator* 6 (May 1848): 500–501. See also Sherburne (New York) Free Church, 5; *Christian Investigator* 2 (Nov. 1844): 184; ibid. 3 (Oct. 1845): 268.

60. *Christian Investigator* 1 (Dec. 1843): 88ff.; *Liberty Leaguer* 1 (May 1849): 16.

61. Mason and Douglass, 80–94; Peterboro (New York), Church of Peterboro, *Resolutions, Church of Peterboro, June 1st, 1849* (Peterboro, N.Y.: n.p., 1849?); G. Smith, *To The Church of Peterboro;* Peterboro (New York), Church of Peterboro, *Proceedings of the Church of Peterboro, at their Meeting held Nov. 27, 1849* (Peterboro, N.Y.: n.p., 1849?); Gerrit Smith, *Gerrit Smith's Reply to Colored Citizens of Albany,* 13 Mar. 1846, Gerrit Smith Papers.

62. Dox, *Rev. Philip Wieting,* 177–81.

63. Burgess and Ward, 615; Dox, *Rev. Philip Wieting,* 180; Van Alstine et al., 14–15; Kreider, 158; *Liberty Party Paper* (12 Feb. 1851); Nichols, *Presbyterianism,* 113.

64. Antoinette Brown to Gerrit Smith, 26 Dec. 1851, Gerrit Smith Papers; Doan, *Miller Heresy,* 16–30, 215–28.

65. Mason and Douglass, 80–93; J. Hatch, 93.

66. *Union Herald* 6 (5 May 1841): 3; ibid. (11 Aug. 1841): 60; ibid. (23 Sept. 1841): 82; *Christian Palladium* 7 (15 Sept. 1838): 154; ibid. (1 Nov. 1838): 200; ibid. 8 (1 Oct. 1839): 170; ibid. (15 Oct. 1839): 185–87; *Liberty Leaguer* 1 (May 1849): 12, 14. See also Henry T. Cheever, *A Tract for the Times* (New York: J. A. Gray, 1859). Several ecclesiastical abolitionists wrote tracts against perceived unorthodoxy, particularly against universalism. Luther Lee, *Universalism Examined and Refuted* (Watertown, N.Y.: Knowlton and Rice, 1836); Nicholas Van Alstine, *Modern Universalism at War with the Bible and Reason* (Baltimore: Evangelical Lutheran Church, 1847), viii, x.

67. Free Baptist leaders in the 1850s were viewed as "liberal clergymen" (see Stanton, Anthony, and Gage, 1:76), but by the beginning of the twentieth century, most rural Free Baptist churches in New York state were bastions of fundamentalism. Many of them eventually joined the fundamentalist General Association of Regular Baptist Churches. See Elton (New York) Free Baptist Church, records, Freedom, N.Y.

68. J. Hatch, 93. See Hotchkin, 360, 491, 515; Rowe, "Elon Galusha," 259.

69. Most of the key leaders of the Wesleyan Methodist Connection returned to the Methodist Episcopal Church in 1866. Part of the reason that Luther Lee, Cyrus Prindle, and others reunited with Methodist Episcopacy was their deep disappointment at the failure to create an ecumenical union church of reform-minded Methodist Protestants and Wesleyan Methodists. Haines and Thomas, 65–66.

70. Van Alstine et al., 14–15; Van Alstine, *Historical Review,* 18; Dox, *Rev. Philip Wieting,* 185.

71. Haines and Thomas, 69–73; Mason and Douglass, 95–98.

72. Non-Episcopal Methodist Convention, 7, 37, 38, 41, 43.

73. Ibid., 29–30, 43, 45; Seneca County (New York), 172.

74. For the history of the postbellum Holiness movement, see Dieter; Charles E. Jones, *Perfectionist Persuasion: The Holiness Movement and American Methodism, 1867–1936* (Metuchen, N.J.: Scarecrow, 1974); William C. Kostlevy, *Holiness Manuscripts: A Guide to Sources Documenting the Wesleyan Holiness Movement in the United States and Canada* (Metuchen, N.J.: Scarecrow, 1994).

75. Victor B. Howard, *Religion and the Radical Republican Movement, 1860–1870* (Lexington: Univ. Press of Kentucky, 1990), 146; James M. McPherson, *The Abolitionist Legacy* (Princeton, N.J.: Princeton Univ. Press, 1975), 15n., 232.

76. Howard, 31, 63, 67, 82, 135, 163, 193, 204; Haines and Thomas, 70.

77. Crooks was a prominent pastor and editor of the Wesleyan Methodist denominational paper in the postwar period. Haines and Thomas, 64–65.

78. Wilcox, 27.

79. Milton B. Powell, "The Abolitionist Controversy in the Methodist Episcopal Church, 1840–1864" (Ph.D. diss., State Univ. of Iowa, 1963), 196–98, 202–5.

Epilogue

1. *American Jubilee* 1 (Mar. 1855): 88. See ibid. (Apr. 1855): 94; "National Liberty Party," 30 Sept. 1852, Gerrit Smith Papers; Perkal, 329–31; Harlow, 464–65.

2. Gerrit Smith, *Speeches of Gerrit Smith in Congress* (New York: Mason, 1856); Harlow, 312–35.

3. *American Jubilee* 1 (Mar. 1854): 1. See G. Smith, *To the Voters of . . . Oswego and Madison;* idem, *To the Liberty Party.* Liberty writers and speakers often restated Lysander Spooner's argument that the Constitution was an antislavery document. Lysander Spooner, *The Unconstitutionality of Slavery* (Boston: B. Marsh, 1845); Gerrit Smith, *Letter of Gerrit Smith to S. P. Chase, on the Unconstitutionality of Every Part of American Slavery* (Albany, N.Y.: S. W. Green, 1847).

4. "The Liberty Party," 28 Nov. 1850, Gerrit Smith Papers; *American Jubilee* 1 (June 1854): 11, 14; ibid. (Feb. 1855): 74, 78; ibid. (Mar. 1855): 88; Ripley, 3:44, 336n., 350; 4:27–29, 44, 91n.; *Impartial Citizen* (24 Oct. 1849), in *Black Abolitionist Papers* (microfilm), 6:0198, 0521, 0650; Douglass, 44–47, 67–68, 74–85.

5. The perfectionists' ideals may have had an indirect effect on public policy decisions during the Civil War. For example, during Goodell's two visits to the White House in 1862, Lincoln expressed his appreciation for Goodell's abolitionist paper, the *Principia,* which the president read regularly. Goodell believed that Lincoln was moved by their discussions to frame the theoretical basis for the Emancipation Proclamation on the principle of "justice, and not merely military necessity." Perkal, 302–8; McPherson, *Struggle For Equality,* 5, 16–20.

6. Sellers, 404. See also *American Jubilee* 1 (July 1854): 22; ibid. (Nov. 1854): 51.

7. "Christian Union" congregations established in the 1860s became centers of Holiness advocacy (Kostlevy, *Holiness Manuscripts,* 86). Various Holiness groups—such as the "holiness bands," the Church of God (Anderson, Ind.), the Churches of Christ in Christian Union, and the forerunners to the Church of the Nazarene—were all radically antisectarian. Jones, 47–61, 90–92; John W. V. Smith, *The Quest for Holiness and Unity: A Centennial History of the Church of God (Anderson, Indiana)* (Anderson, Ind.: Warner, 1980), 46–48; Timothy L. Smith, *Called Unto Holiness: The Story of the Nazarenes* (Kansas City: Nazarene, 1962), 28–38. This same kind of anti-institutionalism was prevalent within early Pentecostalism, especially in the Church of God (Cleveland, Tenn.) and in another Pentecostal group that carried the name "Christian Union." Robert M. Anderson, *Vision of the Disinherited: The Making of American Pentecostalism* (Peabody, Mass.: Hendrickson, 1992), 35–37.

8. On Roberts, see Benson Howard Roberts, *Benjamin Titus Roberts. Late General Superintendent of the Free Methodist Church. A Biography* (North Chili, N.Y.: Earnest Christian Office, 1900); and Clarence Howard Zahniser, *Earnest Christian: Life and Works of Benjamin Titus Roberts* (Circleville, Ohio: Advocate Publishing House, 1957). On evangelical social concern in the late nineteenth century, see Norris Magnuson, *Salvation in the Slums: Evangelical Social Work, 1865–1920* (Metuchen, N.J.: Scarecrow, 1977). On the Holiness legacy, see T. L. Smith, *Revivalism and Social Reform;* D. Dayton, *Discovering;* Hardesty.

9. Winthrop S. Hudson (*Religion in America,* 4th ed. [New York: Macmillan, 1987], 289) points to the publication of Henry M. Dexter's *The Moral Influence of Manufacturing Towns* (Andover, Mass.: W. H. Wardwell, 1848) as the beginning of a corporate understanding of social problems, but by that date (1848) the Liberty League had already been articulating such views for several years. For an example of the transition from evangelical perfectionist revivalism to progressive social reform within the ecclesiastical abolitionist constituency, see John Barnard, *From Evangelicalism to Progressivism at Oberlin College, 1866–1917* (Columbus: Ohio State Univ. Press, 1969).

10. Blanchard, 10, 13, 15.

11. Liberty Party, *Proceedings of the National Liberty Convention . . . 1848,* 30; Resolution of the Rochester Annual Conference in 1847, meeting at Eagle Harbor, Orleans County, N.Y., cited in S. Wright et al., 18. See also Goodell, *Address of the Macedon Convention,* 6–8.

12. Goodell, *Address of the Macedon Convention,* 10.

13. *Christian Investigator* 5 (Nov. 1847): 458; ibid. 6 (Apr. 1848): 496; ibid. 6 (June 1848): 507–8.

14. *Christian Investigator* 4 (Sept. 1846): 356; *Liberty Leaguer* 1 (May 1849): 12–13.

15. Roth, 299–310, describes the difficulties encountered by persons in the burned-over district(s) who attempted to balance the tension between liberty and order.

16. *Lutheran Herald* 2 (16 Sept. 1840): 69.

17. Tocqueville, 265–75

Appendix A

1. Local, county, and regional histories and congregational and denominational sources used for identifying church reform activity in upper New York are found in the bibliography. They are also listed separately in Strong, "Organized Liberty," 383–93.

2. Examples of laypersons or pastors who were known to be antislavery church reformers

(and thus help to identify their congregations as abolition churches and their towns as ecclesiastical abolitionist communities) include Huntington Lyman in Truxton, Arcade, and Warsaw; H. A. Sacket in Franklinville; John Keep in Medina (Ridgeway) and Arcade; Gershom Welles in Castile; George Goodyear in Rensselaerville and Gaines; Calvin Gray in Wales, Aurora, Arcade, and Darien; Joseph Plumb in Lodi (Collins); Charles C. Foote in Salisbury; J. Heustis in Honeoye Falls (Mendon); John J. Butler in Clinton (Kirkland); William Dick in Norway and Middlefield; and Hiram Whitcher in Newport, Whitestown, Poland (Russia), and Unadilla Forks (Plainfield). Hotchkin, 417, 532; *Christian Investigator* 1 (June 1843); ibid. (Sept. 1843); ibid. (Dec. 1843): 88; *Liberty Press* 3 (16 Nov. 1844): 5; ibid. (15 Feb. 1845): 59; *Morning Star* 18 (8 Nov. 1843): 114; Burgess and Ward, 91, 162, 692.

3. New York (State), Secretary of State, *Census . . . for 1845,* Recapitulation no. 6 and no. 7; and idem, *Census . . . for 1855,* 478.

4. The listings of planned Wesleyan Methodist churches in the 1844 and 1845 Rochester Conference Minutes were compared with the listing (and membership numbers) of existing congregations given in the 1847 Rochester Conference Minutes and the 1846 St. Lawrence Conference Minutes in order to ascertain which churches were actually established. "Minutes of the Rochester Conference of the Wesleyan Methodist Connection," 1844, 1845, 1847; "Minutes of the St. Lawrence Conference," 1846, Wesleyan Church Archives.

5. See e.g. *Union Herald* 6 (29 July 1841): 53; Pembroke (New York) Bicentennial Committee, *Town of Pembroke Bicentennial History* (n.p.: n.d.), 57–58.

6. See e.g. John A. Haddock, *Haddock's Centennial History of Jefferson County, New York* (Philadelphia: Sherman, 1894), 707; John Durant, *History of Jefferson County, New York* (Philadelphia: J. B. Lippincott, 1878), 158; H. P. Smith, ed., *History of Essex County* (Syracuse, N.Y.: D. Mason, 1885), 596.

7. See e.g. Hotchkin, 290, 419, 459, 570–71; Sherburne (New York) Free Church.

8. Hotchkin, 360, 397–98, 567.

9. See e.g. *Christian Investigator* 3 (Jan. 1845): 199; ibid. 5 (June 1847): 415–17; Arthur O. Northrup, ed., *One Hundred Years for Christ, 1842–1942* (n.p.: Champlain Conference, Wesleyan Methodist Church, 1942), 29; G. Smith, *Christian Union Convention,* 2.

10. A list of most of the abolition churches in New York state can be found in Strong, "Organized Liberty," 339–82. Due to further research since the writing of "Organized Liberty," about fifty additional abolition churches have been identified that were not included in the earlier list. These recently identified churches have been incorporated into the data presented in this appendix.

11. Again, for the purposes of this study, upper New York is determined to be the forty-five counties north and west of the Catskill Mountains, i.e., that portion of the state north and west of the southern boundaries of Rensselaer, Albany, Schoharie, and Delaware counties.

12. Data obtained from Holley; T. C. Smith, 97. New York Liberty votes for 1844 can also be found in Strong, "Organized Liberty," 339–81. Upstate New York voters provided 24.8% of the 62,323 Liberty votes cast nationally in 1844.

Bibliography

Manuscript and Archival Sources

Arcade (New York) Historical Society. Archives. Arcade, N.Y.

Blanchard, Jonathan. Jonathan Blanchard Papers. Wheaton College, Wheaton, Ill.

Burlington (New York) Free Baptist Church. Records. Library, New York State Historical Association, Cooperstown, N.Y.

China (New York) First Congregationalist Church. Records. Archives, United Church of Christ, Congregational, Arcade, N.Y.

Finney, Charles G. Papers. Special Collections, Mudd Library, Oberlin College, Oberlin, Ohio.

Franckean Evangelic Lutheran Synod. Records. Krauth Memorial Library, Lutheran Theological Seminary, Philadelphia, Pa.

Freewill Baptist Connection. Papers. American Baptist Historical Society, Rochester, N.Y.

Goodell, William. Papers. Berea College Library, Berea, Ky.

Seneca Falls (New York) Methodist Episcopal Church. Records. Archives, United Methodist Church, Seneca Falls, N.Y.

Seneca Falls (New York) Wesleyan Methodist Church. Records. Seneca Falls Historical Society, Seneca Falls, N.Y.

Short Tract (New York) Wesleyan Methodist Church. Minutes of Quarterly Meetings, 1850–1906. Wesleyana Room, Willard J. Houghton Library, Houghton College, Houghton, N.Y.

Smith, Gerrit. Papers. George Arents Research Library, Syracuse Univ., Syracuse, N.Y.

Warsaw (New York) Congregational and Presbyterian Churches. Records. Archives, United Church of Warsaw, Warsaw, N.Y.

Wesleyan Methodist Connection. Records. Wesleyan Church Archives, Indianapolis, Ind.

Publications of Anonymous or Collective Authorship

American Baptist Free Mission Society. *Review of The Operations of The American Baptist Free Mission Society, For The Past Year.* Bristol, England: Mathews Brothers, 1851.

Baptist Missionary Convention, State of New York. *Proceedings of The Twenty-First Anniversary of the Baptist Missionary Convention of the State of New York. Held with the Baptist Church in Rome, October 19 and 20, 1842.* Utica: Bennett, Backus, and Hawley, 1842.

———. *Proceedings of the Twenty-Third Anniversary of the Baptist Missionary Convention of the State of New York. Held with the Second Baptist Church in Rochester, October, 16 and 17, 1844.* Utica: Bennett, Backus, and Hawley, 1844.

Bethany (New York). *A History of the Town of Bethany.* N.p.: n.d.

Buffalo Presbytery. *Trial of the Rev. Asa T. Hopkins, Pastor of the First Presbyterian Church,*

Buffalo, Before A Special Meeting of the Buffalo Presbytery: Commencing October 22, and Ending October 31, 1844. Buffalo: n.p., 1844.

Franckean Evangelic Lutheran Synod. *Constitution and Standing Ordinances of the Franckean Evangelic Lutheran Synod. Together with A Discipline, Recommended as a Guide for the government of Churches.* Cooperstown: H. and E. Phinney, 1839.

———. *Journal of the Annual Sessions of the Franckean Evangelic Lutheran Synod.* Albany, Fort Plain, Milford, West Sandlake, Leesville, Rochester: 1837–1851.

Franklin (New York) Congregational Church. *A Statement of Facts Connected with the Late Difficulties in the Congregational Church in Franklin, N.Y.* N.p.: 1841?

Free Presbyterian Church. *Distinctive Principles of the Free Presbyterian Church of the United States.* Mercer, Pa.: Wm. F. Clark, 1850.

Freewill Baptist Anti-Slavery Society. *Fifth Annual Report of the Free-Will Baptist Anti-Slavery Society, Read at Lebanon, Maine, October 9, 1851.* Dover, N.H.: Wm. Burr, 1851.

Freewill Baptist General Conference. *A Treatise on the Faith of the Free-Will Baptists: With an Appendix, Containing A Summary of Their Usages in Church Government.* 4th ed. Dover, N.H.: Free-will Baptist Printing Establishment, 1848.

General Association of New York [Congregational]. *Minutes of the General Association of New York, at Their Meeting in Champion, Jefferson County, August 25th, 1842; with an Appendix.* Utica: R. W. Roberts, 1842.

Genesee and Wyoming Counties (New York). *Churches of Genesee and Wyoming Counties.* Batavia: D. L. Martin and E. B. Shaw, 1897.

Herkimer County (New York). *History of Herkimer County, New York.* New York: F. W. Beers, 1879.

Lane Theological Seminary. *Lane Theological Seminary, General Catalogue of 1828–1881.* Cincinnati: Elm Street, 1881.

Lebanon (New York). *Church Records, Lebanon and Hamilton, Madison County, New York.* Minneapolis: Daughters of the American Revolution, 1948. Typed manuscript. New York State Library, Albany, N.Y.

Liberty Party. *Emancipator Extra, Tracts, nos. 1–6.* Boston: J. W. Alden, 1843.

———. *History of the Erection of the Monument on the Grave of Myron Holley.* Utica, N.Y.: H. H. Curtiss, 1844.

———. *The Liberty Party. Its Origin, Principles, and Measures (Tract No. 1).* Boston: n.p., 1847.

———. *Proceedings of the Great Convention of the Friends of Freedom in the Eastern and Middle States, Held in Boston, Oct. 1, 2, & 3, 1845.* Lowell, Mass.: Pillsbury and Knapp, 1845.

———. *Proceedings of the National Liberty Convention, Held At Buffalo, N.Y., June 14th and 15th, 1848; Including the Resolutions and Addresses Adopted by That Body, and Speeches of Beriah Green and Gerrit Smith on That Occasion.* Utica: S. W. Green, 1848.

———. New York [State] Convention, 1842. *Address of the Peterboro State Convention to the Slaves and Its Vindication.* Cazenovia, N.Y.: L. R. Myrick, 1842.

New Hartford (New York) Presbyterian Church. *Centennial Day of the Presbyterian Church, New Hartford, New York.* Utica, N.Y.: T. J. Griffiths, 1891.

New York (State), Secretary of State. *Census of the State of New-York, for 1845.* Albany, N.Y.: Carroll and Cook, 1846.

———. *Census of the State of New-York for 1855.* Albany, N.Y.: Charles Van Benthuysen, 1857.

Niagara County (New York). *History of Niagara County, New York.* New York: Sanford, 1878.

Non-Episcopal Methodist Convention. *Minutes of the Non-Episcopal Methodist Convention, Held in Cincinnati, Ohio, May 9–16, 1866.* Springfield, Ohio: Western Methodist Protestant Office, 1866.

Oakfield (New York). *Bicentennial History Book. Oakfield, New York.* N.p.: 1976.

Oberlin College. *General Catalogue of Oberlin College, 1833–1908.* Cleveland: O. S. Hubbell, 1909.

———. *Semi-Centennial Register of the Officers and Alumni of Oberlin College, 1833–1883.* Chicago: Blakely, Marsh, 1883.

Oswego County (New York). *History of Oswego County, New York.* Philadelphia: L. H. Everts, 1877.

Otisco (New York) Church of Christ in Christian Union. "80th Anniversary of the Church of Christ in Christian Union of Otisco, New York." Typed manuscript. 1977.

Pembroke (New York) Bicentennial Committee. *Town of Pembroke Bicentennial History.* N.p.: n.d.

Peterboro (New York), Church of Peterboro. *Church of Peterboro.* [Peterboro, N.Y.: Gerrit Smith, 1843?].

———. *Proceedings of the Church of Peterboro, at their Meeting held Nov. 27, 1849.* [Peterboro, N.Y.: Gerrit Smith, 1849].

Seneca County (New York). *Manual of Churches and Pastors of Seneca County.* Seneca Falls, N.Y.: Courier, 1896.

Sherburne (New York) Free Church. *Organization and Membership of the Free Church of Sherburne, 1847–1856.* N.p., n.d. Typed manuscript. New York State Library, Albany, N.Y.

Warsaw (New York) Congregational Church. *Manual and List of Members of the Congregational Church, Warsaw, N.Y.* Warsaw, N.Y.: Dudley and Merrill, 1871.

———. "The Story of One Hundred Years: The First Congregational Church, Warsaw, N.Y." Typed manuscript. Church Office, United Church, Warsaw, N.Y.

———. "Warsaw Congregational Church." Typed manuscript. Wyoming County Historian's Office, Warsaw, N.Y.

———. *Year Book and Church Directory of the First Congregational Church, Warsaw, New York.* Warsaw, N.Y.: n.p., 1932.

Warsaw (New York) Presbyterian Church. *Schism the Offspring of Error, Illustrated in Historical Sketches of the Presbyterian Church of Warsaw, Genesee County, N.Y.* Buffalo: Robert D. Foy, 1841.

Waterloo (New York) Yearly Meeting of Congregational Friends. *Earnest and Affectionate Address to All People, and Especially Religious Professors of Every Name, and an Address to Reformers: from the Yearly Meeting of Congregational Friends, held at Waterloo, N.Y.* Auburn: Oliphant's Press, 1849.

———. *Proceedings of the Yearly Meeting of Congregational Friends, held at Waterloo, N.Y. from the 4th to the 6th of the Sixth month inclusive, 1849. With an Appendix.* Auburn: Oliphant's Press, 1849.

Wayne County (New York). "Fragmentary Notes on Slavery in Wayne County." Undated clipping in Palmyra Library file, Palmyra Town Historian, Palmyra, N.Y.

Wesleyan Methodist Connection. *The Discipline of the Wesleyan Methodist Connection of America.* Boston: O. Scott, 1843.

Westmoreland (New York) First Congregational Church. *Exercises in Commemoration of the Centennial Anniversary of the First Congregational Church of Westmoreland, N.Y., Tuesday, September 20th, 1892.* Clinton, N.Y.: J. B. and H. B. Sykes, 1893.

Works Projects Administration. *Inventory of the Church Archives of New York (Excluding New York City): Presbyterian Churches.* Philadelphia: Presbyterian Historical Society, 1965.

Wyoming County (New York). *History of Wyoming County, New York.* New York: F. W. Beers, 1880.

Books and Articles—Primary

Baird, Robert. *Religion in the United States of America; or, An Account of the Origin, Progress, Relations to the State, and Present Condition of the Evangelical Churches in the United States. With Notices of the Unevangelical Denominations.* Glasgow: Blackie and Son, 1844.

Barnes, Gilbert H., and Dwight L. Dumond, eds. *Letters of Theodore Dwight Weld, Angelina Grimke Weld, and Sarah Grimke, 1822–1844.* New York: D. Appleton-Century, 1934.

Beecher, Lyman. *A Plea for the West.* Cincinnati: Truman and Smith, 1835.

Birney, James Gillespie. *Debate on "Modern Abolitionism," in the General Conference of the Methodist Episcopal Church, May, 1836.* Cincinnati: Ohio Anti-Slavery Society, 1836.

———. *A Letter on the Political Obligations of Abolitionists, by James G. Birney: With a Reply by William Lloyd Garrison.* Boston: Dow and Jackson, 1839.

———. *Letters of James Gillespie Birney, 1831–1857.* 2 vols. Edited by Dwight L. Dumond. New York: D. Appleton-Century, 1938.

Black Abolitionist Papers, 1830–1865. Microfilm. Sanford, N.C.: Microfilming Corp. of America, 1981.

Blanchard, Jonathan. *A Perfect State of Society.* Oberlin, Ohio: James Steele, 1839.

Butler, John J. *Natural and Revealed Theology. A System of Lectures, Embracing the Divine Existence and Attributes; Authority of the Scriptures; Scriptural Doctrine; Institutions and Ordinances of the Christian Church.* Dover, N.H.: Freewill Baptist Printing Establishment, 1861.

———. *Thoughts on the Benevolent Enterprises, Embracing the Subjects of Missions, Sabbath Schools, Temperance, Abolition of Slavery, and Peace.* Dover, N.H.: Trustees of the Freewill Baptist Connection, 1840.

Cheever, Henry T. *A Tract for the Times.* New York: J. A. Gray, 1859.

Christy, David. *Pulpit Politics; or, Ecclesiastical Legislation on Slavery, in Its Disturbing Influences on the American Union.* Cincinnati: Faran and McLean, 1862.

Colton, Calvin [A northern man, pseud.]. *Abolition a Sedition.* Philadelphia: G. W. Donahue, 1839.

——— [Junius, pseud.]. "Political Abolition." In *The Junius Tracts.* New York: Greeley and McElrath, 1844.

——— [A Protestant, pseud.]. *Protestant Jesuitism.* New York: Harper and Brothers, 1836.

———. *Thoughts on the Religious State of the Country; with Reasons for Preferring Episcopacy.* New York: Harper and Brothers, 1836.

Cowles, Henry. *The Holiness of Christians in the Present Life.* Oberlin, Ohio: J. Steele, 1840.

Dexter, Henry M. *The Moral Influence of Manufacturing Towns. A Discourse Delivered at the Dedication of the Franklin Street Church in Manchester, New Hampshire, December 22, 1847.* Andover, Mass.: W. H. Wardwell, 1848.

Douglass, Frederick. *The Life and Writings of Frederick Douglass,* vol. 2, *Pre–Civil War Decade, 1850–1860.* Edited by Philip S. Foner. New York: International Publishers, 1950.

Dox, Henry L. *Christ the Foundation: A Synodical and Dedicatory Discourse, Delivered at Gardnersville, Schoharie Co., N.Y., June 7th, 1849.* Albany, N.Y.: J. Munsell, 1849.

———. *Memoir of Rev. Philip Wieting, a Pastor Forty Years in the Same Field.* Philadelphia: Lutheran Publication Society, 1870.

Dyer, Oliver. *Oliver Dyer's Phonographic Report of the Proceedings of the National Free Soil Convention at Buffalo, N.Y. August 9th and 10th, 1848.* Philadelphia: Dyer and Webster, 1848.

Edgerton, Walter. *A History of the Separation in Indiana Yearly Meeting of Friends; Which Took Place in the Winter of 1842 and 1843, on the Anti-Slavery Question.* Cincinnati: Achilles Pugh, 1856.

Finney, Charles G. *Lectures on Revivals of Religion.* Reprint. New York: Fleming H. Revell Co., 1868.

———. *Lectures on Systematic Theology, Embracing Lectures on Moral Government, Together with Atonement, Moral and Physical Depravity, Regeneration, Philosophical Theories, and Evidences of Regeneration.* Oberlin, Ohio: James M. Fitch, 1846.

———. *Memoirs of Rev. Charles G. Finney: Written by Himself.* New York: A. S. Barnes, 1876.

———. *Views of Sanctification.* Oberlin, Ohio: J. Steele, 1840.

Fitzhugh, George. *Cannibals All! Or Slaves Without Masters.* Edited by C. Vann Woodward. Cambridge, Mass.: Belknap, 1960.

Foner, Philip S., and George E. Walker, eds. *Proceedings of the Black State Conventions, 1840–1865.* 2 vols. Philadelphia: Temple Univ. Press, 1979.

Foot, Joseph I. *Discourses on Modern Antinomianism, Commonly Called Perfectionism.* Syracuse, N.Y.: J. P. Patterson, 1834.

Foote, C. C. "Woman's Rights and Duties." *Oberlin Quarterly Review* 3 (Oct. 1849): 383–408.

Fowler, Philemon H. *Historical Sketch of Presbyterianism within the Bounds of the Synod of Central New York.* Utica, N.Y.: Curtiss and Childs, 1877.

Galusha, Elon. *Address of Elder Elon Galusha, with Reasons for Believing Christ's Second Coming, at Hand.* Rochester: Erastus Shepard, 1844.

Garrison, William Lloyd. *Principles of the Non-Resistance Society.* Boston: n.p., 1839.

Goodell, William. *Address of the Macedon Convention By William Goodell; And Letters of Gerrit Smith.* Albany, N.Y.: S. W. Green, Patriot Office, 1847.

———. *Address Read at the New York State Liberty Convention, Held at Port Byron, on Wednesday and Thursday, July 25 and 26, 1845.* Albany, N.Y.: Albany Patriot (extra), 1845.

———. *The Democracy of Christianity; or An Analysis of the Bible and Its Doctrines, in Their Relation to the Principle of Democracy.* 2 vols. New York: Cady and Burgess, 1852.

———. *Slavery and Anti-Slavery; A History of the Great Struggle in Both Hemispheres; With a View of the Slavery Question in the United States.* New York: William Goodell, 1853.

Gordon, Joseph. *The Life and Writings of Rev. Joseph Gordon.* Cincinnati: Free Presbyterian Synod, 1860.

Green, Beriah. *Sketches of the Life and Writings of James Gillespie Birney.* Utica, N.Y.: Jackson and Chaplin, 1844.

Hatch, Joel, Jr. *Reminiscences, Anecdotes, and Statistics, of the Early Settlers and the "Olden Time" in the Town of Sherburne, Chenango County, New York.* Utica, N.Y.: Curtiss and White, 1862.

Hawley, Silas. *"A Declaration of Sentiments." Reported by S. Hawley to the "Christian Union Convention," Held in Syracuse, Aug. 21, 1838.* Cazenovia, N.Y.: Luther Myrick, 1839.

Hodges, Willis A. *Free Man of Color: The Autobiography of Willis Augustus Hodges.* Edited by Willard B. Gatewood, Jr. Knoxville: Univ. of Tennessee Press, 1982.

Holley, O. L., ed. *The New-York State Register, For 1843.* Albany, N.Y.: J. Disturnell, 1843.

——. *The New-York State Register, for 1845.* New York: J. Disturnell, 1845.

Hotchkin, James H. *A History of the Purchase and Settlement of Western New York, and of the Rise, Progress, and Present State of the Presbyterian Church in That Section.* New York: M. W. Dodd, 1848.

Keep, John. *Congregationalism and Church Action: with the Principles of Christian Union, etc.* New York: S. W. Benedict, 1845.

Lawyer, John D. *Letter to the Hon. Lewis H. Sandford, Assistant Vice Chancellor.* Albany, N.Y.: E. H. Pease, 1846.

Lee, Luther. *Autobiography of the Rev. Luther Lee.* New York: Philips and Hunt, 1882.

——. *Discussion on the Doctrine of the Trinity between Luther Lee, Wesleyan Minister, and Samuel J. May, Unitarian Minister. Reported by Lucius C. Matlack.* Syracuse, N.Y.: Wesleyan Book Room, 1854.

——. *Five Sermons and a Tract by Luther Lee.* Edited by Donald W. Dayton. Chicago: Holrad, 1975.

——. *Universalism Examined and Refuted.* Watertown, N.Y.: Knowlton and Rice, 1836.

——. *Wesleyan Manual: A Defense of the Organization of the Wesleyan Methodist Connection.* Syracuse, N.Y.: Samuel Lee, 1862.

Lee, Luther, and E. Smith. *The Debates of the General Conference, of the M. E. Church, May, 1844.* New York: O. Scott, 1845.

Lyman, Huntington. *Address Delivered Before the Temperance Society of Franklinville [N.Y.], at Their Annual Meeting, in Sept., 1830.* Utica, N.Y.: Gardiner Tracy, 1833.

Mahan, Asa. *Out of Darkness into Light.* Boston: Willard Tract Repository, 1876.

——. *Principles of Christian Union, and Church Fellowship, a Sermon, by Rev. Asa Mahan, president of Oberlin Collegiate Institute, preached at Oberlin, May 1836.* Elyria, Ohio: A. Burrell, 1836.

——. *Scripture Doctrine of Christian Perfection; with Other Kindred Subjects, Illustrated and Confirmed in a Series of Discourses Designed to Throw Light on the Way of Holiness.* Boston: D. S. King, 1839.

Marks, Marilla, ed. *Memoirs of the Life of David Marks, Minister of the Gospel.* Dover, N.H.: Free-Will Baptist Printing Establishment, 1846.

Marsh, Luther Rawson, ed. *Writings and Speeches of Alvan Stewart on Slavery.* New York: A. B. Burdick, 1860.

Matlack, Lucius C. *The Antislavery Struggle and Triumph in the Methodist Episcopal Church.* New York: Phillips and Hunt, 1881.

——. *The History of American Slavery and Methodism, from 1780 to 1849: And History of the Wesleyan Methodist Connection of America; in Two Parts, With an Appendix.* New York: Lucius C. Matlack, 1849.

——. *The Life of Rev. Orange Scott.* New York: C. Prindle and L. C. Matlack, 1851.

Merrell, Bildad, Jr. *The Utica City Directory, For 1845–'46. 1846–'47. 1847–'48. 1848–'49.* Utica, N.Y.: H. H. Curtiss, 1845, 1846, 1847, 1848.

Morris, B. F., ed. *The Life of Thomas Morris: Pioneer and Long a Legislator of Ohio, and U.S. Senator from 1833 to 1839.* Cincinnati: Moore, Wilstach, Keys, and Overend, 1856.

Noyes, John H. *The Way of Holiness.* Putney, Vt.: J. H. Noyes, 1838.

Peck, George. *Early Methodism within the Bounds of the Old Genesee Conference from 1788 to 1828; or, The First Forty Years of Wesleyan Evangelism in Northern Pennsylvania, Central and Western New York, and Canada.* New York: Carlton and Porter, 1860.

Pegler, George. *Autobiography of the Life and Times of the Rev. George Pegler. Written by Himself.* Syracuse, N.Y.: Wesleyan Methodist Publishing House, 1879.

Phelps, Amos A. *Lectures on Slavery and Its Remedy.* Boston: New-England Anti-Slavery Society, 1834.

Quaw, James E. *The Wolf Detected, or Political Abolition Exposed.* Detroit: Geiger and Christian, 1845.

Richards, William, compiler. *The Utica Directory: 1842-'43.* Utica, N.Y.: John P. Bush, 1842.

————. *The Utica City Directory, For 1844-'45.* Utica, N.Y.: H. H. Curtiss, 1844.

Ripley, C. Peter, ed. *The Black Abolitionist Papers.* 5 vols. Chapel Hill: Univ. of North Carolina Press, 1985.

Roct, J. I., et al. [pseud.?]. *An Account of the Trial of Luther Myrick, Before the Oneida Presbytery.* Syracuse, N.Y.: J. P. Patterson, 1834.

Sanford, Lewis H. *State of New-York. In Chancery. Philip Kniskern and Others, v. Philip Wieting, the Evangelical Lutheran Churches of St. John's at Durlach, and St. Peter's at New Rhinebeck in Sharon; and others. Opinion of the Honorable Lewis H. Sandford, Assistant Vice-Chancellor, July 17th, 1844.* New York: William Osborn, 1845.

Scott, Orange. *An Appeal to the Methodist Episcopal Church.* Boston: David H. Ela, 1838.

————. *Church Government.* Boston: O. Scott, for the Wesleyan Methodist Connection, 1844.

————. *The Methodist E.[piscopal] Church And Slavery.* Boston: O. Scott, for the Wesleyan Methodist Connection, 1844.

Smith, Gerrit. *Abstract of the Argument, in the Public Discussion of the Question: "Are the Christians of a Given Community the Church of Such Community?" Made by Gerrit Smith, in Hamilton, N.Y. April 12th, 13th, 14th, 1847.* Albany, N.Y.: S. W. Green, 1847.

————. *An Address Reported By Gerrit Smith to the "Christian Union Convention" Held in Syracuse, August 21st, 1838.* N.p.: n.d.

————. *Letter of Gerrit Smith to S. P. Chase, on the Unconstitutionality of Every Part of American Slavery.* Albany, N.Y.: S. W. Green, Patriot Office, 1847.

————. *Speeches of Gerrit Smith in Congress.* New York: Mason, 1856.

————. *Substance of the Address, Delivered by Gerrit Smith, Before the Annual Meeting of the American Temperance Society, In the City of New-York, May 7, 1833.* Utica, N.Y.: Gardiner Tracy, 1833.

————. *To the Church of Peterboro.* Peterboro, N.Y.: Gerrit Smith, 1849.

————. *To the Liberty Party of the County of Madison.* Peterboro, N.Y.: Gerrit Smith, 1846.

————. *To the Voters of the Counties of Oswego and Madison.* Peterboro, N.Y.: Gerrit Smith, 1852.

————. *Union of Christians.* [Peterboro, N.Y.: 1841?].

Smith, [Gerrit], and [A.] Brown, Jr. *Two American villages: Peterboro' and Auburn, the one reformed and the other unreformed; the result of a careful visitation.* Preston, N.Y.: J. Livesay, n.d.

Smith, Gerrit, and Cassius M. Clay. *Cassius M. Clay, of Lexington, Ky., to the Mayor of Dayton, O., with a Review of it by Gerrit Smith, of Peterboro, N.Y.* Utica, N.Y.: Jackson and Chaplin, 1844.

Spooner, Lysander. *The Unconstitutionality of Slavery.* Boston: B. Marsh, 1845.

Sprague, William B. *Religious Ultraism: A Sermon Delivered August 25, 1835, at the Installation of the Rev. John H. Hunter, as Pastor of the First Congregational Church in West Springfield, Massachusetts.* Albany, N.Y.: Packard and Van Benthuysen, 1835.

Stanton, Theodore, and Harriot Stanton Blatch, eds. *Elizabeth Cady Stanton as Revealed in Her Letters, Diary, and Reminiscences.* New York: Harper, 1922.

Taylor, Nathaniel W. *Concio ad Clerum: A Sermon Delivered in the Chapel of Yale College.* New Haven, Conn.: Hezekiah Howe, 1828.

Tocqueville, Alexis de. *Democracy in America.* Edited by J. P. Mayer and Max Lerner. New York: Harper and Row, 1966.

Tucker, J. N. T., ed. *The Liberty Almanac, For 1844.* Syracuse, N.Y.: I. A. Hopkins, 1844.

———. *The Liberty Almanac, No. Two, 1845.* Syracuse, N.Y.: Tucker and Kinney, 1844.

Van Alstine, Nicholas. *Historical Review of the Franckean Evangelical Lutheran Synod of New York.* Philadelphia: Lutheran Publication Society, 1893.

———. *Modern Universalism at War With The Bible and Reason.* Baltimore: Evangelical Lutheran Church, 1847.

Van Alstine, Nicholas, et al. *A Reunion of Ministers and Churches, Held at Gardnersville, May 14–17, 1881.* Philadelphia: Lutheran Publication Society, 1881.

Ward, Samuel Ringgold. *Autobiography of a Fugitive Negro: His Anti-Slavery Labours in the United States, Canada, and England.* London: John Snow, 1855.

Wesley, John. *The Works of John Wesley.* Edited by Thomas Jackson. London: Wesleyan Book Room, 1872.

Wood, James. *Facts and Observations concerning the Organization and State of the Churches in the Three Synods of Western New-York and the Synod of Western Reserve.* Saratoga Springs, N.Y.: G. M. Davison, 1837.

Books, Articles, and Dissertations—Secondary

Abzug, Robert H. *Passionate Liberator: Theodore Dwight Weld and the Dilemma of Reform.* New York: Oxford Univ. Press, 1980.

Adams, William, ed. *Historical Gazateer and Biographical Memorial of Cattaraugus County, New York.* Syracuse, N.Y.: Lyman, Horton, 1893.

Altschuler, Glenn C., and Jan M. Saltzgaber. *Revivalism, Social Conscience, and Community in the Burned-Over District: The Trial of Rhoda Bement.* Ithaca, N.Y.: Cornell Univ. Press, 1983.

Anderson, Robert M. *Vision of the Disinherited: The Making of American Pentecostalism.* Peabody, Mass.: Hendrickson, 1992.

Bagg, M. M. *The Pioneers of Utica.* Utica, N.Y.: Curtiss and Childs, 1877.

———, ed. *Memorial History of Utica, N.Y. from Its Settlement to the Present Time.* Syracuse, N.Y.: D. Mason, 1892.

Baird, Samuel J. *A History of the New School, and of the Questions Involved in the Disruptions of the Presbyterian Church in 1838.* Philadelphia: Claxton, Remsen, and Haffelfinger, 1868.

Baldwin, Lewis V. *"Invisible" Strands in African Methodism: A History of the African Union Methodist Protestant and Union American Methodist Episcopal Churches, 1805–1980.* Metuchen, N.J.: Scarecrow, 1983.

Banner, Lois W. "Religious Benevolence as Social Control: A Critique of an Interpretation." *Journal of American History* 60 (June 1973): 23–41.

Barkun, Michael. *Crucible of the Millennium: The Burned-Over District of New York in the 1840s.* Syracuse, N.Y.: Syracuse Univ. Press, 1986.

Barnard, John. *From Evangelicalism to Progressivism at Oberlin College, 1866–1917.* Columbus: Ohio State Univ. Press, 1969.

Barnes, Gilbert H. *The Antislavery Impulse, 1830–1844.* New York: D. Appleton-Century, 1933.

Barnes, Katherine. *A History of the United Community Church, Castile, N.Y.* N.p.: n.d.

Barrett, Selah Hibbard, ed. *Memoirs of Eminent Preachers in the Freewill Baptist Denomination.* Rutland, Ohio: n.p., 1874.

Barron, Hal S. "Staying Down on the Farm: Social Processes of Settled Rural Life in the Nineteenth-Century North." In *The Countryside in the Age of Capitalist Transformation: Essays in the Social History of Rural America,* edited by Steven Hahn and Jonathan Prude, 327–43. Chapel Hill: Univ. of North Carolina Press, 1985.

———. *Those Who Stayed Behind: Rural Society in Nineteenth-Century New England.* Cambridge: Cambridge Univ. Press, 1984.

Bassett, Ancel H. *A Concise History of the Methodist Protestant Church, from its Origin: Embracing the Circumstances of the Suspension of the Northern and Western Conferences in 1858, the Entire Career of the Methodist Church, and the Reunion of the two Branches in 1877.* Pittsburgh: James Robison, 1877.

Baxter, Norman Allen. *History of the Freewill Baptists: A Study in New England Separatism.* Rochester: American Baptist Historical Society, 1957.

Benson, Lee. *The Concept of Jacksonian Democracy: New York as a Test Case.* Princeton, N.J.: Princeton Univ. Press, 1961.

Birney, William. *James G. Birney and His Times: The Genesis of the Republican Party.* New York: D. Appleton, 1890.

Bishop, Lewis H. "Our Historical Heritage: An Address Delivered at the 150th Anniversary Service in the United Church, Sunday, July 13, 1958, at 10:00 a.m." Typed manuscript in church office, United Church, Warsaw, N.Y.

Bloch, Ruth H. *Visionary Republic: Millennial Themes in American Thought, 1756–1800.* New York: Cambridge Univ. Press, 1985.

Blue, Frederick J. *The Free Soilers: Third Party Politics, 1848–54.* Urbana: Univ. of Illinois Press, 1973.

Bodo, John R. *The Protestant Clergy and Public Issues, 1812–1848.* Princeton, N.J.: Princeton Univ. Press, 1954.

Bozeman, Theodore Dwight. *Protestants in an Age of Science: The Baconian Ideal and Antebellum American Religious Thought.* Chapel Hill: Univ. of North Carolina Press, 1977.

Brackney, William H. "The Fruits of a Crusade: Wesleyan Opposition to Secret Societies." *Methodist History* 17 (July 1979): 239–52.

Brewster, J. M. *Fidelity and Usefulness. Life of William Burr.* Dover, N.H.: F. Baptist Printing Establishment, 1871.

Brewster, J. M., et al. *Centennial Record of the Freewill Baptists, 1780–1880.* Dover, N.H.: The Printing Establishment, 1881.

Briggs, Erasmus. *History of the Original Town of Concord, Being the Present Towns of Concord, Collins, North Collins, and Sardinia.* Rochester: Union and Advertisers, 1883.

Brooks, Charles Wesley. *A Century of Missions in the Empire State, as Exemplified by the Work and Growth of the Baptist Missionary Society of the State of New York.* Philadelphia: American Baptist Publishing Society, 1909.

Bruce, Dwight H., ed. *Onondaga Centennial.* Boston: Boston History, 1896.

Bunnell, H. O. *Dansville: 1789–1902: Historical, Biographical, Descriptive.* Dansville, N.Y.: Instructor, 1902.

Burgess, G. A., and J. T. Ward. *Free Baptist Cyclopaedia. Historical and Biographical.* Chicago: Women's Temperance Publication Association, 1889.

Burke, Ronald Kevin. "Samuel Ringgold Ward: Christian Abolitionist." Ph.D. diss., Syracuse Univ., 1975.

Burnham, W. Dean. *Presidential Ballots, 1836–1892.* Baltimore: Johns Hopkins Univ. Press, 1955.

Butler, Jonathan M., and Ronald L. Numbers. *The Disappointed: Millerism and Millenarianism in the Nineteenth Century.* Bloomington: Indiana Univ. Press, 1987.

Carroll, Paul. "Historic [Griffins Mills Presbyterian] Church Seeking Minister." *The Buffalo News* (16 Oct. 1995).

Carwardine, Richard J. *Evangelicals and Politics in Antebellum America.* New Haven, Conn.: Yale Univ. Press, 1993.

Cave, Alfred A. *An American Conservative in the Age of Jackson: The Political and Social Thought of Calvin Colton.* Fort Worth: Texas Christian Univ. Press, 1969.

Cazden, Elizabeth. *Antoinette Brown Blackwell: A Biography.* Old Westbury, N.Y.: Feminist Press, 1983.

Child, Hamilton. *Gazateer and Business Directory of Wyoming County, New York, for 1870–71.* Syracuse, N.Y.: Journal Office, 1870.

Clark, Christopher. *The Roots of Rural Capitalism: Western Massachusetts, 1780–1860.* Ithaca, N.Y.: Cornell Univ. Press, 1990.

Clarke, T. Wood. *Utica For a Century and a Half.* Utica, N.Y.: Widtman, 1952.

Clayton, W. W. *History of Onondaga County, New York.* Syracuse, N.Y.: D. Mason, 1878.

Coe, Richard L. "A History of the Western Presbyterian Church of Palmyra, up to 1860." Typed manuscript. Palmyra Town Historian, Palmyra, N.Y.

Cole, Charles C., Jr. *The Social Ideas of the Northern Evangelists, 1826–1860.* New York: Columbia Univ. Press, 1954.

Conable, Francis W. *History of the Genesee Annual Conference of the Methodist Episcopal Church, from its Organization by Bishops Asbury and M'Kendree in 1810 to the Year 1872.* New York: Nelson and Phillips, 1876.

Conover, George S., ed. *History of Ontario County, New York.* Syracuse, N.Y.: D. Mason, 1893.

Cookinham, Henry J. *History of Oneida County, New York.* Chicago: S. J. Clarke, 1912.

Coppedge, Allan. "Entire Sanctification in Early American Methodism: 1812–1835." *Wesleyan Theological Journal* 13 (Spring 1978): 34–50.

Cowles, George W., ed. *Landmarks of Wayne County, New York.* Syracuse, N.Y.: D. Mason, 1895.

Crissey, S. S. *Centennial History of the Fredonia Baptist Church, 1808–1908.* Buffalo: Matthews-Northrup, 1908.

Cross, Whitney R. *The Burned-Over District: The Social and Intellectual History of Enthusiastic Religion in Western New York, 1800–1850.* Ithaca, N.Y.: Cornell Univ. Press, 1950.

Curtis, Gates. *Our County and Its People: A Memorial Record of St. Lawrence County, New York.* Syracuse, N.Y.: D. Mason, 1894.

Davidson, James West. *The Logic of Millennial Thought: Eighteenth Century New England.* New Haven, Conn.: Yale Univ. Press, 1977.

Davis, David Brion. "The Emergence of Immediatism in British and American Antislavery Thought." *Mississippi Valley Historical Review* 49 (Sept. 1962): 209–30.

———. *The Problem of Slavery in the Age of Revolution, 1770–1823.* Ithaca, N.Y.: Cornell Univ. Press, 1975.

———, ed. *Ante-Bellum Reform.* New York: Harper and Row, 1967.

Davis, Hugh. *Joshua Leavitt: Evangelical Abolitionist.* Baton Rouge: Louisiana State Univ. Press, 1990.

Dayton, Charles H., and John Garth Coleman. *A Brief History of the Presbytery of Geneva and a Tribute to Some Early Ministers.* Shortsville, N.Y.: Geneva-Lyons Presbytery, 1955.

Dayton, Donald W. *Discovering an Evangelical Heritage.* New York: Harper and Row, 1976.

———. "Millennial Views and Social Reform in Nineteenth Century America." In *The Coming Kingdom: Essays in American Millennialism and Eschatology,* edited by M. Darrol Bryant and Donald W. Dayton, 131–47. Barrytown, N.Y.: International Religious Foundation, 1983.

Dayton, Lucille Sider, and Donald W. Dayton. "'Your Daughters Shall Prophesy': Feminism in the Holiness Movement." *Methodist History* 14 (Jan. 1976): 85–86.

Dibble, C. H. *Centennial History of the Presbytery of Genesee, 1819–1919.* Batavia, N.Y.: Daily News Job Press, 1919.

Dieter, Melvin Easterday. *The Holiness Revival of the Nineteenth Century.* Metuchen, N.J.: Scarecrow, 1980.

Doan, Ruth Alden. *The Miller Heresy, Millennialism, and American Culture.* Philadelphia: Temple Univ. Press, 1987.

———. "Millerism and Evangelical Culture." In *The Disappointed: Millerism and Millenarianism in the Nineteenth Century,* edited by Ronald L. Numbers and Jonathan M. Butler, 118–38. Bloomington: Indiana Univ. Press, 1987.

———. "Perfectionism in the Adventist Tradition." Unpublished paper read at the Wesleyan/Holiness Study Conference, Asbury Theological Seminary, Wilmore, Ky., 11 June 1988.

Donald, David H. "Toward a Reconsideration of the Abolitionists." In *Lincoln Reconsidered: Essays on the Civil War Era,* edited by David H. Donald, 19–36. New York: Knopf, 1956.

Dorr, Rheta Childe. *Susan B. Anthony: The Woman Who Changed the Mind of a Nation.* New York: AMS, 1970.

Douglass, Harry S. "Congregationalism in Arcade." *Historical Wyoming* 17 (July 1964): 91–103.

———. *Famous Sons and Daughters of Wyoming County.* N.p.: Wyoming County Newspapers, 1935.

———. "Origins of Abolitionist Movement." *Historical Wyoming* 16 (Oct. 1959): 22–24.

———. *Progress With a Past: Arcade, New York, 1807–1957.* Arcade, N.Y.: Arcade Sesquicentennial and Historical Society, 1957.

———. *United Church of Christ, Congregational. Arcade, New York, 1963.* Arcade: Tri-County Weekly Publications, 1963.

Drake, Thomas E. *Quakers and Slavery in America.* New Haven, Conn.: Yale Univ. Press, 1950.

Duberman, Martin, ed. *The Antislavery Vanguard: New Essays on the Abolitionists.* Princeton, N.J.: Princeton Univ. Press, 1965.

DuBois, Ellen. "Women's Rights and Abolitionism: The Nature of the Connection." In *Anti-*

slavery Reconsidered: New Essays on the Abolitionists, edited by Lewis Perry and Michael Fellman. Baton Rouge: Louisiana State Univ. Press, 1979.

Dumond, Dwight Lowell. *Antislavery Origins of the Civil War in the United States.* Ann Arbor: Univ. of Michigan Press, 1939.

——. *Antislavery: The Crusade for Freedom in America.* Ann Arbor: Univ. of Michigan Press, 1961.

Durant, John. *History of Jefferson County, New York.* Philadelphia: J. B. Lippincott, 1878.

——. *History of Oneida County, New York.* Philadelphia: Everts and Farriss, 1878.

Dykstra, Robert R. *Bright Radical Star: Black Freedom and White Supremacy on the Hawkeye Frontier.* Cambridge, Mass.: Harvard Univ. Press, 1993.

Ellis, Franklin. *History of Cattaraugus County, New York.* Philadelphia: L. H. Everts, 1879.

Emerson, Edgar G., ed. *Our County and Its People: A Descriptive Work on Jefferson County, New York.* Boston: Boston History, 1898.

Fairchild, James H. "The Doctrine of Sanctification at Oberlin." *Congregational Quarterly* 18 (Apr. 1876): 237–59.

——. *Oberlin: The Colony and the College, 1833–1883.* Oberlin, Ohio: E. J. Goodrich, 1883.

Filler, Louis. *The Crusade Against Slavery, 1830–1860.* New York: Harper and Brothers, 1960.

Fladeland, Betty. *James Gillespie Birney: Slaveholder to Abolitionist.* Ithaca, N.Y.: Cornell Univ. Press, 1955.

Fletcher, Robert Samuel. *A History of Oberlin College From Its Foundation Through the Civil War.* 2 vols. Oberlin, Ohio: Oberlin College, 1943.

Flexner, Eleanor. *Century of Struggle: The Woman's Rights Movement in the United States.* Cambridge, Mass.: Belknap, 1959.

Foner, Eric. *Free Soil, Free Labor, Free Men: The Ideology of the Republican Party Before the Civil War.* New York: Oxford Univ. Press, 1970.

Formisano, Ronald P. *The Birth of Mass Political Parties: Michigan, 1827–1861.* Princeton, N.J.: Princeton Univ. Press, 1971.

——. *The Transformation of Political Culture: Massachusetts Parties, 1790s–1840s.* New York: Oxford Univ. Press, 1983.

Fortenbaugh, Robert. "American Lutheran Synods and Slavery, 1830–1860." *Journal of Religion* 13 (Jan. 1933): 72–92.

——. "The Representative Lutheran Periodical Press and Slavery, 1831–1860." *Lutheran Church Quarterly* 8 (Apr. 1935): 151–72.

Fox, Dixon Ryan. *Yankees and Yorkers.* New York: New York Univ. Press, 1940.

Friedman, Lawrence J. *Gregarious Saints: Self and Community in American Abolitionism, 1830–1870.* Cambridge: Cambridge Univ. Press, 1982.

——. "'Historical Topics Sometimes Run Dry': The State of Abolitionist Studies." *The Historian* 43 (Feb. 1981): 177–94.

Frothingham, Octavius Brooks. *Gerrit Smith: A Biography.* New York: G. P. Putnam's Sons, 1878.

Frothingham, Washington. *History of Fulton County.* Syracuse, N.Y.: D. Mason, 1892.

Gaddis, Merrill E. "Christian Perfection in America." Ph.D. diss., Univ. of Chicago, 1929.

Gardepe, Carol Dates, and Janice Dates Regester. *A History of the Town of Yates in Orleans County.* Ann Arbor, Mich.: Edwards Bros., 1976.

Garrison, Wendell Phillips, and Francis Jackson Garrison. *William Lloyd Garrison, 1805–1879: The Story of His Life Told by His Children.* 2 vols. New York: Century, 1885.

Gilbert, Helen Josephine White. *Rushford and Rushford People.* N.p.: Chautauqua Print Shop, 1910.

Ginzberg, Lori D. *Women and the Work of Benevolence: Morality, Politics, and Class in the Nineteenth Century United States.* New Haven, Conn.: Yale Univ. Press, 1990.

Glickstein, Jonathan A. "'Poverty is not Slavery': American Abolitionists and the Competitive Labor Market." In *Antislavery Reconsidered: New Essays on the Abolitionists,* edited by Lewis Perry and Michael Fellman, 195–218. Baton Rouge: Louisiana State Univ. Press, 1979.

Goen, C. C. *Broken Churches, Broken Nation: Denominational Schisms and the Coming of the American Civil War.* Macon, Ga.: Mercer Univ. Press, 1985.

Goodheart, Lawrence B. *Elizur Wright and the Reform Impulse: Abolitionist, Actuary, Atheist.* Kent, Ohio: Kent State Univ. Press, 1990.

Gordon, John O. *An Historical Sermon Preached in the Presbyterian Church, Rensselaerville, New York, July 2nd, 1876.* Albany, N.Y.: Van Benthuysen, 1876.

Gravely, William B. *Gilbert Haven, Methodist Abolitionist: A Study in Race, Religion, and Reform, 1850–1880.* Nashville: Abingdon, 1973.

Graybill, Ronald D. "The Abolitionist-Millerite Connection." In *The Disappointed: Millerism and Millenarianism in the Nineteenth Century,* edited by Ronald L. Numbers and Jonathan M. Butler, 139–52. Bloomington: Indiana Univ. Press, 1987.

Griffin, Clifford S. *Their Brothers' Keepers: Moral Stewardship in the United States, 1800–1865.* New Brunswick, N.J.: Rutgers Univ. Press, 1960.

Gundry, Esther D. *Churches of Napoli, Cattaraugus County, New York,* vol. 2, *Wesleyan Methodist.* Typed manuscript. New York State Library, Albany, N.Y.

Hackett, David G. *The Rude Hand of Innovation: Religion and Social Order in Albany, New York, 1652–1836.* New York: Oxford Univ. Press, 1991.

Haddock, John A. *Haddock's Centennial History of Jefferson Co., N.Y.* Philadelphia: Sherman, 1894.

Hagan, Elizabeth, ed. *Poland, New York: Past and Present.* Poland, N.Y.: Poland Bicentennial Committee, 1976.

Hahn, Steven, and Jonathan Prude, eds. *The Countryside in the Age of Capitalist Transformation: Essays in the Social History of Rural America.* Chapel Hill: Univ. of North Carolina Press, 1985.

Haines, Lee M., and Paul William Thomas. *A History of the Wesleyan Church.* Marion, Ind.: Wesley, 1985.

Hamm, Thomas D. *The Transformation in American Quakerism: Orthodox Friends, 1800–1907.* Bloomington: Indiana Univ. Press, 1988.

Hammond, John L. *The Politics of Benevolence: Revival Religion and American Voting Behavior.* Norwood, N.J.: Ablex, 1979.

Hand, H. Wells, ed. *Centennial History of the Town of Nunda.* Rochester: Rochester Herald, 1908.

Hanley, Mark Y. "The New Infidelity: Northern Protestant Clergymen and the Critique of Progress, 1840–1855." *Religion and American Culture* 1, no. 2 (Summer 1991): 203–26.

Hardesty, Nancy A. *Women Called to Witness: Evangelical Feminism in the Nineteenth Century.* Nashville: Abingdon, 1984.

Hardin, George A., ed. *History of Herkimer County, New York.* Syracuse, N.Y.: D. Mason, 1893.

Harlow, Ralph Volney. *Gerrit Smith: Philanthropist and Reformer.* New York: Henry Holt, 1939.

Haroutunian, Joseph. *Piety Versus Moralism: The Passing of the New England Theology.* New York: Henry Holt, 1932.

Harrold, Stanley. *Gamaliel Bailey and Antislavery Union.* Kent, Ohio: Kent State Univ. Press, 1986.

Hart, Albert Bushnell. *Salmon Portland Chase.* Boston: Houghton, Mifflin, 1899.

Hatch, Nathan O. "The Christian Movement and the Demand for a Theology of the People." *Journal of American History* 67 (Dec. 1980): 545–67.

———. *The Democratization of American Christianity.* New Haven, Conn.: Yale Univ. Press, 1989.

———. *The Sacred Cause of Liberty: Republican Thought and the Millennium in Revolutionary New England.* New Haven, Conn.: Yale Univ. Press, 1977.

Hayne, Coe Smith. *Baptist Trail-Makers of Michigan.* Philadelphia: Judson, 1936.

Heiman, Elmer. *Town of Darien, 1832–1982.* N.p.: 1982.

Hendricks, John R. "The Liberty Party in New York State, 1836–1848." Ph.D. diss., Fordham Univ., 1959.

Hersch, Blanche Glassman. "'Am I Not a Woman and a Sister?' Abolitionist Beginnings of Nineteenth-Century Feminism." In *Antislavery Reconsidered: New Perspectives on the Abolitionists,* edited by Lewis Perry and Michael Fellman, 252–83. Baton Rouge: Louisiana State Univ. Press, 1979.

———. *The Slavery of Sex: Feminist-Abolitionists in America.* Urbana: Univ. of Illinois Press, 1978.

Hewitt, Nancy A. "The Perimeters of Women's Power in American Religion." In *The Evangelical Tradition in America,* edited by Leonard I. Sweet, 233–56. Macon, Ga.: Mercer Univ. Press, 1984.

———. "The Social Origins of Women's Antislavery Politics in Western New York." In *Crusaders and Compromisers: Essays on the Relationship of the Antislavery Struggle to the Antebellum Party System,* edited by Alan M. Kraut, 205–33. Westport, Conn.: Greenwood, 1983.

———. *Women's Activism and Social Change: Rochester, New York, 1822–1872.* Ithaca, N.Y.: Cornell Univ. Press, 1984.

Hodgson, William. *The Society of Friends in the Nineteenth Century: A Historical View of the Successive Convulsions and Schisms Therein During that Period.* 2 vols. Philadelphia: Smith, English, 1876.

Horton, John, Edward Williams, and Harry Douglass. *History of Northwestern New York.* New York: Lewis Historical Publishing, 1947.

Hough, Franklin B. *History of Jefferson County in the State of New York.* Albany, N.Y.: Joel Munsell, 1854.

———. *History of Lewis County, New York.* Syracuse, N.Y.: D. Mason, 1883.

Hovet, Theodore. "Phoebe Palmer's 'Altar Phraseology' and the Spiritual Dimensions of Women's Sphere." *Journal of Religion* 63 (July 1983): 264–80.

Howard, Victor. *Religion and the Radical Republican Movement, 1860–1870.* Lexington: Univ. Press of Kentucky, 1990.

Howe, Daniel Walker. "The Evangelical Movement and Political Culture in the North during the Second Party System." *Journal of American History* 77, no. 4 (Mar. 1991): 1216–39.

———. *The Political Culture of American Whigs.* Chicago: Univ. of Chicago Press, 1979.

Hudson, Winthrop S. *Religion in America.* 4th ed. New York: Macmillan, 1987.

Hunter, Carol M. *To Set the Captives Free: Reverend Jermain Wesley Loguen and the Struggle for Freedom in Central New York, 1835–1872.* New York: Garland, 1993.

Ingle, H. Larry. *Quakers in Conflict: The Hicksite Reformation.* Knoxville: Univ. of Tennessee Press, 1986.

Johnson, Crisfield. *History of Washington County, New York.* Philadelphia: Everts and Ensign, 1878.

Johnson, Curtis D. *Islands of Holiness: Rural Religion in Upstate New York, 1790–1860.* Ithaca, N.Y.: Cornell Univ. Press, 1989.

Johnson, Paul E. *A Shopkeeper's Millennium: Society and Revivals in Rochester, New York, 1815–1837.* New York: Hill and Wang, 1978.

Jones, Charles Edwin. *Perfectionist Persuasion: The Holiness Movement and American Methodism, 1867–1936.* Metuchen, N.J.: Scarecrow, 1974.

Kaufman, Paul Leslie. "'Logical' Luther Lee and the Methodist War Against Slavery." Ph.D. diss., Kent State Univ., 1994.

Kelley, Robert. *The Cultural Pattern in American Politics: The First Century.* Washington, D.C.: Univ. Press of America, 1979.

Kleppner, Paul. *The Cross of Culture: A Social Analysis of Midwestern Politics, 1850–1900.* New York: Free Press, 1970.

Kostlevy, William C. *Holiness Manuscripts: A Guide to Sources Documenting the Wesleyan Holiness Movement in the United States and Canada.* Metuchen, N.J.: Scarecrow, 1994.

———. "Luther Lee and Methodist Abolitionism." *Methodist History* 20 (Jan. 1982): 90–103.

Kraditor, Aileen S. *Means and Ends in American Abolitionism: Garrison and His Critics on Strategy and Tactics, 1834–1850.* New York: Pantheon, 1967.

Kraut, Alan M. "The Forgotten Reformers: A Profile of Third Party Abolitionists in Antebellum New York." In *Antislavery Reconsidered: New Essays on the Abolitionists,* edited by Lewis Perry and Michael Fellman, 119–45. Baton Rouge: Louisiana State Univ. Press, 1979.

———. "The Liberty Men of New York: Political Abolitionism in New York State, 1840–1848." Ph.D. diss., Cornell Univ., 1975.

———. "Partisanship and Principles: The Liberty Party in Antebellum Political Culture." In *Crusaders and Compromisers: Essays on the Relationship of the Antislavery Struggle to the Antebellum Party System,* edited by Alan M. Kraut, 71–99. Westport, Conn.: Greenwood, 1983.

Kraut, Alan M., and Phyllis F. Field. "Politics Versus Principles: The Partisan Response to 'Bible Politics' in New York State." *Civil War History* 25 (June 1979): 101–18.

Krieder, Harry J. *History of the United Lutheran Synod of New York and New England.* Philadelphia: Muhlenberg, 1954.

Kuenning, Paul Phillip. "New York Lutheran Abolitionists: Seeking a Solution to a Historical Enigma." *Church History* 58 (Mar. 1989): 52–65.

———. *The Rise and Fall of American Lutheran Pietism.* Macon, Ga.: Mercer Univ. Press, 1988.

Kutolowski, Kathleen Smith. "The Social Composition of Political Leadership: Genesee County, New York, 1821–1860." Ph.D. diss., Univ. of Rochester, 1973.

Lamos, Aldis M., ed. *One Hundred and Twenty-Five Years for Christ 1843–1968: History of the Champlain Conference of the Wesleyan Methodist Church of America.* N.p.: [1968?].

Lane, Helen, et al. *The Story of Walton, 1785–1975.* Walton, N.Y.: Walton Historical Society, 1975.

Lasser, Carol, and Marlene Deahl Merrill, eds. *Friends and Sisters: Letters Between Lucy Stone and Antoinette Brown Blackwell, 1846–93.* Urbana: Univ. of Illinois Press, 1987.

Lerner, Gerda. "The Political Activities of Antislavery Women." In *The Majority Finds Its Past: Placing Women in History,* edited by Gerda Lerner, 112–28. New York: Oxford Univ. Press, 1979.

Lesick, Lawrence T. *The Lane Rebels: Evangelicalism and Antislavery in Antebellum America.* Metuchen, N.J.: Scarecrow, 1980.

Loveland, Anne C. "Evangelicalism and Immediate Emancipation in American Antislavery Thought." *Journal of Southern History* 32 (May 1966): 172–88.

Ludlum, David M. *Social Ferment in Vermont, 1791–1850.* New York: Columbia Univ. Press, 1939.

McCormick, Richard P. *The Second American Party System: Party Formation in the Jacksonian Era.* New York: Norton, 1973.

McCulley, Mary, ed. *History of Genesee County, 1890–1982.* Interlaken, N.Y.: Heart of the Lakes Publishing, 1985.

McElroy, James Logan. "Social Reform in the Burned-Over District: Rochester, New York, as a Test Case, 1830–1854." Ph.D. diss., State Univ. of New York at Binghamton, 1974.

McInerney, Daniel J. "A State of Commerce: Market Power and Slave Power in Abolitionist Political Economy." *Civil War History* 37, no. 2 (June 1991): 101–19.

McIntosh, W. H. *History of Wayne County, New York.* Philadelphia: Everts, Ensign, and Everts, 1877.

McKelvey, Blake. *Rochester on the Genesee: The Growth of a City.* Syracuse, N.Y.: Syracuse Univ. Press, 1973.

McKivigan, John R. "The Antislavery 'Comeouter' Sects: A Neglected Dimension of the Abolitionist Movement." *Civil War History* 26, no. 2 (June 1980): 142–60.

———. "Vote As You Pray and Pray As You Vote: Church-Oriented Abolitionism and Antislavery Politics." In *Crusaders and Compromisers: Essays on the Relationship of the Antislavery Struggle to the Antebellum Party System,* edited by Alan M. Kraut, 181–91. Westport, Conn.: Greenwood, 1983.

———. *The War Against Proslavery Religion: Abolitionism and the Northern Churches, 1830–1865.* Ithaca, N.Y.: Cornell Univ. Press, 1984.

McLeister, Ira Ford, and Roy Stephen Nicholson. *Conscience and Commitment: History of the Wesleyan Methodist Church of America.* 4th. ed. Marion, Ind.: Wesley, 1976.

———. *History of The Wesleyan Methodist Church.* 3rd ed. Marion, Ind.: Wesley, 1959.

McMahan, Helen G. *Chautauqua County: A History.* Buffalo: Henry Stewart, 1958.

MacMorris, Mary MacDougall. *Argyle: Then—Now—and Forever.* N.p., n.d.

McPherson, James M. *The Abolitionist Legacy.* Princeton, N.J.: Princeton Univ. Press, 1975.

———. *The Struggle for Equality: Abolitionists and the Negro in the Civil War and Reconstruction.* Princeton, N.J.: Princeton Univ. Press, 1964.

Magnuson, Norris. *Salvation in the Slums: Evangelical Social Work, 1865–1920.* Metuchen, N.J.: Scarecrow, 1977.

Marini, Stephen A. *Radical Sects of Revolutionary New England.* Cambridge, Mass.: Harvard Univ. Press, 1982.

Marsden, George M. *The Evangelical Mind and the New School Presbyterian Experience: A*

Case Study of Thought and Theology in Nineteenth-Century America. New Haven, Conn.: Yale Univ. Press, 1970.

Marvin, Edward P. *Semi-Centennary Sketch of the Presbytery of Niagara, 1824–1874.* Lockport, N.Y.: Daily Union Office, 1875.

Mason, Jeffrey C., and Harry S. Douglass. *Alive in the Spirit Since 1813: The Arcade United Church of Christ, Congregational.* Interlaken, N.Y.: Heart of the Lakes Publishing, 1990.

Mathews, Donald G. "Orange Scott: The Methodist Evangelist as Revolutionary." In *The Antislavery Vanguard: New Essays on the Abolitionists,* edited by Martin Duberman. Princeton, N.J.: Princeton Univ. Press, 1965.

———. *Slavery and Methodism: A Chapter in American Morality, 1780–1845.* Princeton, N.J.: Princeton Univ. Press, 1965.

Mathews, Lois Kimball. *The Expansion of New England: The Spread of New England Settlement and Institutions to the Mississippi River, 1620–1865.* Boston: Houghton Mifflin, 1909.

Mayfield, John. *Rehearsal for Republicanism: Free Soil and the Politics of Antislavery.* Port Washington, N.Y.: Kennikat, 1980.

Mead, Sidney E. *Nathaniel William Taylor, 1786–1858: A Connecticut Liberal.* Chicago: Univ. of Chicago Press, 1942.

Melton, J. Gordon. "Reformed Methodist Church." In *Encyclopedia of World Methodism,* edited by Nolan B. Harmon. Nashville: United Methodist Publishing House, 1974.

Merideth, Robert. "Edward Beecher: A Conservative Abolitionist at Alton." *Journal of Presbyterian History* 42 (June 1964): 92–103.

Meyer, Donald H. *The Instructed Conscience: The Shaping of the American National Ethic.* Philadelphia: Univ. of Pennsylvania Press, 1972.

Miller, James A. *The History of the Presbytery of Steuben.* Angelica, N.Y.: Allegany County Republican, 1897.

Minard, John S. *Allegany County and Its People.* 3 vols. Alfred, N.Y.: W. A. Ferguson, 1896.

Moorhead, James H. "Between Progress and Apocalypse." *Journal of American History* 71 (Dec. 1984): 524–42.

———. "Social Reform and the Divided Conscience of Antebellum Protestantism." *Church History* 48 (Dec. 1979): 416–30.

Murray, David, ed. *Delaware County, New York.* Delhi, N.Y.: William Clark, 1898.

Myers, John L. "The Beginning of Anti-Slavery Agencies in New York State, 1833–1836." *New York History* 43 (Apr. 1962): 149–81.

Nassau, Joseph E. *Seventy-Fifth Anniversary of the Presbyterian Church of Warsaw, NY.* Warsaw, N.Y.: H. A. Dudley, 1885.

Nichol, Francis D. *The Midnight Cry: A Defense of William Miller and the Millerites.* Washington, D.C.: Review and Herald, 1944.

Nichols, Robert Hastings. "The Plan of Union in New York." *Church History* 5 (Mar. 1936): 29–51.

———. *Presbyterianism in New York State.* Philadelphia: Westminster, 1963.

Noll, Mark. "Common Sense Traditions and American Evangelical Thought." *American Quarterly* 37 (1985): 216–38.

North, Safford E., ed. *Genesee County, N.Y.* Boston: Boston History, 1899.

Northrup, Arthur O., ed. *One Hundred Years For Christ, 1842–1942.* N.p.: Champlain Conference, Wesleyan Methodist Church, 1942.

Noyes, George Wallingford. *Religious Experience of John Humphrey Noyes.* New York: MacMillan, 1923.

Nutt, Rick. "'The Advantages of Liberty': Democratic Thought in the Formation of the Methodist Protestant Church." *Methodist History* 31 (Oct. 1992): 16–25.

Padgett, Chris. "Hearing the Antislavery Rank-and-File: The Wesleyan Methodist Schism of 1843." *Journal of the Early Republic* 12 (Spring 1992): 63–84.

Painter, Levinus K. *The Collins Story.* Gowanda, N.Y.: Niagara Frontier, 1962.

Parker, Mary Shaw. *History of the Baptist Church of Lockport, New York.* Lockport, N.Y.: n.p., 1928.

Parsons, Levi. *History of Rochester Presbytery From the Earliest Settlement of the Country.* Rochester: Democrat-Chronicle Press, 1889.

———, compiler. *Centennial Celebration, Mt. Morris, New York, August 15, 1894.* Mt. Morris, N.Y.: Mt. Morris Union, 1894.

Pearson, Samuel C. "From Church to Denomination: American Congregationalism in the Nineteenth Century." *Church History* 38 (Mar. 1969): 67–87.

Peck, William F. *Landmarks of Monroe County.* Boston: Boston History, 1895.

Perkal, M. Leon. "William Goodell: A Life of Reform." Ph.D. diss., City Univ. of New York, 1972.

Perry, Lewis. *Radical Abolitionism: Anarchy and the Government of God in Antislavery Thought.* Ithaca, N.Y.: Cornell Univ. Press, 1973.

Persons, Silas E. *A Historical Sketch of the Religious Denominations of Madison County, New York.* Cazenovia, N.Y.: Madison County Historical Society, 1906.

Peters, John L. *Christian Perfection and American Methodism.* New York: Abingdon, 1956.

Plunkett, Margaret Louise. "A History of the Liberty Party With Emphasis Upon its Activity in the Northeastern States." Ph.D. diss., Cornell Univ., 1930.

Polmenteer, Vaughn. "Reynolds Arcade Was the City's Classic: An Address of Distinction." *Rochester Museum and Science Center Focus* 23 (Spring 1989): 22–23.

Pope, Earl A. *New England Calvinism and the Disruption of the Presbyterian Church.* New York: Garland, 1987.

Porter, Peter A. *Souvenir History of Niagara County, N.Y.* Reprint. Niagara Falls, N.Y.: Graphic Services, 1987.

Potash, P. Jeffrey. *Vermont's Burned-Over District: Patterns of Community Development and Religious Activity, 1761–1850.* Brooklyn, N.Y.: Carlson, 1991.

Powell, Milton B. "The Abolitionist Controversy in the Methodist Episcopal Church, 1840–1864." Ph.D. diss., State Univ. of Iowa, 1963.

Quarles, Benjamin. *Black Abolitionists.* New York: Oxford Univ. Press, 1969.

Quist, John. "The Great Majority of Our Subscribers are Farmers": The Michigan Abolitionist Constituency of the 1840s." *Journal of the Early Republic* 14 (Fall 1994): 325–58.

Raser, Harold E. *Phoebe Palmer: Her Life and Thought.* Lewiston, N.Y.: Edwin Mellen, 1987.

Rayback, Joseph G. *Free Soil: The Election of 1848.* Lexington: Univ. Press of Kentucky, 1970.

Reynolds, John F. *The Almond Story: The Early Years.* Hornell, N.Y.: John F. Reynolds, 1962.

Roberts, Benson Howard. *Benjamin Titus Roberts. Late General Superintendent of the Free Methodist Church. A Biography.* North Chili, N.Y.: Earnest Christian Office, 1900.

Roberts, Frank D. *History of the Town of Perry, New York.* Perry, N.Y.: C. G. Clark, 1915.

Roberts, Millard F. *A Narrative History of Remsen, New York, Including Parts of Adjoining Townships of Steuben and Trenton, 1789–1898.* N.p.: Millard F. Roberts, 1914.

Robinson, Laura Bristol, ed. *History of the Centennial Celebration: Warsaw, Wyoming County, New York, June 28–July 2, 1903.* Warsaw, N.Y.: Western New Yorker, 1903.

Root, Mary R. *History of the Town of York, Livingston County, New York.* Caledonia, N.Y.: Big Springs Historical Society, 1940.

Roth, Randolph A. *The Democratic Dilemma: Religion, Reform, and the Social Order in the Connecticut River Valley of Vermont, 1791–1850.* Cambridge: Cambridge Univ. Press, 1987.

Rowe, David L. "Elon Galusha and the Millerite Movement." *Foundations* 18 (July–Sept. 1975): 252–60.

———. "A New Perspective on the Burned-Over District: The Millerites in Upstate New York." *Church History* 47 (Dec. 1978): 408–20.

———. *Thunder and Trumpets: Millerites and Dissenting Religion in Upstate New York, 1800–1850.* Chico, Calif.: Scholars, 1985.

Ryan, Mary P. *Cradle of the Middle Class: The Family in Oneida County, New York, 1790–1865.* Cambridge: Cambridge Univ. Press, 1981.

Scott, Donald M. "Abolition as a Sacred Vocation." In *Antislavery Reconsidered: New Essays on the Abolitionists,* edited by Lewis Perry and Michael Fellman, 51–74. Baton Rouge: Louisiana State Univ. Press, 1979.

———. *From Office to Profession: The New England Ministry, 1750–1850.* Philadelphia: Univ. of Pennsylvania Press, 1978.

Scribner, J. Woodbury. "Centennial Paper for the New Hampshire Yearly Meeting, 1892." [Freewill Baptist Connection.] Handwritten manuscript. American Baptist Historical Society, Rochester, N.Y.

Seaver, Frederick J. *Historical Sketches of Franklin County and Its Several Towns With Many Short Biographies.* Albany, N.Y.: J. B. Lyon, 1918.

Seilhamer, Frank H. "The New Measure Movement Among Lutherans." *Lutheran Quarterly* 12 (May 1960): 121–43.

Sellers, Charles. *The Market Revolution: Jacksonian America, 1815–1846.* New York: Oxford Univ. Press, 1991.

Sernett, Milton C. *Abolition's Axe: Beriah Green, Oneida Institute, and the Black Freedom Struggle.* Syracuse, N.Y.: Syracuse Univ. Press, 1986.

Sewell, Richard H. *Ballots for Freedom: Antislavery Politics in the United States, 1837–1860.* New York: Oxford Univ. Press, 1976.

Signor, Isaac S., ed. *Landmarks of Orleans County.* Syracuse, N.Y.: D. Mason, 1894.

Silbey, Joel H. *The American Political Nation, 1838–1893.* Stanford, Calif.: Stanford Univ. Press, 1991.

Smith, H. P., ed. *History of Cortland County.* Syracuse, N.Y.: D. Mason, 1885.

———, ed. *History of Essex County.* Syracuse, N.Y.: D. Mason, 1885.

———, ed. *History of the City of Buffalo and Erie County.* Syracuse, N.Y.: Smith and Bruce, 1884.

———, ed. *History of Warren County.* Syracuse, N.Y.: D. Mason, 1885.

Smith, James H. *History of Chenango and Madison Counties, New York.* Syracuse, N.Y.: D. Mason, 1880.

———. *History of Livingston County, New York.* Syracuse, N.Y.: D. Mason, 1881.

Smith, John E. *Our County and Its People: A Description and Biographical Record of Madison County, New York.* Boston: Boston History, 1899.

Smith, John W. V. *The Quest for Holiness and Unity: A Centennial History of the Church of God (Anderson, Indiana).* Anderson, Ind.: Warner, 1980.

Smith, Theodore Clarke. *The Liberty and Free Soil Parties in the Northwest.* New York: Longmans, Green, 1897.

Smith, Timothy L. *Called Unto Holiness: The Story of the Nazarenes.* Kansas City: Nazarene, 1962.

———. "The Doctrine of the Sanctifying Spirit: Charles G. Finney's Synthesis of Wesleyan and Covenant Theology." *Wesleyan Theological Journal* 13 (Spring 1978): 92–113.

———. *Revivalism and Social Reform: American Protestantism on the Eve of the Civil War.* Baltimore: Johns Hopkins Univ. Press, 1980.

Staiger, C. Bruce. "Abolitionism and the Presbyterian Schism of 1837–1838." *Mississippi Valley Historical Review* 36 (Dec. 1949): 391–414.

Stange, Douglas C. *Radicalism for Humanity: A Study of Lutheran Abolitionism.* St. Louis: Oliver Slave, 1970.

Stanton, Elizabeth Cady, Susan B. Anthony, and Matilda Joslyn Gage, eds. *History of Woman Suffrage.* 6 vols. New York: Fowler and Wells, 1887.

Stewart, James Brewer. *Holy Warriors: The Abolitionists and American Slavery.* New York: Hill and Wang, 1976.

———. *Joshua R. Giddings and the Tactics of Radical Politics.* Cleveland: Case Western Reserve Univ. Press, 1970.

———. "Peaceful Hopes and Violent Experiences: The Evolution of Reforming and Radical Abolitionism, 1831–1837." *Civil War History* 17 (Dec. 1971): 293–309.

Storke, Elliot G. *History of Cayuga County, New York.* Syracuse, N.Y.: D. Mason, 1879.

Strong, Douglas M. "The Crusade for Women's Rights and the Formative Antecedents of the Holiness Movement." *Wesleyan Theological Journal* 27 (1992): 132–60.

———. "Organized Liberty: Evangelical Perfectionism, Political Abolitionism, and Ecclesiastical Reform in the Burned-Over District." Ph.D. diss., Princeton Theological Seminary, 1990.

———. "Partners in Political Abolitionism: The Liberty Party and the Wesleyan Methodist Connection." *Methodist History* 23 (Jan. 1985): 99–115.

———. *They Walked in the Spirit: Personal Faith and Social Action in America.* Louisville, Ky.: Westminster John Knox, 1997.

Sutton, William R. "Benevolent Calvinism and the Moral Government of God: The Influence of Nathaniel William Taylor on Revivalism in the Second Great Awakening." *Religion and American Culture* 2, no. 1 (Winter 1992): 23–47.

Swaney, Charles Baumer. *Episcopal Methodism and Slavery, With Sidelights on Ecclesiastical Politics.* Boston: Richard G. Badger, 1926.

Sylvester, Nathaniel Bartlett. *History of Saratoga County, New York.* Philadelphia: Everts and Ensign, 1878.

Thomas, Allen C. "Congregational or Progressive Friends." *Bulletin of Friends' Historical Society of Philadelphia* 10 (Nov. 1920): 21–32.

Thomas, George M. *Revivalism and Cultural Change: Christianity, Nation Building, and the Market in the Nineteenth Century United States.* Chicago: Univ. of Chicago Press, 1989.

Thomas, Howard. *The Life of a Village: A History of Prospect, New York.* Prospect, N.Y.: Prospect, 1950.

Thomas, John L. "Antislavery and Utopia." In *The Antislavery Vanguard: New Essays on the*

Abolitionists, edited by Martin Duberman, 240–69. Princeton, N.J.: Princeton Univ. Press, 1965.

———. *The Liberator: William Lloyd Garrison, a Biography.* Boston: Little, Brown, 1963.

———. "Romantic Reform in America." *American Quarterly* 17 (Winter 1965): 656–81.

Thomas, Robert David. *The Man Who Would Be Perfect: John Humphrey Noyes and the Utopian Impulse.* Philadelphia: Univ. of Pennsylvania Press, 1977.

Trump, Clara K. *First Presbyterian Church of Westfield, New York, 1808–1968: A History.* Westfield, N.Y.: Westfield Republican, 1968.

Tully, William K. *Historical Sermon concerning the First Presbyterian Church, Medina, New York.* Medina, N.Y.: Hurd and Taylor, 1876.

Tuttle, William H. *Names and Sketches of the Pioneer Settlers of Madison County, N.Y.* Interlaken, N.Y.: Heart of the Lakes Publishing, 1984.

Tuveson, Ernest Lee. *Redeemer Nation: The Idea of America's Millennial Role.* Chicago: Univ. of Chicago Press, 1968.

Venet, Wendy Hamand. *Neither Ballots Nor Bullets: Women Abolitionists and the Civil War.* Charlottesville: Univ. Press of Virginia, 1991.

Volpe, Vernon L. *Forlorn Hope of Freedom: The Liberty Party in the Old Northwest, 1838–1848.* Kent, Ohio: Kent State Univ. Press, 1990.

Wager, Daniel E., ed. *Our County and Its People: A Descriptive Work on Oneida County, New York.* Boston: Boston History, 1896.

Walsh, John J. *Vignettes of Old Utica.* Utica, N.Y.: Utica Public Library, 1982.

Walters, Ronald G. *American Reformers, 1815–1860.* New York: Hill and Wang, 1978.

———. *The Antislavery Appeal: American Abolitionism After 1830.* Baltimore: Johns Hopkins Univ. Press, 1976.

———. "The Boundaries of Abolitionism." In *Antislavery Reconsidered: New Perspectives on the Abolitionists,* edited by Lewis Perry and Michael Fellman, 3–23. Baton Rouge: Louisiana State Univ. Press, 1979.

Ward, Ferdinand D. *Churches of Rochester.* Rochester: Erastus Darrow, 1870.

Ward, John William. *Andrew Jackson: Symbol for an Age.* London: Oxford Univ. Press, 1953.

Warfield, Benjamin B. *Perfectionism.* New York: Oxford Univ. Press, 1931.

Watson, Harry L. *Liberty and Power: The Politics of Jacksonian America.* New York: Hill and Wang, 1990.

Wayland, John Terrill. "The Theological Department in Yale College, 1822–1858." Ph.D. diss., Yale Univ., 1933.

Welch, Edgar Luderne. *Grip's Historical Souvenir of Seneca Falls.* Syracuse, N.Y.: Grip, 1904.

Wellman, Judith M. "The Burned-Over District Revisited: Benevolent Reform and Abolitionism in Mexico, Paris, and Ithaca, New York, 1825–1842." Ph.D. diss., Univ. of Virginia, 1974.

———. "The Seneca Falls Women's Rights Convention: A Study of Social Networks." *Journal of Women's History* 3, no. 1 (Spring 1991): 9–37.

Wesley, Charles H. "The Participation of Negroes in Anti-Slavery Parties." *Journal of Negro History* 24 (Jan. 1944).

White, Charles E. *The Beauty of Holiness: Phoebe Palmer as Theologian, Revivalist, Feminist, and Humanitarian.* Grand Rapids, Mich.: Francis Asbury, 1986.

White, Philip L. *Beekmantown, New York: Forest Frontier to Farm Community.* Austin: Univ. of Texas Press, 1979.

Wilcox, Leslie D. *Wesleyan Methodism in Ohio.* N.p.: n.d.

Wiley, Samuel T., and W. Scott Ganer. *Biographical and Portrait Cyclopedia of Niagara County, N.Y.* Philadelphia: Gresham, 1892.

Williams, Norman, et al. *Vermont Townscape.* New Brunswick, N.J.: Center for Urban Policy Research, 1987.

Winslow, Hubbard. *The Former Days: History of the Presbyterian Church of Geneva.* Boston: Crocker and Brewster, 1859.

Wright, James A. *Historical Sketches of the Town of Moravia from 1791 to 1918.* Auburn, N.Y.: Cayuga County News, n.d.

Wright, Stanley W., et al. *One Hundred Years of Service for Christ in the Wesleyan Methodist Church, 1844–1944* [Rochester Conference]. N.p.: n.d. [1944?].

Wyatt-Brown, Bertram. *Lewis Tappan and the Evangelical War against Slavery.* Cleveland: Case Western Reserve Univ. Press, 1969.

Young, Andrew W. *History of the Town of Warsaw, New York.* Buffalo: Sage, Sons, 1869.

Zahniser, Clarence Howard. *Earnest Christian: Life and Works of Benjamin Titus Roberts.* Circleville, Ohio: Advocate Publishing House, 1957.

Periodicals

All publication locations listed are in New York State, unless otherwise indicated.

The Abolitionist, Cazenovia

American Citizen, Warsaw; Perry

American Jubilee, New York City

Baptist Register, Utica

Christian Investigator, Whitesboro; Honeoye

Christian Palladium, Union Mills; West Mendon

Christian Union, Ripley, Ohio

Emancipator, New York City

Friend of Man, Utica

The Impartial Citizen, Syracuse; Boston, Mass.

Liberator, Boston, Mass.

Liberty Leaguer, Honeoye

Liberty Party Paper, Syracuse

Liberty Press, Utica

Lutheran Herald, Fort Plain; Milford; West Sand Lake

Madison County Abolitionist, Cazenovia

Morning Star, Dover, N.H.

New York Evangelist, New York City

Niles' Register, New York City

Oberlin Evangelist, Oberlin, Ohio

Principia, New York City

Radical Abolitionist, New York City

True Wesleyan, Boston, Mass.

Union Herald, Cazenovia

Wesleyan Review, Syracuse

Western New Yorker, Warsaw

Wyoming Democrat, Warsaw

Index

Abolition churches, 2, 57, 114, 125–26, 133, 157, 173–79, 220. *See also* Church reform; Ecclesiastical abolitionism

Abolitionism: church reform connected to, 2–3, 11, 47, 93; democratization and, 7–8, 39; evangelical conversion and, 28, 72; evangelical perfectionism and, 4, 7, 73, 93; historiography of, 5–7, 8–10, 47, 78–79, 93; immediate, 25, 28, 71–72; new measures revivalism and, 25–26, 28; in New York state, 25; women's rights and, 78. *See also* Ecclesiastical abolitionism; Garrisonian abolitionism; Liberty Party; Racial equality

Accommodation plans, 16–17, 50–51, 55, 176

Adventists, 112–14, 118, 128–29, 158, 174, 218

African Americans, 44–45, 63, 88, 96, 101, 134, 162–63, 209

American and Foreign Anti-Slavery Society (AFASS), 78–79, 119–20

American Anti-Slavery Society (AASS), 69, 78–79

American Baptist Free Missionary Society, 111

Ames, N.Y., 98, 184

Anarchism. *See* Perfectionism, anarchistic

Antinomianism, 34, 37–38, 40, 63. *See also* Perfectionism, anarchistic

Antislavery Baptists. *See* Baptists, Antislavery

Antislavery church reform. *See* Church reform

Arcade, N.Y., 24, 75, 127, 129, 137–39, 182

Bailey, Gamaliel, 119, 148

Bailey, Wesley, 82–83, 99–100, 101, 125

Ball, Rachel, 222, 225

Baptists (Regular), 17–19, 105, 109–12, 116

Baptists, Antislavery, 109–12, 114, 154, 174

Baptists, Free. *See* Free Baptists

Beecher, Edward, 119

Birney, James G., 76, 120, 144–45, 156, 222, 226, 228

Blanchard, Jonathan, 30

Brown, Antoinette, 44–46, 55, 57–58, 135, 154, 156, 201, 225

Brown, William Wells, 134

Buffalo, N.Y., 66–67, 134, 182

Burned-over district, 9, 23–24, 29, 87–88, 94, 190, 201, 226

Calvinism, 16, 27, 34, 38, 55, 58, 137

Cazenovia, N.Y., 34, 53, 125, 181

Cedar of Lebanon, 82–83

Central Evangelical Association, 53–54, 143

Chase, Salmon P., 119, 148

Chautauqua County, N.Y., 111, 180

Chenango County, N.Y., 126–27, 153

China, N.Y. *See* Arcade, N.Y.

Chinese Americans, 134

Christian Church (Disciples of Christ), 193

Christian Connection, 19, 47, 112, 176

Christian Investigator, 63, 64, 150, 155, 176–77

Christian perfection. *See* Entire sanctification; Perfectionism, evangelical

Christian Union. *See* Church reform; Union churches

Church reform: abolition and, 47, 52–53; Adventists and, 113; African Americans and, 62–63; agenda of, 57–61; Baptists and, 109, 111; Congregational churches and, 54–55; conventions, 91, 93; decline of, 92, 140–41, 153–58; doctrine, 58–59, 61; evangelicalism of, 61, 63–64; evangelical perfectionism and, 7–8, 48, 61–62, 65, 93; Franckean Lutherans and, 96–97; Free Baptists and, 107–8; Goodell and, 63–65; Green and, 62–63; growth of, 62, 113–15; historiography of, 47, 93; Holiness movement and, 163; leaders, 218; Liberty Party and, 3, 44, 64–65, 92, 114, 122, 124–29, 133, 149–50, 173, 179, 222; Myrick and, 53–56; network, 92–93; Oberlin and, 62; ordination and, 57–58; polity (church government), 59–61, 92, 163; Presbyationalists and, 51–52, 54–55; restructuring of American religion and, 2–3, 47–48, 53;

Jackson, James C., 79, 88, 156, 204, 206
Jay, William, 119, 148

Keep, John, 62, 127, 204, 233
King, Leicester, 148

Land use reform, 134, 162
Latourette, James, 33
Lawyer, John, 25, 56, 97, 98, 156
Leavitt, Joshua, 55, 76, 148, 149
Lee, Luther: abolitionism of, 25, 99, 101;
   church reform of, 101–3, 104–5, 158;
   Franckean Lutherans and, 95, 210; Liberty Party and, 85, 101, 125; racial equality
   and, 101; social status of, 88; Syracuse
   Church Reform Convention and, 102, 115;
   women's rights and, 201, 216, 225
Lewis, Samuel, 148
Liberty League, 133–34, 150, 232
Liberty Party: African Americans in, 88, 134,
   162–63, 204; antislavery societies and,
   78–79; campaign strategy, 81, 124, 144–45;
   church reform and, 3, 11, 47, 64–65,
   67–68, 98, 101, 107, 113, 114, 122, 124–29,
   133, 137, 149–50, 177, 221–22, 223; coalitionist faction, 147–52; comprehensive social reform strategy of, 131–34, 150;
   constituency of, 86–89; decline of, 140,
   146, 152–53; election results of, 123–29,
   152–53, 177–86, 190, 208, 221, 227, 233;
   evangelicalism of, 6, 63–65, 189, 204;
   evangelical perfectionism in, 4–5, 65, 67,
   71–73, 75, 83–86; factionalism in, 136,
   145–52; founded, 75–76; growth of, 2, 86,
   121, 217; mediating position of, 79–81;
   nonperfectionists in, 119–20; social status
   of, 88–89; universal reform faction,
   148–52; viewed as an abolition church, 3,
   92, 142, 187; women in, 79–80, 88, 135–36,
   162, 225; women's rights advocacy in,
   134–36, 206, 225
Liberty Party conventions: Albany (1840), 75,
   101, 128; Arcade (1840), 75, 128; Arcade
   (1844), 128; Buffalo (1843), 66–67, 204;
   Buffalo (1848), 134, 150, 152; Macedon
   Lock (Liberty League, 1847), 133; Port
   Byron (1845), 133, 225; Warsaw (1839), 13,
   75
Liberty Press, 67, 82–83, 100, 101
Lincoln, Abraham, 231
Local orientation of ecclesiastical abolitionists, 25, 26, 90, 105, 122–23, 141–42, 164,
   208–9

Lockport, N.Y., 113, 125, 140, 181
Lockwood, Lewis C., 64, 115, 117, 199, 220
Loguen, Jermain W., 134
Lutherans (General Synod), 94–95, 96–97,
   157, 210
Lyle, W. W., 158–59
Lyman, Huntington, 25, 127, 137, 139–40, 141,
   233

Macedon Lock Convention of the Liberty
   League (1847), 133
Madison County, N.Y., 34, 123, 152–53, 154
Mahan, Asa, 35, 197, 225
Manlius, N.Y. *See* High Bridge, N. Y.
Market culture, attitudes toward the, 8–9,
   23–24, 31, 87–89, 141–42
Marks, David, 106–7
Matlack, Lucius, 159
Merritt, Timothy, 33
Metcalf, Jonathan and Joseph, 129, 118, 224
Methodists (Methodist Episcopal Church), 2,
   17–19, 32, 34, 49, 65, 99, 116, 129, 197
Methodist Protestants, 19, 47, 99, 158
Mexican War, opposition to, 96, 134
Michigan, 9, 144
Millennialism: abolition and, 30, 86, 112, 116;
   anarchism and, 40; church reform and,
   113, 115, 116; Finney and, 118; Garrison
   and, 40; Miller and, 112, 118; politics and,
   81, 113, 118–19, 152. *See also* Government
   of God; Postmillennialism; Premillennial-
   ism
Miller, William, 112, 218
Millerism, 112–13, 117–18, 219
Moral law, 27, 34, 36, 52
Moral suasion, 5, 40, 68–71, 74, 77
Myrick, Luther: antislavery and, 99; church
   reform and, 42, 53–54, 56, 58–59, 210;
   Liberty Party and, 64, 88, 121, 125, 203;
   perfectionism of, 33–35, 39, 95; trial of,
   33–34, 50–51; Union churches established
   by, 53

Native Americans, 134
Nativism, opposition to, 134
New birth. *See* Evangelicals
New England emigration, 14–16
New measures revivalism, 13, 22–23, 26–27,
   28, 50, 94, 117, 210. *See also* Evangelicals
New York state, upper, 9, 86–87, 177, 190–91,
   200, 233. *See also* Burned-over district
New York State Anti-Slavery Society, 50, 52,
   95, 102, 109, 204, 214

Nonresistance, 37–38, 40
North Elba, N.Y., 203
Noyes, John Humphrey, 37–38, 112

Oberlin College: abolitionist training at, 25; Big Tent of, 36–37, 66–67, 83; burned-over district of New York connected to, 35, 37, 62, 66, 127, 190; church reform at, 62, evangelical perfectionism of, 35–36, 66, 106, 142, 155; Franckean Lutherans and, 95; Free Baptists and, 106, 148; Free Soil Party and, 148; Liberty Party and, 66–67, 92; opposition to, 142–43; social restraint viewed as necessary at, 42, 148; women at, 225. *See also* Finney, Charles G.
Ohio, 6, 9, 35, 200
O'Kelly, James, 193, 213
Oneida Institute, 25, 62, 89, 92, 96, 125, 142–43, 155
Oneonta, N.Y., 107
Ordination, importance of, 57–58, 201

Palmer, Phoebe, 197–98, 214, 226
Panic of 1837, 31, 69, 140
Parish, N.Y., 97, 184
Payne, Daniel A., 96
Pegler, George, 99–100
Pentecostals, 163
Perfectionism, anarchistic, 38, 39–40, 198, 219. *See also* Antinomianism; Garrisonian abolitionism
Perfectionism, evangelical: affective religious experience of, 4, 10, 30–31, 32, 34–35, 42, 83–84; anarchistic perfectionism contrasted to, 84, 198–99; beliefs about sin and, 7–8, 29, 41–42, 63; biblical authority and, 198–99; in burned-over district of New York state, 33; comprehensive social reform and, 132, 150; the moral law and, 34; mediating views (middle course) of, 7–8, 41–43, 145; Myrick and, 33–35; the new birth and, 61, 84; Oberlin and, 35–36, 197; political action and, 4, 65, 71–73, 83–85, 150–51, 205; Presbyterian opinions about, 33–34; women's rights and, 134–35. *See also* Entire sanctification
Perfectionist moment, 113–15, 117–21, 142, 161
Perry, N.Y., 113, 128, 129, 181
Peterboro, N.Y., 63, 123–24, 125, 175, 181, 203
Pietism, 94–95, 210

Plan of union. *See* Accommodation plans
Plumb, David, 58
Political millennium, 118–19, 132, 136. *See also* Government of God
Politics: antislavery and, 74–75, 77; campaign tactics and, 81–83, 123–24, 144–45; Finney and, 76, 77, 81; Garrison and, 37–38, 40, 77–78; Green and, 77; popularity of, 74, 121; religion and, 66, 76–78, 80–83, 167–69, 205; revivalism and, 74, 83; sanctification and, 78, 83, 123; single-issue, 131, 150; social change and, 131; Ward and, 44, 77. *See also* Liberty Party
Postmillennialism, 30, 111, 118
Premillennialism, 111–12, 118
Presbygational churches, 16–17, 50–52, 54–55, 126, 128, 175–76
Presbyterians: accommodation plans and, 16–17, 50–51; antislavery and, 50, 103; Calvinism of, 12–13, 34; church reform and, 2; Congregationalists and, 16, 51; New School, 50, 51; in New York state, 12–14, 17, 33, 50; Old School, 50–51; perfectionism and, 33–34, 50–51, 58, 142; polity of, 17; Unionists drawn from, 103, 215
Prindle, Cyrus, 99, 104–5, 222
Progressive evangelical groups, 168–69
Prohibition, 159, 162. *See also* Temperance movement

Quakers, 108, 201

Racial equality, 96, 100, 150, 163, 167. *See also* Civil rights
Racism, 48, 133–34, 150
Radical Abolitionist Party, 161–62
Ray, Charles B., 134
Reconstruction, 158
Reformed Methodists, 19, 99, 214
Regular Baptists. *See* Baptists (Regular)
Religious right, 168–69
Republican Party, 139, 161, 163
Revivalism. *See* Evangelicals; New measures revivalism
Roberts, B. T., 163
Rochester, N.Y., 24, 69, 75, 84, 181, 226

Salvation Army, 163
Sanctification, 28, 29, 31–32. *See also* Entire sanctification; Perfectionism, evangelical
Scott, Orange, 99, 104, 215–16, 226

Perfectionist Politics: Abolitionism and the Religious Tensions of American Democracy was composed in 10.25/14 Bulmer MT in QuarkXPress 4.04 on a Macintosh by Kachergis Book Design; printed by sheet-fed offset on 60-pound, acid-free Glatfelter Natural Smooth, and Smyth-sewn and bound over binder's boards in Arrestox B-grade cloth with dust jackets printed in 3 colors and laminated by Braun-Brumfield; designed by Kachergis Book Design of Pittsboro, North Carolina; published by Syracuse University Press, Syracuse, New York 13244-5160.